SELECTIONS

FROM THE

LETTERS

OF

THOMAS B. GOULD,

A

MINISTER OF THE GOSPEL IN THE SOCIETY OF FRIENDS;

WITH

MEMOIRS OF HIS LIFE.

BY

WILLIAM HODGSON.

"Let it not be a light thing in thine eyes, that He now accounteth thee worthy to suffer among His choice lambs, that He might make thy crown weightier, and thine inheritance the fuller."—Letter from I. Penington, in Aylesbury Jail, to T. Ellwood, a prisoner at Oxford.

PHILADELPHIA:

FOR SALE BY THE EDITOR, NO. 714 ARCH ST.,
AND BY ISRAEL BUFFINTON, FALL RIVER, MASSACHUSETTS.

PRINTED BY C. SHERMAN & SON.
1860.

At a Meeting for Sufferings of New England Yearly Meeting of Friends, held at Newport, R. I., 3d of 8th month, 1860,—

The reading of the Writings and Memoirs of our dear departed Friend, Thomas B. Gould, prepared by Wm. Hodgson, Jr., of Philadelphia, which has occupied several sittings of this meeting, at various times, has been now concluded. During the time in which we have been thus engaged, we have been much comforted and edified by this record of the remarkable faithfulness and devotion of our dear Friend to the cause of Truth and Righteousness in the earth; and believing that usefulness would result from a more general circulation and perusal of these Writings, the Editor is left at liberty to publish the same; and the Clerk is requested to furnish him with a copy of this minute.

Signed on behalf of the Meeting aforesaid.

GEORGE F. READ,
Clerk.

CONTENTS.

CHAPTER VI.

CHAPTER VII.

CHAPTER VIII.

PREFACE.

It may be well to premise to the following work, a few general remarks, for the encouragement of a living remnant, and for the information of that portion of its readers who may not have had a clear understanding of the ground, nature, and tendency of the sorrowful lapse which has spread over a large portion of the Society of Friends, within the past twenty-five years, through the introduction of doctrines contrary to those always held by its faithful members from the beginning.

True Friends have ever believed that this people was raised up of the great Head of the church universal, to testify to the almost forgotten truth, that the Light of Christ in the soul is the immediate divine source of all true religion; and to bear a living witness to the life-giving efficacy of the Gospel, as "the power of God unto salvation to every one that believeth." This great truth, which lies as a corner-stone to that fabric of practical doctrine which has distinguished the Society of Friends from other professors of the Christian name, was announced on various occasions and in divers manners, by our blessed Lord and his apostles. They spoke of "the true Light that lighteth every man that cometh into the world"—"the ingrafted Word, which is able to save the soul"—"the Word nigh in the heart"—the Light that "maketh manifest"—"the Grace of God, which bringeth salvation [and] hath appeared unto all men"—the "Comforter," the Holy Spirit, who should "bring all things to remembrance," and "guide into all truth"—"Christ in you the hope of glory"—even come a "second time, without sin, unto salvation" to all them that believe and obey his voice. Our Saviour's own words were—"Abide in me, and I [will abide] in you"—"he that is with you shall be in you"—"I in them, and thou in me"—and "whosoever loveth me, my Father will love him, and we will come unto him, and make our abode with him." Holy and blessed promise! And who can doubt that a substantial reality was intended by these repeated assurances?

It was through submission to the humbling and purifying operations of this Spirit in the soul, and obedience to its successive manifestations, that our predecessors were brought to know by experience for themselves the blessed truths of the Gospel; and were made quick of understanding to perceive the falsifications and perversions by which the profession of Christian doctrine had been beclouded, in the long and dark night of apostasy, which the dawn of the Reformation from Popery had then only partially dispelled. The "dayspring from on high," which mercifully shined into their souls, and to which they faithfully gave heed, brought them to a clear appreciation of the "perfect day" of the Gospel dispensation; and they were enabled to put away those corruptions and man-made accompaniments and impediments to Christianity, with which carnal contrivance had burdened it, and under the delusive influence of which, many were "ever learning, and never able to come to the knowledge of the truth."

Obedience to this principle of Light and Grace in the soul, and simple dependence upon its teaching, produced also a clear sight and sense of their duty to God, and of the ways of His providence to mankind; and the doctrines of the Gospel, in accordance with the testimony of Holy Scripture—mysteries unknown to the merely natural mind—were thereby opened to them and sealed upon their understandings; so that they could say, they *knew* the truth, and the truth had made them free. Herein they were made stewards of the mysteries of God, saw, eye to eye, the deep things of His Kingdom, spoke one language, and promulgated an entire harmony of doctrine. It is doubtful whether any other religious body would be able to present so large an amount of writings, controversial, didactic, and biographical, in support of heir own faith, published during an equal period, as the Society of Friends produced during the first thirty years of its distinct existence as a body; and all this was of one and the same faith with that of succeeding periods, notwithstanding the bold assertions to the contrary, put forth by recent authors. Indeed it is wonderful, considering the great variety of mental character, and of the circumstances of life and education under which they had previously been placed, how great was the uniformity of doctrine among them from the very first; and this fact seems clearly to confirm us in the belief that the Lord himself was their Leader and their Teacher.

The various Christian testimonies which they were thus led to promulgate to the world, were parts of one great divine law,—fruit of one tree—branches of the one stem,—even of the principle of Light and Life in the hearts of the faithful. They found that a close adherence to this holy law written in the heart brought them into a true unity and fellowship with Christ and one with another; and they saw that all departures from the unity of this faith had their beginning in a departure from this law of the Spirit of life in Christ Jesus, by which an entrance was allowed to the Tempter to beguile and lead astray; so that none who had once known the truth could depart from and oppose any part of this fabric of doctrines, but they who had first departed in heart from that which was the corner-stone thereof. Thus their endeavors to restore transgressors and those who had fallen away from any of the testimonies of their profession, were principally or primarily directed towards awakening again a sincere and humble dedication of heart to the Lord in his inward manifestations; knowing that if the Witness for truth could be raised again into dominion in that heart, the branches which had withered would soon recover their vitality and health. Yet they ceased not, for all this, to point out the errors which such were in, and faithfully and openly to testify against them.

Clear and sound they were in the faith, that He who was the eternal Word and Son of God, was manifested in the flesh, and "bore our sins in his own body on the tree," as an atonement for the sins of the whole world, was raised again for our justification, and now sitteth at the right hand of the Father as our Intercessor and Advocate. Yet entirely consistent with this was their belief, that even that blessed offering for sin, once for all, without the gates of Jerusalem, can only be made available to mankind individually, as they submit in heart and mind to the cleansing and purifying operations of His visiting Grace and indwelling Spirit, and walk in obedience to the leadings of the light thereof. So that it was, in their view, no less hazardous to the soul's welfare, to reject the inward coming of Christ into the soul,—to enlighten it by His universal and saving Light to see the nature and depth of sin, and Him its Saviour to deliver it from sin; to refine and purify it by the washing of regeneration, and the renewing of the Holy Ghost; to lead and guide it into all truth, and qualify and strengthen it, according to His will, for every good thought, word, or deed,—than it was, to discard and deny His miraculous coming in the flesh, for that perfect example, and great offering for sin, and all that He did for us, without us, in that prepared body in which He was "seen of men." They knew, that while "no man can come to the Father but by Christ," yet no man can availingly "call Jesus, Lord, but by the Holy Ghost;" and that therefore, the immediate revelation of Christ to the soul being that which alone affords to every individual any true and solid foundation for his own hope in Christ, an attempt to invalidate this great fundamental truth, must be at least equally offensive in the Divine sight, and as dangerous to the souls of men, as the denial of the eternal Sonship of Him who was made flesh and offered Himself an atonement for the sins of the whole world—awful and ever to be avoided as such denial surely is! They could say from living experience, "We *know* that the Son of God is come, and hath given us an understanding that we may know Him that is true;" and they were well assured, that they who have received this manifestation, and abide true to it, never can deny that which He hath outwardly done for man in that acceptable offering; for these are of all men the most sensible of its efficacy and blessed sweetness to their souls.

It can scarcely have escaped the notice of candid persons conversant with the writings of our forefathers, how eminently sensitive they were to any misrepresentations of their faith or doctrines, and how ready they always appeared to defend the truth and to disprove the allegations of its opponents. They held that pure divine truth was more to be cherished than any other possession with which it had pleased Divine Wisdom to intrust them, for the best welfare of mankind. Many were the occasions on which, either through the enmity of their persecutors, or the envy and malice of false and apostatized brethren, their zeal was aroused in defence of the doctrines of the Gospel. George Fox himself set an example, in stepping forward with his pen to the rebuke of gainsayers and the clearing of the church from perversion or reproach. And on the occasion of that extensive and sore trial to Friends by the apostasy of Wilkinson, Story, and Rogers, many eminent members were engaged in controverting their errors and opposing their schism, both orally and in printed or written communications. The most prominent ministers and elders in the Society were often, and for a long time together, laboriously engaged in this work; and this they did promptly and openly, for the preservation of the flock, and the clearing away of reproach from the precious cause which they espoused. And greatly blessed was their labor of love and true zeal, to the confirmation of many, and to the conviction and restoration of some that had erred. But where this was not the result—even where error succeeded in drawing away disciples after it—the faithful servant having done what he could was clear; and the church was clear by issuing and maintaining its testimony against such errors, and against those engaged or led away therein. And they who stood to the original acknowledged faith of the body, were always accepted as the true members of the Society, without question from friends or foes.

Robert Barclay, in his "Apology for the true Christian Divinity," in mentioning the characteristics of a true and living church of Christ, gives this as a distinguishing one, that it consists of those who are not only gathered into a belief of the true principles and doctrines of the Christian faith, but who are also concerned "to bear a joint testimony *for the truth* and *against error, suffering for the same,* and so becoming, through this fellowship, as one family and household."

About the time of the defection of Wilkinson, Story, and Rogers, above mentioned, R. Barclay published his celebrated Treatise on Church Government, entitled "The Anarchy of the Ranters," &c.; in which he clearly advocated the necessity of separating those from the communion of the gathered church, who persist in promulgating doctrines adverse to its ancient faith; and, without regard to the question of numbers, sustained the undeniable position of those who remain firm and faithful to the original principles of the Society. In this work he says:

"Now if any one or more so engaged with us, should arise to teach any other doctrine or doctrines, contrary to these which were the ground of our being one, who can deny but the body hath power in such a case to declare, 'This is not according to the truth we profess; and therefore we pronounce such and such doctrines to be wrong, with which we cannot have unity, nor yet any more spiritual fellowship with those that hold them.' And so, such cut themselves off from being members, by dissolving the very bond by which they were linked to the body." . . . . "As, if a body be gathered into one fellowship by the belief of certain principles, he that comes to believe otherways, naturally scattereth himself; for that the cause, that gathered him, is taken away."

What R. Barclay had in view, in speaking as above of "the body," was not *necessarily* the plurality, or majority, as is manifest from the following passage taken from his Postscript or "Vindication" of his work on Church Government, viz.: "The power of decision is only and alone in the Spirit, not necessarily tied to a general assembly; but if it please God to make use of such an assembly, yet neither to the plurality of them, but in and through such of His servants as He sees meet. And that none are capable or can be supposed to be members of such an assembly, or esteemed such from whom such a judgment can be expected, or ought to be received, unless they be men in whom the Grace of God not only is, but hath truly wrought to mortify and regenerate them in a good measure: in whom the judgment of truth really proceeding from the Spirit, will be manifest to all who are truly faithful," &c.

Again R. Barclay says, in the same treatise: "Suppose a people really gathered unto the true and certain principles of the Gospel; if any of these people shall arise and contradict any of those fundamental truths, whether have not such as stand, good right to cast such a one out from among them, and to pronounce positively,—This is contrary to the truth we profess and own; and therefore ought to be rejected, and not received, nor yet he that asserts it, as one of us? And is not this obligatory on all the members, seeing all are concerned?" &c. And again: "For seeing it is so, that in the true church there may men arise, and speak perverse things contrary to the doctrine and Gospel already received; what is to be the place of those that hold the pure and ancient truth? Must they look upon these perverse men still as their brethren? Must they cherish them as fellow-members? Or must they judge, condemn, and deny them?"

And further on, he remarks: "If God has gathered a people by this means into the belief of one and the same truth, must not they, if they turn and depart from it, be admonished, reproved, and condemned? Yea, rather than those that are not yet come to the truth; because they crucify afresh unto themselves the Lord of Glory, and put Him to open shame." . . . "Were such a principle to be received or believed, that in the church of Christ no man should be separated from, no man condemned or excluded the fellowship and communion of the body, for his judgment or opinion in matter of faith, then what blasphemies so horrid,—what heresies so damnable,—what doctrine of devils—but might harbor itself in the church of Christ? What need then of sound doctrine, if no doctrine make unsound?" &c. . .

"So that from all that is above mentioned, we do safely conclude, that where a people are gathered together into the belief of the principles and doctrines of the Gospel of Christ, if any of that people [mark, without limitation as to a small or a large number] shall go from their principles, and assert things false and contrary to what they have already received; *such as stand and abide firm in the faith,* have power by the Spirit of God, after they have used Christian endeavors to convince and reclaim them, upon their obstinacy, to *separate from such,* and to exclude them from their spiritual fellowship and communion: for otherways, if this be denied, farewell to all Christianity, or to the maintaining of any sound doctrine in the church of Christ."

A few pages afterwards, R. Barclay adds: "Or on the other hand, that those that abide faithful, and have a discerning of those evils, ought to be silent, and never ought to reprove or gainstand them, nor yet warn and guard others against them; and that it is a part of the commendable unity of the church of Christ, to suffer all such things without taking notice of them—I know none [that] will say so; but if there be any so foolish as to affirm it, let them consider these Scriptures," &c., &c. . . . . . . "For though Christ be the Prince of peace, and doth most of all commend love and unity to His disciples; yet I also know He 'came not to send peace, but a sword,' that is, in dividing man from the lusts and sins he hath been united to. And also it is the work of His disciples and messengers to break the bands and unity of the wicked, wherein they are banded against God and His truth, and the confederacy of such as stand in unrighteousness, by inviting and bringing as many as will obey, unto righteousness; whereby they become disunited and separated from their companions, with whom they were centred, and at peace, in the contrary and cursed nature. And indeed, *blessed are they,* that are sent forth of the Lord to scatter here, that they may gather into the unity of the life: and they are blessed, that, in this respect, even for righteousness' sake, are scattered and separated from their brethren, that they may come to know the brotherhood and fellowship which is in the Light; from which none ought to scatter, nor to be scattered, but be more and more gathered thereunto."

Concerning the right and power of decision in the church, R. Barclay says: "The only proper judge of controversies in the church, is the Spirit of God; and the power of deciding solely lies in it; as having the only unerring, infallible, and certain judgment belonging to it: which infallibility is not necessarily annexed to any persons, person, or places whatsoever, by virtue of any office, place, or station any one may have or have had in the body of Christ. That is to say, that any have ground to reason thus,—because I am or have been *such an eminent member*, therefore my judgment is infallible; or, *because we are the greatest number;* or, that we live in such a noted or famous place, or the like;—though some of these reasons may and ought to have their *true weight* in case of contradictory assertions; yet not so, as upon which, either mainly or only, the infallible judgment is to be placed: but upon the Spirit, as that which is the firm and unmovable foundation."

Near the close of this treatise, he says: "This infallible judgment is only and unalterably annexed and seated in the Spirit and power of God; not to any particular person or persons, meeting or assembly, by virtue of any settled ordination [he might have said 'organization'], office, place, or station that such may have, or have had, in the church; no man, men, nor meeting, standing or being invested in any authority in the church of Christ upon other terms, than so long as he or they abide in the living sense and unity of the life in their own particulars; which, whosoever, one or more [mark that expression—*one or more*], inwardly departs from, *ipso facto* loses all authority, office, or certain discerning, he or they formerly have had; though retaining the true principles and sound form, and (may be) not fallen into any gross practices, as may declare them generally to be thus withered and decayed."

This work of Robert Barclay's, on "Church Government," as well as his great work, the "Apology," has received the official sanction of the Society of Friends from its first publication; and the candid reader will excuse the extent of the above quotations therefrom, on the consideration of the remarkable adaptation of the positions advanced therein, to the circumstances of the present times in the Society, and to the subjects alluded to throughout the following volume. And does it not follow from R. Barclay's reasoning, that if an individual member, or a meeting of the Society, or even a number of meetings, large or small, associated together, should persist in giving countenance to fundamental error or departure from the ancient faith of the body, such individuals or meetings must thereby lose their standing in the church, and all right authority therein which they might have had whilst living and abiding in the truth? And if so, how can the still living branches of the Vine hesitate in withdrawing from communion with such, and declaring them separated from that of whose sap and life they are permitted to partake; lest by continuing connected with them, and thus conniving at their lapse, they should themselves be infected by contact with a lifeless portion of the body?

The Society, though abounding in the good things of this life, and enjoying the esteem, instead of the enmity of the world—and perhaps in part as a consequence thereof—has of late years been laden with distress and perplexity. The past thirty-five years have seen it sorrowfully torn by two fearful defections from the faith of our forefathers, far surpassing any or all previous ones in the extent of the devastation produced within its borders, and of the reproach thereby brought upon the cause of truth. The one was, in effect, a denial of the outward, or what our Saviour has done for us without us—the other, a discarding of the inward, or what He is to do for us individually, within us. The first, the heresy of Elias Hicks and his coadjutors, was characterized by a denial of the miraculous birth and divine Sonship of our Lord and Saviour Jesus Christ, and his atonement for the sins of the whole world; by a light esteem of the Holy Scriptures; and by a general laxity of religious faith and life, bordering more or less on deism, and clearly evincing their departure in heart from Him who is the Sanctifier and holy Leader of his people. Against this defection many faithful brethren openly testified, and labored diligently to expose its awfully delusive and destructive nature, and to preserve the flock, as much as might be, from its poisonous effects. But in some places the power and influence of popular leaders induced great numbers to go off in the schism, leaving in many instances but a small remnant to sustain the true Society in certain localities. Yet to these was readily accorded by the Society elsewhere, the undoubted claim to recognition and fellowship, without any further regard to the smallness of their numbers than as their sympathies were thereby additionally aroused on their behalf, as the records of those days will amply show. The question was, which party faithfully adhered to the ancient doctrines and practices—not, which had the numerical majority, or retained the meeting-houses, in any portion of the heritage.

The other great defection from the true foundation of Quakerism, in our day, has been that distinguished by the name of its chief author and prominent promoter, Joseph John Gurney, which was of a far more insinuating and widely delusive character. In this instance, the cunning enemy adapted his stratagem to suit the proclivities of a people rich and full, learning to court the world and avoid the humiliating submission to the cross of Christ, and placing too great a reliance upon mere human learning and acquirements; and accordingly the system now presented for the acceptance of the unwary, was based upon the idea that a knowledge of religious truth and duty was to be obtained through an intellectual belief and study of the Holy Scriptures; and characterized by views of a worldly nature, disparaging to the inward work of Divine Grace as the groundwork; and discarding several of the spiritual doctrines of our early Friends, and their published works as expositions of what was now to be believed. The "Beacon" schism in England, of 1835 and 1836, was merely the premature offshoot hereof, or the premonitory symptoms of the disease which had already begun to lurk in secret, and was thwarting the application of preventives or remedies adequate to the danger.

When we consider the different features of these two successive defections, we are, even at first sight, repelled and disgusted by the coarse character of the wild unbelief of Elias Hicks, in regard to that which our blessed Lord Jesus Christ did for mankind in that prepared body in the days of his flesh; and might almost be induced to look with leniency on the later departure, so fraught with a plausible show of what appears outwardly good unto men; did we not find, on a near inspection and comparison of it with what has already been seen in the Light to be the path which the vulture's eye hath not seen, that in this heresy lurks a still greater danger to the integrity of the church, on the very account of its insinuating nature, by which it would appear, as it were, as an angel of light, to the unwary mind, and thereby is calculated to draw away great numbers who would not have dared to embrace the open errors of Hicksism. The system of J. J. Gurney came over the Society so stealthily, so amiably as it were, so beautifully in its superficial aspect, so pleasingly to the natural affections and to the benevolent tendencies of cultivated minds, so attractively to the great bulk of nominal professors,—it was so calculated to win for Friends the good will and esteem of others, instead of their jealousy and enmity,—and so apparently parallel at first were its paths (to the eye that looked at it but slightly) with that which by many was looked upon as the true path of their profession,—that great multitudes were entangled in it, before they suspected anything more than supposed improvements of sentiment and language, conformable to the polish of the nineteenth century. Yet there were, even early in the inroads of this great defection, some deeply experienced and faithful servants of the Most High, whose inward eye being kept in the Head, and open to the unfoldings of His wisdom, was renewedly anointed and enabled to detect the snare thus laid for the unwary; and these mourned over the lapse which they saw impending over this people. For J. J. Gurney, by his position in the community at large, and in the Society, attracted to his support the influence of many standing as leaders and occupying posts of much power; and though he was not without admonition, even early in his career as an author, yet preferring his own ways, and the learning of the schools, to the wisdom of those who had learned it at the school of Christ, he proceeded to add volume to volume in great profusion, spreading whole editions of some of his works gratuitously; and soon acquired great authority, and almost superseded the previous publications of the Society on the tables of the members, by the overwhelming numbers of his own.

This seed produced its natural fruit; for notwithstanding the testimony openly borne against it, by such servants of Christ as Thomas Shillitoe, John and Lydia Ann Barclay, Sarah L. Grubb, George and Ann Jones, John Harrison, Thomas Hancock, and others in England, and many gifted and faithful ones in America, the voices of the multitude in favor of a popular religion prevailed to such an extent, as to render the primitive principles and practices of the Society distasteful to a very large proportion of the members. It is needless here to trace the successive steps of this sad departure. The inquiring reader may find them in some of the published official documents of Philadelphia and New England Yearly Meetings, and may learn many features of its progress by an attentive perusal of the "Journal of John Wilbur," and the letters contained in this volume.*

Thomas B. Gould was one of the first in New England, who clearly discerned the nature of this awful defection, and the probable results to be apprehended from its being allowed to spread unrestrained over the land; and was constrained to stand in the breach, in conjunction with his beloved and honored friend John Wilbur, and other honest-hearted and unflinching servants of Christ, in an early stage of its appearance in this country. His letters, written during the troubles brought by this schism upon the Society in New England, show the constancy of his zeal in testifying against its inroads, and in warning his friends to beware of its fascinations. Many of these letters are too ample in their details for insertion in this work, and may furnish valuable material for the future historian; but the portions selected for our present purpose will almost furnish of themselves a con-

* For distinct and detailed information relative to the nature of this defection, and the essential difference of doctrine and practice between the position taken by the Gurney party, and that of Friends from the beginning, the reader is referred to the "Appeal for the Ancient Doctrines," &c., published by Philadelphia Yearly Meeting in 1847; the "Report on the Division in New England Yearly Meeting," issued by the same Yearly Meeting in 1849; the "Journal and Correspondence of John Wilbur, 1859;" and an "Examination of the Memoirs and Writings of J. J. Gurney," by W. Hodgson, Philadelphia, 1856.

nected narrative of the exercises and trials which, from time to time, were his portion, in opposing the progress of innovation, or in defending the truth and his own position in it. These letters may possibly appear to some to dwell much on his own affairs. But it will be well to remember that they were addressed, in most instances, to his intimate and familiar friends, who, as he knew, felt a lively interest in whatever concerned him and the cause, and were desirous of such intelligence from time to time. It was also the aim of the editor, in making the selection, to present especially such portions of the correspondence, as alluded most particularly to the successive events and circumstances forming the main features of his pilgrimage; and many portions of a different character have necessarily been omitted, as their insertion would have swelled too voluminously the bulk of the work.

It will be seen by the reader, that Thomas B. Gould partook largely of the distresses brought upon a sensitive mind by the machinations of a crafty and envious party spirit, whose evil reports continually assailed him in one way or another, either secretly or openly. Yet these things turned him not from his steadfastness. "The archers shot at him—but his bow abode in strength, and the arms of his hands were made strong by the mighty God of Jacob." And he had not only the unity of the faithful, in standing firmly as he did for the truth, but also the inward testimony of the blessed Comforter, from time to time vouchsafed, that his labors in this cause were acceptable in the sight of Him with whom he had to do.

As a citizen, Thomas B. Gould was known and acknowledged, through his native city and island, for unquestionable candor, integrity, and uprightness. His every-day demeanor was that of a disciple of Christ, with a sobriety and gravity which bespoke his earnestness, and at once impressed those who met with him, that he was endeavoring in sincerity to walk worthy of his high vocation and holy profession. He was diligent in his outward business when health and intervals from religious engagements permitted, often toiling through a great portion of the night, to take advantage of favorable weather, and make up for time unavoidably spent in other avocations or duties; and he was conscientiously careful in fulfilling all his pecuniary obligations. He had a keen relish for the beauties of the outward creation, and loved at times to point out to his familiar friends the admirable works of the Creator. Yet he was religiously concerned to keep the world under his feet, in view of that better country in which his hopes were centred; esteeming the riches and gratifications of this world but as a worthless bauble, in comparison with the pearl of great price, and the sweet evidence of acceptance with Him who said unto Simon Peter, "Lovest thou me more than these?"

As a minister of the Gospel, he was justly esteemed by his fellow-citizens; who knew the sincerity of his heart, and divers of whom, including ministers of various denominations, occasionally hearing him, were deeply affected by his appeals to the unflattering Witness in their souls, and could not refrain from the inward acknowledgment, and sometimes the open and even public avowal of their conviction, of the wisdom and power and unction attending his advocacy of the pure doctrines of the Gospel. Having been very early in life made acquainted with the principles of truth, and having measurably conformed his life in obedience to the successive manifestations of the Light of Christ as his Leader, his spiritual faculties strengthened and matured beyond those of most young men of his years; and thus, being advanced to the stature of "a man in Christ Jesus," he knew whereof he affirmed, from a degree of blessed experience, and could boldly declare, with the holy men of old, yet in humility and fear of the Lord alone, "We know that he is come, and hath given us an understanding, that we know Him that is true," and "that which we have known and seen and handled of the good word of life, that declare we unto you."

He was of a tender spirit, and willing to cherish the good in all, and was many times enabled to develop the inward movements of the heart in those whom he addressed, or with whom he conversed in relation to their everlasting welfare. And it is believed that none were able to charge him with hardness of feeling towards any, or with conduct on any occasion inconsistent with Christian kindness and civility. Yet in his testimony against the inroads of error and schism in the church, he was open and uncompromising, from a conviction of duty and of the vital nature of the case: and though comparatively young in years, it may be said of him, as T. Ellwood said of George Fox, that "he was valiant for the truth, bold in asserting it, patient in suffering for it, unwearied in laboring in it, steady in his testimony to it, immovable as a rock—zealously earnest where the honor of God, the prosperity of truth, and the peace of the church were concerned: for indeed, the care of the churches of Christ was daily upon him, the prosperity and peace whereof he studiously sought." And we may add, to the honor and praise of the great "I AM," that it was all of Divine Grace—all in the ordering of the goodness and wisdom of God, who condescended to make the child of faith a partaker of heavenly gifts in Christ Jesus.

He was eminently acquainted with the history of our religious Society, and with the didactic and controversial publications of our early Friends; and loved to dwell on their works of faith and labors of love, and constancy under suffering for the testimony of Jesus. But particularly and above all other books did he value the Holy Scriptures; which from his boyhood he had diligently read, with his inward eye directed to Him who only hath the key of David, and can open and unfold their heavenly mysteries, and thereby "make the man of God perfect, thoroughly furnished unto all good works," and "wise unto salvation through faith which is in Christ Jesus." He quoted largely from them in his ministry and writing, "comparing spiritual things with spiritual," greatly to the comfort and edification of those whom he addressed, and whose inward ear was anointed to hear and receive the truths of the Gospel.

And what if some, through party spirit and prejudice, did not believe and would not receive? "Shall their unbelief make the faith of God without effect?" Or shall it weaken our confidence in His eternal truth, and cast down our hands from His holy altar? And what if even "twenty-and-two thousand men," who had at first gone forth against the Midianites, should have become "fearful and afraid," after beholding the hosts encamped against them, and so "returned" from the warfare; shall we all fear with their fear and be afraid, as if there had been no "dew on the fleece?" And what if, of the "ten thousand" still in the field, even nine thousand seven hundred should be found unworthy to be trusted for the battle, and be set aside, leaving a remnant, as it were, but three hundred, to stand openly in the conflict against the enemies of Israel: shall all this mighty defection turn the truth of God into a lie? Or shall it persuade us, that what we have heretofore seen in the Light to be the will of the Lord for us to do, is not to be done, because the multitude command it not? Or shall we forsake that "narrow way that leadeth unto life," to join a confederacy of men that turn aside, to please the world and the carnal mind? Nay, verily; but let the remnant of true-hearted Israelites be content to be accounted even as the three hundred that lapped in the army of Gideon, if haply they may be found worthy to suffer in defence of so good a cause; and let them hold on to the shield of faith which has heretofore been anointed, knowing that what they have been contending for, these twenty years and more, is no other than "the faith once delivered to the saints," but now despised and discarded and perverted, by some of the very descendants of those who suffered grievous persecutions, rather than give away, or barter away, one tittle of that which had been made known to them as the unchangeable truth of Christ.

Let us then be still livingly concerned to rally to primitive principles and primitive practices, remembering that Truth is truth, though all men may forsake it; and go on with the help of the Most High, as we may be graciously endued with a little renewal of strength from Him, for the accomplishment of His will, though to the humiliation and reduction of the creaturely will and wisdom into nothingness before Him. May neither the open assaults of the enemy, nor his secret insinuations and snares, weaken our constancy, or slacken a godly zeal, or efface from remembrance the deliverances which have heretofore been experienced at the Lord's hand, and the blessed, and heavenly, dying experience of this our brother, and those of his fellow-laborers who with him have gone before us to the heavenly inheritance, and received the end of their faith, even the salvation of their souls; remembering how they were sweetly supported, in their closing hours, by the sustaining presence of the Most High, and how they were enabled to sing of His mercies, from a living and sensible feeling and foretaste of the joys in store for them. Let us bear in mind also, how they had aforetime walked among us, steadfast in the one faith; and how they endeavored to encourage and animate the flock, to stand firmly in the testimony which the Lord had given us against gainsayers, and to live over them by a godly life, as well as by word and pure doctrine. Thus, as each one is renewedly concerned to maintain individually a fervent exercise of mind after the one baptism, which baptizeth by the one Spirit into the one body, the church may be edified, and our meetings, large and small, may be kept more and more in the power and wisdom of Truth; the Lord alone may be known to be their crown and diadem, the vacancies in the ranks may be filled up by living worshippers, and "the shout of a King" may still be heard in our camp.

PHILADELPHIA, 3d month, 1860.

LIFE AND LETTERS

OF

THOMAS B. GOULD.

CHAPTER I.

THOMAS B. GOULD was the son of Henry and Abigail Gould, of the city of Newport, on Rhode Island, and was born there on the 22d of the sixth month, 1813.

His father, Henry Gould, who still survives him, was of the fourth generation in descent from the first settler of that name in Rhode Island, Daniel, the son of Jeremy and Priscilla Grovier Gould, of Great Britain, who emigrated to America and settled in this colony about the year 1642, when about sixteen years of age. Daniel married Waite Coggeshall; and, about the year 1658, was convinced of the principles of truth professed by Friends, to which he steadily adhered through the trials of that day of persecution in New England. He joined William Robinson and Marmaduke Stevenson, at Salem, in the autumn of 1659, after they had been banished from Massachusetts on pain of death; travelled with them over the colony for four weeks, and returned with them to Salem and Boston. They were all three imprisoned in the common jail of Boston, with several other Friends, who had accompanied them to that city, and were treated with great harshness. After the martyrdom of William Robinson and M. Stevenson, several of the remaining prisoners were whipped through the streets, Daniel Gould receiving thirty lashes on his bare back. But he continued faithful to his religious convictions; and, in 1671, accompanied John Burnyeat on his second visit to Virginia, where many who had, a few years before, been involved in the defection of John Perrot, were favored with ability to retrace their steps. In the ministry of the Gospel, he also travelled in various parts of New England, Staten Island, Long Island, New York, New Jersey, Pennsylvania, &c., the Lord blessing his labors to the convincement of divers of those who heard him.

He is said to have been "a man richly furnished with the gifts of the Holy Spirit; patient under exercises, grave in behavior, pleasant and exemplary in conversation; his ministry weighty and deep, tending to the consolation and comfort of God's people;" and "his understanding and memory in his latter years had more than common brightness." In his last sickness he often expressed great resignation to the Lord's will, and endured much bodily suffering with exemplary patience. He greatly enjoyed the company of his friends, and when drawing near to his close, expressed his full assurance of life eternal, and encouraged all to walk in the unchangeable Truth to which he had endeavored faithfully to bear witness, with the animating language, "Let death come when it will, my reward is sure." He died in the year 1716, a minister about forty-five years, and in the ninety-first year of his age. Successive generations of the family have continued to reside at and near Newport to the present day.

Thomas, the subject of the present memoir, was a child of remarkable promise, showing an unusual degree of clearness of mental perception, maturity of intellect and sentiment, and integrity of purpose and walk, at a very early age. He was favored with the privilege of having tender and religiously-concerned parents, and was carefully brought up by them in the nurture and admonition of the Lord.

In the absence of many incidents of his early life, his

childhood and youth can scarcely be better portrayed than in some of the language of his surviving friends in their memorial of him issued soon after his decease.

"He was naturally of a slender constitution, and subject to frequent attacks of illness. He was a dutiful child, and religiously inclined from very early life, having been heard to say in maturer years, that he did not remember the time when he had no religious impressions. As an evidence of the heed he early gave to the inward monitions of the Heavenly Teacher, the following incident may be related. At a time when he was quite young, military displays were often made at some little distance from his father's house, and he felt a strong desire and curiosity to go and see them. One day, seeing a number of his playfellows going to the grounds, the temptation became very strong, and he followed them without the knowledge of his parents, who, he knew, would disapprove of it. As he walked on, a sense of his disobedience pressed heavily upon him; which, as he proceeded, became more and more oppressive, until at length he could feel no peace but in turning back; which he did, without ever again desiring to go to such places.

"When but seven or eight years of age, his father, who was a miller, was in the practice of sending him about the town to supply his numerous customers; in which vocation he won the attachment and affection of the town's people almost without exception; being of a kind and obliging disposition, scrupulously exact and honest in his dealings, and his conversation with them generally of a serious or religious cast.

"When about twelve years of age, he was brought so low by a severe attack of sickness, that his life was despaired of. After his recovery from this illness, his religious impressions appear to have deepened, and his experience to have ripened, in a remarkable manner for one so young. About this time, he commenced keeping a written account of his feelings and exercises, with incidents of visits of friends in the ministry, as well as of others; and continued the practice for some years: but subsequently destroyed most of his productions in this line, as it would appear, from an humble opinion of himself; and in after life said, he did not think it was required of him to keep a journal.

The following was written during the sickness above alluded to.

"Oh! how sure is the Rock of Ages! But how unlike is Satan, the grand adversary, who defileth everything he entereth into. But He who descended from heaven, not to destroy but to save life, influences me by His Spirit to love and serve Him. My desires are at times very strong to be enabled to distinguish between the voice of Satan and that of the King of Heaven; as also, when the voice of the true Spirit is distinguished, that I may be enabled to be obedient thereto."

From his early childhood, he sought and greatly enjoyed the company of those who, as he believed, were servants of the Most High; and from the position of his parents and some beloved connections at Newport, he often had the privilege of association with eminently gifted members of the Society of Friends, in their temporary sojournings at that central location of the Society in New England. He was a great favorite, while a boy, with that valuable woman and faithful minister of the Gospel, Abigail Robinson, and spent much time with her, profiting by her instructive conversation and example, and by the opportunities thus afforded, at her residence, of mingling with the wise and good. The impressions then received had a marked effect on his mind in more mature age.

Thus, by the immediate touches of the tendering hand of the Shepherd of Israel, and by giving heed to the precepts and admonitions of those who were concerned for his welfare, he was enamoured of the love of God, and brought into a degree of acquaintance with His truth, remarkable for one of his years. Yet he had fluctuations in his religious course, the enemy assailing him powerfully, and at times gaining a little upon him, weakening his faithfulness for a season, and giving him occasion subsequently to mourn over the ground he had lost, by allowing him an entrance with his insinuations. The following memorandums, found among other papers after his decease, appear to allude to such seasons.

"Another year has passed over my head, and awful to remember the sorrowful neglect of Divine Goodness, unwatchfulness, and lukewarmness that have prevailed! Oh, that the Lord would be pleased to spare me yet a little longer, that I may be more watchful, more careful to obey the dictates of His divine anointing principle within."

"On looking over some memorandums this evening made in the twelfth year of my age, my spirit hath been greatly humbled in consideration of the tender mercy and condescension of Almighty Goodness, in that he was pleased, in that season of childhood, to vouchsafe a sense, a deep and spiritual sense, of His purity and holiness; and also of the means by which purity and holiness of life and conversation might be attained, through which alone a conversion into a similitude and likeness of His own nature, might be known and witnessed, even in earthen vessels. But oh! since then, the vessel has been broken through unbelief, and the precious treasure suffered to escape, by which (if retained) the vessel might have been preserved in innocence and purity. It is a truth beyond all doubt with me, that nothing short of a measure and manifestation of divine Grace, inwardly and spiritually communicated, ever could have conveyed that sense of divine truth which I was then favored with, and such conformity to, and uniformity with scripture terms and doctrine. Well, if this is the case, and that communication has been interrupted, how necessary that the old paths should be diligently sought! Where is the old way?—for truly I am in a way which neither myself nor my fathers in the truth heretofore walked in! Oh, Thou who art the healer of breaches, and the restorer of paths for the lame to walk in, wilt Thou be pleased this once more to pluck my feet out of the mire and the clay, and to set them upon that Rock against which, as an establishment thereon is known, the gates of hell would never be able to prevail! Here, oh here, I have once been favored to behold thy face, and to meditate on thy law with great delight! And should I again be favored to have light in my dwelling and on my path, then, O my soul, would thou be enabled to pursue thy journey with alacrity; and that true advancement would be known, which would be a source of comfort unto thee in this life, and would prepare thee for celestial enjoyment when time shall be no more!"

Submitting to these convictions, he grew in grace and in the saving knowledge of the Most High; and though still a youth, his mind was endued with a clear appreciation of the pure doctrines of Christianity, and a qualification was given to discern truth from error, either in principle or practice. He was favored with ability to wait on the Lord in the silence of all flesh, and to know the benefit thereof, above all merely outward performances, in the renewing of his strength, and the reception of a capacity to know and do the will of the Almighty. He alludes to this exercise in the following beautiful though brief memorandum.

"Divine worship, I believe, implies a patient waiting to know, and a faithful and scrupulous engagement to do the will of our Heavenly Father. But how hard have I often found it, to be so divested of active self, as to get into that true silence, humility, and lowliness of mind, where we can stand perfectly still, separated from any dependence on, or attention to any other than the great object of our adoration and praise! Nevertheless, I have at times been made sensible, to my humbling admiration, of the glory of the Lord descending and filling the outward temple, so that there was no place for, nor any disposition to engage in any official duties, but only to stand quite still, and behold the great glory and magnificence of the Shepherd of Israel."

His mind was often brought into serious concern for the religious welfare of his friends, and especially for those, like himself, in the early walks of life; and giving up in obedience to what he believed was of divine requiring, he was made willing to visit such at times, both in his native city and in places more or less remote, and in humility and love to deliver to them the burden which rested upon him on their account. His labors were often owned by the Witness for truth in the hearts of those visited, to the tendering of their spirits, and he was favored to return home in peace. At other times his concern for his brethren was manifested by epistolary communication, addressed in affectionate and earnest expostulation, encouragement, or admonition. The following is a portion of one of these epistles, showing the earnestness of his desire to be found faithful to his feelings of duty in this respect.

MY DEAR FRIEND:

Having been at times (as I believe thou art sensible) baptized into sympathy and fellow-feeling with thee in thy many trials and besetments, as well as into exercise on thy account, and renewedly and feelingly so at this time, I thought I could not easily get from under the burden, without spreading the concern which I have felt, a little before thee, as I may be enabled, and in this epistolary way, notwithstanding I have the favor and privilege of thy company at times.

I have observed with humbling admiration the bountiful goodness and preserving power of an All-wise Providence, not only in thy preservation from evil communications in good measure, but from evil habits also, in thy temporal and relative accommodations and blessings, but above all other considerations, in bringing thee to a knowledge of the ever-blessed truth in some good degree; and while I am writing, my soul bows in thankful acknowledgment on thy behalf, and can adopt the language, "This is the Lord's doing, and it is marvellous in mine eyes." And the fervent breathing of my spirit is, that neither one thing nor yet another may cause the work to be marred upon the wheel, but that thy hands, which are often ready to hang down, may be mercifully strengthened, and thy feeble knees confirmed; for I believe thou art often exceedingly stripped, and that thou feelest exceedingly the want of the sensible influence and perceptible guidance of Divine Good. But be entreated, in these seasons of deep proving, to hold fast the profession of thy faith without wavering, nothing doubting but that He that hath been with thee in six troubles will be with thee in the seventh.

The point, however, to which my mind has been the most forcibly turned in relation to thee, is, that thou mayst be increasingly gathered into the patient waiting for Christ in the way of His coming, and increasingly guarded with respect to those things which are likely to obstruct His appearance, or becloud thy vision. Oh, bear with me, my dear friend, as with one who would gladly have been excused, if relief might have been obtained in any other way than in the way of duty, while I entreat thee to shun all those things. I believe that the adversary of our happiness always enters at the weakest side, and that, well knowing in what things he would seek in vain to betray thee, he is making use of his pernicious influence to weaken thy hands, by casting temptations before thee adapted to thy situation and circumstances.

I find, if I obtain relief, as Thomas Shillitoe says, "the whole counsel committed unto me must be communicated;" that I must come right to the point; that I must entreat thee to resist bravely all solicitations to attend the meetings of other religious societies. I am sensible that here the cross may possibly be exceedingly heavy for thee to take up and to bear; but, my dear friend, I have seen with the eye of faith what the result would be, if this testimony should not be faithfully supported, in connection with some others which thou art, I believe, acceptably engaged in the support of. And I also feel a concern affectionately to recommend thee to take into thy serious consideration the subject of the common use of heathenish names for the days of the week, and months, as well as all complimentary titles and distinctions, and in connection with the use of the plain Scripture language, endeavor to bring them to the Light which will make all things manifest; and I do verily believe that thou wilt be favored to see, clearly to see, that the same precious principle which has led thee into one, will lead thee into the other. Nothing can be farther from my best feelings than in thus addressing thee, either to draw thee outward in thy views, or towards me as an instrument. My object is no other than that of all rightly administered instrumental labor, even to bring home to the true Teacher; and as thou art concerned to wait day by day to feel its quickening power, thou shalt be enabled to go on in that power, conquering and to conquer, even until judgment shall be sent forth unto victory. . . . . . .

During much of his youth, Thomas was liable to frequent attacks of bodily indisposition, and at times was brought very low by sickness, and thereby his schooling was considerably interfered with; but possessing an active mind, acute perceptions, and an uncommonly clear and retentive memory, his subsequent application and industry enabled him amply to compensate, in useful acquirements, for the time apparently lost to literary pursuits. His mind being thus stored beyond many of his years, and his conversational powers, naturally good, being improved by constant and familiar association with enlightened men and women greatly his superiors in age and attainments, his company and conversation, as he advanced in life, became attractive and instructive to his acquaintances of all ages, and especially to those whose faces were in reality set Zionwards. These could feel the true life in him answering to the witness in their own hearts, and were attracted towards him by ties stronger than those of natural brotherhood, because pertaining to the heavenly relationship.

His letters to his friends were many times fraught with deep instruction, and often contained very graphic descriptions of incidents or conversations in which he had been engaged, and in which he knew that his friends felt a lively interest. A portion of such descriptive epistles, (written in more mature life) selected for their value in developing the events of his own day, the sad departure of multitudes from the ancient landmarks of the Society, and his own efforts to warn his friends of the unsound doctrines insidiously introduced, and the mischievous devices of those engaged in promoting them, will furnish the reader of the following pages with something approaching to a narrative of the most remarkable events of his life, in the absence of any regular journal or autobiography. Being brought up by his father to the milling business, many of the most valuable and weighty of his epistles were written in his windmill, during the hours usually devoted to sleep, some of them being finished long after midnight or towards dawn of day. The following letter written to a relation, when about sixteen years of age, delineates familiarly some interesting particulars of a visit of George and Ann Jones to the Island of Canonicut.

FROM THOMAS B. GOULD TO ——.

NEWPORT, 21st of 6th mo. (1st day), 1829.

ESTEEMED COUSIN: I may inform that on the 20th G. and A. Jones appointed a meeting on Canonicut, at the eleventh hour. Aunt Mary, Lydia Ann, and myself having an inclination to attend, went over in the horse-boat, with G. and A. Jones, and E. Pitfield. The wind being against us made hard work for the horses, and it was nearly eleven when we arrived on shore. A very solid company was convened, and George was engaged to minister; beginning: "To be carnally-minded is death, but to be spiritually-minded is life and peace;" and went on to show that the carnal mind was indeed at "enmity with God." Ann followed him: "It is not in man that walketh to direct his steps;" showing our utter inability, as men and creatures, to do anything to the glory and honor of His glorious, holy name, unassisted by that divine principle, "a measure and manifestation" whereof has been given unto us "to profit withal;" that as we are engaged to know a co-working with that precious principle, it would work out for us a "far more exceeding and eternal weight of glory," even an entrance into that glorious, holy city, whose "walls are salvation and whose gates are praise;" that a mere historical faith in Christ's sufferings, death, resurrection, mediation, and intercession, would do nothing for us; that we must indeed witness the powerful operations of the Holy Ghost and fire, this being the only effectual, saving baptism; and be enabled to say, "It is not by any mighty works which we have done, but by the washing of regeneration and the renewing of the Holy Ghost." Dear Elizabeth Pitfield followed her, and sweetly encouraged those that were ready to say, "Can it be, that Christ died for so vile a worm as I am? Can it be, that I am an object of divine regard?" A precious meeting it was. Oh, that it may be to me like bread cast on the water, which returned after many days. This gave us a valuable opportunity of being in the company of these faithful advocates of the cause of truth and righteousness in the earth. . . . . . .

The wind blew so heavy, it was thought improbable the horse-boat would come over, and Ann Jones not being well, she thought most proper to leave at four o'clock, and the wind continuing to blow very heavy, the spray broke over into the boat to such a degree that it wet our friends very much, although they had umbrellas and cloaks. I crawled under the cuddy, where I should have been dry, if the water had not dripped through the planks. However, I esteem it another merciful favor that we were preserved from any other damage than wetting our clothes. Elizabeth thought it might be a specimen of crossing the Atlantic, but Ann told her it was not a comparison to it. Ann remarked, while on board the horse-boat, that it reminded her of a saying in her country, of putting to sea in a post-chaise. . . . . . .

The following memorandum is dated in 1830, when Thomas B. Gould was about seventeen years of age.

"It has been clearly manifested to me, that conscience is not the proper rule and guide which the Almighty, in His infinite wisdom and goodness, has provided for the regulation of the actions of His creature, man; because conscience, like reason, being a natural gift, may, when unenlightened, become depraved and identified with, or rather adulterated by, our evil propensities. But that the Holy Spirit of Christ, which He promised He would send in His name (which is often put for His power), is the guide and rule by which our conduct is to be regulated; for though in us, it is not of us, but is a most precious gift, being the same Rock that followed Israel, and that Rock was Christ. This never can be depraved, but, as minded and submitted to in its gentle movings and leadings, would subdue and overcome all that the Lord's holy controversy is against, and would gain for us an admittance into that city, the walls whereof are salvation, and whose gates are praise; it being the purchase of that most satisfactory sacrifice on Calvary's Mount, whereby He hath forever perfected them that are sanctified, and cast up a way for the ransomed and redeemed of our God to walk in; which, although an exalted situation, and one that of ourselves we are wholly incapable of attaining unto, yet it is so plain and so simple, that the wayfaring man, though a fool as to the things of this world, may not err therein. Well may we exclaim, 'Great is the mystery of godliness!'"

FROM THOMAS B. GOULD TO ——.

DEAR WILLIAM,—for so I believe I may address thee, having, from a feeling of pure love, been induced to make this exposure of myself, entirely independent of any outward information whatever.

I may remark that when thou wast here, a few weeks since, I felt such a nearness of sympathy and brotherly love for thee, as is entirely out of my capacity to convey; but intended, however, to have manifested it by more attention and being a little more in thy company, which was pleasant. But circumstances out of my control prevented the accomplishment of my intentions. There would not, probably, have been any other effect from these feelings, but the other day, as I sat in meeting, engaged in a train of thought which would not come under the term worship, but which I think was not altogether unprofitable, thou wast very unexpectedly and feelingly brought to my remembrance, accompanied with a belief that it would be best for me to write to thee; and although I had some openings, yet the end and design of the concern was not made known. The subject passed off; but soon after, something transpired, which tended to strengthen the feelings. I was sincerely desirous to do the thing that was right, and like Mary formerly, "kept all these things and pondered them in my heart:" and now having given the subject due deliberation, and endeavored to feel after the mind of truth, I am persuaded that I shall not be quite clear without submitting a few simple remarks for thy consideration.

Thou hast, I believe, been mercifully preserved from many of the evils and dangers incident to youth (of which

I have no doubt thou art sensible), but still thy path, as well as my own, is thickly strewed with Satan's baits, prepared by his subtle hand, in a way and manner in which thou art least likely to discover them, in order to detect and resist them. Thou must be brought into a feeling of thy own unworthiness and inability to do any good thing, before thou wilt be in a suitable state rightly to apply for assistance where alone it can be found. By attending simply to this, to "the Grace of God, which brings salvation, and hath appeared unto all men," thou wilt be enabled to discover clearly the way in which thou must go, wilt be made sensible of the exceeding corruption and depravity of the human heart, of the necessity there is for watchfulness; and as thou keepest thine eye single, wilt in due time experience deliverance from the house of bondage, which is sin, or the nature of the first Adam, from spiritual Egypt, where is darkness, but into which darkness the light of the Lord hath shined, as it is written: "They which sat in darkness saw a great light, and to them which sat in the region and shadow of death light is sprung up." And the evident design of the arising of this light, is to bring thee forth out of Egypt, from under the dominion of sin; and, if I am not mistaken in my feelings, it hath required thee to go as it were three days' journey into the wilderness, to sacrifice unto the Lord thy God; being made sensible, as the children of Israel formerly were, that it will be inconsistent with His will and pleasure to offer sacrifice unto Him, before thou hast witnessed and known a departure out of. Egypt. And this passover thou must be willing to eat in the way and manner that Divine Goodness has been pleased to direct, although it may be with bitter herbs, with the loins of thy mind girded, shoes upon thy feet, and a staff in thy hand, a full resolution and willingness being wrought to forsake the pleasures of Egypt, in order to journey forward and to possess the land of promise: and thou mayest remember that it is the willing and obedient that He will give to eat of the good fruit of that land. And thus, with a high hand and with an outstretched arm, thou wilt be enabled to go forth, by His assistance, not of thyself or thy own power; and when the sea is divided, and thou art made sensible of the wonderful power of the Lord, the horse and his rider being drowned in the midst of it, while to thee it is a wall on either side, the pillar of cloud going before thee by day, and the pillar of fire by night,—after thou hast known this, thou mayst believe thyself to be on the banks of deliverance.

Here thou wilt probably sing His praise, and mayest be ready to conclude that the warfare is accomplished, and that thou hast already arrived almost beyond the reach of trouble and danger. But I entreat thee to remember that thou art but just brought out and allured into the wilderness, and on the very outset and beginning of thy journey towards the heavenly Canaan; that here thou art to receive the dispensation of the law, and to be instructed in it, to be made acquainted with divers washings and cleansings, trying, perhaps, in their nature and administration; but be assured they are necessary in order to do away all Egypt's nature; for thou canst no more be fit to enter into that "good land," before this work is accomplished, than thou wast to offer sacrifice, before thou hadst taken some steps in thy journey thither. And be not anxious that this wilderness state may be suddenly gone through with, but rather be attentive to the hand of the Lord which may be observed herein. Remember that He fed His people formerly with bread from heaven and flesh to the full, that He clave the rocks for them, and encamped round about them, that the cloud rested upon the door of the tabernacle, and they journeyed not until it was lifted up. (He that readeth, let him understand.) For "when the cloud was taken up from over the tabernacle, the children of Israel went onward in all their journeys; but if the cloud were not taken up, then they journeyed not till the day that it was taken up. For the cloud of the Lord was upon the tabernacle by day, and fire was on it by night, in the sight of all the house of Israel, throughout all their journeys." Exodus 40 : 36, 37, 38.

Thus, my dear friend, be encouraged to keep thine eye singly upon Him who leadeth out His own sheep, calleth them by name, and goeth before them: so thou wilt be preserved from making any idol, and worshipping it, while, in His infinite wisdom, He is pleased to withhold Himself from thee, in order to prove thee and deepen thy love for Him. And thy journey in this wilderness will be shortened; thou wilt be favored to overcome all opposition; and although Balak may see thee approaching, be afraid, and call Balaam to curse thee, yet it will be turned into blessing altogether; and in the Lord's due and appointed time, when all that sinneth and lusteth after Egypt shall fall in the desert, thou wilt be enabled to pass over Jordan, and to bring up from the very bottom thereof stones of living memorial, showing where thou hast been dwelling, even under the preparing, fashioning hand of the Lord. On the other hand, if thou art disobedient, and hearkenest to the voice of the evil one, who will endeavor to retard thy progress by suggestions like those whereby he discouraged Israel, through the instrumentality of the evil spies (who being sent over to view the land, plainly discovered it to flow with milk and honey, were favored to taste of the fruit thereof and to bring back some with them to the camp, saying, this is the fruit of it, nevertheless discouraged them by saying "that the cities are walled and very great, and there are Anakims in the land, in comparison with whom we are like grasshoppers),"—listen not to the adversary, lest, after thou hast been raised up to view it, thou receive the intelligence, "Thou shalt not go over thither." But oh, that the spirit, the holy resolution which was in Caleb, may be in thee, who stilled the people by saying, "Let us go up at once and possess it, for we are well able to overcome it." Remember, the strength of the people who dwell there is departed from them, and that "there is none like unto the God of Jeshurun, who rideth upon the heaven in thy help and in His excellency on the sky. The eternal God is thy refuge, and underneath are the everlasting arms." As thy dependence is here, all these Canaanites will be driven out; for the command is, utterly to destroy them and drive them out; and unless this is accomplished, they will be a continual vexation and cause of stumbling.

This is my fervent desire and prayer for thee, as well as myself; and although it may seem strange to thee that I thus write, and in such a metaphorical manner, yet my excuse is the same as Balaam's was, "Whatsoever is put into my mouth, that I must speak, less or more;" my desire also has been like his, "Let me die the death of the righteous, and let my last end be like his."

The spring having closed, I must end as I began, that is, with reference to the pointings of truth, having no knowledge, when I put pen to paper, as to the matter or manner of my writing. I may however request that if thou receivest this and feelest freedom, thou would just give me some hints respecting thy apprehensions, especially if there is anything in it thou dost not clearly understand. I conclude,

Thy tenderly affectionate friend and well-wisher,

THOMAS B. GOULD.

FROM THOMAS B. GOULD TO ——.

MY DEAR FRIEND:

Notwithstanding I was strengthened to communicate a few words expressive of my belief of the divine nature of the visitation with which thou hast been visited (though very much in the cross), yet I felt afterwards so comfortably quiet, that I took it as a precious and abundant reward for this attention to what I have long believed to be incumbent on me. But the interruptions to which thou knowest I have been so much subjected, and which were repeated this evening, prevented me from fully relieving my mind; and the concern remaining weightily upon me, I have believed it to be right for me, in order to unburden my mind, and to discharge my duty towards thee, to submit a few simple remarks in writing, for thy consideration.

Thou wilt find it recorded in the Scriptures of truth, that "in the beginning God created the heavens and the earth." I have no doubt thou wilt readily acknowledge to the truth of this declaration; and in acknowledging to this, thou wilt admit the subsequent account, given by the inspired penman, of the six days' work, and also the divine authority of the Holy Scriptures. And thou wilt find that, after the whole creation was finished, and the fowls of the air, the fish of the sea, and the beasts of the field had been made, the Lord said, "Let us make man in our image, after our likeness;" that the Lord looked upon all that He had made, and "behold, it was very good;" that "in the image of God created he him, male and female created he them." Here thou wilt observe that he was created in the image and after the likeness of God; and as it is reasonably understood that a likeness, in the common sense of the term, bears some considerable resemblance to the original, so we may conclude that he partook largely of the divine nature, and was good. "And the Lord God planted a garden eastward in Eden, and there He placed the man whom he had formed." He was placed in a state of happiness and enjoyment in the favor of his Almighty Creator, having full liberty and permission to eat of the fruit of every tree of the garden but of the tree of knowledge of good and evil; and upon this the Almighty was pleased to lay his prohibitory command, and to pronounce a curse upon him in case of disobedience: "In the day that thou eatest thereof thou shalt surely die." And so long as the obedience of our first parents kept pace with their knowledge, they continued to relish and enjoy this union and communion with their Almighty Creator; but when, through the subtlety of the serpent, they had been prevailed upon to transgress the divine command, then they were made sensible of it; and when they heard the voice of the Lord walking in the garden, in the cool of the day, a time favorable to reflection, they hid themselves, knowing that they had sinned. But the Lord was pleased to call them, in a manner similar, I believe, to that in which thou hast been called when running contrary to the divine will inwardly revealed, "Adam! Adam! where art thou?" And his answer was, "I heard thy voice, and I hid myself, because I was naked." "Who told thee that thou wast naked? hast thou eaten of the fruit of the tree which I commanded thee not to eat?" His answer was, "The woman which thou hast given me gave me of the fruit, and I did eat:" and when the woman was questioned, she answered, "The serpent beguiled me, and I did eat."

Thus, my dear friend, I want thee to observe the excuses that were made, and compare them with the lines of thy own experience. Examine thy own heart; let the examination be impartial; and see how the thing will preponderate; see if it will not bear some comparison to this evasion, which was made by our primitive ancestors in a case exactly parallel. Remember also the judgment that was pronounced upon them. This judgment and the promise that was then made, are of the highest importance unto us, even in this glorious Gospel day in which we live, and to which it referred. It is fraught with deep instruction to the minds of those who rightly apply unto the Lord for help and instruction. To such as these our adorable King is pleased to open the Scriptures of truth by His eternal Spirit, and to seal on their minds those deep and important truths contained in them. And to this I would earnestly call thy attention; to an attentive perusal of the Scriptures, with the eye of thy mind fixed upon Him who alone can open the seals, and with thy spiritual ear open and attentive to that Spirit which can alone convey that soul-sustaining intelligence and encouragement, which will nourish it up unto eternal life.

But to return to the judgment that was pronounced upon the serpent, upon whom I think it was first passed: "I will put enmity between thee and the woman, and between thy seed and her seed; it shall bruise thy head, and thou shalt bruise his heel. Cursed art thou above all cattle: upon thy belly shalt thou go, and dust shalt thou eat all the days of thy life." And unto Adam He said, "Cursed is the ground for thy sake; in sorrow shalt thou eat of it all the days of thy life; thorns also and thistles shall it bring forth unto thee, and thou shalt eat the herb of the field." Here thou wilt perceive a great change to have taken place in the condition of our first parents, so lately enjoying sweet union with their Maker, and now being driven forth to till the ground from whence they were taken, and to eat the "herb of the field." And lest he should put forth his hand and partake of the tree of life, and live forever, there were placed at "the east of the garden of Eden, cherubim, and a flaming sword, which turned every way, to keep the way of the tree of life." This is a subject that has often engaged my serious attention, it remaining to be a sealed truth, that no man can attain unto the tree of life, but by passing under this flaming, two-edged sword; and this view of the subject coincides with the testimony of the Apostle Paul, who described the sword of the Spirit, as being a quick discerner of the thoughts and intents of the heart, and that it divided between soul and spirit, joints and marrow. By this thou wilt discover that we are prone by nature to act contrary to this Spirit of Grace, and to do despite unto it, in that all have sinned and fallen short of the glory of God, in that we have all partaken of the sad effects of this fall of our first parents from that state of happiness and goodness in which they were created; as it is written, after Adam was driven out of Paradise, that he "begat a son in his own image, and after his own likeness."

And this corrupt nature of the natural man must be done away, this image and likeness of the first Adam; and there is no way by which it can be accomplished, but through the glorious way of escape promised by Infinite Goodness, almost as soon as His divine command had been transgressed, viz.: "I will put enmity between thee and the woman, and between thy seed and her seed; it shall bruise thy head and thou shalt bruise his heel." Now, thou mayst remark, that the head is a vital part of the body, and when the head is wounded we are justly said to be wounded all over; and this is agreeable with the testimony of the apostle: "For this purpose was the Son of God manifested, that He might destroy the works of the devil;" and with this the testimony of the holy patriarchs, prophets, and apostles agrees. Moreover, the promise of this seed of the woman was renewed to Abram; and in token of his favor and acceptance with the Almighty, and also of the change of heart and disposition that had taken place, his name was changed to Abraham, and the promise was renewed: "In thee and in thy seed shall all the families of the earth be blessed." It was renewed to

Isaac, and to Jacob, whose name was also changed to Israel, because he wrestled and obtained the blessing, saying, "I will not let thee go except thou bless me." The Lord Almighty was pleased, however, before He introduced the glorious dispensation of the Gospel of our Lord and Saviour, Jesus Christ, to bring in, between the fall and the way of escape from the fall, another dispensation, consisting of divers washings and cleansings, which never "made the comer thereunto perfect," but pointed to that which did. It pointed to the last and lasting dispensation, by which we are enabled emphatically to draw nigh unto God; by which, and by which alone, we can possibly be placed in a capacity to rise above the first nature; which is fallen, degenerate, and dead, but through this propitiatory sacrifice, which in due time was offered up for our sins, there has been a gift of God purchased, a little divine seed and agency placed in the corrupt heart of man in the fall, which counteracts and opposeth the evil seed and the first nature; and as it is attended to in its appearances, however small they may be, it would overcome, it would subdue all of a contrary nature, and finally would effect a change of disposition and a change of heart; all old things would be done away, all things would become new, and all things of God. Here thou wouldst be raised out of the fall and the effects of it, and having in this passed under the flaming sword, or in other words, known Him whose right hand is to rule and to reign, to come into thy heart, and to sit there as a refiner with his fire and as a fuller with his soap, to purge away the dross, and the tin, and the reprobate silver, thou wouldst be favored to partake of the tree of life; and if thou continued faithful unto death, a crown of life would be given thee, eternal in the heavens, which fadeth not away. . . . .

[WRITTEN IN THE YEAR 1832.]

"I have of late made so little progress, and in my heart was so far gone back into Egypt, that I have been ready to wish that I never had been favored in the way that I am, rather than those things that are so very near and dear to me should be called for. O, Lord, be thou pleased to forgive the thought of my corrupt heart; seeing Thou hast been tempted in all points like as we are, sin only excepted: and oh! enable me to return thanks unto thee, that thou hast, in unbounded mercy, been pleased to lengthen the thread of my natural and spiritual life, and that thou didst not cut me off altogether! And enable thou me, if it be consistent with thy holy will, to walk more humbly and consistently before thee; that so I may not dishonor thy holy cause in the earth!"

MEMORANDUM, FOUND AMONG HIS PAPERS, DATED SEVENTH MONTH, 1832.

"Strong desires are at times raised in my heart, that the good work that I humbly hope has been begun, may be in mercy carried forward, that I may know a progression from this state of childhood to that of a young man, and to a strong man in Christ Jesus; He being the Author of every good work; and if the state alluded to is ever attained, it must be only by Him. And I thought I might adopt the language, in allusion to the small progress that has been made hitherto: 'By Thee I have run through a troop, and by my God I have leaped over a wall;' notwithstanding I have yet much to pass through, and am daily passing under the just judgments of an offended God, in one way or other. Yet being sensible that I have a baptism to be baptized with, I am at times exceedingly straitened that it may be accomplished; and at this time I am encouraged to believe, that as I sincerely endeavor to keep near the unfailing Helper of His people, although His waves and His billows may pass over my head (which I sincerely hope may be the case, that the old and corrupt nature may be washed away), I shall be preserved from sinking. For I am firm in the belief, that by no other means than by baptism can any man become a member of the Church of Christ; and I also believe that out of that Church there is no salvation." ["If I wash thee not, thou hast no part with me." John 13 : 8.]

FROM T. B. G. TO GEORGE F. READ.

NEWPORT, 23d of 10th month, 1834.

MY DEAR FRIEND:

I have taken up my pen this afternoon to answer thy acceptable letter of last sixth month; and although I have deferred it so long, I can assure thee that I cannot charge myself with either negligence or forgetfulness, but in truth I can inform thee I have not since that time been in a situation to communicate anything which would have been worth thy perusal. I have been an inhabitant of a dry and barren land, in which there has been neither dew, nor rain, nor field of offering; and as it has, for a long time, been a settled principle with me, not to open my inward exercises and trials to any, without feeling that liberty in the truth to do it which alone could make such a disclosure safe, I have forborne to burden thee with complaints, choosing rather, as I might be favored, to abide in my tent, and endeavor to search for the cause of this great desertion and leanness; for even Jerusalem was to be searched with lighted candles. Oh! my dear friend, the preciousness, as well as the importance, of having the candle lighted and on the candlestick! If it is on the candlestick and not lighted, it is worse than useless, because profession without possession is hypocrisy; and if it has, through adorable Mercy and condescending Goodness, been lighted, and remains under the bushel, it must unavoidably go out again, for it cannot burn in unsuitable and unprofitable confinement. The declaration of our blessed Lord still continues to hold good: "Ye have not chosen me, but I have chosen you, and ordained you, that ye should go, and bring forth fruit, and that your fruit should remain." And again: "Ye are the salt of the earth, and the light of the world; and a city that is set on a hill cannot be hid." Now those that have been called and chosen by Him, and through and by His holy help, enabled not only to labor but to bring forth fruit, these certainly do season and give light unto others; but when they cease to season and give light unto others, then the salt has lost its savor; it is thenceforth good for nothing, and is cast out and trodden under foot of men; and the light which shone through them being obscured, finally will be put out; for we read that the candle of the wicked shall be put out. But as our hope of *preservation* is in the unfolding of that Light which makes manifest, and as a measure and manifestation of this Light has been given unto every man to profit withal, so I believe it does become our weak and childlike state to abide in our tent with the little we may be intrusted with, until that Light moveth and goeth before. Then we may safely follow, because that same direction which it takes will be the path for us to walk in. I have often instructively remembered the account we have of the dealings of the Lord with the children of Israel, in bringing them forth out of the land of Egypt, through the Red Sea and the wilderness, in general; and in particular, the manner in which they journeyed. It is declared that a pillar of a cloud rested on the tabernacle by day, and a pillar of fire by night, in the sight of all the house of Israel, and throughout all their journeys; and that they journeyed not until the cloud was lifted up. Well, as surely as the cloud rested on the outward tabernacle visibly, so surely does it rest on our tabernacles spiritually, yet sensibly; and I believe, the more closely we are engaged to watch its movements, when it goes before and leads the way for us, or to abide in our tents when it remains stationary, the more profitably we shall get along for ourselves, and for those among whom we may be walking; for the tabernacle of God, agreeably to the testimony of the Apostle John, remains to be with men; and he says that God Himself shall be with them, and wipe away all tears from their eyes, and be their God. And this was written when the temple of the tabernacle of witness in heaven was opened. Doubtless it is in them only, who, by an attention to the manifestation of His Spirit, are engaged to prepare His way in the wilderness, and to make His paths straight, that the precious promise above alluded to will be realized. If, as a general thing, those who are thus under exercise, should unadvisedly open their state to such as are not qualified to understand the same, and of consequence not skilful to make such an application as the case requires, they would lay themselves liable to serious injury. It was a cause of complaint against some formerly, that they had healed the wound of the Lord's people slightly; and against others, that they had been daubing with untempered mortar. Now I believe that if we rightly seek that wisdom that is profitable to direct, we shall be preserved from opening our condition to such as these; and on the other hand, those that dwell near the Spring of Divine Life in themselves, feeling a sympathy for and a fellowship with us in that life, without any outward information whatever, are often enabled to speak a word in season to them that are weary, and according to the apostolic description, the secrets of hearts are made manifest; for prophecy (which is a speaking to edification and comfort) came not in old time by the will of man, but holy men of old spake as they were moved by the Holy Ghost.

These openings and advices, coming from a pure and unerring spring, must be abundantly more safe and useful than those which originate merely in the unauthorized and unassisted invention of the human mind.

Thus, my dear friend, I have simply made these remarks as they have renewedly and feelingly opened to the view of my mind; though I have long been confirmed in the belief of their truth, and I also believe, as I am more and more concerned to be thus governed, that I shall be favored to stand in my lot at the end of my days. But weakness and infirmity of flesh and spirit are so much mine, that except in some brighter and more favored moments, discouragement prevails in a great degree. That I may have the sympathy of thy spirit, and that thou mayst favor me with a line, I most sincerely ask, not waiting or deferring it because of my long silence: for the reasons for my not writing, above given, are true and honest reasons.

I am often sensible of deep exercise and concern on account of our religious society, in general and more particularly, so that I feel like a cask which wants vent, but no way often opens by which I can find relief. I go about under the weight of the exercise, wearing sackcloth as the king of Israel did, in the time of the famine in Samaria, inwardly upon his flesh, when the city was besieged until an ass's head was sold for five pieces of silver. I know not but my case may be like that of the lord on whose hand the king leaned; who, when the prophet prophesied of better things, said, "If the Lord should make windows in heaven, might these things be;" [might *such a thing be?*] and indeed the denunciation pronounced against him, "Thou shalt see it with thine eyes, but shalt not eat thereof," seems sometimes to apply, for I am as it were in the sight of food, but am not permitted to eat thereof. But I have been comforted in the remembrance of the four leprous men who sat at the gate of the city. Thou mayst remember, they said one to another: "Why sit we here until we die? If we enter into the city, the famine is in the city, and we shall die there, and if we sit still here we shall die also. Now let us fall into the camp of the Assyrians; if they save us alive, we shall live, and if they kill us, we shall but die." But when they came, they found no man there, but horses tied and asses tied; for the Lord had caused them to hear the sound of chariots and horsemen, and they said, "The king of Israel hath hired the kings of Egypt and the kings of the hills against us;" so they fled and left the camp as it was. Just so the leprous men found it; and they went into one tent and ate and drank, then into another; but presently they were awakened to a sense of the importance of their standing. "What are we doing?" was the query which arose in their minds, no doubt under the influence of the same Divine Light of which I have been speaking: "This is a day of good tidings, and we hold our peace; if we stay here until the morning light, some mischief will befall us: now therefore come, that we may go and tell the king's household." If I ever should be sent with a message to the king's household, or be permitted to carry good tidings there, it may afford some relief; but at present it seems as if the language was binding: "To thy tent, oh Israel!" And indeed this is a place of safety and comfort when it is our proper place, and if we have not, by our own rebellion, unfitted ourselves for running with a message in the way of the divine and holy commandments.

I hope thou wilt excuse the length of this, and permit me again to request thee not to do as I have done. If the candle of the Lord is shining upon thy dwelling, remember those that sit in darkness. For the face of the whole earth is not often covered with clouds at the same time. Had my state admitted it, I should have answered thine long ere this, as I have frequently attempted it, and as frequently destroyed the production.

After saying that my health has been very poor since the yearly meeting, till within a few weeks (having been grievously afflicted with asthma), I conclude this by requesting thee to excuse all imperfections, and believe me to be thy sincere friend,

THOMAS B. GOULD.

11th of second month, 1835.

In an interview with a beloved cousin, an elder in the Society, to-day, on a religious account, there was a degree of encouragement afforded, which I had no expectation of, and which I had no right to expect; but I have reason to think it was right, although it was something quite new to me in the manner of its falling out. Yet it was formerly, and in more favored and better days in our religious society, very common, and would be so now if the rightly exercised elders were more frequently to be found, and more faithful in the discharge of their duty in the encouragement of tender-spirited and rightly-exercised friends, in the more retired and secluded ranks of religious society. How would those who stand in need of help and encouragement be felt out, and their feeble hands and trembling knees confirmed and strengthened! And thus the great end of religious associations would be promoted, and the cause of Truth might gain ground among the nations, even until all flesh should see it together. T. B. G.

[The elder alluded to was, no doubt, Stephen Gould.]

To George F. Read.

Newport, 12th of second mo., 1835.

My dear Friend,—

My mind is very frequently and affectionately turned towards thee, and has been so, even before I was personally acquainted with thee, but particularly since the reception of thy last letter, which tended to confirm me in the belief, however it may end, that our correspondence had a right beginning.

There is a marked coincidence in my own views of the purifying tendency of those spiritual trials alluded to, with thine; and I am firm in the belief (the state of the church considered), that it would be a sign of death rather than life, to be without them. Indeed I have seen it proved to be so. "Plant ye vineyards, and eat the fruit of them, for ye shall not go into captivity," is in the mouths of many of the false prophets of the present day; whereby they are deceiving themselves and the people, while the precious seed is already so oppressed and captivated in themselves, that they are without a correct knowledge of their own condition. That interesting and important query, "By whom shall Jacob arise, for he is small?"—uttered by the holy prophet, who well understood the state of things in his day, and through the medium of prophetic vision, saw far beyond, even through supervening ages into the glorious Gospel day in which we live, is often raised in my heart, and sometimes on my tongue; and verily, I do believe, notwithstanding the cry of light, knowledge, effort, religious effort, and reformation, that there never was a day when this precious and immortal seed was more overlooked, borne down, and oppressed, than in the present. I do not suppose indeed that there are many without the pale of our own Society who would unite with me in the sentiment; but truly the sense that I have of these things is very deep and strong; and I am firm in the belief, that if it should please the Great Disposer of events to raise up and qualify such instruments as our early Friends were in His hands, the world would come as near being turned upsidedown as it did then; and that the same persecuting spirit would be as widely spread through the nations. I do not indeed think that it is likely many would be put to death for religion; but I do think, if any were concerned to take the same steps they did, that they would be very severely persecuted, and by those, too, that make the highest profession of religion without the actual possession of it. I know indeed that the enemy's power is a limited power; but if he should be disturbed, in his Popish cloak under the high-sounding name of Protestantism, there is no doubt that his enmity would be greatly excited to destroy that which threatened the destruction of his kingdom: for the better he can make that appear, the more subjects he will have. And there is great reason to fear that many of those who are so active in the present day, are far from being rightly influenced in their labors, even among the members of our own Society. I would not however wish to be understood as charging any among Friends with Popery, but some other professors of religion are evidently leaning that way, while they are actively engaged in endeavors to pull it down and destroy it; and how much these rudiments of it still visible among them tend to weaken their hands, it requires no great degree of discernment to discover.

Too great an intimacy and union with the world has, almost imperceptibly to themselves, leavened many into its spirit and maxims, and the cross of Christ has become of none effect. There are many who seem to hail the increasing disposition to mingle with them, with great joy. For my own part, I look upon it as a mark of a declined Society, and a great and manifest cause of the death and darkness so prevalent in our assemblies. Oh, that the time may be hastened, when the church shall come forth out of the wilderness, fair as the moon, clear as the sun, and terrible as an army with banners! We have become a great and respectable people, and we may be killed with kindness; and in proportion as we mix, unadvisedly, with others, our own peculiar testimonies will go into disuse; indeed I think there is a danger of some of them being lost: and I do verily believe that we are as much bound to dwell alone, and not to be reckoned among the nations, as ever ancient Israel was, and that there are as peculiar testimonies given us to bear.

There is nothing, I apprehend, more irksome and contrary to the natural mind, than those necessary and salutary restraints imposed upon us by an entire dependence upon, and a reverent waiting for, the word of divine commandment and the unfolding of divine counsel, so absolutely necessary to the acceptable performance of religious duties. The check is too severe to be submitted to by many, and hence arises that superficial and unbaptizing ministry so prevalent among us, as well as among other professors of Christianity. An ardent desire to do good and to promote the great cause in the earth, may even proceed from the transformations of the adversary, if the creaturely will is not so completely reduced as that there is none left. And here there will be no chance for him to work, as it comes to be so reduced and slain; for he cannot work upon that measure of divine grace; with which we have all been favored in a greater or less degree; and when this is suffered to come into dominion, then all his deceitful baits will be brought to light and to judgment; and this he cannot endure; there is nothing he more sincerely hateth, and therefore he must and will flee. The solicitude I feel is very great, that all those concerned may be careful to know the putting forth of the holy finger, and the limitations also: then should not only those on whom the labor was bestowed be helped and strengthened, but the instrument also; those that preach the Gospel should in reality live of the Gospel: and the Apostle Paul gives this plain reason: " For the laborer is worthy of his hire."

It was very satisfactory to me to receive the intelligence that thou hadst been reading Friends' books. I do sincerely wish it was more generally the case. Next to the Holy Scriptures, I believe them to be the most profitable kind of reading in which we can be engaged; and I am firm in the belief, if it was more generally the case among our young Friends, as well as some older ones, there would be less disposition to mingle with the world, and to copy its customs and manners. It has been very convincing and confirming to me to meet, in them, with views which accorded exactly with openings I had been previously favored with; and although at the time I had no doubt of their divine original, yet I have been ready to compare it to a threefold cord that is not easily broken.

That thou and I may be increasingly careful to seek for and to follow Him who was given for a light unto the people, a leader and a commander of the people, is what I greatly desire. Here I believe we should be favored with that holy help which is sufficient to supply every lack, and to heal every wound; and thus coming to receive with meekness the engrafted Word, should be nourished and grow thereby, and be favored to fill our several allotments with religious propriety.

Thou wilt perceive that I have continued my scrawl to considerable length again; and after requesting thee to excuse all imperfections (for I have written it in the mill, and while it has been going, as I do nearly all that I do write), I conclude,

Thy sincere friend,
THOMAS B. GOULD.

FROM THOMAS B. GOULD TO ——.

Third month, 5th, 1835.

In looking a little towards thee lately, my spirit has been impressed with this language: "Thus saith the Master, my time is at hand; I will keep the passover at thy house with my disciples." Thou mayst remember it was addressed by our blessed Lord to one of His disciples, in answer to the query, "Where wilt thou that we prepare for thee to eat the passover?" And they were commanded to enter into a certain city, and informed that they should meet a man bearing a pitcher of water, whom they should follow into that house wherein he entered, and should salute the good man of the house with that salutation above quoted; and they were further informed that he should show them a large upper room, furnished and prepared, where they should make ready for Him to eat the passover.

Now, my dear friend, I apprehend that thy spiritual ear has been saluted with a similar language; but whether the large upper room has been furnished and prepared, this is the point; and further, I am firm in the belief that thou hast met the man bearing the pitcher of water, so that thou art at no loss what house to enter into. Well, this sign having been given and punctually fulfilled, I have thought that there was a strong claim upon thee to comply with the conditions which the Master has been pleased to fix, in order to the fulfilment of the promise, "I will sup with him, and he with me." I am not aware that there ever was an unconditional promise of this kind given: how necessary, then, that the terms be complied with! Oh, why wilt thou keep Him out? His head is already wet with the dew, and His locks with the drops of the night! Open unto Him: be entreated to seek for His counsel, and to follow in the way of His leading, even in that measure of divine light He has been pleased to enlighten thee withal, and of grace with which he has favored thee. So shall thy soul be filled with fat things, and thou wilt be enabled to run with patience the race set before thee, remembering that they that run in a race run all; and I verily believe, not only a large field of labor would open before thee, but of usefulness also. The Egyptian tongue would cease to be heard in thy camp, and the pure language would be heard there, and thyself made instrumental in turning the people unto it; and not only so, but as thou submitted unto His yoke, it would be made easy, and His burden would become light; rough places would be made smooth, and crooked paths straight.

Nothing but the opposition of our own corrupt wills stands in the way of our advancement, in conjunction with the transformations of him who is seeking to deceive those one way whom he cannot destroy in another. I have not been so explicit as I might have been, from a belief that thou canst understand what I allude to; and if I am not mistaken in my feelings, thou wilt understand it. . . . . .

MEMORANDUM, 1835.

"Departed this life, on the eleventh of third month, 1835, my endeared friend, Abigail Robinson. In her death, the Society of which she had been an eminently useful member from early life, and minister for forty years, (she being in the seventy-seventh year of her age) has met with no common bereavement. She was a woman of uncommon intellectual strength and clearness, united with much improvement in the literary way; and over and above all other considerations, was added that of deep religious experience, so that she became, like Deborah, a mother in Israel. And oh! how few such she has left behind her; in the consideration of which, how doth my spirit mourn! And I can adopt the language: 'The fathers, where are they? the prophets, do they live forever?' O, Thou, who raised her up, fitted and qualified her for eminent usefulness in thy church, be pleased to cause the mantles of the Elijahs of the present day to rest upon the Elishas; even a double portion of thy Spirit, that so there may be a succession of standard-bearers and testimony-bearers continued in the church, that the precious testimonies of everlasting truth may be faithfully supported, and may never be suffered to fall to the ground!

"As it respects myself, in this afflicting bereavement, my greatest desire I think is, that I may be enabled to seek out what this dispensation is speaking unto me in particular; that so I may be enabled to turn it to a good account; being firm in the belief that trouble ariseth not out of the dust, nor affliction out of the ground, but that every affliction is suffered to fall upon us for some wise and benevolent end. And if this has a tendency to drive me closer home, even into a nearer and more intimate union with that Friend who sticketh closer than a brother, I may witness improvement by it as the instrumental means.

"14th of third month, at two o'clock, attended the funeral of my dear departed friend, at her late residence on the Point. Although the ground was exceedingly wet, it was largely attended, and by the most respectable inhabitants of the town; and we were favored, as I apprehend, with the overshadowing wing of Ancient Goodness, through a longer sitting than usual; in which a short but living testimony was borne to the Christian virtues, exemplary life, and peaceful close of the dear deceased, and to the precious truth she made profession of, and lived in the possession of. My mind was weightily impressed with that injunction of our blessed Lord, 'Watch therefore, for ye know not when the master of the house cometh, at even, or at midnight, or at the cock-crowing, or in the morning. Blessed are those servants, whom the Lord, when he cometh, shall find watching: verily I say unto you, that He shall gird himself and make them to sit down to meat, and will come forth and serve them.' Although I cannot help thinking that this relates to that intimate union which subsists between the adorable Head, and the humble, watchful members of the militant church on earth, yet I do not think it would be straining the text, to apply it to that watchfulness and earnest expectation with which the mind redeemed from the earth waits for the coming of the Lord Jesus, to conduct it safely through the dark valley of the shadow of death to the church triumphant in heaven. And from my personal knowledge of the state of her mind for a long time before, but particularly near the close of her probationary existence, I think it may in this case apply to it. Indeed it seemed to be the posthumous language of my precious friend to me in particular, and powerfully exhorted me to such a life of dedication to the cause, and patient waiting for the power of truth, by which that bread is still mercifully broken, and handed in secret, for the sustenance and the strengthening of the hungry soul, enabling it to hold up the head and journey forward in the line of divine appointment, however hard to the fleshly part. And nothing else can give strength adequate to the performance of this great and all-important work."

MEMORANDUM, WITHOUT DATE, PROBABLY 1836.

"Our transgressions are multiplied before thee, and our sins testify against us; for our transgressions are with us, and as for our iniquities, we know them." Isaiah 59: 12.

Yet I feel bound with thankfulness to acknowledge, that this day in meeting I was favored, while reviewing and bemoaning my sad condition, with a renewed and lively sense of this truth, namely: that as I was engaged to stand still in that Light which made the evil manifest, I should be favored with power and strength to withstand the fiery darts of the devil; the Light being nothing less than the Seed of the woman, which is alone able to bruise the head of the serpent, and to which the promise is that it shall do it. Notwithstanding this is no new doctrine with me, but one that I have long believed in, yea, at times (in better days perhaps) have felt concerned to recommend to others, yet the revival of it in my remembrance at a time when I was ready to adopt the language above quoted, and other parts of this fifty-ninth chapter of Isaiah, did convey encouragement to my distressed mind, believing it to have been produced by the influence of the Holy Spirit, which is also called the Comforter; and it was declared concerning him, by the Master, while on earth, that when he was come, he should not only reprove or convince the world of sin, of righteousness and of judgment, but should bring all things into their remembrance, whatsoever he had spoken unto them; and further, "He shall take of mine and show it unto you."

Although I am far from believing that the Holy Spirit influences only in subordination to the Scriptures, or rather only through them as instruments, and through providential occurrences, yet I believe it is not inconsistent with the will and pleasure of Almighty Goodness, powerfully and profitably to impress the mind through these mediums. With respect to the Scriptures, I readily and heartily subscribe to the sentiment, that whatsoever any do, pretending to the Spirit, contrary to them, may be justly accounted a delusion of the devil.

From Thomas B. Gould to ——.

Newport, 27th of 3d mo., 1835.

My dear Friend:

Although I greatly desire to be preserved from presumptuous sins, yet I am at times favored to feel a living concern to be found faithful in the work of my day; and a part of that work may possibly be to "comfort those that mourn, to preach deliverance to the captives, and the opening of the prison doors to them that are bound." I do not, however, mean to be understood, in the line of public ministry, or that I possess any power or might of my own, sufficient for these things; but as I do myself highly value instrumental labor, and have realized its blessed effect in some measure, so I am inclined to believe that it is sometimes bestowed on others, not only with the appearance, but with the efficacy and power of truth. Under these impressions, then, permit me to expostulate a little with thee, and to recommend the apostle's advice, "Whereto we have already attained, let us walk by the same rule, let us mind the same thing." If thou hast not been sensible of earnest and living desires having been raised in thy heart, similar to that of the church to the spouse, "Tell me, oh thou, whom my soul loveth, where thou feedest, where thou makest thy flock to rest as at noon," I am greatly mistaken in my feelings and views concerning thee. And if this is the case, which I am confident it is, then let nothing prevent thee from continuing thy search until thou hast found Him whom thou seekest. Although it is not an impossibility that "the Lord whom thou seekest" may come "suddenly into his temple," thy heart, with great power, majesty and might, so that it may be filled therewith in a remarkable manner, yet "if he tarry, wait for him;" and in the meantime be entreated to remember, that through that long journey the children of Israel took, through the Red Sea and the wilderness, their garments "waxed not old, neither did their feet swell;" and that the Lord would not bring them by the way of the land of the Philistines, though that was near, lest peradventure, their heart should melt when they saw war, and they should turn back into Egypt; but brought them up by the way of the Red Sea and the wilderness, yea, "he led them about and instructed them."

Oh, that thy faith in him may be strengthened, that thou mayst indeed believe him near, as indeed he is about our bed, and about our path, and spieth out all our ways: so that neither thou nor any other hath need to say, and the apostle says, "Say not, who shall ascend into heaven, to bring Christ down from above, or who shall descend into the deep, to bring him up again from the dead?" I want thee to pay particular attention to this caution, and also to the remarkable testimony to his inward appearance, which immediately follows: "But what saith it? The word is nigh thee, even in thy heart and in thy mouth." He also adds, "This is the word of faith which we preach." Now it was by an attention to this same word of faith, that the elders obtained a good report; and it is a living efficacious faith, by which a man may even live, and it works by love to the purifying of the heart. They whose conduct is governed by this divine principle of life and power, are not stimulated to holiness of life and conversation by fear of punishment, but by love. They love the Father because He first loved them, and gave his only-begotten Son a ransom for them, that whosoever believeth in Him should not perish, but have everlasting life; and the apostle says, "The life that I now live in the flesh, I live by faith in the Son of God;"—faith in his inward appearance, as well as his outward and visible appearance, no doubt. So thou wilt perceive that "without faith it is impossible to please God:" hence the great desire and concern that I feel for thee, that thy faith may be strengthened in the reality of those divine requirements that may be made at thy hands; being firm in the belief that among those that have been doomed to everlasting destruction from the presence of the Lord, not a few of them have been so from the fact that they refused to admit the truth of this doctrine; and others, who admitted it, yea, were convinced of its truth beyond a doubt, refused to comply with its requisitions because they were so small; in like manner as it was said of the Master himself, "Is not this the carpenter's son? are not his brethren and sisters all with us?" So that there is great danger of overlooking this "grain of mustard-seed," this "little leaven," or, to change the similitude, this "one talent," which the man to whom it was committed hid in a napkin, because it was but one; while it would have been as sufficient for him as the two or the five were for those to whom those numbers were committed.

I want thee truly and honestly to give these hints that weight they may appear to deserve, notwithstanding the weakness of the instrument, or the homely and bungling manner in which they are thrown out; for I apprehend that my views in this are of a more exalted nature than to have attempted any display, had I been capable of it. And suffer me to add that I firmly believe, as thou art concerned to act consistently with the light thou art favored with, thou wilt in due time become wiser than thy teachers, and wilt witness the restoration of paths for the lame to walk in, by His holy help who remains to be the "repairer of breaches;" that the mists and the clouds that the enemy has been permitted to raise, will be dispelled by the brightness of the arising of the Sun of righteousness, which has been predicted and signified by the morning star already appearing in thy horizon; which is a sure guide to further illumination, as it is attended to: that so thou mayst happily experience the work to go progressively on, and be enabled to cast off thy old garments as they become burdensome, which they soon will, if thou art faithful; for I do believe, that as thy eyes become afresh anointed with the eye-salve of the heavenly kingdom, thou wilt see thyself to be clothed in rags, as all have ever been favored to see, that have been concerned to obtain the "linen pure and white, which is the righteousness of saints," and to be clothed upon by it. As this becomes thy happy experience, thou wilt see the dead formality in which the generality of the professors of the Christian name are living, and their ministers are preaching, and wilt be prepared to adopt the language of Job, "Can that which is unsavory be eaten without salt, or is there any taste in the white of an egg?" also to see how much their labor is to keep people in the dark, that all they have may come through them. And how much they contribute to this end, the present state of the churches bears ample evidence to those who have had an eye opened to discover the signs of the times, which are indeed gloomy; for the tongues of the sucking children cleave unto the roofs of their mouths for thirst; yea, when the children ask bread, no man breaketh it unto them.

But under this gloomy view of things, I have been comforted, while writing, in the renewed belief that the foundation of our God standeth sure, having this seal, the Lord knoweth them that are His; and that He is still redeeming by His precious blood, sprinkled indeed upon their hearts and consciences, to the remission of sins that are past, through His forbearance; and by the powerful operation of His Holy Spirit, redeeming from the power of sin such as shall be saved *if they continue faithful.* Here thou wilt be favored, by the immediate openings of the pure truth upon thy mind, and by living experience, to know what it is to have thy heart sprinkled from an evil conscience, and thy body washed with pure water,—the baptism which alone saveth,—and to eat clean provender which has been winnowed with the shovel and the fan, even to eat the flesh and to drink the blood of the Son of man; not any outward flesh or material blood, but in the mystery; thou shalt eat, and thy soul be satisfied with marrow and fatness, for His flesh is meat indeed, and His blood is drink indeed; His words, they are spirit and they are life, and whosoever drinketh the water that He gives, they thirst not, neither go to any inferior spring to draw, for it remains in them a well of living water, springing up unto everlasting life. Here He is known to be the resurrection and the life, and whosoever believeth in Him, though he were dead, yet he comes to be renewed, quickened, and made truly alive unto God. And as thou goest on in the heavenly race, thou shalt experience further this truth, "he that liveth and believeth in me shall never die;" and here coming to this blessed experience, thy curiosity about the resurrection of the body will be stayed, and thou shalt be made quite willing to leave it where the Holy Spirit left it in the Scriptures. However, "thy flesh shall rest in hope," having seen the Father; for whosoever hath seen the Son hath seen the Father also, for "no man knoweth the Father, save the Son and he to whom the Son shall reveal Him;" and the revelation of the Son to profit is only in and by the Spirit. For notwithstanding the disciples of our blessed Lord had been so long time with Him, had seen the mighty works which He wrought, yet they knew Him not; as is plain by the reply that Philip made to the declaration of the Master, when he said, "Show us the Father, and it sufficeth us." The reply made by our blessed Lord is very striking: "Have I been so long time with you, and yet hast thou not known me, Philip?" for it appears that He had told them, that "whosoever had seen the Son had seen the Father also;" to which he returned, "Show us the Father, and it sufficeth us." Oh! it seems to me that this is sufficient to convince any, that they knew Him not, as He was the living and eternal Son, until He had been revealed unto them by the Spirit; for He expressly declared to Peter, that flesh and blood had not revealed it unto him, "but my Father who is in heaven;" and strengthened and confirmed this view by saying, "Yes, thou art Peter, and on this rock I will build my church, and the gates of hell shall not prevail against it." But Peter was a poor, frail man, although an eminent disciple: but all those that have known their foundation to be on this immovable Rock of divine immediate revelation, on these, as they keep their feet, all storms and tempests beat in vain, because they are founded on a rock, an immutable rock, the foundation laid in Zion. "Behold I lay in Zion, for a foundation, a stone, a tried stone, a sure foundation; whosoever believeth thereon shall not make haste." This is that upon which David was favored to know his feet established, that was higher than he, when he had the new song put into his mouth, even high praises to His name, who had established him thereon that he could not be removed, because He had made "a covenant with him, ordered in all things and sure," even the "sure mercies of David;" than whom none I believe of the servants of the Lord in those days experienced a greater degree of illumination in the way that we contend for it. Hence arose those very numerous testimonies to its excellency; as when he implied it by saying, "Oh, send out thy light and thy truth; let them lead me; let them bring me to thy holy hill and to thy tabernacles:" then, said he, "I will teach transgressors thy way, and sinners shall be converted unto thee." Oh! the preciousness of being brought to the holy hill and tabernacle of God, by the arising of this Divine Light in the soul, and the establishment of truth there! Here an experience is attained of offering unto the Lord an offering in righteousness, even a pure offering; for I do assuredly believe that when we are favored with a just sense of the relation in which we stand to our Father who is in heaven, as we abide under that influence by which the sense is given, we are favored by the same influence to see that the living only can praise Him acceptably, that "the dead cannot praise" Him. From this, ardent desires are raised in the soul, to be quickened and made truly alive unto Him; and as this is the case, our prayers (though they may be but sighs or groans rightly begotten, or tears shed in truth) will arise before Him as "sweet incense," and the "lifting up of our hands as the evening sacrifice;" yea, they will be abundantly more acceptable than the most eloquent words or sublime expressions uttered when the heart is far from Him, because they are the strugglings and the groanings of His seed under oppression, as it was in Egypt under the hard taskmasters. But the precious and consoling language uttered on that occasion still continues to hold good: "I have seen, I have seen the affliction of my people who are in Egypt, and have heard their groaning, and am come down to deliver them." Notwithstanding thy task may be doubled, and thou mayst be required to make brick as it were without straw, verily I say unto thee, as thou art concerned to follow Moses thy leader, thou shalt be delivered; yea, when darkness covers all the land of Egypt, thou shalt have light in thy Goshen; for all the children of Israel, the true seed, the wrestling seed of Jacob, "had light in their dwellings;" and when the destroying angel shall be sent through all the land to destroy the first-born, "from the first-born of Pharaoh that sitteth on the throne, to the first-born of the beggar that sitteth on the dunghill," the destruction shall not come nigh thee, "the lintel and the two side-posts of thy door" having been sprinkled with blood, although surely it may have been by a bunch of hyssop (a bitter herb) dipped therein.

That thou mayst come to experience these things, is what I greatly desire for thee; and may I not say, I travail with thee, that "Christ may be formed in thee;" for except this is the case, all that He has done for us, without us, will be of no avail to us. This then is the work of regeneration, by which we become "new creatures," having new faculties communicated and dispensed unto us, that "as we have borne the image of the earthly, we may also bear the image of the heavenly," and may be enabled to taste the doctrines and try the fruits of others. The spirit also of true judgment will be given, as it is written, "I will be a spirit of judgment to them that sit in judgment;" and strength will be afforded to "turn the battle to the gate:" at which gaining an entrance by following the Captain who never yet was foiled in battle, nor his armies put to flight, thou wilt gain an admission into that city, "whose walls are salvation, and whose gates are praise." . . . T. B. GOULD.

The novel doctrines of the party which seceded about this period from the Society in England, known commonly under the name of the "Beacon" secession, had for some time been favorably received and promoted by Elisha Bates of Ohio, and by some in high standing and great influence in New England Yearly Meeting. They went so far in their desire to spread these innovating views, as to make a remarkable, though at that time an unsuccessful attempt, to introduce the book entitled "The Beacon," into the Boarding School at Providence, R. I., under the charge of the Yearly Meeting. Seth and Mary Davis, who were then superintendents of that institution, and that faithful elder Moses Brown, one of the committee, then in very advanced age, were firm and decided in their opposition to the introduction of such a work, and by their steadfastness incurred the hostility of those who promoted the innovation. Some of the publications of the Beaconite schism reached the hands of Thomas B. Gould. He was not slow to perceive their unsound nature, and endeavored to warn his friends against their dangerous tendency. He saw, too, that these attacks upon the faith of our forefathers were of the very same origin as the errors of Joseph John Gurney, and that the writings of the latter had indeed been greatly instrumental in promoting those outward and superficial views, into which these people sought to leaven the Society.

FROM T. B. G. TO SETH AND MARY DAVIS.

NEWPORT, 15th of 3d mo., 1836.

MY DEAR FRIENDS, SETH AND MARY DAVIS:

. . . . I believe I can say in truth, that I have felt my mind drawn into near sympathy and unity with you in your many trials and exercises in the midst of a crooked and perverse generation, and a deeply revolted and backslidden people; and in your honest and faithful labors to exalt the standard of Truth, and support the testimonies thereof, amongst those who are turning their backs upon the one, and trampling the other under their feet.

I have not been altogether ignorant of the persecution which has fallen to your lot since you left your own peaceful abode, and undertook the arduous care of the Institution; but, my dear friends, "if ye be reproached for the name of Christ, happy are ye, for the spirit of glory and of God resteth upon you." This, I have no doubt, you have witnessed to your consolation and support, while the cloud of dust, which the enemy has been permitted to raise against you, has been returned with accumulated strength into the very faces of those who have been instrumental in promoting his wicked designs; for you may remember the Apostle immediately adds, "On their part he is evil spoken of, but on your part he is glorified."

I could have wished, for the Truth's sake, that your healths would have admitted your longer stay; for I do assuredly know that your management, and the wisdom which has been displayed therein, has given satisfaction to all those whose vision is sufficiently clear to discriminate between thing and thing, and who are yet able to give the "living child to the right mother." But alas!

the number of these is small indeed, compared with those who either openly deny, or undervalue, or disregard the only appointed and consecrated means of attaining the spirit of a sound mind, and of true judgment: for it is written, "I will be a spirit of judgment to them that sit in judgment;" and if *He* who is, indeed, the *Wonderful Counsellor*, is rejected, and not suffered to bear rule, and the government to *rest* upon *His shoulder*;—which you well know may be the case, even while there is a loud cry of "Lord! Lord!"—it is no marvel that there should be confusion, and that the language should be confounded,—that one should be crying "Lo, here!" and the other "Lo, there!"—for this has been the distinguishing characteristic of all the Babel-builders, from the days of Noah even until now. However, I do believe, that the stone which has been set at nought and rejected by these wise builders, is indeed the Headstone of the corner, the Rock on which the true Church is built, and against which the gates of hell can never prevail. I also believe that the object of the saints' faith is unchangeable; that it has been the same in all ages, and will so continue; that none but those who come by their faith in the same way that Peter did, are members of this Church, or true believers in the Lord of life and glory, or can possibly inherit, or will receive the blessing pronounced upon him, "Blessed art thou, Simon Barjonah, for flesh and blood hath not revealed it unto thee, but my Father who is in heaven."

Now if we can obtain true and saving faith, and justification thereby, in any other way than the saints in former ages did, even by divine, immediate revelation, then a man may call God, Father,—and Jesus, Lord, and not by the Holy Ghost; which would be and is, a manifest contradiction of plain Scripture doctrine.

I should not probably have blundered on these things at this time, if I had not most surely believed that the ground of the opposition which has been manifested to you, is the same as that which is seeking to overturn those precious principles and doctrines which I have briefly hinted at; indeed they seemed to lie so much in my way, that I could not well get over them; but while I have been writing, I have been forcibly reminded of the striking similarity there is between your case and that of the prophet Daniel, against whom his adversaries were forced to confess they should not be able to find an occasion, except concerning the law of his God.

Well, my dear friends, may you continue to go on in this your might, and fight valiantly for the faith which was once delivered to the saints, and has been testified unto by a cloud of witnesses, even down to the present day, and in it, notwithstanding it is a day of so deep revolt from the law and the testimony. For the Lamb and His followers will have the victory, seeing He never was foiled in battle nor His armies put to flight, so long as they fought with reference to His divine counsel and under His banner; and as I am a believer in the doctrine that the weapons of this warfare are not carnal, I cannot help being grieved to see those who have begun in the Spirit, seeking to be made perfect by the flesh, which, indeed, profiteth nothing. . . . .

I suppose you have seen Elisha Bates's "Vindication." . . . . I have greatly feared that it would do much hurt, and even tend to separate some still more widely from the Truth, who have already lost their innocency and integrity, as well as wisdom and judgment. Oh, it seems as if the language of lamentation might be rightly taken up, "How are the mighty fallen, and the weapons of war perished! Tell it not in Gath, publish it not in the streets of Askelon,—lest the daughters of the Philistines rejoice, lest the daughters of the uncircumcised triumph!" It has, with me, utterly failed of vindicating his character; for if the principles and doctrines he has there defended be the doctrines of the Gospel,—to say nothing about Quakerism,—I never understood them at all: and if the doctrine of Justification by Faith, which we hear so much about, be a justification while sin remains, by imputed righteousness, without good works being in very deed produced by the Spirit—I deny it. For this is "another Gospel;" seeing the very purpose for which the Son and sent of the Father was manifested in the flesh, was, to "destroy the works of the devil," to finish transgression, to put an end to sin, and to bring in everlasting righteousness.

There is another expression which he has used in the "Vindication," and in his public ministry,—I have often heard others use it of late—other ministers—viz., "silent meditation." Now this does not convey to my mind the same idea which I have been led to believe *silent waiting upon the Lord* to mean: it seems rather to mean something which we may propose to ourselves to reflect upon,—some subject—some theme—and not that patient waiting for Christ, for the arising of His precious and Divine Life in the soul, or for the renewal of strength there, agreeable to that of the prophet Isaiah,—"they that wait upon the Lord shall renew their strength; they shall mount upwards with wings as eagles,—they shall run and not be weary,—they shall walk and not faint." Now I can conceive of a state in which there may be outward silence, and there may be meditation, it may be on subjects that are good in themselves, and proper in their places; and yet there may be no waiting on the Lord,—no mounting upwards above our own thoughts,—no renewal of strength, spiritually,—nothing in it all which would enable us to run in the way of the Lord's commandments and not be weary, or to walk therein and not faint. No, but it would effectually prevent us from coming to a knowledge of what His mind and will concerning us is, because it would be doing our own works, and thinking our own thoughts, while the holy Apostle spoke of a state, in which "every thought" was brought "into subjection to the obedience of Christ." This I conceive to be the only way in which a preparation to perform true and acceptable worship can be attained to, agreeably to the well-known principles of truth as professed by Friends formerly, but which now appears to be too strait for these "sons of the prophets" to dwell in. It would have been well for them and us, however, before they undertook to enlarge their dwelling, if they had consulted the true prophet, and said, "Be content, we pray thee, and go with us;" but this does not appear to have been the case,—it is evident they have gone alone, and gone where, had they followed His leading, they never would have been found. The axe-head, too, has fallen into the water; it appears in some instances to have been "borrowed," but for my part I see little probability of its being made to "swim" again, for I very much fear there will not be an application to that Heavenly Power which alone can make it.

Indeed, I am entirely at a loss to reconcile his manner of treating the doctrine of the resurrection of the dead, and of judgment, with what I believe to be the truth; as well as his specious endeavor to elevate the Scriptures above the place in which Friends have held them; and the subject of missions, the latter being one with which Friends have nothing to do, as they are at present conducted. . . . .

After requesting to be excused for the liberty I am taking, as well as all other imperfections (seeing I have written in my mill, while it has been grinding fast), I conclude by asking you to accept my dear love; I would add, in the everlasting and unchangeable Truth, if I were not afraid of presuming beyond what I have yet attained to, even a possession therein; which, however, I am, I trust, at times sincerely desirous may be the case.

THOMAS B. GOULD.

FROM T. B. GOULD TO —— ——.

NEWPORT, 1st of 6th mo., 1836.

MY ENDEARED FRIEND AND LONGED-FOR IN THE LORD:

My mind has been very deeply exercised and concerned on thy account, the whole time I have been awake, since I left thy house on first-day evening; so that tears have been as my sorrowful meat, while my spirit has been impressed with this language, in the firm belief that it is sorrowfully verified in thy case: "A certain man went *down* from Jerusalem to Jericho, and fell among thieves, who robbed him, and wounded him, leaving him half dead." Now, my dear friend, I believe thou hast very lately been favored with a renewed sight of Jerusalem, the quiet habitation, the tabernacle that should not have been taken down. Not one of the cords thereof should have been broken, nor one of the stakes should ever have been removed, if thou hadst steadily and singly kept thine eye to that Light by which, and by which alone, thou couldst possibly be enabled so to see it. But instead thereof, thou hast descended from Jerusalem to Jericho, the city that was destined to utter destruction; and here thou hast fallen among thieves, who have robbed thee of the precious sense of good with which thou wast renewedly favored, and which it should have been thy care by all means to have kept; agreeably to the solemn injunction, "Keep that which thou hast, and let no man take thy crown." Yea, they have wounded the precious life, which is more than the meat which perisheth, and have left thee "half dead," as to any sensible feeling and enjoyment of it. For thou mayst remember the declaration of our Divine Lord and Master, "the life is more than meat, and the body than raiment." Now, although thou mayst obtain food for that part in thee which is designed for utter destruction, by thus descending as from Jerusalem to Jericho, yet it will only increase thy woe and misery; it will render thee barren and unfruitful in that which is most excellent. And this is what the Apostle recommended should be preferred and sought after; and not only so—for except the branch abide in the vine it cannot bear fruit of itself, but shall be "cast forth as a branch," and when it is so cast forth, "men gather them, and they are burned." Truly, my dear friend, hast thou not experienced this sorrowfully to be the case, when, for want of abiding in the Vine of life which has been made to shoot forth in thee, and for want of keeping the house and abiding in thy tent, thou hast gone forth without the sacred inclosure?—how have the men of the world gathered thee, and thou hast been burned by their scorching, withering, and blasting influence! On the other hand, when thou hast kept better company, hast thou not been at times sensibly leavened with good? Hast thou not been sensible of the prevalence of earnest and living desires raised in thy heart after an advancement in the just man's path, which is declared to be as a shining light, which shineth brighter and brighter, unto the perfect day?

Oh! turn in, I beseech thee, to that measure of divine light and grace with which thou art favored: occupy with the precious gift, yea, obey the injunction, "Occupy till I come;" and I do verily believe thou wilt find very little more required of thee at present, than thus to occupy with it, and watch its movements, and follow its gentle leadings. Cast all thy care upon Him who hath in great mercy favored thee with that and numberless other blessings, and He will, in His own due and appointed time, enlarge thy dwelling; yea, He will introduce thee into the glorious liberty of His children, by delivering thee from under the hard task-master, who is seeking, by all possible means, thy utter destruction; who is seeking to harden thy heart, and persuading thee to turn a deaf ear to the reproofs of instruction, which are the way of life and salvation; so that the time will come when thou wilt have to say, in the anguish and bitterness of thy soul, "Oh that I had not hated instruction and despised reproof, for the harvest is past, the summer is ended and gone, and I am not healed!" For most assuredly every knee shall bow and every tongue confess, either in mercy or in judgment, that Jesus Christ is Lord, to the glory of God the Father! But oh! that this awful stroke may in great mercy be averted!—that thou mayst be enabled to leave those things that are behind, and journey forward; for thou hast encompassed this mountain in the wilderness long enough, while the language of thy heart has been, I remember the leeks and the onions which I did eat in Egypt freely. Thus I believe thou hast lusted after the flesh-pots of Egypt; but these must be given up, and thou must not suffer thyself to lust after them any more at all, but press forward towards the promised land, which indeed flows with milk and honey; and if thou art willing and obedient, thou shalt eat of the good fruit of that land; but if thou art disobedient, thy carcass will fall in the desert, and then, what an evil savor will arise from it! For truly my mind seems to be deeply impressed with the belief, that thou wilt fall into greater evils than ever thou hast yet known, except thou listen to the voice of thy teachers, and incline thine ear to them that instruct thee, not calling in question the manner in which it may be conveyed, or the means which may be used to convey it.

Oh, dear friend, if the light in thee become darkness, how great will that darkness be! As eye hath not seen, nor ear heard, neither hath it entered into the heart of man to conceive the good things which the Lord hath in store for them that love Him, so I feel deeply concerned to tell thee, that thou little thinkest how much worse thy last state will be than the first, if thou dost not yield obedience to that good hand and power of the Lord, which hath shown thee clearly what things his controversy is against. And now, after having in vain tried to obtain relief, without again alluding in plain terms to a subject concerning which I have spoken to thee before, I find I must come to the point; I must call upon thee, I must beseech thee, and entreat thee, in the bowels of love,—even that love which passeth the understanding of the natural man,—to forsake that company of which I spoke to thee the other day, lest it prove thy utter ruin: and suffer me to quote for thy encouragement a very precious blessing pronounced upon that man who pursues the course which I recommend to thee, viz.: "Blessed is the man who walketh not in the counsel of the ungodly, nor standeth in the way of sinners, nor sitteth in the seat of the scornful, but whose delight is in the law of the Lord, and therein he doth meditate day and night. He shall be like a tree planted by the rivers of water,—his leaf also shall not wither, and whatsoever he doeth shall prosper." Yea, I say unto thee, in the fear and dread of the majesty of heaven, that if thou wilt give up in these things to follow the Captain of thy salvation, He will lead thee into the green pastures of life, and cause thee to lie down beside the still waters thereof, where nothing can hurt thee or make thee afraid. And not only so, but He will teach thee wondrous things out of His law, which He will daily write in thy heart, and cause thee to joy in the Lord, and rejoice in the God of thy salvation. . . . .

From T. B. G. to ——.

Newport, 23d of 11th month, 1836.

My dear Friend:

I have thought so much of thee lately, in connection with the events of this eventful day, that I concluded to let thee hear from one whom, among thy many friends, I suppose thou hast nearly forgotten, though I hope my name remains on the list.

I have called this an eventful day, and I think I have not misapplied the term, even if it should be confined to the comparatively narrow limits of our own borders; for I think there have not, within the time we have been a people, such occurrences taken place amongst us as at the present. When I look at the almost unparalleled sufferings which our worthy predecessors underwent, after that long and dark night of apostasy (emphatically so to thousands and tens of thousands who were waiting for the consolation of Israel, and panting after the true bread and water of life), in publishing the glad tidings of the everlasting Gospel in its primitive purity, and seeking the sheep who were scattered upon the barren mountains of an empty profession, and the desolate hills of lifeless forms and ceremonies, and not only seeking them but finding them and gathering them out from amongst the various ceremonial worships into the true sheepfold, where the true Shepherd was known and felt, feeding His flocks, and making them to rest as at noon in the green pastures of life, and beside the still waters thereof, where nothing could hurt them or make them afraid; I say, when I consider their almost unparalleled sufferings, their unfeigned faith, their matchless love, their truly Christian spirit, and harmless demeanor among men, I am almost disposed to envy them their happiness, even amidst all their sufferings; for they gave unquestionable evidence that they were the people the Lord had formed for himself, by their showing forth his praise in a manner not equalled since the primitive church. . . . .

To Peleg Mitchell.

Newport, 1st month, 20th, 1837.

My dear Friend :

[After relating many circumstances connected with the apostasy of Elisha Bates, he says]:

I thought I could not close this, notwithstanding the length to which it has already been carried, without alluding to a communication made by E. B. in our yearly meeting, either the first or second time he attended it, I am not certain which. If thou attended that year, I have no doubt thou wilt recollect it; if not, it may not be altogether void of interest; to say nothing about the evidence which, I apprehend, is contained therein, of the truth of our primitive and precious doctrine of divine, immediate revelation, and the unfolding of the light of Christ to His humble, devoted children and servants. Such I believe he then was, notwithstanding his awful fall and apostasy since: like as Judas by transgression fell from his ministry and apostleship, though he had received power over "unclean spirits, to cast them out," in common with the rest of the apostles. Luke 9 : 1, 2.

Elisha had been engaged in a weighty testimony, in which he adverted to the Hicksite separation, to the ravages which that desolating spirit had made in the other yearly meetings; and spoke in a deeply touching manner of our having been hitherto in a great degree preserved: but in an awfully solemn manner he warned those present to stand upon the watch, for the enemy was within our borders; that he was nearer many of us than we were aware of; that he was seeking to deceive those in one way, whom he could not destroy in another; that he would transform himself into an angel of light, in short, that he had done so; that we should not escape a sifting; that there were those then present, and standing in the most conspicuous stations in society, who, if it should now be told them the evil they would do unto the Lord's people, in the latter days, would say with Hazael, the Syrian: "Is thy servant a dog, that he should do this thing?" I well remember the power and unction attending this communication, at least to my understanding. It made a deep impression upon me, which is not yet effaced, and was sufficient at the time to beget faith in my mind that it would be even so; although I had not the least idea then, that it would ever apply to him.

I have so nearly filled my paper with what has "come to my knowledge," that I have little room left for what has been "passing in my own mind," in relation to these things. However, I have this general remark to make, and with it I shall conclude: that, in my belief, this spirit of opposition, which is now developing in many places (for it is not local), against those intrepid advocates for truth, the truth itself, and the principles of truth, is the same, in the root and ground of it, with that which, when "the truth first broke forth" after the long night of apostasy, persecuted those who bore testimony to it, even unto death; that it has only changed the mode of its operation in such a manner as to entrap many, who, if it had appeared under its old garb, would peradventure have seen it, and, it may be, escaped the snare. For truly "in vain is the snare laid in the sight of any bird." In a measure of that love which is sensibly felt to flow in an especial manner towards those "who are of the household of faith," I subscribe myself thy sincere friend,

THOMAS B. GOULD.

FROM THOMAS B. GOULD TO —— ——.

NEWPORT, 11th of 2d mo., 1837.

BELOVED FRIEND:

From the time thou appeared in our preparative meeting to the present, the subject of thy request and desire to be admitted a member of our religious Society has very frequently been weightily with me. I have felt my mind introduced into lively exercise on thy account, and on account of the very precious, and important, and peculiar testimonies given us as a people to bear. But within the last day or two, it has increased, and become so burdensome that it has appeared to me I could not safely, either to myself or to thee, carry it much longer. I have thought of seeking an opportunity with thee; but as this has not been practicable, I have believed it to be right in this way briefly to advert to some things of vast importance to thyself, to the Church, and to those among whom thou art conversant.

To be a member of our religious Society, and thus publicly profess the holy name of Christ our Lord, involves an awful responsibility, inasmuch as we make a higher and more holy profession than any other people whatever, in divers very important particulars, some of which I shall name. And as thy case has engaged my attention to-day, that solemn query put by our blessed Lord to the mother of Zebedee's children and to them, on that deeply interesting occasion, when she requested of Him for them, that they might sit the one on His right hand and the other on His left in His kingdom, has been weightily and constantly with me: "Are ye able to drink of the cup that I drink of, and to be baptized with the baptism that I am baptized with?" Now, my beloved friend, although the Society of Friends have ever declined the use of outward forms and ceremonies, and of water-baptism, yet they have ever as strongly asserted and as firmly believed that it is by baptism, and by that alone, that any can be joined unto the Lord, so as to become of one spirit with His people, or in other words, true and living members of His Church: that it is necessary for us that we should be "buried with Him by baptism into death" to sin, "that like as He was raised from the dead by the power of the Father, even so we also should walk in newness of life," having "put off the old man with his deeds, and crucified the flesh, with the affections and lusts, and put on the new man, which, after God, is created in righteousness and true holiness."

As this is a subject which is most intimately connected with life and salvation, it cannot do either of us any harm most seriously to consider what we have known of this great and important work to be begun and carried on in our hearts, by "the faith of the operation of God," who will work in us both "to will and to do of His own good pleasure," and unmerited mercy; and who hath graciously declared: "Behold I stand at the door and knock; if any man hear my voice and open the door, I will come in and sup with him, and he shall sup with me." By thus submitting thyself unto Him, and turning at His reproofs, even at the "reproofs of instruction, which are the way of Life," thou wilt find thyself quickened and renewed in the spirit of thy mind, from time to time; for it is written that "the first man Adam was made a living soul," but the second Adam is the Lord from heaven, "a quickening spirit." This is He who is the Judge both of the quick and dead, those that are dead in trespasses and sins, and those who have been made truly alive unto Him by an attention and submission to that Word of eternal life, which wakes the dead, and causes even those that are in the graves to come forth unto the resurrection of life—even He who is the resurrection and the life. "I am the resurrection and the life," saith Christ, "he that believeth on me, though he were dead, yet shall he live, and he that liveth and believeth on me shall never die." "And you," saith the apostle, "hath he quickened, who were dead in trespasses and sins; wherein in time past ye walked, according to the course of this world, according to the prince of the power of the air, the spirit that now worketh in the children of disobedience. But God, who is rich in mercy, for His great love wherewith he loved us even when we were dead in sins, hath quickened us together with Christ: (by grace ye are saved.)" Ephesians, 2: 1, 2, 4, 5.

Now if thou hast in truth known something of this work begun in thy heart, thou must have been made sensible that it is impossible for thee to be kept alive, except thou receive day by day thy daily bread. It is as impossible for the soul to live without food of a nature or quality corresponding to its own high destinies, as it is for the body to subsist without its proper food. "Except ye eat the flesh and drink the blood of the Son of man, ye have no life in you." These were pronounced by some formerly to be hard sayings; they exclaimed, "who can bear them," and it is recorded that from that time some went back from Him, and walked no more with him. But turning to His disciples, He said unto them, "Will ye also go away?" One of them replied, "Lord, to whom shall we go? Thou hast the words of eternal life." And again, it was declared, that a man should not "live by bread alone, but by every word that proceedeth out of the mouth of God." With regard to others, it was positively asserted that they were even "made clean by the word spoken unto them."

This I apprehend thou wilt find to be the true Supper of the Lord; for as thou wilt observe, (and, I earnestly desire, mayst richly experience), it is made to depend upon hearing the words of Christ, upon opening unto Him, when he knocks by His Spirit at the door of thy heart, upon waiting for, and when favored to hear, listening, in the silence of the fleshly part, unto His voice, which is sweet, that thou wilt come to a view of His countenance, which is comely, yea, wilt come to experience the lifting up the light of His countenance upon thee, and to taste of the rivers of unspeakable pleasures which are at His right hand for evermore. This is indeed a being brought into "His banqueting house," and here the banner of His love is spread over us, and we know and are sure that if we continue to walk in the light, as Christ is in the light, we have fellowship one with another, and that the blood of Jesus Christ will cleanse us from all sin: yea, that our fellowship and communion is with the Father, and with the Son, and with the Holy Ghost. This is the high and advanced ground (however feebly advocated or set forth by me) which the Society of Friends have taken, and still as a people maintain; and this is the true ground of initiation among, or communion and fellowship with them; although it must be acknowledged that it is not maintained by many who are nominally in profession with us.

With regard to our testimonies against war, slavery, and all oaths, together with the giving and receiving of complimentary and flattering titles, and honors, falsely so called, I have no doubt thou hast been convinced of their inconsistency with the Gospel of Christ. But I want thou shouldst also be convinced of, and be willing (however much it may be in the cross) practically to keep to the use of the plain Scripture language, on all occasions and in all companies, as well as simplicity of behavior and apparel. I think it will not be amiss to say that I never knew an instance, where an individual prospered in the best things, that balked his testimony in these things, or where that "covetousness which is idolatry" prevented him from the due and diligent attendance of meetings both for worship and discipline; those held on the middle of the week, as well as those on that day set apart for the purpose, by the common consent of those called Christians, the world over.

But after all that has been said, or that can be said or written, if thy mind is not convinced of and converted to a belief in the divine "Light of Christ within,"—"as God's gift for man's salvation,"—which is our main distinguishing point or principle, and, as William Penn said, in his preface to George Fox's Journal, "is as the root of the goodly tree of doctrines which grew or branched out from it,"—it will be impossible for thee, or any other, to support those doctrines and testimonies; the support of which, however, cost our worthy and ever memorable predecessors in the pure truth of our God, everything that was near and dear in this life, and even life itself. But they counted it all as loss and dross, in comparison to the excellency of the knowledge of Christ, their dear Lord; and esteeming the reproach of Christ greater riches than all the treasures of Egypt, they cheerfully relinquished their hold on the things of this life, even an unlawful hold on lawful things, that they might secure an incorruptible inheritance in the world to come.

As all things that are reprovable are made manifest by the Light, and as whatsoever maketh manifest is Light, and, as John testified concerning Him who is the true Light that lighteth every man that cometh into the world, that the end and design was, "that all men through Him might be saved;" so let me, in conclusion, commend thee, in the language of an apostle, unto God and to the word of His grace (mark that), which is able to build thee up, and to give thee an inheritance among all them that are sanctified. . . . . .

THOMAS B. GOULD.

To Peleg Mitchell.

Newport, 7th of 4th mo., 1837.

My dear Friend:

. . . . I fully unite with thee in the sentiment "that the signs of the times are awful," and with thy other expressions in connection therewith. But although it was foretold by the Lord's servants, the prophets (thou wilt not here understand it of those recorded in Scripture), has it not come upon many "as a thief in the night?" It certainly has found but a few comparatively,—a little remnant,—watching. Still, I believe there will in great mercy be a remnant preserved, as the "two or three berries upon the top of the uppermost bough, four or five upon the outermost fruitful branches thereof;" yet surely they would seem to be as "the gleaning grapes that are left in it, or as the shaking of an olive tree." "At that day shall a man look to his Maker, and his eyes shall have respect to the Holy One of Israel." Isaiah 17 :.6, 7. Oh, that it may be realized! I have no doubt this is the effect that it is designed to have upon us as a people, for has there not been a looking to "the altars, the work of men's hands?" "But these strong cities have become as a forsaken bough." "Because thou hast forgotten the God of thy salvation, and hast not been mindful of the Rock of thy strength, therefore shalt thou plant pleasant plants, and shalt set it with strange slips. In the day shalt thou make thy plant to grow, and in the morning shalt thou make thy seed to flourish; but the harvest shall be a heap in the day of grief and of desperate sorrow." Ibid. 10, 11.

I believe there has been an improper trust in man amongst us in the general, and in particular, a receiving what this great man or the other great man has said, or done, or written, without bringing things to the true touchstone, the balance of the sanctuary, which the Lord Almighty has been pleased to place in every sincere mind. This would have placed a curb upon those who are as "the horse or the mule, who have need to be held in with bit and bridle;" and at the same time that it would have rendered "tribute to whom tribute was due, and custom to whom custom was due," it would have rendered "unto God the things that are God's:" who in all things will have the pre-eminence, and whose right it is to rule and reign, by virtue of His law of love and life, which is written in the heart and placed in the mind.

It seems to me sometimes, that the blood of all the prophets will be required of this generation, who are now acting over again [in a sense] the awful tragedy which was performed upon those faithful "witnesses" and "martyrs of Jesus," who "counted not their lives dear, in order that they might finish the ministry which they had received of the Lord Jesus, to testify the Gospel of the grace of God." Can we too frequently advert to them? Shall they ever be forgotten? No! "their memorial is on high." "They that be wise shall shine as the brightness of the firmament, and they that turn many to righteousness, as the stars forever and ever." "The righteous shall be had in everlasting remembrance, but the name of the wicked shall rot." "Woe to the multitude of many people, which make a noise like the noise of the seas, and to the rushing of nations, that make a rushing like the rushing of mighty waters." "And behold at evening-tide trouble, and before the morning he is not; this is the portion of them that spoil us, and the lot of them that rob us."

I verily believe it is applicable in both its parts: "Inasmuch as ye did it (or did it not), to one of the least of these, ye did it (or did it not) to me;" for it is an assured truth, that the Lord accounteth that which is done unto His members, as done unto Himself: aside from the hurt done unto the great cause of truth and righteousness in the earth. . . .

Thy assured friend,
THOMAS B. GOULD.

TO PELEG MITCHELL.

NEWPORT, 1st of 8th month, 1837.

MY DEAR FRIEND:

. . . . . I can truly say that I have thought much of

thee in the time, not only on account of that mutual bond of union and fellowship which subsists between us, but in relation to that change which I suppose has taken place in thy situation, since I last communicated with thee. Although I am not in possession of experimental knowledge on the subject, I may peradventure be allowed the expression of a sentiment. I have ever entertained, I believe, an exalted sense of the propriety of that step, as well as its importance, and have frequently recurred to those instances we have on record, where the parties were led and guided therein by the good hand and power of the Lord, and, when the consummation of their prospects arrived, had their testimony to bear (and this is a peculiar testimony) that they were sensible of the Master's presence and power accompanying them and uniting them together. Oh! precious experience and acknowledgment! It often proved an earnest of future happiness in time, and a prelude to that which is eternal. I hope it has been thy experience in the former, and that it may be in the latter.

It is doubtless unnecessary to make any remark to thee on the subject; but I have often thought that no less evidence of divine illumination and revelation was to be found in the distinguishing views of Friends on the subject of marriage, than in any other point on which we differ from other people. It might almost amount to a proof of it (seeing we *reason* in these days as well as *walk* backwards), to consider that it is becoming, according to my sense and observation, of less and less concern with the generality under our name, to violate it. Witness the number of children, who either speak half Jew and half Ashdod, or pure Ashdod—I might rather have said, impure.

I fully unite with thee in sentiment on the subjects referred to in thy letter, and assuredly believe that multitudes of our members are laboring under a sad delusion with regard to the subject of slavery (or more properly, the abolition of it), and which, while it professes to exalt that testimony, is sapping the very foundation on which it rests, and weakening their attachment to, and crippling them in the support of, others not less important.

[SAME LETTER, LATER DATE.]

. . . . There is, indeed, a diversity of gifts and talents, as well as different degrees of growth and experience; but whereunto we have already attained, as we have all walked by the same rule and minded the same thing, a uniformity of faith and principle must of course be the effect. Was this ever so beautifully exemplified as among our primitive Friends? Shall we ever see it so exemplified again? Alas! I fear we shall not. When I happen to express such a sentiment, I am told, not to despair; but I cannot help it, I *have* despaired of it long since. Indeed, Peleg, my faith is at a low ebb: if others are not better off than we are, here on Rhode Island, there is certainly a cause for it. I sometimes express such a sentiment to some who ought to be judges; they say they are not in a better condition than we are. Indeed the most alarming feature in my view is, that so many are saying "we are rich and full, increased with goods, and have need of nothing," when they are poor, and blind, and naked, and have need of everything,—or of that in which all good things are included.

With regard to the prominent difficulties in Society, I hear but little said about them. It seems to me, however, that even some of the upright-hearted are in some measure deceived, supposing that the danger is over on that score from which truth's testimonies have of late suffered so severely. I may acknowledge myself of a different judgment; for although there are signs, on the part of some, of a willingness to sign a truce, yet I am well satisfied that true repentance and conviction have not had their perfect work. The state of things, as I view them, seems to be this: that there has been, and now is (for, in comparison with the defection and departure from the principles and testimonies of the Society, very few have been disowned by it), a large number of individuals, who stand in membership in the Society, many of them in high stations, ministers, elders, &c., who either never understood the principles for the support of which we were originally gathered to be a separate and distinct body, or, having received a literal, book-knowledge of them into the brain, have adopted so much of them as would promote them to offices and confer power upon them; or another sort, who, having been convinced of and converted to the truth, in former and better days, and grown up into a good degree of its heavenly virtue and power, so as to be decked and adorned as with the Lord's heavenly jewels and gifts; for want of abiding in the simplicity of little children, and in deep humility and dependence upon the Lord, the Giver of every good and perfect gift, have become puffed up and exalted above the pure witness in themselves, have taken the Lord's jewels and made merry over them, and then, by a further delusion and snare of the grand adversary, have been tempted to deny the testimony of His "faithful and true witness," until by the continual grieving and despite done unto it, they have for the present slain it, and their "house is left unto them desolate," "given over to a strong delusion, even to believe a lie." Of such as these, nothing less can be expected, but that they will persecute "the woman," and the "remnant of her seed," as they are now doing. But I confess I do not so much fear the consequences of this kind of trial, as I do that of the other class first mentioned; who, though they have "secretly joined themselves to the broken army of Magog" (see Edward Burrough's works), and have all along been in league with him, yet now, for political reasons, are very willing to have it appear they are very good Quakers, "saying they are Jews, and are not," but are of that synagogue from which the floods of opposition come. These, since they have failed to undermine the Society, I am firm in the belief, are now trying another scheme, and by smooth words and fair speeches, are deceiving the hearts of the simple; they are very willing to pass for sound, and, as much as in them lies, to use sound words,—to build the sepulchres of the prophets. Indeed, to use the words of one of the prophets (I. Penington), their structure now is "built in imitation of Zion, painted just like Zion," and looks like Zion; but it is only in appearance; although there is as much art in setting it forth as can be imagined, and the paint is very skilfully laid on, yet in secret, the simplicity and purity of the truth, the straitness of the gate, and the narrowness of the way, are despised and condemned.

I do not know how it may appear to thee; but I am not satisfied with the manner in which the Englishman now travelling in this country has got along. He has now such a load of books on his back, as I should be very unwilling to carry: some of them containing anything but Quakerism, others with just enough that "looks like it," to give them a pass, and cause them to do fourfold more harm. When he left his home, he had but just deserted the ranks of "Beaconism," and ceased openly to oppose the "little ones." (A friend in our neighborhood, who has seen him at his house, can testify.) How it is possible he should be cleansed of his leprosy so quick, I am at a loss to determine. I think at least he should have been "kept without the camp seven days." And as there is so much proof of the "plague" being in the very "wall" of his "house," it would have been more satisfactory to me, if there had been some evidence that it had been pulled down to the very ground, and rebuilt upon a better foundation, a new foundation, the Foundation "laid in Zion." Then, I am satisfied that the first work he would have found to do, would have been to unsay a great deal that he has said, and to contradict a great deal that he has written. I expressed sentiments something like this to our mutually dear friend John Wilbur; and in the course of the conversation he said, that he had asked a friend if the Lord's mountain and the mount of Esau were so near together that men could pass from one to the other at a single leap. . . . .

I am aware that there is much said now against judging; the labors of those who have been tinctured with the new views have been from the first directed against it: they introduced cautions against it into the Epistles of the yearly meeting; no man was to be judged for his unsoundness, nothing must be thought, much less said, about it. Well, was not this a snare of the crafty fowler? Did it not answer the end completely? All mouths closed, every lip silent, and every tongue dumb, while they were carrying on their warfare unmolested, and even turning those institutions which were ordained and set up for a defence round about the city, into engines of destruction to it! The epistles which have been sent back and forth, between our own yearly meeting and that of London, are a witness to the truth of this remark; I mean for several years last past. Is not the language applicable: "Judgment is turned away backward, truth has fallen in the streets, and equity cannot enter?" And did not all those who were favored to have their eyes open, see in these things a clear evidence and legitimate fruit of that spirit "which genders to bondage;" which has brought and is still bringing many back again under that grievous and cruel yoke of bondage, which was laid upon the nations by the hard task-master, in the night of darkness, and in the time of apostasy from the light, spirit and power of Christ, even many who had known some good degree of deliverance from it?—which light, spirit, and power, those sons of the morning of the Gospel day, after the long night of darkness and apostasy, were so preciously instrumental and so eminently successful in proclaiming, and gathering the people into, so that the language began to be fulfilled,—the language of prophecy, "It shall come to pass in the last days, that the mountain of the Lord's house shall be established in the top of the mountains, and exalted above the hills (of an empty profession); and many people shall go and say, Come and let us go up to the mountain of the Lord, to the house of the God of Jacob, for He will teach us of His ways, and we will walk in His paths; for out of Zion shall go forth the law, and the word of the Lord from Jerusalem." And "He shall judge among the nations," &c. "In this mountain shall the Lord make unto all people a feast of fat things, of fat things full of marrow, of wines on the lees well refined; and shall destroy the face of the covering which is spread over all people, and the veil that is over the nations." Now I am abundantly satisfied that the true believers in Christ, the Light, are established on this holy mountain, and that to all that are in this holy hill, He that reigneth King in Zion will give a spirit of judgment. "I will be a spirit of judgment to them that sit in judgment," &c. "He that is spiritual judgeth all things." "And upon all the glory there shall be a defence." How should any be able to defend those glorious testimonies which arise out of that law which goeth forth of Zion, and are required by that Word from Jerusalem, unless they had power to judge that which seeks to subvert them?

In short, my dear friend, I unite with thee in the sentiment, that we are to keep our ranks in that "city whose walls are salvation, and whose gates are praise" (very clear and comprehensive, in my view, is the doctrine and instruction contained in this description); and not by any means to suffer "the strength and concern ordained to flow through us as a people," to be mixed with the "water" ("their gold and their silver is cankered and their wine mixed with water") which remains in those that "are without." However we may rejoice in those things in which they may appear to be nearing us (by the way, I greatly fear we are nearing them, much faster than they are coming towards and embracing the Truth), we ought not in the least to incur the danger of diminishing or obscuring the light of that "city which is set on a hill," and which, if we were faithful, "could not be hid."

Thy assured friend,

THOMAS B. GOULD.

CHAPTER II.

In the course of the visit of Joseph John Gurney to the United States—a visit sorrowfully disastrous to the Society of Friends in this land—he attended the Yearly Meeting of New England, held at Newport, in 1838. Thomas B. Gould had by this time become familiar with some of his writings, and in common with a large number of other Friends of that yearly meeting, as well as in other parts of the land, was clearly convinced that his published sentiments were calculated to produce a departure from the ancient standard of our Christian profession—that he was unsound in many points of doctrine which our forefathers in the truth held most dear,—and that there was extreme danger, from the influence of his position, his wealth, his tact and activity, and his reputation, truly or falsely estimated, for benevolence, learning, and eloquence, that large multitudes would be turned aside from the simplicity and spirituality of our true and ancient faith. On this occasion therefore, when some of those who had obtained the pre-eminence in that yearly meeting, were urging the claims of J. J. Gurney to implicit acceptance, and beguiling the minds of many honestly disposed, but more or less superficial members, who placed undue confidence in eminent men, Thomas B. Gould felt it to be his religious duty plainly to bear his testimony, as way opened for it, against the erroneous doctrines of this voluminous author, and to show the reasons of his disunity with them. This attracted the attention, of course, of the individual thus testified against, as well as of those whose efforts were directed to promote his cause; and from that time Thomas was marked and watched, as in their opinion pertinaciously endeavoring to obstruct their course, and as a person disaffected and dangerous to their favorite scheme of bringing over the whole Society to the views and practices of Joseph John Gurney and others like him in England, where the seed so widely sown in his numerous and unchecked publications, had taken root in the hearts of very many of the members, and sprung up to the covering of that once beautiful garden of the Lord with the noxious weeds of superficial and carnally-minded profession.

Joseph John Gurney soon took an opportunity of calling at Henry Gould's residence, and Thomas candidly opened to him his uneasiness, but without receiving any satisfaction from him. This interview—in which Thomas plainly charged him with promulgating unsound doctrines, and exhorted him to disavow and condemn them, and also expressed to him his dissatisfaction with his ministry—ending as it did in no concession on the part of J. J. Gurney—T. B. Gould considered himself not only clearly at liberty, but bound by his sense of duty, to speak of it openly, and to warn his fellow-members of the disastrous results likely to follow to the Society from the popularity of this unsound author. As a consequence of his faithfulness herein, he was, in common with his friend and fellow-testimony-bearer, John Wilbur, made the object of a long-continued persecution, by those who scrupled not to pervert the discipline of the Society to their unholy purposes. Yet no cause could be found against him, except concerning the law of his God. Efforts were even made to spread an idea that his mental powers were impaired, and many were the vituperations cast upon his character, particularly after the interview above-mentioned. Much talk and misrepresentation having been made about it, he wrote the following notes of the occurrence, and sent copies to some of his intimate friends, in order that his fellow-members might have a correct version of what transpired on that occasion.

NOTES OF T. B. G.'S INTERVIEW WITH J. J. GURNEY.

Between the hours of five and six on the afternoon of

seventh day, the 16th of sixth month, 1838, Joseph John Gurney and Henry Hinsdale called at my father's house, Thomas B. Buffum being with them. Thomas P. Nichols was present. My parents and sister were also in the room; when the following conversation ensued.

After some general remarks made by him (and he seemed very much disposed to talk), I took my seat by his side, and said: "I suppose thou hast heard that I have said a good deal on the subject of the unsoundness of thy writings; I now take this opportunity to acknowledge that I have done so, and to convince thee that I am not disposed to keep it a secret from thee." He interrupted me by saying, "Oh, my dear friend, I did not come here on that account at all, I only came to manifest my love for thee and for the family." I continued, "There are many sentiments in them contrary to our acknowledged principles and testimonies. I am exceedingly dissatisfied with them. Now, wilt thou acknowledge that there is unsoundness in them, and by so doing, remove the obstructions to thy service, that exist in my mind, out of the way?" He replied, "All that I have to say to thee, my dear friend, is, that I have nothing to say on the subject of my writings. I do not consider it to be my present business; I am here on another concern, and my mind is very much exercised with it." I replied, "The minds of Friends in this country are very uneasy in relation to much which thou hast written—as well as myself—and it is a very serious obstruction to thy work and service. It is impossible that it should accomplish the professed object, or reach the same end, until these obstructions are removed; and if thou wilt acknowledge that there is unsoundness in them, and so remove the offence out of the way, I believe there are those who would receive thee with open arms." He replied, "My dear, I feel a great deal of love for thee, and I did when thou spoke in meeting the other day. I admire thy candor and uprightness, but I must decline entering upon the subject of my writings: they are very extensive, and all I have to say to thee is, that it is none of my business, and, to tell thee the truth, I do not consider it to be thine." I answered, "'If thou bringest thy gift to the altar, and there rememberest that thy brother hath aught against thee, leave there thy gift before the altar, first go and be reconciled to thy brother, then come and offer thy gift.' This I believe is a doctrine of Scripture; thou makest great professions of regard for the Scriptures, and settest them above the mark at which Friends have ever held them; now thou ought to conform to this precept, and deny or condemn such parts of thy writings as have given so much uneasiness to me and a multitude of other Friends; by so doing thy path would be rendered more easy, and the minds of Friends would be relieved. I do consider that it is thy duty to satisfy both me and them." He again made large professions of love for me, put one arm around me, and laid the other hand upon my knee, in a very plausible and seemingly affectionate manner, saying, "All I can say is, to recommend thee to the Master, to whom thou must leave me, simply doing what He requires of thee; and mayest thou more and more come under the very power of the Lord's Spirit, with which I believe thou art acquainted. Keep in the quiet, dear Thomas, simply doing what He requires of thee." (He did make some further remarks here, by way of preaching to a very small extent, which, however, I do not remember.) I replied, "It has been required of me to do what I have done; my mind has been very deeply exercised on the subject of the unsound doctrines promulgated and propagated by thy books amongst us; it has deprived me of much sleep, and even affected my health;—but," I said, "I am not aware that my mind has been impaired,"—appealing to my two intimate and dear friends, T. P. N. and T. B. B., to know whether they had discovered that any distraction or derangement of mind had taken place, remarking, "they both know me well; we are frequently together, and converse on these subjects." T. P. N. said that he believed I was "of perfectly sound mind," with emphasis. T. B. B. sat silent, with his hat drawn down over his eyes. He evidently was unwilling to take any part in the matter between us, although he had previously conversed freely and frequently with me upon the subject of my concern with J. J. G.: such is the pernicious influence which great names and popular applause exert upon even honest hearts.

I then appealed to J. J. G. again in an affectionate manner, as he had it in his power to relieve me from this weight and burden, to do so, and thus take the ground of offence against him away; at the same time remarking that if he would do so, I should be able to inform friends who felt the same uneasiness with myself, that he had condemned whatever was in his books contrary to our acknowledged principles and testimonies, and thus open his way with them, where I assured him it was now entirely closed. He utterly refused, again and again, to enter into any discussion, as he chose to call it, upon the soundness of his writings, or to acknowledge they were unsound; but said nothing about his certificates, or his having been well received by some friends. He never alluded to it at all. I replied: "I wish no discussion, I have asked for no such thing, but only for thee to condemn such parts of them as are contrary to our acknowledged principles, and have given friends so much uneasiness." He manifested great uneasiness at this time, and said something about humility, which I do not distinctly remember, and again refused to make any the least concession.

After a short pause, I found my mind engaged to testify against his ministry, which I did in the following manner: "I must say to thee, that I am not satisfied with thy manner of preaching: thou puttest the cart before the horse; thou laborest to induce a belief in the doctrines testified of in the Scriptures, by the mere force of reason and argument, and the bare reading or hearing of them; and then speakest of the gift of the Spirit as a consequence of that belief or acceptance. This is contrary to that Scripture doctrine, 'as no man knoweth the things of a man save the spirit of man which is in him, even so no man knoweth the things of God but the Spirit of God.' Now," said I, "it was because of the absolute necessity there was and is for men and women to come to this Spirit, to have their understandings opened and their hearts quickened by its power, that our ancient friends labored to exalt the testimony to the true Teacher, and to bring them under its power and teaching; and they well knew that when people come to this ground and foundation, there is no danger of their undervaluing the Scriptures, for it is impossible; the manifestation of the Spirit now will not contradict the revelation of the same Spirit in days that are past. They knew it, and I know it. But thou, instead of laboring to bring the minds of the people to the true Teacher, who promised to teach His people Himself those great doctrines and fundamental truths of the Gospel, and bringing in the Scriptures, as a collateral evidence of, and testimony to the truth of them, goest about to persuade people to accept them in 'simple faith,' or to convince them merely by thy own powers of reasoning and argument, and holdest forth that the gift of the Spirit is consequent upon that kind of belief or acceptance. Now this is contrary to the principles of truth as professed by Friends." He did not attempt to deny that this was true, and said, "I am satisfied of thy sincerity and faithfulness, and am willing to be further instructed as a Christian should be."

Here some of the family remarked that Moses H. Beede was at the door; and Jonathan Nichols (who had just stepped up) inquired if I was willing he should come in; whereupon I invited them both in. J. J. G. had risen up and put on his hat in the interim, and seemed exceedingly unwilling that anything further should be said. Thus I was prevented from fully relieving my mind, as it related to him. But I did say to J. J. G., "As thou hast refused to give me any satisfaction, I want thee distinctly to understand that I shall consider myself at liberty to speak against thy writings, at such times and in such manner as I shall think proper,—and with thy understanding it to be so, thou must leave me thus at liberty." He said, "I do not give thee liberty, but leave thee to the Master, who is able to keep us both." I told him that it was contrary to common sense and reason, that he should be at liberty to write and publish what he pleased against the Truth, and I should be denied the liberty and exercise of my conscience, in bearing my testimony against and exposing the unsoundness of his writings, while he was travelling amongst us and refused to condemn them. I had previously told him that my objections to his writings were not of recent date, that I had been familiar with them from my childhood, and had had unity with the first edition of his "Religious Peculiarities" (with some small exception), which had interested me in what came from his pen, and led to the reading of it; and the time had been when I sincerely wished he might be sent over to this country; but long before he came, my feelings had been changed, and now I had cause to regret it exceedingly. He said, "that he had heard me patiently, and that he felt great love for me." It was evident, however, that he was not willing to hear me, and that it gave him much uneasiness.

When the subject was first opened, he seemed disposed to make light of it, and laugh it off. After discovering that this would not discourage or prevent me from prosecuting the concern, he attempted to drown it by large and gratuitous professions of love and good will for me. Finding that plan would not work, and especially while I was enforcing the obligation he was under, to leave his gift at the altar until he was reconciled to his brethren, I must say that he seemed somewhat affected by it; at any rate, he was more silent, and apparently sensible that it was just.

I have read the above notes to T. B. B. and T. P. N.; they both acknowledge them to be substantially correct. I took them down immediately after the interview, and where they are marked as quotations, I am satisfied the language is given as it was used. I am willing to acknowledge that Joseph John did not say much. What he did say (as will be seen) was, with two or three exceptions, a repetition of the determination at first expressed, or of his professions of love for me. This may account for my so repeatedly insisting upon his condemning the unsound and offensive parts of his writings. If he had called for it, I could readily have referred him to such parts as are so diametrically opposed to our acknowledged principles, as they stand recorded in our approved and standard works, that "he who runs may read" and understand the difference. As for T. B. B.'s silence when I appealed to him, he has since said to me that he considered it altogether unnecessary to make such an appeal (he was not aware however of the reason why I made it), and that he should be willing to bear testimony to his full conviction of my entire sanity to J. J. G., should an opportunity offer. THOMAS B. GOULD.

NEWPORT, 29th of 6th mo., 1838.

FROM T. B. GOULD TO J. AND E. NICHOLS.

[Accompanying a copy of the Notes of his Interview with J. J. Gurney.]

NEWPORT, 29th of 6th month, 1838.

MY DEAR FRIENDS, J. AND E. NICHOLS:

. . . .

Indubitably satisfied and convinced I am, that the very tendency of this man's labors is to make us a will-worshipping people; and although he does not now acknowledge it in words, yet it is very evident that he dreams, that Jerusalem, the holy city, whither the tribes go up to the testimony of Israel, the city which the Lord hath chosen, to place His name there, to manifest His power there, is too far off;—and those, who are concerned to yield obedience to the divine commandment, "Thou shalt not offer thy burnt-offerings nor thy sacrifices in every place that thou seest, but in the place which the Lord thy God shall choose, to cause His name to dwell there," are likely to maintain their allegiance to David their king, and to say, "Thine are we, David, and on thy side, thou son of Jesse." Oh, that the eyes of the upright-hearted may be opened by the effectual application of the eye-salve of the Kingdom, which is inward and spiritual,—(the worship is spiritual, the offerings are spiritual, the temple and the altar are spiritual, and the worshippers are spiritual, such as worship in spirit and in truth)—to see the mystery of iniquity; for truly, great is the mystery of iniquity, as well of godliness. None can understand either the one or the other, but those, and those only, who have been taught by Him who is the alone sufficient Teacher of His people, who "teacheth them to profit," and as no man ever spake or taught. He still continues to show to a little, poor, and despised remnant, the depths of Satan on the one hand, and on the other, the "unsearchable riches" (unsearchable to the wise and prudent of this world, the letter-learned), which are in Himself, with whom are hid all the treasures of wisdom and knowledge. But it is now, as it was formerly: "He is a stone of stumbling and a rock of offence" to the high-professing, self-righteous Jews. "They stumble at that stumbling-stone." And to the worldly-wise Greeks (both characters are frequently united in the same subject) "foolishness." But to those who believe, to those who receive their gift of faith from Him, who has been the object of the saints' faith in all ages of the world, the Author and Finisher of it, "Christ is the power of God and the wisdom of God."

Your afflicted, but not forsaken friend,
THOMAS B. GOULD.

[Postscript.]

. . . . I do not believe the impressions he makes will last longer than the "veil which is spread over all nations" who have not come to the mountain of the Lord's house, to the house of the God of Jacob, where He teacheth them His ways, and they receive strength from Him to walk in His paths—remains upon them; for it is in "this mountain" that the face of the covering is removed, and the veil is destroyed. I was ready to add, in the renewed feeling and sense of its truth, "We have a strong city: salvation hath God appointed for walls and for bulwarks:" for I have been, at times and seasons, comforted in the firm faith given unto me that the foundation stands sure—for faith remains to be an heavenly gift, the gift of God; and it still is the "substance of things hoped for, and the evidence of things not seen." (Not J. J. Gurney's "*simple faith—mere credence*," which, he said, in his communication on fifth-day of yearly meeting, formed a fundamental link in the great chain of Christian doctrines.) "The foundation stands sure;" and because He lives who is the Rock of ages, upon which the true Church is built (not upon the Scriptures), those who are prophesying in sackcloth shall live also; and the storms and tempests, though they may beat vehemently, shall not be able to overthrow such.

. . . . I should be glad to receive a letter from you; and with the assurance of true love I conclude. If you are uneasy with any part of my conduct, be sure to let me know of it.

THOMAS B. GOULD.

FROM T. B. G. TO GEORGE F. READ.

NEWPORT, 4th of 7th mo., 1838.

MY DEAR FRIEND, G. F. READ:

Having understood by good authority that the fact of my having had an interview with J. J. Gurney on the subject of his writings, &c., has caused much remark in Providence, and subjected me to actual abuse from some individuals (all which I sincerely wish may be mercifully forgiven them, seeing they know not what they do), I thought it would be best for me to inclose thee a copy of the memorandums I made, of what passed between us, in order that thou might know how far I am justly censured.

Thou art aware that in the time of yearly meeting I made no scruple of expressing my objections to his printed books. I did consider I had as much right to do so, as he had to print and publish them. I am of the same judgment still. I know they are not Quakerism; I also know he is no Quaker, if he holds the same sentiments, whatever else he may be. And the fact being proved that he will not condemn them, shows that he is still accountable for all that he has written. Friends might just as well have received thee into membership with thy Baptist notions, and licensed thee to remain and propagate them, as to suffer him to travel as a minister, with his Episcopalian principles; and much better, as thy influence would not have been anything near so extensive.

As to my right to express my concern to J. J. G., which I understand has been called in question, I am not at all afraid to say, that no one who understands the principles of Friends, and retains his integrity and allegiance to them, will hesitate for a moment to acknowledge it. However, I am not the first who has been judged and condemned by false and envious brethren, for doing that which was required of him. Joseph was hated by his brethren, when he told them his dreams, and carried "their evil report" to Jacob his father. Moses was inquired of by one of his brethren, in outward fellowship, no doubt, "Who made thee a prince and a judge over us?" And Eliab, David's proud and envious eldest brother, whose "anger was kindled against him," said to him, "Why camest thou down hither, and with whom hast thou left those few sheep in the wilderness? I know thy pride, and the naughtiness of thine heart." I believe I may with propriety adopt the answer that David made, "What have I now done?"—and "Is there not a cause?" A man travelling as a minister, with certificates from his monthly, quarterly, and select yearly meetings, the last drawn in such a manner as to cover that essential part in which it is wanting (it does not say that he was liberated in the unity, but "after an expression of much unity"), and obtained contrary to the solid sense and judgment of the faithful, weighty, and sound part of the body in England; who has volumes of books in circulation which Friends in England and in this country *know* were at the root of that declension from our principles, which has shaken the Society there to its centre; which has carried so many back again into those things out of which our predecessors in the Truth were gathered by the immediate extension of the Lord's Eternal Arm of Power —such a man, so travelling in this country, and the reputed "watchmen" on the walls slumbering at their posts, or so overcome by that spirit which has spread far and wide in our Society in this land as well as in England (a dark, uncertain, unbelieving spirit), as not to be able to distinguish between thing and thing,—really I did, and now do believe, there was a cause for me to bear my testimony against it, and so clear myself of the weight and burden laid upon me.

But I do not think it strange that such as in their hearts and by their conduct, if they do not acknowledge it in words, deny the present continuance of Divine immediate Revelation, and its being still the "primary, adequate rule of faith and practice," and are setting up the Scriptures as such a rule,—as the "more sure word of prophecy,"—should be disposed to call in question the propriety of such an one as I am, meddling in this matter. Nothing less can be expected from such. If we reject the principle that a measure and manifestation of Divine Light and Grace has been given to every man to profit withal; that this Light is that medium through and by which men and women are shown what their duty is, and the manner and time in which it is to be performed, as well as qualified to perform it,—and if we set up the Scriptures in the place of this Light and Grace,—make them *the foundation* of all religion and morality,—say that human learning, outward information, is a *necessary* qualification in order to come to a right judgment in matters relating to faith and worship, in things of a divine, spiritual, and heavenly nature,—then I believe we shall find that we are indeed dependent upon our fellow men, for authority to act in the Church, and that we have cast off our allegiance to the great Head of the Church, except so far as words go;—these may still be retained, for the enemy does not regard the use of words merely, he does not regard the bare assertion that Christ is the Head of the Church, that He is the President and Master of our assemblies,—so long as he can rule in the will,—so long as he can virtually have the government. This he can manage to retain, where the Scriptures are the "primary rule," and while they are "interpreted like all other books, according to the common and intelligible rules of language, and not without a reference to innumerable facts and circumstances which throw light on their meaning." Here is ample room to shuffle about, and to evade their true meaning. . . . . . Not so with those who do not acknowledge them to be the "primary rule," or the "ultimate appeal," but accord both terms to that source from whence they emanated. They are bound, by the same Spirit and power by which the Scriptures were given forth, and by which only they are truly opened and understood, or savingly, profitably, and comfortably applied to the heart, to yield obedience to the precepts, to obey the commandments recorded in them. These have the sanctified use of them, although they openly acknowledge that they are only a secondary rule, completely subordinate to the Spirit.

Thou art aware, my dear friend, that it is no picture of the imagination, which has suddenly darted across my organs of vision; but that it is something which I have long seen and felt was coming upon us. My former letters to thee will bear testimony to this fact. Yea, I have seen and felt this spirit at work for years; many of my most intimate friends know it. I have seen it in that Light which never deceived me. When I say that it is a "dark, uncertain, unbelieving spirit," I know what I say. "For darkness hath covered the earth, and gross darkness the people,"—"they grope for the wall, like the blind at noon-day;" and the reason is, "they love darkness rather than Light, because their deeds are evil." They are not willing to bring their deeds to the Light, lest they should be made manifest,—to the Light of Christ which shines in the heart, and makes a true discovery between thing and thing. There is no evading this swift witness, this faithful and true witness. But there is such a thing as resisting, until it ceases to strive; for it is written, "my Spirit shall not always strive with man." It is for this reason that the natural, corrupt heart of man is constantly seeking out some easier way, is "climbing up some other way." But equally true and certain it is, that these are all "thieves and robbers." "I am the door (into the true sheepfold), by me if any man enter in, he shall be saved, and shall go in and out and find pasture." And the sheep of Christ hear his voice, and they follow Him; "and the voice of the stranger they will not follow, for they know not the voice of strangers." It is their distinguishing characteristic, that their Lord and Master, as their eyes are kept single unto Him, in the obedience of Faith, gives them a true discernment, a true judgment (for he is a "spirit of judgment to them that sit in judgment" rightly), between that which is really and truly of Him (whether passing in themselves, or appearing in others), and that which is not. Here is the real, substantial ground of judgment. Such as these are the humble whom the Lord teaches of his ways, and the meek whom he guides in the paths of true judgment. There is much said now against judgment; no man is to be judged for his unsoundness, let him be ever so much so; if he professes to believe in "the religion of the Bible," with his lips and his tongue, it is all to be suffered and borne. It is said, he is an evangelical friend, or a "Bible Christian." The spirit of the age is against judgment—the spirit of the world is against it,—and both are very prevalent in our religious society. But I am satisfied that when judgment ceases to go forth, to be passed upon and set over wrong things amongst us, as R. Barclay said, "though one or more, few or many," we shall cease to be a true Church of Christ, though we may retain the bare name, and even glory in it.

With regard to its being an "uncertain spirit," I apprehend it might be easily proved to be so. And it cannot be sure, it cannot be certain, when that main fundamental point or principle is denied or rejected, which William Penn said, was "as the root of the goodly tree of doctrines, which grew or branched forth out of it,"—that principle of divine immediate revelation, which enabled the disciples of our blessed Lord to see through and "beyond the veil" of flesh with which the eternal Word and Son of God was clothed or covered, in the days of his outward manifestation, to that which dwelt "within the veil." No others could discover it, no others could acknowledge it then. No others could answer with certainty and assurance, when the question was asked, "Whom do men say that I, the Son of man, am?" There was a diversity of sentiments, a variety of conflicting opinions among men. Some guessed one thing, and some another: "Some say thou art Elias, some John the Baptist, and some, one of the old prophets risen again." But when his immediate followers and disciples were asked,—those who had left all to follow Him,—to whom it was given to know the mysteries of the kingdom, which is an inward and spiritual kingdom;—when they were inquired of, "Whom do ye say that I, the Son of man, am?"—they could answer with certainty, with full assurance of faith, "Thou art the Christ, the Son of the living God." For Simon Peter not only spoke for himself, but for his fellow-disciples and believers, as was the case on many other occasions; when they were all addressed, one answered for all. Oh, the preciousness of the doctrine and instruction contained in the blessing pronounced upon this confession of faith in Him, who is Lord of all, Head over all things to his Church and people, and not only so, but the everlasting and sure foundation laid in Zion, the Rock of Ages, the foundation upon which the Church is built. "Blessed art thou, Simon Barjonah, for flesh and blood hath not revealed it unto thee, but my Father, who is in heaven!" Yes, "thou art Peter; and upon this Rock will I build my Church, and the gates of hell shall not prevail against it."

Thou art aware that the Society of Friends has ever professed and believed, that the revelation of Christ in spirit, is the foundation upon which the Church is built, upon which every member of it is established; and other foundation can no man lay than that which is laid, which is, Christ Jesus. Thou art aware also that this principle is controverted in that book which I showed thee; a book, which, if it was made public, I am satisfied would have a tendency to open the eyes of such amongst us as still retain their integrity and uprightness of heart; however it might be with those who are overcome by the "dark, uncertain, unbelieving spirit." These, it is probable, would not see, for the god of this world hath blinded the eyes of them that believe not; and truly it is no less unbelief and infidelity, to deny Him as he is, the Lord from heaven, a quickening spirit, to deny the inward and spiritual appearance of Christ in the heart, to deny the plain declaration made by Himself, "I will not leave you comfortless, I will come to you,"—to make distinctions and separations between the "three that bear record in heaven,"—which "three are one,"—to bring down the doctrine of the indwelling of Christ by his Spirit in the heart, to "simple faith—mere credence," in the Scriptural account of Him, and of what he has done and suffered without us, or to speak of it as a mere "influence." This is not true faith; it is not the "substance of things hoped for,"—it is not a living, efficacious faith, such as is able to save the soul. This is not Quakerism, but it is what the most carnal professors in the world would allow. It is their principle, not ours, and the world loveth its own. They are all ready to join with this spirit. They are all rejoicing at the rapid strides which multitudes called by our name are making towards them.

When I say that it is unbelief, practical unbelief, I know what I say. And if such as are in this spirit had lived in the time of the outward manifestation, they would as surely have rejected it; they would as surely have said, "We will not have this man to reign over us," notwithstanding the loud cry they make about the Scriptures, notwithstanding their professions of faith in Christ, as ever the high professing Jews did. These were as anxiously looking for Christ to come, as those are confident that he has come and suffered for us. The Jews were as well acquainted with the prophecies of their own prophets, as any of the description I have been speaking of, and much better; still they rejected Him on account of His mean appearance, and said, "Can any good thing come out of Nazareth? Search and look, for out of Galilee there ariseth no prophet." Ah! they searched the Scriptures, and thought to have eternal life in them, but they would not come unto Him, that they might have life. They had not His Word abiding in them. They thought to know Him by comparing him with the prophetical account which had been given forth by the spirit of prophecy concerning Him. But notwithstanding the astonishing clearness, the wonderful precision with which the time and manner of His coming had been foretold and recorded, they failed in making a right application of those prophecies to Him, when He appeared. And why? Because, for all their professions of regard to the letter of Scripture, they were not true believers even in them,—they were not led by the Spirit,—they were not subject to the Power, in and by which the Scriptures were given forth. We have "the word of a King" for it—the testimony of the King, immortal, eternal, and invisible to the carnal eye of man, however mighty he may be in the literal, head knowledge of the Scriptures. Had they truly believed Moses and the prophets, they would have believed in Him; for, says

He, "Moses wrote of me;"—"But if ye believe not his writing, how shall ye believe my words?" Is it not clear that they were not true believers in the Scriptures of the Old Testament, although they had as much "simple faith, mere credence" in them, as the Scribes and Pharisees of the present day, and they are numerous amongst us? There are those amongst us who do indeed go "in long robes," and "love greetings in the markets, and the uppermost seats in the synagogues, and for a show make long prayers;" who when they fast, fast to be seen of men, and all under an appearance of great humility; but it is only in appearance, for it is impossible that any man can be in an humble frame of mind, while he is calling in question, not only the united judgment of the Church in its collected and official capacity, from the time when we were first raised up and gathered into a distinct religious society to the present, but also the individual soundness of those worthies who died triumphantly in that faith, for a testimony to which they suffered, in many instances, even unto death. Of this faith, of some of the most important of these principles and testimonies, it is now declared, that they lead to or "involve the danger of a very fatal heresy." If this is true humility, it is of a different kind from that which I have ever desired to know or be acquainted with. But it appears in some instances to have had a wonderful effect, in leading many "silly women captive."

To return,—it is a fundamental doctrine of Truth,—it is one of those testimonies to the Truth, which we were raised up as a people to bear—it is a doctrine abundantly testified of in the Scriptures,—that no man can come unto Christ, except the Father, who sent Him into the world, draw him; that no man can savingly believe in Christ, except he receive the gift of faith, from Him who is the author and finisher of the saints' faith. For faith is the gift of God, and "without faith it is impossible to please Him." There must be "an understanding" given, before any can "know Him that is true." There must be a preparation of the heart in man, by the Spirit and Power of the Lord. He who is the Way, the Truth, and the Life, must open our understandings, before we can understand the Scriptures; and unless this is the case, we shall as surely fail of the right understanding of them, as ever the Scribes and Pharisees formerly did. Notwithstanding, it is roundly asserted, in open violation of our acknowledged principles, and in direct contradiction to their own testimony, "that they must be interpreted like all other books, according to the common and intelligible rules of language, and not without a reference to innumerable facts and circumstances which throw light on their meaning." Who shall ever be able to refer to these innumerable facts and circumstances? Can that which is innumerable ever be numbered or referred to, any more than that which is wanting? The Scriptures are, indeed, able to make the man of God perfect (not the natural man), but only through faith which is in Christ Jesus. "For the natural man understandeth not the things of the Spirit of God, neither can he know them, because they are spiritually discerned." . . . .

My health is very poor—scarcely able to attend to my business. I am afflicted, but not forsaken, in the best sense; and what I have to feel for "the afflictions of Joseph," are my greatest sufferings. My dear love is to thee.

T. B. Gould.

To Peleg Mitchell.

Newport, 30th of 7th month, 1838.

My dear Friend:

Thy letter was received four days after its latest date. The several items of intelligence were very interesting, not only to me, but to all the family; and it was a great comfort to us all, to find thou hast the very same sense and judgment, in relation to all the subjects touched upon, that we have been favored with. As to myself, a very humiliating, and somewhat more public line of service has been my lot, in relation to the state of society now, than has yet been required of them, although I believe they have stood faithfully at their several posts. From the course which I have felt called upon to pursue, much persecution and abuse has been visited upon me, both by open and avowed enemies to the truth, and by those who have hitherto professed much love and esteem for me, and allegiance to the principles of truth. Although I had no reason to doubt, yea, I was and have been sensible all along, of the unity and sympathy of thy spirit—I mean, at times and seasons when the renewed feeling of that hidden fellowship one with another, which still follows, and is a consequence of "walking in the Light," is vouchsafed—still the expression of it was and is truly sweet, precious, and strengthening. "Words fitly spoken," or written, "are like apples of gold, in pictures of silver." Apples are a very pleasant fruit, and both these metals are called "precious." How good it is!

There was a written copy of a book which J. J. G. had printed in Norwich, England, for private circulation only, sent to me by a friend in New York, entitled "Brief Remarks upon Impartiality in the Interpretation of Scripture." In the time of the yearly meeting, I thought it right occasionally, in expressing my dissatisfaction with his other writings, and with his being suffered to travel as a minister amongst us, while he refused to condemn them, sometimes to refer to and produce it, to prove that he was essentially and radically unsound in the faith, and not only so, but that in this case he had attacked the principles of the Society, although, like Joab, under an hypocritical and deceitful profession of kindness. As I made no secret of my uneasiness, believing myself called upon to proclaim as upon the housetop, that which was done as it were "by night" ("it was night," according to one of the evangelists, when Judas betrayed his Master), so I believed the full time had come for me to do what I did, and to do it openly. This made a wonderful stir amongst Gurney's friends; it really seemed as if they were afraid "the house of Dagon, their god," would be pulled down on their heads! Rowland Greene, who by the way professed to me that he was entirely ignorant of Gurney's having written anything unsound, told me that I was not aware "how much I was hurting his service"—that many friends were prepared to receive him as a dear brother, he had good certificates, &c. &c. I told him, if he was really ignorant, it was a very culpable ignorance,—if he was a watchman on the walls of Zion, he ought to know what the enemy was about; that he ought to watch for him, and give the alarm when he was coming, &c.; and then, with some difficulty, I prevailed upon him to listen to some parts of that book, which strikes at the very foundation of Quakerism, which we know to be primitive Christianity. He said, in excuse to the company for listening to the book and to me, that he should not have done so, but for the great love and esteem he *had* had for me. This was about all the satisfaction I got from him; but I felt a peace flow from the sense that I had done that which was my duty to do, which the loss of his favor and my good name with him, could not take from me. There were about twenty-five friends present. The thing was much more extensively gone into than I have room to give thee an account of.

It happened one day that we had a large company to dinner, between thirty and forty. While some were at dinner, L. T. and a young woman present got into a conversation about Joseph J. Gurney; they continued it for half an hour perhaps, saying many things in his favor, until there was a misstatement made by the female, with regard to his reception by friends in Philadelphia. I had sat entirely silent until this time, although my burden had been increasing: but as I attended Philadelphia Yearly Meeting, I happened to know how he stood with many friends there; so I corrected the mistakes she had made, and perhaps added my own sentiments with regard to him. One thing led on to another, until the subject spread pretty wide, among us three, no other person in the room taking any part in it. In the midst of it, the friends from the first dinner-table came in. What I said seemed to produce much uneasiness in J. Meader; I could perceive it plainly before he said anything; but he soon took the subject out of the hands of the young friends, by attacking me for expressing my sentiments before so large a company. I told him I held no objection to J. J. G., or opinion concerning him, which I wished to conceal, that he had been guilty of a public offence, and was so far from being willing publicly to condemn it, that he would not do it privately. Putting me upon my proof, I told him, I knew it by the testimony of as reputable friends as any there were in Philadelphia Yearly Meeting. He said, that was too far off, he might have condemned them before this time. I then told him, "I knew he had not, by the testimony of John Wilbur, who visited him yesterday upon the subject, and called upon him to condemn them, but he refused."

. . . . . There was a great deal said, both doctrinally and disciplinary (that is, with regard to the "order of society," and J. J. G.'s formal certificates; which were obtained contrary to that power which only makes the form truly valuable); and I *know* that many valuable friends, ministers and elders present, had unity with me in it.

. . . . . . I had told J. M. that he (J. J. G.) was like Absalom, "who stole away the hearts of the people from David his father;" and that while the true ministry had a tendency to gather to Christ, the true Teacher, and to produce a silent waiting state upon Him, this man's labors had a contrary effect, and gathered only to the speaker, begetting a desire after more words. . . . . . Sometime while they were here, I was led into an expression of my objections to the "—— Association," and the reasons why I *could not* attend their meetings, by a friend saying he was sorry I had not been there. J. M. treated it with contempt, if not with scorn. I hope I shall be *enabled to bear* the sneers of false brethren; but I cannot take any part or lot in the matter. I never have felt myself at liberty to join any "separate" society. The same thing has *restrained* me, that has *led* me into the acquaintance I *have* with the Truth. I have been earnestly solicited to unite, years ago, with Bible, Tract, Temperance, Anti-Slavery, Anti-Masonic, and even *Literary* Societies. Oh! the gate is strait, and the way is narrow, that leadeth unto *life;* and there is no other way of entering the strait gate, or being preserved in the narrow way, but by *following* the Light, *by walking in the Light.* Some appear to think, some that have, I believe, *entered* at the strait gate, and *walked for a time* in the narrow way, that they might take more liberty to look about them, to see what other people are doing, or stop and abide with them awhile; and that the way is so plain there is little danger of missing it; that their own powers perhaps are sufficient to keep them in it. But alas! there are so many byways and crooked paths, which appear at first sight (as the deeply-experienced and divinely-illuminated author of the "Short History of a Long Travel from Babylon to Bethel" said) to lie almost or quite parallel to it, that if the Light is not believed in and followed to the end of the race, where only the crown is to be obtained, such will assuredly make shipwreck of their faith and a good conscience at the same time; for it is not they that run well for a season, but they that hold out to the end, that are saved. The invincible shield of faith, and armor of light, is as able to repel all the fiery darts of the wicked as ever, blessed be His name in whom is Life, and the life is the light of men; in whom is Light, and there is no darkness at all in Him! But darkness covers all the land of Egypt; and many there are who have gone back into it, and their darkness is to be felt indeed, yea, thick darkness is their hiding-place; they are stumbling upon the dark mountains, and all the while crying, "The temple of the Lord, the temple of the Lord are these;" but the Lord is not among them; for where the Spirit of the Lord is there is liberty, but there is bondage in Egypt.

. . . . . . I herewith send thee a copy of the notes I took, of what passed between us. I have felt the greater necessity to do so, from the fact that my having spoken to him has been an additional cause of suffering and persecution to me, although R. Greene and John Meader both advised me to do so; they both thought, however, I have no doubt, it would be the last thing I should do or say in the matter. If they did, they were mistaken. He was not permitted to give my "flesh to the fowls of the air," nor to "the beasts of the field;" but he "despised my youth," as well as that simplicity in which I appeared before him, as much as ever Goliath of Gath did David's, and his sling and stones. Although I am not about by any means to compare myself with David, yet I am satisfied that he might be compared to Goliath; he has as truly despised the armies of the living God and their spiritual weapons, he is as truly harnessed "with a coat of mail" spiritually, as Goliath was literally. In this respect, however, there is a wide difference: the one appeared in his own native character; he was a Philistine, and we have no account that he ever sought to pass for anything else. The other is in the Philistine nature; he is seeking to "stop the wells which the children of Israel have digged,"—yet says, he is a Jew, but is not. He is not even a Jew outwardly; he has not got even the form of sound words: and oh, how far removed from being "in the spirit, and not in the letter;"—he is in the letter, and not in the spirit, and his praise is of men, and not of the Lord. . . .

. . . Poor —— —— is in a Sardis, but has not defiled his garments. Oh, how I have felt for such as have been seeking the Pearl of great price, and made willing to sell all that they had, in order to purchase the field in which the Pearl lay hid; when these have, through deep baptisms and humbling exercises, come among us, and have found such unsoundness, lukewarmness, and unfruitfulness, how must they feel? They cannot help seeing that the whole head is sick and the whole heart faint, with many who are accounted leaders of the people. These are they who cause them to err; these are they who are now destroying the way of the paths of righteousness. Yea, they that are leading captive the simple, who depend upon them without sufficiently bringing their spirits to the balance of the sanctuary, are requiring a song, and they that are spoiling us are requiring of us mirth, saying, Sing us one of the songs of Zion. This was literally the case in the time of the yearly meeting. But how can the Lord's song be sung in the city of a strange land? The harps of the faithful are hung upon the willows; mourning, and lamentation, and woe, is written within, and on the backside of the book which is open before them. They weep when they remember Zion! The wall thereof is broken down, and the gates burnt with fire. The wild boar of the forest is making ravages in the midst of the camp; there is an enemy in the midst of the camp, nourished and caressed there. But there is a small remnant preserved. These are becoming increasingly near to each other. Oh, their fellowship with each other, and with their holy Head, is sensibly increased and increasing! By the three hundred men who lapped water as a dog lappeth, the Lord saved Israel out of the hand of Midian. None of the fearful and afraid were permitted to remain; they were sent home. I have had a language sounding in my ears for many years: The people are too many, the people are too many! I verily believe they will be sifted as corn is sifted in a sieve. The pure wheat will bear it; gold will abide the fire. But such as have been building with wood, hay and stubble, these will suffer loss of all! There is great confusion now among them; it seems as if they were afraid of their own shadow. Some of them flee when no man pursueth them.

. . . . I am frequently suffering great difficulty of breathing, and have a troublesome cough, although I have been more comfortable the whole of the last week, till to-day, than at any time since the yearly meeting; having never, in the course of my disease, been reduced so low as since that time; "my heart and my strength" having both "failed" me. In this respect, however, I hope not to be misunderstood; for my faith never was stronger than it has been of late. But, as R. Barclay said, "all comparisons halt in some part," so I believe quotations may sometimes. "My heart has failed me," in respect to the honor of Truth being maintained by the Society in a general way; and in particular, by some who have stood high, whom few suspected at all, and of whom I had hoped better, much better things. These have discernment enough to see my bodily strength is wasted and wasting, and they lay hold of that, to weaken and take off the force of my concern in respect to "the better part;" of which David said, in immediate connection, I think, with the above quotation, "But God is the strength of my heart, and my portion forever."

I should not have hinted at those small matters and light afflictions, but in order more effectually to encompass a point I have had in view all the while; which is, that thou mayst be induced to consider more weightily the obligation, not to expose what comes to thee in black and white, from thy "weak brother," and which is written under so many unfavorable circumstances. Still, if there may any, the least, good arise from it, I should not prohibit it, believing thou art acquainted with that "wisdom which is profitable to direct,"—although additional suffering and persecution should follow. As dear John Barclay, of England, said, in a letter to John Wilbur, which I have before me, dated 8th mo., 1837 (it was the last he ever wrote to him): "Now I have relieved my mind in the above respect, how shall I do to set forth all I could say on our present, past, and probable future posture, as a religious body, in this land? I trust on many points thou art ably and fully addressed by many Friends of this country. I shall then only touch at things that come before me, and thou must give me credit for entire union with thee and all those who still remain wholly on the Lord's side, and one with our holy ancient ones and valiants, even the primitive stock, who came forth in the powerful Name which is above every name, and unto which every other name, however high and lifted up, must bow! Ah, beloved friend, thou that saw the first seeds and dawning of that which has now manifested itself in degree, knowest well enough, how much of the same nature and root we still have, to oppress and afflict us, and of which it is difficult to particularize, or speak closely of, in the abstract, without allusions to individuals who give uneasiness." This quotation may halt in some part, but in others I am sure it will "hold fast." I had intended, when I commenced, to inquire of thee what thou hadst known of this John Barclay, and whether thou hadst seen any of his writings; also to have given thee an extract from his "Preliminary Observations (to Jos. Pike's and Jos. Oxley's Journals), chiefly addressed to the Society of Friends," on the subject of religious controversy, and the state and condition of the Society in England. He was a descendant of R. B. *in the life and power*, as well as in name and character; none in membership with the Society in this day having, in my judgment, come out in writing with equal clearness and soundness to him, and to the same extent. He was a minister also. . . . . Thy friend,

THOMAS B. GOULD.

FROM T. B. GOULD TO W. C. T.

NEWPORT, 15th of 2d mo., 1839.

MY DEAR FRIEND:

. . . . I cannot say that I have read the whole of William Allen's "Selections from Barclay's Apology," or that I have compared it throughout with the original work; my eyes have been so weak this winter, and other things intervening have prevented me. But I have examined it sufficiently to warrant my saying, that I do not approve of it; and if the limits of an ordinary letter would admit, I could give many solid reasons why I do not. As the case is, I shall confine myself to—first, in regard to the original work "containing much controversial matter [which was] better suited to the period in which it was written than to the present time." Inasmuch as it is a notorious fact, that many of the principles and practices which are controverted in the "Apology" (and which, so far as sound reason and argument, supported by the testimony of the Holy Scriptures, can do it, are therein and thereby entirely overthrown), are now promulgated and strenuously advocated by some of the members and ministers (so called) of that very Society, for "an explanation and vindication of [whose] principles and doctrines" it was originally written, and by whom it has been officially, and, until a recent date, unanimously approved, and more extensively circulated by the Society than any other book: I say, inasmuch as these are notorious facts, I do not approve of the controversial part, nor any other part of the work, being omitted; neither do I believe that it is "too voluminous for the generality of readers."

Secondly: In this "Selection," divers fundamental principles and doctrines which the Society has always held, and until recently (as a body) faithfully supported, are entirely omitted, the same principles and doctrines being now called in question, and undervalued, and denominated mistakes and heresies, by some who stand in high stations in the Society! viz.: First,—"Concerning the true (ground and) foundation of (religious) knowledge"—a whole proposition omitted. Secondly,—concerning the "adequate primary rule of faith and manners, the Spirit the first and principal leader." And to pass over many other important omissions, and some alterations not very creditable to him who made them, I come, thirdly and lastly, to "the communion or participation of the body and blood of Christ." Under this head or proposition, thou wilt find that all that R. B. has said, about "what that body and what that flesh and blood is" which is eaten,—supported as he is by the testimony of the Scriptures, and by the "most sound and solid reason," to say nothing about the hitherto undeviating testimony and principle of the Society,—is entirely omitted (being several pages, or nearly three sections); and no allusion, that I have been able to discover, made therein to any other sect or people whatever, except in the third section, where he does allude to the Papists, Lutherans, and Calvinists. And in the latter part of this third section, W. A. recommences his "Selections;" which are wholly, or nearly so, aimed against the ceremonial use of bread and wine; and it seems to me that it requires but little discernment, to see that what is here omitted is in no wise of so controversial a character as that which is retained or "selected;" inasmuch as the important, fundamental truth, advocated by R. B. in what is left out of W. A.'s book, has never been asserted by any that I know of, except by our blessed Lord and His apostles, the primitive Friends, and those of the same faith, and led by the same unerring Spirit, light, and grace, in the present day; and by Augustine, whose spiritual understanding of, and declaration concerning "the body of Christ which is eaten," R. B. quotes; viz.: "Ye shall not eat of this body which ye see, and drink this blood which they shall spill which crucify me. I am the living bread, who have descended from heaven. He calls Himself the bread who descended from heaven, exhorting that we might believe in Him," &c.

And R. B. goes on and says: "If it be asked, what that body, what that flesh and blood is?" I answer: "It is that heavenly seed, that divine, spiritual, celestial substance, of which we spake before, in the fifth and sixth propositions. This is that spiritual body of Christ, whereby and through which He communicateth life to men, and salvation to as many as believe in Him and receive Him; and whereby also man comes to have fellowship and communion with God." Then follows his Scripture proof of this doctrine. I feel the more reason to disapprove of W. A.'s omitting this part, because J. J. Gurney, in his "Brief Remarks on Impartiality in the Interpretation of Scripture," which was printed in 1836 (W. Allen's book was printed in 1837), has expressed opinions on the flesh and blood of Christ (as well as on many other fundamental and important points of doctrine), utterly at variance with our original principles. I shall inclose thee all he says on this subject in that book, and I do earnestly request thee to compare it with R. B.'s thirteenth proposition throughout, and the latter with W. Allen's "Selections." These new views, I have the best authority for saying, have obtained about London, to an alarming extent, so that the Morning Meeting some time since refused to pass a tract written by Samuel Rundell, on account of its containing extracts from R. B.'s "Apology," and the doctrine it contained being in conformity with it. The title of the tract is, "Observations on the Redemption of Man, on Divine Worship, and on the Partaking of the Flesh and Blood of our Lord Jesus Christ." I have it now by me, and it is an excellent thing: but I understand that J. J. G. "objected to the whole scope and tendency of it," when it was examined in the Morning Meeting, "as partaking of mysticism," &c. I also know, that after the Morning Meeting rejected it, the author, who is a minister, and lives at Liskeard, Cornwall, was induced to republish it by the encouragement given him by Daniel Wheeler. It had been printed before.

Notwithstanding I have written so much, I cannot seem to get clear of the weight of the subject of the hue and cry now raised against controversy, by those who are disposed to drop the original principles of the Society of Friends, and to adopt new notions utterly at variance with them. R. Mott, when last here, on his return from New Bedford after yearly meeting, in a large meeting called together on his account, publicly condemned all "polemical controversy," saying, "it had been a waste of time and talents, a lavish waste," and that he "had no particular class of controversialists in view;" "I condemn them all," said he. I suppose, and some of his own admirers say, that the articles lately inserted in "The Friend," over the signature M. R., belong to him. In the last of them there is another hint and nod or two at controversy, strictures, rejoinders, &c., under the cover of "Gospel family order." . . . . . .

At a time, at this time, when it cannot be denied that there is an attempt making, both from within and without the Society,—"when both ingenuity and industry are taxed, for the purpose of giving to Quakerism another form and character than that which it has ever known" (see William and Thomas Evans's address to their subscribers, on the cover of the first month of the third volume of the "Library"),—it does not seem remarkable to me, that such as unite with those who are engaged in this work should be afraid of controversy. It is a very natural fear, and it has been a very common one too! The adversaries of the Society, whether within or without its pale, always feared the force of truth and justice erected for the defence and spread of its principles. The Hicksites cried out against it: no man was to be condemned for his opinions on religious subjects; they were not to be controverted in the least; no, no! Their cry was, "We must all live in love together, and every man enjoy his own opinion."

At the very first appearance of these things in England, before the days of Beaconism, every effort was made to create a prejudice against the controversial writings of our early Friends. Some said, "they had better never been written;" and others, that "they ought to be gathered into a heap and burnt." These artful men well knew, that so long as they continued to be read and justly valued, they never would be able to bring in the very notions, to controvert which these writings were written, in the openings and requirings of the Lord's divine light and Spirit; which light never had any fellowship with darkness, but always manifested it and reproved it, as did those who walked in the light and were led by the Spirit. See the Apostle: "Have no fellowship with the unfruitful works of darkness, but rather reprove them:" and a multitude of Scriptures might be produced, to prove that this subterfuge, that wrong things, unsound things, and those who err from the faith and bring in strange doctrines, doctrines of devils, must not be controverted, is anti-scriptural. It can be proved that such ought to be "rebuked sharply, that they may be sound in the faith," and, if that end is not gained, that "their mouths ought to be stopped."

But it does seem not a little remarkable, that any in whom there is left a good degree of honesty and faithfulness to our principles, should be "the subjects of so marvellous a hebetude of vision, as not to discern the fallacy" of their pretensions to charity, love, unity, &c., when they are only made a cover for attacking the everlasting, unchangeable foundation, through those who are endeavoring to build upon it, not with wood, hay, or stubble, but a spiritual and heavenly building which will abide the fire,—even by and through the Spirit and power of Christ,—a habitation for His holy Presence to dwell, to tabernacle in. I am often forcibly reminded, whilst viewing, as it were "by night," the walls of Jerusalem, which are broken down, and her gates, which were once so strongly guarded, and the posts thereof so firmly rooted and established upon that which is sure, but are now burnt as with fire, and the bars thereof removed—I am forcibly reminded of Abner, whom Joab took aside to speak with him in the gate quietly, and smote him under the fifth rib, that he died. Surely, well might David exclaim, "Died Abner as a fool dieth! Thy hands were not bound, nor thy feet put into fetters," &c. And of Judas, who, under a profession of love, betrayed his Master! I may well say, "whilst viewing the walls by night;" for I am not known to "my people," nor to the elders of my people (so called), many of them, except as a "byword," a hissing, and to be reproached; on account of the testimony which I hold, and am constrained to bear, against these things. And firm I am in the belief, that if I am favored to hold fast the beginning of my confidence firm unto the end, I shall know an overcoming: and all those who are faithful will know an overcoming, a getting the victory over the beast and over his image, over his mark, and over the number of his name, and over the false prophets too—those who say they are Jews, but are not, but are of the synagogue of Satan,—"by the blood of the Lamb," and by the word of their testimonies which they have held, not having loved their lives unto the death.

When those disaffected persons in England, before spoken of, had paved the way for it, by creating a prejudice against the controversial writings of Friends, and casting dust upon them (in which unhallowed work they succeeded too well with many honest but unsuspecting Friends), the next step, and it was a short one, was to call their testimonies and doctrines and practices in question; and notwithstanding all their pretensions to faith, charity, and love, the event has proved they were destitute of either of these Christian virtues. I acknowledge that some of these have quite gone off; yet but few compared with the extent of the unsoundness, as divers letters now by me, from sound Friends, ministers and others, in England, would prove. Other facts and circumstances, coming under our own observation, prove it. The language of one of the letters referred to is: "I sometimes think it is only a part of the roughest of the mixture which has been sifted from us. There is much of a more specious and refined nature remaining, which, if I mistake not, is still more opposed to the simplicity of the truth as it is in Jesus. Oh! what a subtle enemy is ours, working in a mystery!" &c.

It is abundantly and sorrowfully evident, that the same spirit which operated in E. Bates and the Beaconites, is still at work in the Society in England and in this country, though under a more subtle and specious, and of course more dangerous, garb. I say, in this country,—yes, in this country,—and time will manifest that what I say is the truth. There are those now living who will, then, have an opportunity to see, and perhaps feel, what all this uproar and outcry against controversy means, and the call which has been heard from Dan even to Beersheba, *to be still and quiet*, and to have patience, and charity, and love, for those things which some of us do assuredly know to be evil: even that it is intended to lay us asleep, as on the lap of Delilah, until they have shorn us of our strength, and put out our eyes;—then they will rejoice over us, as the Philistines did over Samson in the house of Dagon: that it is intended to prevent us from making any the least resistance, until they have penetrated the very heart of our city, and even into the temple, and robbed it of the vessels of gold and of silver, the treasures of the Lord's house, which they will carry away with them to Babylon, and the people to a land of captivity!

And now, my dear friend, in the conclusion of this long letter, allow me to say, may that part of the message which was written unto the Church at Ephesus, which is quoted below, be applied unto thee; may it be verified in thy own experience, through the power and operation of the same Spirit which revealed to John, the beloved disciple and servant of our Lord and Saviour Jesus Christ (who is the faithful and true Witness, the true Light and Life of men, the Alpha and Omega, the first and the last, the beginning and the ending)—"those things which must shortly come to pass;" and who declared, "Blessed is he that readeth, and they that hear the words of this prophecy, and keep those things which are written therein, for the time is at hand." May it be applied unto thee: "These things saith He that holdeth the seven stars in His right hand, who walketh in the midst of the seven golden candlesticks: I know thy works, and thy labor, and thy patience, and how thou canst not bear them that are evil; and thou hast tried them which say they are apostles and are not, and hast found them liars; and hast borne, and hast patience, and for my name's sake hast labored, and hast not fainted."

In much unfeigned love, I am thy friend,

THOMAS B. GOULD.

FROM T. B. G. TO JOHN WILBUR.

NEWPORT, 1st of 3d month, 1839.

MY DEARLY BELOVED AND VERY KIND FRIEND:

. . . . I am very much obliged—we are all very much obliged—by thy minute account of thy providential deliverance. It certainly was not merely a "chance" which happened to thee; for the eye of the Lord is continually upon them that fear Him, upon them that hope in His mercy; not only to deliver their soul from death, and to keep them alive in famine, spiritually; but I am firm in the belief,—notwithstanding He causeth the sun to shine on the evil and on the good, and sendeth rain on the just and on the unjust,—that even in temporal things, in things which relate to these poor bodies, there is not only a difference in the subject, by or from which the event is or may be distinguished and denominated, but also, that whatever is permitted outwardly to befall those who are followers of that which is good, is designed by Him who numbereth the very hairs of the heads of such, to "work together" with those spiritual dispensations which He sees meet to lead into and impart, "for good," and for the promotion and consummation of His own all-wise and inscrutable purposes, in and upon His children and people, as well as for the furtherance and accomplishment of their work and service for His name and truth's sake.

Really I can, according to my small measure and growth, have fellowship and sympathy with thee in mourning and lamentation, on account of Israel's loss, in the removal of that valiant man and honorable elder, Jonathan Evans, who was indeed to many, in this day of warfare with Amalek, as Aaron and as Hur were to Moses in that day when his hands were ready to hang down, by reason of heaviness and sorrow for a highly-favored but stiff-necked and rebellious people, who forsook their own mercies, and turned their backs upon, and trampled under their feet, the testimonies which the Lord had given them to bear.

I was spending the evening at William Nichols's when the sorrowful tidings reached me. I might have adopted, and I believe I did adopt, a part of David's expressions on the death of Abner: "Know ye not that there is a prince and a great man fallen this day in Israel?" Surely I felt weak, and I believe we felt that the little company who are left, and who are still favored to say, "Thine are we, David, and on thy side, thou son of Jesse," are weakened, are stripped and peeled still further. . . . . .

Cannot a remnant now say, in reference to this vine, which was indeed planted a noble vine, wholly a right seed, as the prophet said of old, "I will bewail with the weeping of Jazar the vine of Sibmah; I will water thee with my tears, O Heshbon and Elealeh! for thou hast laid my vine waste, and barked my fig-tree, laying it clean bare, even with the ground?" . . . .

I had not read for some time in either of the Books of Kings, when I received thine; but as I was reading what thou hast so instructively and comfortably written about Elisha, it was revived in my remembrance, how it was with him "when the Lord would take up Elijah into heaven by a whirlwind;" that he, Elisha, knew it, and "went with Elijah from Gilgal;" and that he would not be prevailed on to remain there, but when the Lord sent him to Bethel he said, "As the Lord liveth, and as thy soul liveth, I will not leave thee." And so again at Jericho, where Elijah proved Elisha still further (no doubt by divine requirement, or permission at least) saying, "Tarry here, I pray thee, for the Lord hath sent me to Jordan:" but he continued unwavering, and would not leave Elijah, no, not even when he came to Jordan. Oh! what he would have lost if he had left him! Undoubtedly he would not have received a double portion of the spirit which was in and upon Elijah; he certainly could not have caught the mantle as it fell from him; for it was after they were "gone over" Jordan, that Elijah said, "Ask what I shall do for thee;" and even then, beside his asking a hard thing, there was another condition, that of watchfulness: "Nevertheless if thou see me when I am taken from thee, it shall be done unto thee: but if not, it shall not be done." Are not watchfulness, faithfulness, and obedience inculcated here? I have often thought so before, and renewedly so at this time, as well as when I was reading thine.

Long ago, years ago, when I was a little child, I remember how I loved, and how I was concerned to endeavor to keep near those who kept near the Lord; and how earnestly I desired then to be able to see spiritually who were near Him; and I remember how it was opened to me then, that it was necessary for me to keep my own eyes, the eye of my mind, to Him, and upon Him, and in Him, not only for my own safe condition and standing, but also it was clearly and immediately opened to my view, that even those who had attained to a good condition, to a heavenly and honorable condition, might lose it and fall from it, and yet this might be the case when, as to the outward, there might be little change in the appearance: so that the mind must be kept principally and primarily in the "Head," and not look to men or follow men, any farther than they followed Him and were found in Him. I desire to speak it to the praise of that grace, everlasting loving-kindness, and tender mercy, by which not only I am what I am, but by which alone I have been preserved from still clinging to and following after men, who, having once been favored with it, and richly adorned and eminently qualified by it for usefulness, and thereby made as examples to the flock, have turned from it to wantonness. But how many there are who *practise* upon the false principle, "once in grace, always in grace," however unwilling they may be to own it; so that if a man has once had a name to live, and especially if this reputation has been great and generally acknowledged, when he loses his life and becomes spiritually dead, to all intents and purposes, nothing remaining but a lifeless carcass, and even this unlike that of the prophet who was slain by the lion (for his carcass was not eaten, nor the ass on which he rode torn), he must still be honored and cherished, as if he were a living man!

When I have thought of the course which ——, ——, and many others have of late pursued, I have been forcibly reminded of Jehoshaphat, of whom it is recorded that he did that which was right in the sight of the Lord, walking in the way of Asa his father: howbeit the high places were not taken away (in his reign), but the people still offered and burnt sacrifices in the high places: and he made peace with the king of Israel, he joined affinity with that wicked Ahab, and went at his call to Ramoth-Gilead to battle, saying, "I am as thou art, my people as thy people, and my horses as thy horses." Alas! how nearly it cost him his life! . . . .

The time has come when I can well understand how it was with the prophet when he said, "O, that I had in the wilderness a lodging-place of wayfaring men, that I might leave my people and go from them." And I believe it will be with the *profession* of Quakerism, as it was with the *profession* of Christianity in primitive times; when it became popular, it was adopted and professed by men of worldly wealth and power; kings and princes trading in it and with it; and the true Church was driven into the wilderness *by those who bore her name* and gloried in it, boasting of the constancy of those who had previously suffered martyrdom for the thing itself, which they only had the image and likeness of, and were "persecuting the woman and the remnant of her seed,"—until they drove her out of sight, and for a time, to outward appearance, got rid of her; although she never ceased to exist in the place prepared for her of the Lord, her Maker and her Husband, who still nourished her and loved her in her forlorn and desolate condition. But then was the time of the vain-glory of the false church, when she sat as a queen and no widow, upon the scarlet-colored beast; when the false prophet, with his lying wonders, deceived the nations, upon which the false church sat, and over which she bare rule.

And now, notwithstanding it did please Him who is Head over all things to his Church, to make way for her, several hundred years ago, to come forth out of the wilderness, "clothed" indeed "with the sun," and not only the moon but all changeable things under her feet,—notwithstanding she was brought forth "fair as the moon, clear as the sun, and terrible as an army with banners,"—notwithstanding the Lord was her light, and her God alone her glory,—notwithstanding He was for a crown of glory and a diadem of beauty, unto her, and for a spirit of judgment to them that sat in judgment, and for strength to them that turned the battle to the gate,—notwithstanding the mountain of the Lord's house was exalted, and set upon the top of the mountains, and above the hills, and many people did come and say, "Let us go up to the mountain of the Lord, to the house of the God of Jacob, for He will teach us of his ways and we will walk in his paths,—for out of Zion shall go forth a law, and the word of the Lord from Jerusalem" (though all nations did not flow unto it, neither have they to this day),—notwithstanding, as I firmly believe, our ancient Friends did arrive at and stand upon the very summit of the Lord's mountain, the top of the holy hill of Zion; and standing there, they witnessed, and in them and to them was fulfilled the vision of the evangelical prophet, "In this mountain shall the Lord make unto all people (that come unto it) a feast of fat things, of fat things full of marrow, of wines on the lees well refined; and shall destroy the face of the covering that is spread over the nations, and the veil that is over all people" (that have not known what it is to find and stand upon Mount Zion, the holy hill, which cannot be removed),—notwithstanding this is my faith concerning them and the glorious work which they wrought, through the Lord's eternal spirit and power, and that they were a people "formed for himself," and by himself, and showed forth His praise, the praise of his own work,—and so, I believe, there has been a living remnant from that day to this, preserved upon this everlasting foundation, though not so many in proportion to the numbers who professed the same high and holy calling; and of latter time the number of this remnant has been fast decreasing,—notwithstanding all this, and that I have, I believe, as deep and exalted a sense as I am capable of, of the surpassing strength, excellency, dignity, glory, and beauty of those testimonies which the Society of Friends was raised up to bear, and which they did formerly bear faithfully and nobly;—yet I do believe that those who stand faithful to these heavenly principles (which may be included and comprehended in one word, the Truth) will be excommunicated from the Society (their names are already cast out as evil); that they will be driven back into the wilderness, and go out of sight, very much, as it respects an outwardly gathered, and visible state and condition; while those who have gone from the Spirit, Life, and Power (which joins to the living Head), and are separated from the Vine, and are cast forth as a branch, and are burnt and withered, will retain the image, the name, &c. And by how much the reformation which was wrought under this name and power exceeded, and the ground which was gained, overlooked, surpassed, and was advanced beyond any former age, state, and condition of the visible Church, by so much will those who are clothed with an imperfect image and likeness of it, the more deceive the nations, than any others have done; and by so much the more keen and afflicting will the persecution be, which these inflict upon the "residue of the people who are left," even the remnant of the seed of that "woman" who was "clothed with the sun," had the "moon under her feet, and a crown of twelve stars upon her head." For, as that eminent seer and true prophet, Job Scott, said in his preface to "The Baptism of Christ, a Gospel ordinance:" "Babylon is not yet so fallen as to rise no more: she is still lurking in a mystery; mystery Babylon the great; and still the mother of many harlots; thousands are ensnared among some or other of her daughters, and are not aware of her cup." And this will be the most harmful of all her many and artful sorceries, a doubly refined golden cup, full of the greatest abominations that ever yet made desolate the heritage of the Lord.

On reading this latter part over, what shall I say to thee, my dear friend? I will say, for I can do it in truth, as J. Barclay said to P. Bedford, that when I took up my pen, I had quite another intention, than to have branched out on this subject at this time; although I had thought, some time ago, of expressing my views to thee in a somewhat similar way. But I found myself writing upon it before I was well aware, and then could not seem to leave it sooner. If I have gone too far, please burn it immediately, and deal very plainly with me; although I do not at present think I have, if I have written so as to be understood, which I sometimes think I scarcely do. . . . . .

I have so many things on hand, and am so feeble and poorly, that it seems as if what I have to do must be done quickly; for I can hardly keep or go about. I have also lost my hope that anything will be done in a Society capacity, or that [as such] it will be saved from utter ruin. That truth's testimonies will be lost by it [as a body] I greatly fear; though, of a solitary remnant I am still firmly persuaded, that they will be saved, "as the two or three berries from the top of the uppermost boughs, four or five upon the outermost fruitful branches thereof." But they will surely be as the gleaning grapes that are left in it (in the true faith of the Gospel), or as the shaking of an olive tree: for everything that can be shaken will be shaken, and that only which is founded on the immovable Rock will remain. And if it is not fully accomplished in the days of the fathers, it will be in the days of the children.

Thy sure friend,
THOMAS B. GOULD.*

TO PELEG MITCHELL.

NEWPORT, 8th of 3d month, 1839.

MY DEAR FRIEND, PELEG MITCHELL:

. . . You have been much and often in my remembrance, and I have employed all the time which my feeble state of health, and a proper attention to other incumbent duties, would permit, in making thee a copy of J. J. G.'s "Brief Remarks," &c., which I have now completed, and only await an opportunity to send. . . . It is one of the basest, most offensive, and sophisticated attacks ever

* A portion of this letter has been already published, in the "Journal and Correspondence of John Wilbur." Several other valuable letters from T. B. G., having especial reference to the trials attending J. W., have been included in that volume, the recent publication of which renders it needless to repeat them in this collection.

made on our principles, either from within or without the pale of our religious Society: and still, marvellous indeed must be the "hebetude of" that "vision" which "cannot discern the fallacy of the author's pretensions" to a concern for the "peace and prosperity of our section of the Christian church!" I have been ready to say, as Jehu the son of Jehoshaphat said to Joram (or Jehoram) the son of Ahab (who sold himself to do wickedly): "What peace, so long as the whoredoms of thy mother Jezebel and her witchcrafts are so many?" And truly this man (and many others who are as unsound and corrupt as he) "covets" the "vineyard," or inheritance of our forefathers in the everlasting, unchangeable Truth, which the Lord hath "forbidden" some of us to "sell or exchange for another," as much as Ahab and Jezebel (with her painted face and tired head) coveted that of Naboth the Jezreelite, even for "a garden of herbs." But now, when it cannot be denied that there is a famine in the land, even now, when not only "one," but many, "go out into the field (the world) to gather herbs, and finding a wild vine, and gathering thereof a lapful of wild gourds, come and shed them into the pot of pottage;" there are some of the "sons of the prophets" who are still favored to know or discover that "there is death in the pot;" and there are some also who are neither prophets nor sons of prophets, but whom the Lord hath taken as "they followed the flock," and as they were "gathering sycamore fruit," and showed them that "there is death in the pot;" and hath required some of these "herdmen," at times and seasons, to declare, as "at Bethel," that if the pottage which has been "seethed" is partaken of, "the sanctuaries of Israel shall be laid waste." But "the land is not able to bear all the words" of these, any more than it was in the days of Amos; and those who are called "priests" say now, as Amaziah said to him: "Prophesy not again any more at Bethel, for it is the king's chapel, and it is the king's court!" . . .

. . . Now is it not remarkable that Samuel Gurney, the brother of Joseph John, should have told P. E., who was in London, and attended the yearly meeting there, when J. J. G. got his certificates, that the story which had then gone about, with respect to the objection to his coming in the select yearly meeting, was utterly false! I read it in a letter in P.'s own handwriting, at cousin Stephen Gould's. . . . Truly, if Truth's testimonies are supported in this day of "treading down and perplexity," those who are or may be accounted worthy to suffer for His sake, whose they are and on whom they are based, from the least of them unto the greatest of them, must indeed set their faces as a flint, and be willing to stand as in the gap, to be shot at by every archer. That it may be our experience, and that our bows may abide in strength, and the arms of our hands may be made strong, by the power of the mighty God of Jacob, who is both the "Shepherd and the Stone of Israel," is the sincere desire of thy affectionate friend, for thee and for all the upright-hearted who are of the wrestling seed, as for my own soul.

THOMAS B. GOULD.

TO JOHN WILBUR.

NEWPORT, 22d of 4th mo., 1839.

MY DEAR FRIEND:

. . . And lately, more especially, I have, I think, seen and felt the application of the sorrowful language: "Ephraim is joined to his idols; let him alone;" as it respects some prominent individuals; and more of the necessity of refraining from casting pearls before those who would only trample them under their feet, and turn again and rend such as, even in that "love" which is "without dissimulation," were seeking not to destroy that which had been captivated in the "snare of the fowler," but to lend a hand of help (where the strength was wasted in a fruitless striving to get along, and to make an advancement while covered with the net), to lend a helping hand to remove the net first, and to endeavor to get clear of that, entirely clear, and then to seek for the ancient path, to inquire where is the good old way, and to have the feet turned back again into it. But what can be done for those who plead for the net because it is of so fine a texture, and hug the chains because they are gilded over with a gilding that looks like the finest gold? They are not willing to come near that fire, by which these things must and will eventually be tried; and inasmuch as they will not submit to it now, I fear they will in the end suffer loss of all. . .

. . . . We are a poor priest-ridden people, here in Newport now, and need the "prayers of all saints" that we may be enabled to "keep the faith and the patience of the saints."

. . . . . Father's judgment is, that there has been something of a gathering known to the true Teacher, by some, and he is very much concerned lest they should be scattered. But as far as respects the instrument of this scattering, I fully believe that his building is not to be propped up or supported at all, nor anything to be done that should have an effect to paint it, or make it look any more like the right thing than it now does; but let it manifest itself, and be developed. For there is a sufficient attempt made now to pass it off as sound Quakerism, though the truth will appear, to such as are favored to have their eyes open, notwithstanding all the art and device that can be used.

I will give thee a short extract from H. Battey's last letter, dated 25th of 3d month. She says: "My dear aged father [Joseph Hoag] is with us on a visit. I read both thy letters to him. He says: 'When thou writes to that dear family, remember my love affectionately to them all. Tell them I rejoice to hear, there is yet left in New England one of a hundred and ten of a thousand, that are concerned to abide upon the ancient landmarks;' and then added: 'It reminds me of what I passed through, previous to the breaking out of the schism in our yearly meeting. If I spoke against Elias Hicks's doctrine, the cry was, "Be still! it won't do to say anything!" But I marked these, and when the time of separation came, they went off,—those that were so afraid there should be a word said, lest it should produce a schism.' He further said, 'I have felt the necessity of bearing public testimony, in different places since our division, that one woe is past, behold! another cometh! and I think the second will be worse than the first.'" . . . .

THOMAS B. GOULD.

To John Wilbur.

Newport, 19th of 5th mo., 1839.

My dear Friend:

. . . . . . Sorrowful as it may be, I think there is not much to be expected of any man whose faith is only pinned upon another's sleeve, and who has so little root and discernment in himself, as to be driven about with every wind of doctrine that blows. Surely, if the minds of Friends had not been more in love with and engrossed in their farms and merchandise, and if they had been really convinced of and converted to the truth; if that faith, which was once delivered to the saints, had been delivered to them, and they had kept to the work and operation thereof in themselves, they had not so vilely cast away the shield, as they now have done: and being found without the armor on, the fiery darts of the devil have pierced them, and wounded them to the life. Still, if it shall please the Lord in very deed to reanimate any of these slain; if it please Him to command any of His servants the prophets, to "prophesy to the wind," and as they prophesy, to cause a shaking among them, and to gather them together (who have been scattered), bone to his bone, and to cover them with sinews, and to cause flesh to come upon them and cover them, that they may stand upon their feet, and become a "great army," and by virtue of His quickening and almighty power, be enabled to fight His battles; I hope we shall be favored to acknowledge and own the work in due season. But at present I apprehend some of these are aware that we have at least read the injunction, "Lay hands suddenly on no man." But the unchangeable truth of that Scripture, they must most assuredly first be convinced of, viz.: that there is no manner of fellowship "between Christ and Belial," and that it is impossible to "partake of the Lord's table and the table of devils." That valiant soldier in the Lamb's army, Joseph Hoag, I understand, said lately in his preaching, that "there was nothing the devil liked better than to get his kingdom alongside Christ's kingdom; but though he might make it look never so much like it, he could not get it in, and that he (the devil) never had it in his power to emit one ray of light to illustrate the truth!" How much need some of these Babel-builders have, to learn the "first principles of the doctrine of Christ;" and with all their study and research, what novices they are in those things which are clearly seen and thoroughly understood by mere children and babes, whose youth they so much affect to despise! But the eternal decree and purpose of Him, to whom all his works are known from the beginning, to hide these things forever from that eye which is disposed to pry into them, to "study" them, and search them out, cannot be changed; neither can His holy will and pleasure to reveal them unto babes, any more be changed. The preaching of the cross is as great a stumbling-block to those who say they are Jews now, and are not, as it was to them of old, and as very foolishness to the modern as to the ancient Greeks,—"the learned and polished Greeks." And so also, "to them that believe" in Christ, the Word of faith (who is nigh, in the heart and in the mouth), and whose faith cometh by hearing Him, the living and eternal Word, which was in the beginning, and liveth and abideth forever,—to these He is known to be the wisdom of God, and the power of God, yea, He is made unto these, of the Father, "wisdom, and righteousness, and sanctification, and redemption."

Oh, that men might be brought down, that they might know the wrong eye, the false eye, closed, and the right eye, the true eye, the single eye, opened! Then should their spiritual "bodies" be "filled with light," by Him who is the Fountain of light, and hath His habitation therein forever; and by walking in the light, they would come to have fellowship and communion with him, and one with another. Then indeed would the "blood of Christ" be found precious; then there would be ground for a sure testimony to be borne to the preciousness of His blood, and the benefits of His death and sufferings; for, having known an overcoming by the blood of the Lamb and by the word of the testimony, such would have "right to the tree of life," and the fountain of life, and would have a real interest in, and a joint fellowship with Him in His death and sufferings, having been made conformable thereunto; and thus would enter in "through the gate," and by "the door," into the city, that spiritual, celestial house, habitation, and building, "which hath foundations," whose walls are salvation and her gates are praise, and whose builder and maker the Lord alone is.

I had no intention to have written thus, but a very different one. If I do send this sheet, I hope thou wilt excuse me, on account of the great weight and burden which I am laboring under, in respect to these things, and many other points with which the true believer, the true Quaker, cannot but be familiar. . . . .

We are a tried people here in Newport, or a tried remnant, and "no people" (in the scriptural use of the term); and I sometimes think, if the "three mighty men" were here, who brake through and drew water out of the well which was by the gate of Bethlehem, when David longed for it, they would hardly be able to reach it, and return with it to the king; the Philistines do stop up the wells which the children of Israel have digged, so that there is danger of perishing for want of water, *not for want of words*. . . . .

In much love and near affection, I am thy sure friend,

Thomas B. Gould.

From John Wilbur to T. B. G.

6th mo. 11th, 1839.

. . . . T. Shillitoe's opinion, that if Friends do not what they can to discourage or suppress his [J. J. G.'s] writings, the Society will go down, has come fresh to me within two or three days, and I am confirmed of its truth. The defection has already advanced so far that, although a remnant may be preserved, by the bearing of a faithful testimony against him and his writings, yet I do greatly fear that those who are now prepared to resist the bearing of such a testimony, will go away, and walk no more with our crucified Lord. In reading the last volume of T. S., I met with a particular account of the separation in New York, and of what transpired in the first meeting "thereafter." He says that "Daniel Haviland, a very aged, blind friend, said, the scene we had passed through in this yearly meeting was clearly unfolded to his view before he came to the city, and expressed his thankfulness to his heavenly Father for this great deliverance. But, said he, dear friends, there will yet something come to pass, if my feelings have not deceived me, that will more fully try our foundation."

Thomas Shillitoe, near his close, said: "Oh, let it be known, that I contend to the last, with unremitting confidence and assurance, for the second coming of our Lord and Saviour Jesus Christ, to the saving of the soul. Oh! what should I have been now, if I had not submitted to His baptism, the baptism of fire?" The prophesies and testimonies of these deeply experienced, faithful, and therefore dignified servants, are, in my apprehension, worthy of credence.

When in the neighborhood of the former, I heard enumerated many prophetic declarations which he was heard to utter, which were unfailingly fulfilled; and the present aspect of things fully indicates the approaching fulfilment of the prediction above recited. . . . .

In dear love to all my true friends,

I am, &c.,

JOHN WILBUR.

FROM T. B. G. TO PELEG MITCHELL.

NEWPORT, 7th of 3d mo., 1840.

MY DEAR AND FAITHFUL FRIEND:

. . . I thought I was sufficiently afflicted when I last wrote (and I think I hinted at it), but thine of the 24th ult. reached me under a much keener baptism of suffering. The reflection that I had been unfaithful to thee, only added trouble to my sorrow. I was not in a state to write when I thought to do so: as G. Fox said, when one of the priests advised him to sing psalms; he said, he was not in a condition to sing! Indeed I am sensible that I am a miserable correspondent every way. I almost marvel that I ever commenced such a work, though no one enjoys the letters from his friends better than I do, I am fully persuaded; at least when I can enjoy anything. However, I do not want to be misunderstood: it is not from any attack made upon me by the archers, that I have been thus depressed, neither has it been from any particular apprehension of anything of that sort. I have been remarkably clear of forebodings as it respects myself, of late; and though I cannot say, perhaps, that I feel resigned to whatever of that sort may be permitted to come upon me, yet I can almost say that I feel at the present time nearly indifferent to it, except some faint desire that I may be helped through it, so as not to dishonor the great and good cause. I cannot speak of anything beyond a "faint desire" at present, although I can well remember having had strong ones; for I seem to be "like the heath in the desert," or the pelican in the wilderness. The bare recollection of former experiences (as thou wilt freely admit) will not do to trust in or speak from. Whether this dispensation is preparatory to further service, or still greater suffering, I am not able to say. The first does not seem at all probable; and if time should make manifest, as it respects the last, it is at present hidden from me. . . . .

THOMAS B. GOULD.

EXTRACT OF A LETTER FROM T. B. G. TO ——.

13th of third month, 1840.

MY DEAR FRIEND:

Thine of the first was duly received on the fourth of the present month. I do not know how it could have been more gratefully received, but I do know that I shall not be able adequately to express the satisfaction we all feel, in the evidence afforded us of the remarkable manner in which way has been made for thy dear father [J. W.] to fulfil his mission among the too generally benighted sons and daughters of a highly favored, though degenerated and revolting people, to whom the mournful language of the prophet seems truly applicable, "O Israel, thou hast destroyed thyself; but in me is thy help!" It does seem to be a renewed evidence that He is still graciously disposed to help this people; inasmuch as he is engaging, requiring, and moving His servants to visit them, and to call unto them,—not out of Seir, the mount of Esau, where the scorner stood formerly, as they do now who cry, "Watchman, what of the night?"—but out of Zion, the Lord's holy mountain, where the Lord setteth His watchmen, and commissioneth them, by his own power and Spirit, with great authority, to declare what they see in His Light, both concerning the "morning, and also the night" in which the treacherous dealer hath dealt so very treacherously, and the spoiler hath so grievously spoiled (even some of the vines upon which were tender grapes); and to say unto them, "If ye will inquire, inquire ye: return; come;" for—"why will ye die!"

From T. B. G. to John Wilbur.

10th of fifth month, 1840.

. . . . I cannot divest myself of the fearful persuasion, that they will either be permitted to trample upon me and grind me to powder, or that I shall be left to do or say something that will injure that blessed cause and testimony which I have in times past ventured in a very small degree to espouse, though never to any greater degree than just to bring up the *rear* of the *hindermost* of those ranks who were prepared and concerned to say, "Thine are we, David, and on thy side, thou son of Jesse." And then, oh! then, I shall not only be left alone in this wide, unfeeling world, without even an old building to shelter me; but what is worse, shall have become reprobate concerning the faith and a good conscience, having made shipwreck of both! And those Friends who have been favored to see the tottering and decayed state of the building (in which we have had and still have a joint interest,—our poor Society, I mean),—and whose unity and fellowship, even the unity and fellowship of the clear-sighted, the willing-hearted, and the living in Jerusalem, I have ever desired and esteemed next to the immediate influence of divine love and power, and sweet communion with Him who dwelt in the bush, and has at seasons visited my own soul—such as these, I feel fully persuaded, will all forsake me, if, indeed, they have not already (and some such I suppose have, to save themselves); although I cannot, upon a close self-examination, see wherein I have missed my way, other than on that side which may be accounted for, and possibly claim some allowance, inasmuch as I am both naturally and spiritually so much weaker than other and ordinary men. . . . .

T. B. G.

To Peleg Mitchell.

Newport, 14th of fifth month, 1840.

My dear Friend:

. . . . I was absent from home three weeks lacking one day. I left home on second-day morning, the 13th of fourth month, and crossing the ferries to South Kingston, took the cars to the place of their nearest approach to the house of dear J. Wilbur, where he met me, and took me in his wagon to his home; and on fourth-day night we took the steamboat at Stonington, and reached the house of J. Wood in New York soon after sunrise on fifth-day morning; where we stayed, to mutual satisfaction I believe, till about the same time on sixth-day morning; when we left for Philadelphia, and were favored to arrive there in safety about three o'clock that afternoon. John lodged at Thomas Kite's, and I was very kindly received and entertained by my dear friends, C. and G. W. A large number of true-hearted and honorable guests were at their house. Ezra Comfort, and his brother John, who is one of the most useful and clear-sighted elders in that yearly meeting (as indeed Ezra is a minister), with their children, lodged at C. W.'s, and a very large and precious flock of Comforts they are. J. W. was entirely silent throughout the yearly meeting, except in one of the sittings of the select meeting, and in the public meeting on fifth-day at the Western district house, which is mostly composed of Gurneyites; here he had some close service, and that noted woman from the Cape, A. D. W., undertook to answer it, as I was told, for I was not present.

. . . . Great was the joy to the honest-hearted to have John among them, and the fullest satisfaction was expressed by those of the highest standing and clearest vision and judgment, as I had abundant opportunity to know, both in public and private; and I am satisfied, no other person could have gone from this yearly meeting, who would have been so acceptable. One elder, the mother of Ezra Comfort, and a very aged, clear-sighted Friend, though too far advanced to get out, was led to intercede that he might be sent over to help them, and afterwards, without outward information (as I understood), had a sense he would come. On first-day, after the yearly meeting closed, he attended the North meeting in the morning, and Arch Street meeting in the afternoon. The last was a season of suffering and oppression, and he had but a short testimony, just at the close, which however met the sense, and was in unison with the feelings, of the rightly-exercised. In the first, he was raised up early, and largely opened, both in testimony and supplication; and such was the victory which truth wrought through its own power, that no strange voice was heard; which was to the great comfort of Friends, both on truth's account and on John's; for as —— and —— were there also, a fear was entertained by many Friends, who have a clear sense and understanding of the state she is in at present, that she would anticipate him and block up his way; as she is clearly seen to be in that forward, active spirit, so common in many who are called ministers amongst us now; and by which forwardness and creaturely activity, the pure streams of life are much obstructed, if not turned aside from their due course; and so there is a sad and continued witnessing in spirit, of the wells, which those of the true seed of Abraham and Jacob have digged, being filled up by their enemies! But she was on this occasion silent, and it was truly a solemn and favored season.

But alas, for the general state of the ministry and eldership amongst us! However, there is a living spring kept open in both respects, in that yearly meeting, of which we were favored with renewed evidence, in divers instances. Still it was thought by ample judges, to have been a time of oppression, and even more so than last year, both in the public meetings and in the meetings for business; though the latter part of the closing sitting was remarkably owned. Dear Jacob Green had predicted, on the opening of the meeting, on second-day morning, that it would be so at the close; and now he had to return living vocal praises, for that the Master of all rightly gathered assemblies had magnified His word above all His name, &c.

We left the city early on second-day morning, by railroad, for Bristol, Pennsylvania, about twenty miles; where, by appointment, a Friend met us with his carriage, and took us about six miles further, to his house, where we lodged that night; and the next day the same Friend, James Moon, took us to the house of Christopher Healy, where we stayed till the next sixth-day morning, making and receiving many social and long-to-be-remembered visits from Friends in that neighborhood. John also attended both their select and mid-week meetings, at the Falls, or Falsington, of both which C. H. and J. M. and wife are members.

We reached New York on sixth-day afternoon, and intended to come home the same night; but John finding D. Wheeler had arrived, and was very ill at J. C.'s, did not feel easy to pass on without attempting to see him; and as there was no boat till seventh-day night going round the Point (Judith) to Newport, I concluded to wait, and did accordingly, and after a fine run, reached home on first-day morning. But it served no other purpose than for John to clear himself; for the family would not suffer J. W. and John Wood to see him. After several fruitless attempts, J. Wilbur went alone, and urged it much, as he was writing to England by a packet just ready to sail from New York. He was then permitted to go to his *chamber door*, and *look upon him* while he was asleep, but on his rousing up a little, was taken immediately away, for fear D. W. would recognize him! From what I saw when I was in that house, he appeared to be surrounded with attendants who must be anything but satisfactory, unless, like some others, he has been leavened into the likeness of the company he keeps; for truly there is something in the very air such breathe, and they claim him stoutly. It may be that he has been laboring with them for their outgoings, in order that they may be restored, and that they claim him only for an effect. I do greatly desire this may prove to be the case, and that, if he should be raised up again, he will come out in a clear, bold, and undeviating testimony against them, not giving them even that kind of reason to claim him, which is afforded by his keeping their company, &c., as heretofore. And truly I cannot doubt, if he and others had only come out as clearly and boldly, in private and on all occasions, against this thing, as Ann Jones did against Hicksism, that their company would have been as unacceptable to them as hers was to the Hicksites. . . . .

THOMAS B. GOULD.

CHAPTER III.

During the early part of the year 1840, Thomas B. Gould's mind was frequently introduced into great conflict and exercise, not only from the distress occasioned to his peculiarly sensitive feelings by the continued attempts to undermine his religious standing, on the part of those who could not bear his firm testimony against innovation; but also from the deep baptisms and sore travails of spirit with which he was now visited, preparatory to his coming forth in public testimony as a minister of the Gospel. These were of a searching and humiliating nature, bringing him often very low before the Lord, and tending renewedly to divest him of self-dependence, and reliance on anything short of the power and wisdom of Him who hath the key of David, and who is alone worthy to open the seven seals.

It is evident from many of his letters, that his mind had long been preparing for such a service; and indeed in a private way he may be truly said to have been a preacher of righteousness from his childhood. But now, as the time approached for a more public line of labor, even in the congregations of the people, the baptisms and exercises seemed sometimes almost as close as nature was able to bear. Yet divine Goodness was near throughout, sustaining his soul, and renewing his faith in the mercy and goodness of the Ancient of days; and he was at length enabled to come forth in a clear and lively testimony, to his own great relief and peace, and to the satisfaction and comfort of the honest-hearted. His first public appearance as a minister was about the close of the fifth month, 1840, in his own meeting at Newport. Some of his feelings on the occasion were a little portrayed in a letter written soon after to his dear fatherly friend, John Wilbur. The substance of his testimony on that occasion, as near as can now be gathered, was as follows:

"Behold, the day cometh that shall burn as an oven; and all the proud, yea, and all that do wickedly, shall be stubble: and the day that cometh shall burn them up, saith the Lord of hosts, that it shall leave them neither root nor branch. But unto you that fear my name, shall the Sun of Righteousness arise, with healing in his wings; and ye shall go forth, and grow up as calves of the stall. And ye shall tread down the wicked, for they shall be ashes under the soles of your feet. The zeal of the Lord of hosts shall perform this. For thus saith the Lord, I will work a work in those days, at the hearing of which, both the ears of them that hear it shall tingle: for I will dry up the green tree, and cause the dry tree to flourish; I will open rivers in high places, and fountains in the midst of the valleys. These things will I do for my seed's sake, for my chosen. Therefore, O thou afflicted, tossed with tempests and not comforted, behold I will lay thy stones with fair colors, and thy foundations with sapphires; I will make thy windows of agate, thy gates of carbuncles, and all thy borders of pleasant stones."

From T. B. G. to John Wilbur.

Newport, 1st of 6th mo., 1840.

My dear Friend:

I wrote to thee soon after quarterly meeting, earnestly requesting thee to give me some account of what was done there, but I received no answer. At the time I wrote, I was under an exceeding deep and sore baptism; I can say in truth, that the earth with its bars was round about me, and the weight of mountains upon me; the weeds were wrapt about my head, and I seemed plunged as into the very belly of hell! Thy not writing added to my affliction. . . . Having never, at the time I wrote, been so deeply tried before, no doubt my letter portrayed a state comparable to that of a bullock unaccustomed to the yoke; and my dependence on man not being completely broken up (which was the end, I fully believe, the divine Wisdom had in view, in permitting so close a trial), thy not writing would seem sufficient to add greatly thereto. . . . But I now see, I have cause to be thankful thou didst not write, inasmuch as the undeniable evidence of divine regard, which has since been, in adorable mercy, vouchsafed, and which, both in degree and extent, has far exceeded anything I ever before experienced, has been enhanced in value and clearness by it; blessed forever be that worthy name and power of the Lord, who, as sufferings and tribulations for the seed's sake abounded, in his own due and appointed time, did cause the consolations of the Gospel much more to abound; to his praise alone be it spoken, and let all flesh be silenced and laid in the dust forever!

For several days previous to our monthly meeting, I had been trying what in me lay, to devise some business, or frame some excuse to leave the Island, so as to avoid being at the meeting; but my health had become so much impaired, that that alone would have rendered it improper, if I had eventually dared to do so; which as it drew near, I durst not hazard, though my fears and distress were as great as ever, and I was so reduced in health and strength, that it was with much difficulty and in great weakness that I went to the meeting, and sat in it until near the close of that for worship; when the Lord's light, and invincible power, did spring over all the powers of darkness, and his Word sounded in the ear of my soul, saying, "The treacherous dealer hath dealt very treacherously, and the spoiler hath grievously spoiled: but flee thou unto the strong hold, thou prisoner of hope!" And immediately I did feel myself marvellously strengthened, both inwardly and outwardly, and to such a degree, that had the adversaries and enemies been as strong as Samson, as great as Goliath of Gath, and as numerous as the "host of Midian," I should not have been afraid of them, seeing the language to me was, "Go in this thy might;" and it was enough! . . . .

The next day (which was sixth-day, the 29th of fifth

month) in the afternoon, while my hands were engaged in my usual avocation, my mind was sweetly and powerfully attracted and drawn inward, to the source and centre of all heavenly consolation and divine illumination; and as I yielded to that power which overshadowed me, the approaching yearly meeting was opened before me, and things which shall (if faithfulness is only abode in) most surely come to pass, were seen with the eye of faith (which was opened by the pure power) as clearly as ever the sun was seen with the outward eye at noonday. Yea, I saw the tents of Cushan in affliction, and the curtains of the land of Midian did tremble! . . . After being thus wrapt up in the heavenly vision,—and to such a degree that I was in some doubt for a time, whether I was in the body or out of the body, it was so clear and so bright; though the doubts I had in the above respect sprung more from the marvellous nature of the things I saw, than from any consciousness of mental aberration, for I was perfectly sensible what I was about, and fully aware of everything around me, and my mill, going with much speed, required attention, and had it as fully as at any other time (which, I believe, was permitted to be so, or rather vouchsafed under such circumstances, in order that I might be sure I was not beside myself);—I say, after a time, the vision seemed to close up, and I fell into a train of reasoning. . . . But, then, I can say in truth, and with a good understanding and experience of what I do say, an horror of great darkness fell upon me, even darkness as great as the light had been brilliant; and I felt such a stop in my mind, and so forcibly forbidden to reason upon it,—I mean upon what I had seen and what they would do,—that I could do no other than forbear, which I did, and then the whole thing opened again upon me, and even with greater clearness than before; which continued for some time, gradually closing up, until the most remarkable features had disappeared, and only a sense and recollection of it remained, attended however with a sweet savor and abiding assurance of the reality of those things which I had seen and heard: indeed it left a dew upon my spirit which has not yet wholly dried up; and I was not left without instruction what to keep to myself and what to open to others, as well as when and how to open it: although I did see some things which were not to be uttered at all, at least at present.

Thou mayst well suppose it must have occupied much of my attention since; and indeed it has, though I can assure thee, it has been of too solemn and important a kind to fly out in words. From these I have indeed been much restrained, except when renewedly opened. Oh! the preciousness of the experience of being kept by the Shepherd of Israel in the low valleys where the dew lies long, and of lying down by the side of the still waters, where nothing can hurt or make afraid! I have been too much a stranger to this. I feel it so. I also now feel and taste the sweetness of it.

Last first-day morning, the 31st, as I was preparing to go to meeting, my mind was again very powerfully overshadowed with heavenly good, and also forcibly turned to the subject of the last page of the enclosed sheet, and those things which are now acting upon the stage of our Society; and as I viewed it in the light of truth,—for such I knew what I saw and felt, to be—yea, I knew it to be the light of truth, by its own demonstration and clearness,—the Lord was pleased to give me a sign and pledge, that those things which I had seen should surely come to pass; and it was fully equal to Gideon's fleece, and has been since as signally fulfilled and redeemed. This is all I can say about it at present, or rather, all I think it right to say, though a deal might be said, and a volume written. . . . It [the meeting] was truly a remarkable time, wherein the glorious Lord was pleased to be a place of broad rivers and streams, and to exalt his own name and power over and above all the powers of darkness, for His seed's sake! And my faith is firm that He will yet more and more arise, and plead His own cause, and that, too, through such mean and weak instruments, that the praise and the honor and the glory shall be wholly ascribed unto Him who is alone worthy, worthy, worthy of the praise of his own works, forever and ever!

I made out, with great difficulty, to get down to meeting

in the afternoon, but was unable to sit the meeting through; neither indeed did I expect to when I went, but thought it best to go (in which I had peace), and have been confined to the house ever since, except that on second-day morning I went to the mill; being willing if possible to work, or at least to manifest a disposition, for the cause' sake, and lest it should suffer by my not being there; as the eyes of the people, within and without, were increasingly upon me. Had it been an ordinary occasion, I should not have gone, and as it was, I could not stay. Indeed I have been very much reduced in my bodily health, by the uncommon exercises which I have had to pass through; but my mind has been preserved in a perfect calm; and peace and quietness have reigned there, to a degree never before experienced. This has been spread as a canopy over me, and I can say that I have "sat under His shadow with great delight, and His fruit has been sweet to my taste," and His countenance comely to look upon, yea, the chiefest among ten thousand, and altogether lovely.

Now, my dear friend, I do not pretend to say how it has been or is with thee at present, but I can say that it is in the cross to my natural inclination that I have spread these things before thee. I would gladly have been excused from it, but could not, for some reason or other, feel easy to refrain from giving thee these hints of what has happened here, being fully persuaded thou art no "stranger in Jerusalem," neither at all ignorant of the exercises through which all her children, even the least, are led, seeing she is the mother of all the living. But I believe there is reason to lift up the head in hope, that her borders will be lengthened, and her stakes strengthened; and however dark and gloomy the night may have been, and is, I am persuaded that it is far spent, and the hidden things of darkness will be brought to light, and the nakedness of those who have lifted up their heels against the Lord and His anointed, His chosen, will be discovered, and their heels made bare. For He will arise, and scatter and confound His enemies. But there must be no flinching or manœuvring on our part; that will be going over to their ground, which is enchanted ground. They have been seeking enchantments, and unto those who have familiar spirits, and are astrologers and soothsayers. But the Lord will make their diviners mad! Yea, He will frustrate the designs and the tokens of liars, and turn the counsel of Ahithophel into foolishness. . . . . . .

T. B. Gould.

Extract from a Letter from T. B. G. to ——.

. . . . . . I am decidedly of the opinion that an indiscriminate disclosure of the exercises and trials that are permitted to come upon us, ought to be avoided by all means; as I can testify, from woful experience, to the poverty and leanness that it brings upon the poor mind that has fallen into the error. Nevertheless, as a liberty and freedom is felt, under the guidance of truth, to open to those that are prepared, by a similar course of experience, to feel and to enter into suffering with them that are bound, as bound with them, and them that suffer affliction, as being also of the body, here, I believe, is the patience and the fellowship of the saints; here the advantages of religious society are realized; here the ability to bear one another's burdens is emphatically felt; and it is often very beneficial to the parties; it is frequently a means of building up the feeble members of the body (the church); and by introducing those that are stronger into this suffering, into this exercise, and this patience, is a means of keeping them low and humble, under the weight of their sufferings; and so the great work is promoted, to the praise of the great Head. But there are those that have indulged in it for want of willingness and patience to bear the allotted portion of labor; who have I believe been wisely prohibited [in consequence thereof] from partaking of the benefits of this fellowship. . . . . .

To George F. Read.

Newport, 7th month, 17th, 1840.

My dear Friend:

. . . . . . The times surely call for great watchfulness and care, for they are evil! I greatly desire for myself and for Friends everywhere, that we may be preserved on the unchangeable Foundation; that so, although storms and tempests, both from within and without, may beat vehemently upon us, the building may stand; yea, that we may be kept by the eternal power of God through faith unto salvation, and livingly know, and richly experience, through the abundant mercy and grace of our Lord Jesus Christ, the Lord of glory, *even while here below*, that although our earthly house should be dissolved, we have a building of God, an house not made with hands, eternal in the heavens, and which fadeth not away! And thus having an anchor to the soul, both sure and steadfast, we shall be able to "endure hardness as good soldiers," to fight the good fight of faith, under our unconquered Captain; and not be driven about by every wind of doctrine, nor yet taken by the snares and "cunning craftiness of men who lie in wait to deceive," and who, "if it were possible, would deceive the very elect," as said the apostle.

With much love, I am, as ever, thy sincere and affectionate friend,

THOMAS B. GOULD.

FROM T. B. G. TO C. W——.

NEWPORT, 2d of 9th mo., 1840.

. . . . Truly some of us on this part of the Lord's footstool, have had sufficient employment to "possess their souls in patience," and also great cause to cry mightily unto Him who hath His way in the sea, and his path in deep waters, even the waters of affliction, and whose footsteps are not known, that He, in His mercy and for His truth's sake, would be graciously pleased to strengthen and enable us steadfastly to refuse to sell, or to exchange for another, that vineyard which is our birthright, "the inheritance of our fathers." Many there are, who give sorrowful evidence of being governed by the same spirit that ruled in Ahab, of whom it was declared, that he not only walked in the sins of Jeroboam (who caused Israel to sin), but that he "did more to provoke the Lord God of Israel to anger, than all the kings of Israel that were before him."

And this is not all, for they practise literally upon the counsel of wicked Jezebel (1 Kings, 21 : 7, 8, 9, 10), and openly suffer and encourage her to teach and seduce the people (Rev. 2 : 20), calling her a true prophetess, &c., as was the case in Thyatira; and like some in the church of Pergamos, they "hold the doctrine of Balaam, who taught Balak to cast stumbling-blocks before the children of Israel, and to eat sacrifices unto idols." But there are a few names preserved, even in this, our modern Sardis, who have not defiled their garments; although they are clothed as in sackcloth, and can but lament day and night for the slain of the daughter of the Lord's people, and so, if in no other way, bear witness against the abomination which is making desolate this portion of his vineyard, and standing where it ought not to stand.

Did not the Lord's prophet say, "The vineyard of the Lord of hosts is the house of Israel, and the men of Judah are His pleasant plant; He looked for judgment, but behold oppression, for righteousness, but behold a cry"—a vain and empty cry, of, The temple of the Lord, the temple of the Lord, the temple of the Lord are these! while the Lord is not among them? Our ears are constantly annoyed with this, in substance at least; and as for true judgment, it "is turned away backward, truth has fallen in the streets, and equity cannot enter!" It is those who have been considered, and now consider themselves, leaders of the people, that cause them to err, and destroy the way of the paths, removing the ancient landmarks of the good old way in which the fathers walked; introducing new things, which neither we nor our fathers have known, and so setting up a separate altar—a will-worship, which is as truly idolatry as that calf-worship was, which Jeroboam set up, lest, if the people went to Jerusalem to worship, their hearts should turn away from him to the king of Judah. And when any are raised up to prophesy against it, then the priests which they have made say, there is disaffection to the government, conspiracy against the rulers, elders, &c., and the land is not able to bear all their words: yea, even as Amaziah, the priest of Bethel, said to Amos, "O, thou seer, go, flee thee away into the land of Judah, and prophesy there; but prophesy no more again at Bethel, for it is the king's chapel, and it is the king's court!" But they seem insensible that every hand which has been put forth to set up, or raised to defend, a separate altar, is and must be withered; and that may account at once for their being unable to draw it in again, and for our refusing to regard it as *living*, which is the only binding authority, under the pure and spiritual dispensation of the Gospel. . . . . . .

Oh, Charles, I hardly know how to part with you, even on paper (for it seems as if I must include you all); the very satisfactory and instructive hours spent with you seem, while I am writing, almost realized again. If it be weakness, I frankly acknowledge it; I would not attempt to conceal the emotion which I deeply feel: and if we never meet again in time, I do most fervently desire that neither heights nor depths, principalities nor powers, things present nor things to come, nor any other creature, may ever be able to separate us from Him who, as we keep His commandments and abide in his love, will, I doubt not, in His own time, present us faultless before the presence of His glory with exceeding joy. Farewell.

THOMAS B. GOULD.

TO ETHAN FOSTER.

NEWPORT, 21st of 10th mo., 1840.

. . . . . . Well, my dear friend, may it be our chief concern to cleave to that which shows us the true state of things. Then may we have a well-grounded hope that preservation will be vouchsafed, amidst all the trials which may be permitted to attend us, in our passing along through time: and although Israel may be carried away captive, even into the enemy's land, yet the Lord will have a remnant there. Oh! I am often comforted in reading, and also in the renewed remembrance of the trials and sufferings which the Lord's prophets endured, who testified faithfully against the abominations committed among the children of Israel according to the flesh; inasmuch as it goes far to show that no new thing has happened to those who now suffer. "So persecuted they the prophets which were before you," said our divine Master to His disciples, when he forewarned them of the world's hatred.

The enmity which was placed between the two seeds, immediately after the fall of our first parents, has been the same in all ages, though it has been manifested variously, according to time and circumstances. And, as thou very justly remarkst, they are not less the enemies of Truth who now pretend its authority,—indeed to be the only possessors and expositors of it,—than those who in former times and ages, set up the same pretensions, walked in the same path, and manifested the same bitter fruits, even under a false name, persecuting the true seed. There is however this difference, time has made the first manifest; and, as a shrewd and experienced, though persecuted man, said to one of these modern persecutors of the life, "If time does not [also] make these manifest, eternity will!" . . . May we all be kept by the Lord's power, through faith unto salvation! My faith is firm that we shall be, if we are faithful. . . . .

Thy sure friend,

THOMAS B. GOULD.

TO PELEG MITCHELL.

NEWPORT, 12th mo., 14th, 1840.

MY DEAR FRIEND:

. . . . Dear E. P. had an appointed meeting in the evening here, which was a season of favor, and seemed like a brook by the way, in the midst of this dry and barren land; though I feel inclined to acknowledge, and I do it with feelings of gratitude to Him who still "openeth rivers in high places and fountains in the midst of the valleys," that we have of latter time been renewedly favored in this meeting, when no strangers were present, with a little help out of Zion. For He, by His ancient and new power, hath been graciously pleased in a remarkable manner to fulfil His word: "He hath dried up the green tree, and caused the dry tree to flourish;" and I am more and more convinced that He will yet redeem us out of all our troubles, and deliver us from under the hands of those who oppress us; and that "saviours shall stand upon Mount Zion, to judge the mount of Esau, and the kingdom shall be the Lord's." . . . But as we are favored to keep in the "quiet habitation," we shall, I am fully persuaded, in the Lord's due and appointed time, witness the fulfilment of His ancient promise: "As birds flying, so will the Lord of hosts defend Jerusalem; defending also He will deliver it, and passing over, He will preserve it." . .

Thy sincere friend,

T. B. GOULD.

To JOHN WILBUR.

NEWPORT, 24th of 2d mo., 1841.

MY DEAR FRIEND:

. . . Her [Sophronia Page's] testimony had been clear, sound, searching, powerful, and prevalent indeed, and truly remarkable in reaching the states of some, of whom she could not have been informed by man. The meeting was large, by the procuration of some who had taken her under their care; but things were laid open in such a manner, that there is much reason to believe they sincerely repented having contributed so largely to their own exposure; for her concern lay with the lost sheep of the house of Israel; and circumstances of later time rendered it easy for those who, while they are not members, usually attend meetings, and can distinguish between the living and the dead, to understand and apply what she said with great power and authority, about the famine in this place, "not," said she, "of bread nor of water, but of hearing the word of the Lord!" The meeting ended well, in solemn supplication, which terminated in praise and thanksgiving from prepared hearts and renewedly baptized spirits. But how shall I set forth the favors vouchsafed in the afternoon meeting, early in which she stood up with nearly these words: "It is a very serious consideration, and one which is worthy of more than a passing thought, that all our actions, and even our most secret designs and intentions, are naked and open in the eyes of Him with whom we have to do!" She then proceeded to search out and lay open the hidden things of dishonesty, and of Esau, in such a manner as I have never before heard; describing the double-minded man as being unstable in all his ways, and boldly declaring that the sinners in Zion were afraid, and that fearfulness would more and more surprise the hypocrite. To all such she spake with a voice of thunder, of which they seemed to be sensible. But she was in an eminent degree a daughter of consolation to an afflicted and a poor people, whose peculiar trials and afflictions she was enabled to portray with a degree of skilfulness and accuracy, which plainly showed that it came from Him who, as G. Fox used to say, is indeed the Original. What she said about the preparations which had been made to wage a war of extermination upon this poor and despised remnant, was exceedingly cutting to the usurpers. Nor was it less remarkable, that she should have declared how seriously the former had been led to consider, how they, being so few, &c., should be able to contend with so much of power and authority as was arrayed against them, to all outward and human appearance; but added, "The Lord shall fight for you, and ye shall hold your peace,—stand still, and see the salvation of God," &c. Two kinds of ministry were largely spoken of as existing among us, and clearly and fully distinguished. I have given thee but a very short and imperfect sketch of a long testimony, which it required more than an hour to deliver;—to attempt to speak of the life and power attending it, would be unavailing, or of the awfulness of the pause which intervened;—when one who was sensible of it had something like a seal to set to what had been delivered; soon after which the dear Friend appeared in solemn supplication, very short and full, near access being mercifully granted. Then, a longer period of silence than usual;—and, although it had been a remarkable time from the very commencement of the meeting, yet in the conclusion it might have been said, "The Lord's power was over all!" . .

. . . I believe it was right that all our friends were silent lookers on to-day. But do tell thy wife, that I am not aware of having lost any part of my interest in the success of the good cause. I can feelingly acknowledge that I have nothing to boast of; to me belongeth only blushing and confusion of face; and if that cause could be promoted through so poor a creature as an instrument, I do most sincerely desire that all the honor and all the praise may be ascribed unto Him, who still is pleased at times to call things that are not, as though they were.

Thy sincere friend,

T. B. GOULD.

TO PELEG MITCHELL.

NEWPORT, 26th of 2d month, 1841.

MY DEAR FRIEND:

. . . . He whose place of defence is the munition of rocks, must shake his hands from the holding of bribes. But did I say anything in that letter, which led thee to suppose that I considered "a dead letter ministry" "among the *lesser* features of Gurneyism?" I remember having used the latter expression somewhere in that letter; but if it was susceptible of such a construction, I am confident it must have been owing to the looseness of my style, to the haste in which I wrote, or to incorrect punctuation; as I am sure I never entertained such an opinion, having been virtually prepared, long before the time of my writing to thee, very fully to adopt the expression of Richard Jordan, that "the distempers in the ministry (even in his day) were the *greatest* in the Church!" How much more emphatically true and applicable is it then to these degenerate times, which, it seems to me, would suffer almost or quite as much, by a comparison with those in which R. Jordan lived and labored, as would the chaff when compared with the "principal wheat." . . . . . .

I can feelingly respond to what thou sayest about being more favored when met in select companies, than is generally the case at other times. And it is not strange that it should be so: there is so much of an opposing spirit to be felt in some, yea, many, even when they do not show their true colors openly; surely the darkness and bitterness of their spirits is so great, that I have often thought of the "two witnesses," and of their bodies lying dead, as it were in the streets of "the great city which spiritually is called Sodom and Egypt, where also our Lord was," and is, "crucified." Is there any question that one of these witnesses may be a living Gospel ministry? But still, "the spirit of life from God" does enter into those who are intrusted with that gift, at times and seasons (which are all in His hand), and they are raised up to bear testimony against those who had, to all human appearance, "overcome them and killed them," . . . they are raised up, and enabled to "stand upon their feet." Then it is, that "great fear falls upon them" who had "made merry" over them, and sent gifts one unto another, during all the while they had lain as it were dead; although their bodies were not suffered to be put into graves. . . . . .

28th, first-day eve.

As I do not recollect any other interrogatory in either of thy letters, and suppose that J. W. has before this given you on Nantucket a particular account how he fared at Providence, I will not undertake to make any extracts from his last very interesting letter to me; but instead of it, I will make one from one since received from his son-in-law, my dear friend, Ethan Foster, of Westerly, because it will give you a view which I cannot doubt will be interesting, if not encouraging, and which you would not be likely to obtain from John himself. It is as follows, viz.: "We [Ethan and wife] have had a very interesting visit at father Wilbur's; found him cheerful, and I believe happy, compared with many of those once his friends, but now his accusers and opposers. Our meeting yesterday [they belong to Hopkinton meeting, though they live in Westerly], was an interesting as well as a comforting season. Our dear father was extensively engaged in testimony to the life and power of the Gospel, and to experimental religion, in which he was somewhat doctrinal; illustrating with great clearness the Christian covenant as being two-fold, and that neither part can be dispensed with, without losing the benefit of the whole. He dwelt at length on this point, with a degree of clearness and force which bore the impress of something far above human reason and argument. The meeting seemed much to enter into his feelings, and somewhat to travail with him in exercise. Truth rose into dominion, and an evidence was mercifully afforded, that we are not utterly forsaken, and however dark and gloomy the prospect may appear, that brighter days are yet to be experienced by those who possess their souls in patience, and keep their ranks in righteousness. At the conclusion he appeared in supplication, in which he was evidently favored with near access to the throne of grace. I mention this, not that it is unusual for him to appear in testimony with the evidence of divine assistance; but this was one of those seasons of peculiar favor, when the waters increased, from a small stream, until they became a river to swim in, though of that description wherein there goes no galley with oars, neither does gallant ship pass thereby."

. . . . . We had an acceptable and edifying visit from our dear friends, Enoch and Sophronia Page, of Salem, a week ago last first-day. They attended both meetings, in which Sophronia was largely and eminently engaged, both in testimony and supplication, especially in the afternoon meeting. I thought at the conclusion of the meeting, it might have been truly said, the Lord's power was over all! . . . . .

Believe me to be as ever thy warmly-attached friend,

T. B. Gould.

To Peleg Mitchell.

Newport, 15th of 4th month, 1841.

My dear Friend:

. . . . . Did I tell thee in my last, what an acceptable and truly remarkable visit we had from our dear friend, Sophronia Page, just before I left? I think her service in this meeting exceeded anything of the kind I ever witnessed. Why, Peleg, although she is not very old, she is worthy to be called a mother in Israel. Like Jael, "she put her hand to the nail, and her right hand to the workman's hammer; and with the hammer she smote Sisera." Truly it might have been said, "*So* let all thine enemies perish, oh Lord! but let them that love Him be as the sun when he goeth forth in his might."

I was grieved to hear that dear Mary Davis was not encouraged to proceed in her prospect of attending Philadelphia yearly meeting. She would have been, I have no doubt, a very acceptable visitor there. It does seem to me, that if no one but poor A. S. objected to it, there must have been strength enough in that select meeting to have overruled his objection, had the strength which some there possess, been used. What are Friends afraid of? It seems to me, we have, in far too many instances, just given them the ground. Why, it is shameful to do so! Only think of the last yearly meeting; it was just so there: there were Friends enough present, who felt no unity with his [J. J. G.'s] having that certificate, to have thrown the ranks of the aliens into confusion, if they had only come forth, and manifested on whose side they were. And of what avail is it to be in the right, and to have light, if it be always hidden, always kept under a bushel? Oh! it seems to me, some have need that the pure mind in them should be stirred up; they need to be reminded that whosoever is ashamed of their Lord, or of His cause, which is the same thing, of them will He be ashamed before His Father and the holy angels. I desire that Friends may be encouraged to use what strength they have, in the Lord's time for service, lest, by neglecting to use it, it be taken from them, and be given to those who are faithful. Let them come forward in the true order of the Gospel; let them *keep their ranks*, and say, "Thine are we, David, and on thy side, thou son of Jesse." . . . .

Thy sincere friend,

T. B. G.

From John Wilbur to T. B. G.

Haran Cottage, 15th of fifth month, 1841.

My dear Thomas:

The many unavoidable engagements which have fallen to my share of attention since quarterly meeting, have thus far deterred me, until the present moment, from the pleasing task of responding to thy very interesting letter, in which thou speakest of thy visit to Philadelphia, &c. And truly pleasant and satisfactory was thy account of things which transpired at those places; and the sweet remembrance, and good and living desires of my ever dear friends in those parts, did afford to my afflicted and often drooping spirit the balm of consolation; so that for a time I was almost prepared to thank God and take courage. . . . And I trust thou knowest, Thomas, by living experience, that when we are borne down with sorrow and affliction, with fear and trembling for the safety of Zion, and for the escape of our own souls, that many fears and apprehensions are then ready to arise in our almost desponding minds. . . . . . .

Our dear friend, Prince Gardner, came home with us from Greenwich, and a very good visit we had from him. He tarried three nights. He and Andrew both agree in saying, that one reason, if not the principal one, why the meeting for sufferings refused to enter into an examination of the doctrines of J. J. G., was, as they said, because the morning meeting, or meeting for sufferings in London, had taken all his writings into consideration, in order for correction: but whilst P. G. was here, a letter from A. R. Barclay arrived, which put the question beyond all doubt, that no such thing had taken place in London. Rawlinson says, that Joseph John attended their late quarterly meeting in London, and his preaching was so sad, that the elders, although his admirers, had enough to do to sit with proper decorum. R. seems very desirous that some accredited body in this country should forward to one or the other of their authorized bodies, the objections of sound Friends to the doctrines alluded to. I learn that the applications from myself, and from Nantucket, and from South Kingston monthly meeting, were civilly received and noted on the book, as relating to doctrines; but they pretended, in addition to the foregoing reason, that they were not authorized by discipline to examine books already printed or written by a member of another yearly meeting. And so it seems they have got us fast, that nobody has a right to refuse unsound publications, without the leave of the meeting for sufferings, and they no right to decide whether good or bad, after the impression of types, and the books offered for sale! If these things are so, how forlorn the condition of this people, in a day like this, when heterodoxy of principle is promulgated by the wise and the learned among them! . . . .

JOHN WILBUR.

FROM T. B. G. TO ETHAN FOSTER.

STEAMBOAT MASSACHUSETTS, 22d of seventh mo., 1841.

MY DEAR FRIEND:

. . . . I wrote to thy dear afflicted father soon after I received thine, at thy request; though I feared it only served to aggravate his sufferings; but was rejoiced to get a very kind letter from him last evening. . . . I feel much for him in his manifold afflictions, even as much, I believe, as I am capable of feeling; but I am always most miserable at the expression of condolence. However, it has seemed to me from the first, that there was and is much application to him in the language of Scripture: "Many are the afflictions of the righteous, but the Lord will deliver him out of them all:"—and not to him only, but my mind has often, yea, very often, been drawn into very near sympathy with thy beloved mother; all within me capable of feeling has been made to feel for her, not doubting that she is often ready to exclaim, "Surely there is no sorrow like mine!" Although no afflictions for the present may seem joyous, but grievous, nevertheless they do yield the peaceable fruits of righteousness to those who are rightly exercised thereby; and that she is one of this class, I have no more doubt, than that an entrance will, in the Lord's due and appointed time, be abundantly administered into that everlasting kingdom of rest and peace, where the wicked cease from troubling, where He who was a man of sorrows and acquainted with grief is already entered; and not only so, but He is graciously pleased to enable those who are rightly exercised by the afflictions which arise because of the word, to say at times and seasons: "We are exceeding joyful in all our tribulations," and thus to give them a blessed foretaste and earnest of the reward of the righteous. . . . .

Believe me to be, with love to all,

Thy sincere friend,
THOMAS B. GOULD.

On the 31st day of the eighth month, 1841, Thomas B. Gould was united in marriage, at the Northern District Meeting in the city of Philadelphia, to Martha Smith Ecroyd, a daughter of James and Martha Ecroyd, and formerly of Muncy, in Lycoming County, Pennsylvania, but then residing with her widowed mother in Philadelphia.

FROM SARAH HILLMAN TO THOMAS B. AND M. S. GOULD.

PHILADELPHIA, 1st mo. 11th, 1842.

DEAR FRIENDS, T. AND M. GOULD:

If leisure and inclination for writing had combined with affectionate remembrance and desire for your prosperity and safe-stepping as on the "sea of glass," methinks ere this time many evidences had been received by you from my pen. But somehow I have little aptitude for writing; my talent never ran that way; at school almost any other study was more pleasant. Nevertheless I can say I have you on my heart; and often does my spirit greet you, in desire that the blessing of the Highest may be with you, that He would be pleased to give you those pure nether springs of Divine consolation, which flow from His holy presence: and then, whether the north or the south wind blow upon your garden, the spices will flow forth, as acceptable incense to the King of kings.

Many eyes are upon you, I am well aware. Ye had need be clothed with the whole armor of light, that neither Satan nor any of his ministers gain any advantage over you. Surely he will not be suffered to overturn the foundation, nor to lay waste the hope in the Lord Jesus, of one, not even the very least of the flock, and family, and household of faith, so long as we keep hold of the shield. Ah, no! "Our Redeemer is mighty, the Lord of hosts is His name." He is beholding the tower which the children of men have been and are building; and I believe He has come down and confounded their language, so that the wise Babel-builders understand not each other's language: and He is turning to His people a "pure language, and they shall all call upon His name, to serve Him with one consent." Surely "there is no enchantment against Jacob, neither is there any divination against Israel;" but all these things have happened rather to the furtherance of the blessed Gospel of the dear Son of God, which at the first began to be spoken by Himself, and was confirmed unto us by them that heard Him, and is to this present day spoken by His own blessed Spirit in the hearts of His truly humble, true-born, simple-hearted, obedient little children.

It seems to me that the day is coming, when all the proud, and all that do wickedly, shall be stubble; some that are puffed up and seem to be somewhat, but in conversation add nothing to the true Israel, will be manifested, and the day shall declare them, and burn up all that will not stand the fire of purification; while the remnant that is escaped will be found among the jewels, and spared to magnify the mercy, the long-suffering mercy, of Israel's unslumbering Shepherd. Truly can some of us adopt the language, "Lord, I am not worthy thou shouldst enter under my roof:" yet He has marvellously made bare His arm and helped us hitherto; and have we not at seasons cause to raise new Ebenezers to His praise? Though many afflictions await the righteous, it is no new thing; the disciple need not expect to be above his Master: if he do, he will assuredly be disappointed. What was the path of the dear Son and Sent of the Father? He fasted in the wilderness, He was with the wild beasts, yet angels ministered unto Him. And as surely as He was ministered to by angels, so surely the angel of His presence encampeth round about them that fear Him, and delivereth them. Let us not then be found saying, "a confederacy," to all who would say, a confederacy; but sanctify Him in our hearts, who has revealed Himself secretly to us, whose love, whose mercy towards us, has been and is infinite. Has He not, dear Thomas, attracted thy soul towards Him in very infant years, and amid many temptations kept thee to this day? Yes. For what? To make thee a minister and a witness, not only of what thou hast seen, but also of those things in which He will appear to thee: and He will not now forsake thee!

Interrupted by a visit from Sarah Emlen and Edith Jefferis, who were at meeting this morning, and ministered to us.—Please tell thy sister Lydia, I often remember her kindness to us poor pilgrims, with that of thy dear father and mother; and desire their sloping days may be cheered by the bright shining of the Sun of righteousness, whose I trust they are and will be till death: and then, never fear,—there is a glorious rest, a crown laid up, a house not made with hands prepared, into which their purified spirits, through unutterable love and mercy, will be admitted, and where the arrows of the archer can never come. Till then, may we each fight the good fight of faith, that so we may obtain! Many talk much of faith, whose walk is not in the steps of faithful Abraham, who yet style themselves children. What will they do, in that day when every covering, save that of "my Spirit, saith the Lord," shall be stripped off? . . . I must now conclude. With truest affection, your sincere, sympathizing friend, in which my dear mother and sisters, with dear E. P., unite.

Farewell, says your friend,

SARAH HILLMAN.

FROM T. B. G. TO JOSEPH KITE.

NEWPORT, 25th of 3d mo., 1842.

. . . We have recently been much comforted and refreshed by a visit from dear John Wilbur, who spent a week with us and in the neighborhood, and went home this day week. He seemed better in health than we expected to see him, and green and lively in spirit, weighty and powerful in doctrine, and clearly evincing that patience under suffering, and resignation to whatever degree of it may be yet in store for him, which men may talk about and attempt to imitate, but can never realize or exemplify, unless really endowed with His spirit, who "was led as a lamb to the slaughter," and when "He was reviled, reviled not again." John attended our meeting three times. In the first, on fifth-day, the 10th inst., he was silent; but on first-day morning he was raised up early in the meeting, with the language of the patriarch Jacob, while prophetically engaged in blessing the heads of the tribes of Israel: "I have waited for thy salvation, O Lord!"—proceeding to show very clearly the necessity of so waiting in all similar engagements. And in the opening of large fields of doctrine before him, he seemed more especially led to speak of worship and ministry, and to distinguish between the true and false in both instances; having much encouragement to offer to those who are baptized for the dead, ministering to the spirits that are in prison, speaking prophetically of their enlargement and deliverance, and that, as there was an engagement to tarry at Jerusalem until endued with power from on high, and to "wait for the promise of the father, which ye have heard of me," the number of these rightly exercised and divinely qualified ministers would be increased, and they should yet bear witness of Him to whom all power in heaven and on earth is given, "in Jerusalem, in Judea, at Samaria, and unto the uttermost parts of the earth." And immediately quoting the animating promise, "Lo! I am with you always, even unto the end of the world," he proceeded to show the absurdity of the idea, that there is any "falling off" from the perfection and adaptation of the Gospel to our every need, in these latter days; but that the spiritual presence, guidance, and power of Christ, divine immediate revelation, &c., is still felt and enjoyed by His humble and obedient followers, and graciously offered unto all; and that it was not because it had ceased or diminished in power and efficacy, but because men were not obedient thereto, and had not faith therein, that there were misgivings and unsoundness upon these points. This fell heavy upon some who sat near him, whose actions show how lightly they esteem these fundamental principles of unchangeable truth, and who not unfrequently now dispense sage cautions against deeply spiritual views, though generally coupled with far-fetched encomiums upon the character and writings of the early Friends, and high professions of a divine requiring to extend such cautions. It requires no great degree of discernment, to see the extremely ill grace with which such encomiums fall from the lips of these people, while they are actually, and with a furious though blind zeal, engaged in removing the landmarks, and lowering the standard, which our worthy predecessors were made instrumental in setting up and exalting among the nations: though I confess it requires more discernment than I am possessed of, to discover the foundation of their claim to divine requirement or commission for so doing. But I have digressed, as I am very apt to do.

These people treated John with more civility, and even apparent kindness, than is usual or might have been expected, and the meeting separated under a very solemn covering, Truth having the ascendency for that time at least. Indeed it had been a remarkably solid time from the commencement. One young woman, who happened to be there, habited in a full suit of mourning, by profession an Episcopalian, though remotely descended from Friends, was remarkably tendered in the course of his exercises, and seemed very reluctant to part with him after meeting. So also was her husband, who has regularly attended all our meetings since, though not accustomed to do so. . . .

Oh, how much the tenderly visited, seeking people are to be felt for! I often think, more especially so, when, instead of being instrumentally fed with bread through qualified breakers of it, stones, serpents, and scorpions are poured out upon them. But there is much consolation in the conviction, that He who clave the rock for His chosen people formerly, while journeying outwardly in a desert land, and sent them bread from heaven, can now, and does give to those who hunger and thirst after righteousness, of the bread and water of life, freely and immediately. . .

Seventh month, 1842.

There is with most, such a secret preference of the *form* to the *power*, and such an unwillingness to be identified with a small remnant, with "a despised and afflicted people," that we are likely, in the end, to be relieved of all who are not willing to be truly religious. It is lamentable that there should be so many who, in forming their conclusions respecting the truth of the case now in controversy, are looking wholly at circumstances, and the decision of numbers, rather than to the witness for truth in themselves. . . . .

How many simple, honest-hearted Friends are favored with a sense of wrong things existing among us, but instead of keeping to that which shows them their condition and the state of the church, they begin to look to those whom they consider more experienced than themselves; thus taking men for their guide, and opening their ears to hear them, they lose sight of the true Teacher, fall behind the true Light, become involved in darkness and uncertainty, and finally get into the current, and are swept away by it.

From T. B. G. to Peleg Mitchell.

Newport, 7th month, 1842.

My dear Friend,—

. . . . Thou requested my opinion as to thy addressing a letter to —— ——. Now, my dear friend, I feel rather a delicacy in expressing one, but from my acquaintance with the man, and from the sense and judgment I have of his present state—just coming off, as we *hope*, from a misguided course, and emerging from under a cloud, with perhaps rather a galling sense of the steps taken therein, and the blocks over which he has stumbled, which *may not be entirely removed*—it has seemed to me that it would be rather safer to defer it, at least for the present, as it might have an effect on him to the clear contrary from what was intended. I found my dear M. entertained the same opinion respecting it—and I suppose we have had rather more opportunity to judge of his feelings and character than thyself. If he was able to bear it—it might do. But I cannot—I must not go into particulars, and I trust thou wilt excuse what I have written, and also the freedom used in expressing my view of it.

26th of 8th month. When this was commenced, I fully intended sending it off the next day; but was compelled to lay it aside, without the opportunity of resuming it till this morning. Our dear brother and sister Snowden with their children, have been spending several weeks with us; they left us the day before yesterday, for home. Their visit has been a great consolation to us. Brother Joseph and myself attended South Kingston monthly meeting last second day, from which thou wilt probably hear the particulars ere this reaches thee. It was a sore thing to the committees, that divers members from other monthly meetings were present, and witnessed their disorderly proceedings; though none of them took part in the business of the meeting, save our friend J. T. K. and his brother; upon which D. B. rebuked them, and cautioned them and other friends there present in similar circumstances, from interfering; which was altogether unnecessary, so far as some of us were concerned—indeed there was *no* necessity for it, the South Kingston Friends being fully competent to manage the case themselves. Brother Joseph thought it could not have been more skilfully conducted anywhere or by anybody than it was by them, and they are mostly young men too; but they were evidently equipped for war, and ordered for battle, by Him who never yet was foiled therein, nor his armies put to flight; though every expedient was resorted to, which the ingenuity and malice of the Evil One could invent, to break their ranks and throw them into confusion: and after the report of the committee [clearing John Wilbur from all censure] had been received and recorded in the men's meeting, R. G. and T. A. made three attempts by shaking hands, to close the meeting, while the report of the committee was under consideration by the women—well knowing that if they could prevent the record of *their unity* with it, J. W. would not be restored. But these attempts were severally defeated, through the vigilance and promptness of some.

As soon as the meeting was opened, J. D., in the name and on the behalf of the quarterly meeting's committee, made a long and incoherent speech—part threatening, part coaxing, part unintelligible, and therefore not to be interpreted by the common rules of language, but by the character of the man and the nature of his office. He was replied to by dear old T. H., who is in the eighty-seventh year of his age, and rode near twenty miles to attend that meeting. He briefly went over the ground of the controversy with that monthly meeting, the proceedings of the yearly meeting's committee, the appointment of the committee of that monthly meeting to hear and decide the case, the appointment of the quarterly meeting's committee, &c.,—and then called for the reading of the report of the committee of their monthly meeting, as the best method of coming to an understanding of the state of the case; which being united with by other South Kingston Friends, the report was read, and united with by *many Friends.* But while they were expressing unity with it, H. B. presented a "minority" report, signed by himself and W. S. P.; upon which two or three of the members of South Kingston monthly meeting, and divers of the two grand committees, commenced a desperate attempt to have the "minority report" read and considered, in order to throw them into confusion. It was argued on the part of J. Wilbur's friends, that this report was informal and improper to be read, inasmuch as those two disaffected and disorderly committee-men had been duly notified of the time and place of meeting, when the report signed by seven of the committee had been agreed to. On the other side it was alleged, that six out of the seven, who had signed the report recommending the dismission of the case, were relatives of J. Wilbur, and the understanding was that they would not be impartial judges. There was a great deal said on both sides. They stated again and again, that the monthly meeting's committee had departed from the ground of the complaint, by allowing J. W. to go into an investigation of doctrines: and T. A. was very strenuous, repeatedly declaring that doctrines had nothing to do with the case,—that J. Wilbur had never been charged with any unsoundness of doctrine, and that even the term *doctrine* was not mentioned in the complaint! In the course of their clamorous interference, they had repeatedly urged the reading of the complaint, as well as the "minority report;" both which the meeting now consented should be read, with the express understanding and agreement, however, that a new investigation of the case should not be gone into, and that the report of the committee already before the meeting should receive its undivided attention. Notwithstanding this agreement, the complaint and "minority report" were no sooner read, than the yearly meeting's committee took the very course which had been anticipated and provided against; of which they were forcibly reminded by several Friends; when Wm. J. had the hardihood to declare that no such agreement had been made! And he became so warm on this and several other occasions, that some of his own colleagues, who sat above him in the gallery, thought it necessary to cool him off; which they did by pulling him down and shaking their heads at him! T. A. made an awkward and unsuccessful attempt to extricate himself from his assertion, that the term *doctrine* was not to be found in the complaint; and endeavored to explain it away, continuing to insist that they had departed from the original ground of complaint against J. W., which was the cause of the committees leaving before the termination of the trial, &c. He was replied to by C. P., the clerk of the committee, who said that at their last monthly meeting T. A. had called for the extracts from their minutes upon that subject—they were now present, and he would read them. He accordingly took the paper, and read it.

The reading of these extracts had a powerful effect upon them: though T. A. cavilled a little, and said that they had seen some part of that paper before, but much had been added by they knew not whom. William J. inquired of Charles Perry, whether that paper had not been written since the meeting of the committee when they were present, or something to this effect. To which C. P. replied, that it had not—that it was a true extract from their minutes, with the exception of the explanatory note, which he had clearly identified when he read it. This seemed to close them up. A proposition was made that Friends should again express themselves as to the reception of the report, which they did,—nearly or quite four-fifths of the meeting uniting with its reception and the dismission of the case, while but one man openly objected to it, and three or four others threw cold water upon it, though they did not in so many words object. Nevertheless, T. A., R. G., and D. B. declared that the solid sense and judgment of the meeting was opposed to its reception, and every member of the quarterly meeting's committee, in conjunction with their colleagues from the yearly meeting, did their utmost to have the case referred; but after great deliberation, and almost unparalleled patience, the clerk made an appropriate minute, receiving the report and dismissing the case;—it was then sent to the women, who soon sent it back, with the information that it had been very fully united with in their meeting. But the female members of the quarterly meeting's committee did what they could against it.

The meeting was no sooner closed, than the quarterly meeting's committee stopped Lydia Wilbur and Eunice Foster, and sent Othniel Foster after John Wilbur, who declined going. They then inquired of the two women, whether they had unity with their husbands;—being answered in the affirmative, they were all three advised, in the name of the quarterly meeting's committee, not to attend any more select meetings. As J. Wilbur declined going to the meeting-house at their bidding, and very properly, too, as I believe, they sent J. D. and B. C. immediately to his house, where, in the name of the quarterly meeting's committee at large (for the select committee, which has been so long standing, and so active in dealing with J. Wilbur, was released at the last quarter), they advised him not to attend any more select meetings; to which, considering it merely the effect of their spleen, he made no answer. When they asked his wife if she had unity with her husband, she promptly answered, "Yes, I am no Gurneyite!" . . .

Farewell.

T. B. Gould.

To John Wilbur.

Newport, 25th of 12th mo., 1842.

My dear Friend:

. . . . Indeed, there has nothing occurred which seemed worth writing about, or rather that if written, would have paid for the reading. But I received a letter recently from brother Joseph, in which he says: "Two of our friends lately had a very serious opportunity with —— ——, on his return from Baltimore, in relation to the proceedings in the case of J. W. He seemed in a good disposition, and said he entirely disapproved of the proceedings, and had used his influence in the committee to get them to drop it. The only thing he seemed to justify, was the laying down of the monthly meeting." . . . "He said he did not think the quarterly meeting had any right to annul the proceedings of the monthly meeting, which they had sanctioned by going into an investigation before the committee in J. W.'s case, and in other ways. In fact, he was brought to acknowledge that nearly all the proceedings were wrong! And I have no doubt myself that he would much rather not have anything to do with these things, but, like many others, has not independence enough to withstand the influence of the great men at Providence." . . . I have just written to Joseph, informing him pretty fully of the part which —— —— has actually performed in this business,—of the advices contained in that paper which he signed and presented to your monthly meeting, the report of the committee, &c.,—by which he may see how inconsistent his practice has been with his profession to them; and letting him know withal, that I cannot find sufficient charity, or good ground, for believing that he is in a very "good disposition," being persuaded that he only resorted to that shift, to escape their close questioning, and made use of smooth words and fair speeches in order to deceive them; also expressing a hope that they would be on their guard in future. There is no doubt in my mind, that —— —— was rather reluctantly drawn into this business at first, but I fear he has been for some time fully initiated into all their schemes. His conduct has shown his co-operation therein. . . . Well, my dear friend, let them try their best to effect their purpose. I believe it will all work for good in the end. For surely, if they keep on, and they have not got much farther to go, they will make the most extraordinary and notorious case of injustice, oppression, and persecution, that was ever known since we were a people! . . . .

Our mutual friend, Stephen Chase, of Portsmouth, was here yesterday; he says that Primacy Pearse, relict of Benjamin Pearse, has been very ill for some time, and that she sent for him, a few days ago, to come and see her. On going, he found her so ill that he would not have thought it suitable to say anything to her about the state of Society; but she soon introduced it herself, by telling him of some visits she had received, in which the visitors had employed their time in tirades against thee and some other friends; to some of whom she had replied, that J. Wilbur was a friend she had always highly esteemed, but she had no doubt thou wast tried in the furnace of affliction, and that it was heated seven times hotter than it was wont to be heated; but that her faith was, thou wouldst be delivered without even the smell of fire upon thy garments. She then told Stephen of her meeting with thee in the street after yearly meeting; that it had been so long since she had seen thee, that she would not have known thee, had it not been that T. B. G. introduced thee to her; and added: "When thou seest John Wilbur, give my dear love to him, and tell him that my prayers are for him, both day and night!" Stephen requested me to give thee this account, with his own love affectionately. I have used Stephen's words, I think.

Thus, thou seest, the prayers of the Church are for thee, which, that is, the Church, is, I believe, much represented by, if not composed of, the little and low—the humble and retiring ones—who also are often found in a persecuted, wilderness state. The query often arises, will they not be sought out and gathered?

We have lately had a visit from D. C. He spoke three times in our mid-week meeting. His first communication was remarkable for him, or indeed for any one, as it was not the work of D. C., or of any *man*, I am persuaded, for he got hold of things quite unintelligible to them, and most likely to himself; but his last two showed the weakness of poor mortals, being made very *sickening with love*, &c., to use Christopher Healy's quaint expression. After which the query was revived, "If ye love them that love you, what thank have ye? do not even the publicans the same?" And it was shown that it was a very natural and easy thing to love our friends (which had been the burden of his last communication), but that He who is Lord of all had erected a higher standard to which He gathered His children and people, requiring them to love their enemies, to do good to them that hate them, and to pray for them that despitefully use them and persecute them, and say all manner of evil against them falsely, for His sake; and it was declared, that nothing short of a measure of the Spirit, power, and life of Christ, could enable any man to do this; and also that except our righteousness did exceed the righteousness of the Scribes and Pharisees, we could in no wise enter the kingdom of heaven. After which, M. H. B. undertook to show what a "distracting and disorganizing effect religion [!] produced in the world, to go no farther back than the rise of our Society;" but was hard set to maintain his position, and seemed equally unable to cast anchor, and unwilling to go ashore; to which, however, he at length drifted. . . . .

I wish thou couldst find in thy heart to make us a visit. We get along very comfortably, and I believe it would be more satisfactory to thee than it was last winter,—things are very different in every respect. Those peculiar trials under which we then labored, I have no doubt, were wisely permitted, and that we are more likely, rightly to appreciate the blessings we now enjoy, which are so numerous and unmerited, that I often feel as if my cup did overflow! Surely goodness and mercy have followed me all the days of my life! . . . .

Farewell, from thy affectionate friend,

THOS. B. GOULD.

From John Wilbur to T. B. G.

Haran, 1st month, 6th, 1843.

My dear Thomas:

Thy kind letter was so interesting throughout, that it truly deserved a more ready and better answer than I have been, and shall at this time, be able to give. And first I will speak of the comfortable and peaceful state which thyself and family are enjoying, both in body and mind. Nor am I myself so much below par as to forbid my rejoicing with you; nay, for I will rejoice, that Infinite Goodness, through the abounding of His mercy, has enabled us so far, through this campaign of a cruel warfare from false brethren, to escape with our lives unhurt, amid the storm of arrows so prepared, as for a deadly purpose. Yea, and let the whole remnant of Israel rejoice, give God thanks, and take courage, without foreboding much of the probably greater suffering and greater dangers yet to come; for we clearly see that He is able to cover the heads of those who trust in Him, and to ordain that sufficient unto the *evil* day shall be the *good* thereof; to provide sufficiently for the escape of those whose minds are stayed upon Him, and who trust in Him. I am full in the belief, that no weapon which is formed against these shall prosper, so long as they are thus stayed, in the most pinching seasons of the trial of their faith, upon Him who was never foiled in battle, though all the powers from beneath were arrayed against Him; no, never; nor will He ever be! And the more I see of the concert and the plans which are contrived by that wisdom which is from beneath, the more clearly I have been enabled to see through this "battle of the warriors, and garments rolled in blood:" yes, garments rolled in blood; for many have been slain by them, whose blood will certainly be required at their hands! . . . . . .

Thine as ever,
John Wilbur.

FROM T. B. G. TO GEORGE F. READ.

NEWPORT, third month, 12th, 1843.

MY DEAR FRIEND:

. . . . I cannot longer withhold an acknowledgment of the peculiar satisfaction, comfort, and encouragement which thy last letter was a messenger of to me; and not to me only, but to a few other and strictly confidential friends, who, like thyself, are under bonds and afflictions for the testimonies which they hold, and are constrained to bear, in the midst of a crooked and perverse generation; who having a form of godliness, deny the power thereof, and in this state, as dear Isaac Penington said, "can do no other than persecute those who bear testimony to the one and against the other."

Well, my dear friend, as this is no new thing under the sun,—for so persecuted they the prophets which were before us—I can but respond, and that, too, with sincerity and earnestness, to thy petition, that we may be enabled to endure hardness as good soldiers, to contend zealously for the faith once delivered to the saints, and to fight valiantly the Lord's battles, in His strength and not our own, rallying to His standard, that His banner may cover us; for I am renewedly persuaded that "He hath given a banner to them who fear Him, which shall be unfurled because of the truth."

My desire is, that we may not only be encouraged by "the cloud of witnesses" who have trodden this tribulated path before us; but that we may be unceasingly engaged in looking unto Jesus, and waiting upon Him who is the Captain of our salvation and the Author of our faith; and who, though He is Lord of all, Himself endured the cross and despised the shame, and, loving the church, gave Himself for it, that He might purify and cleanse it, and make it a glorious church, not having spot, or wrinkle, or any such thing. Oh! He will have a clean, pure people, a peculiar people; and He knows what will make them such; therefore He hath set His fire as in

Zion, and His furnace as in Jerusalem, and caused judgment to begin as at the house of the Lord. See also Isaiah 10 : 16, 17, and Obadiah 17, 18, and 21. . . .

With much love, I am thy sincere friend,

T. B. GOULD.

TO ETHAN FOSTER.

NEWPORT, third month, 21st, 1843.

MY VERY DEAR FRIEND:

. . . . . I could not get rid of a very strong and rather peculiar desire to visit you, to see you face to face; so strong indeed that I could scarcely yield to circumstances which seemed to render it wholly improper. To visit the brethren and see how they do, is often as serviceable (if not more so), to the visitors as to the visited, especially when the former are inhabitants of a desert land. Such, journeying southward, sometimes meet with "springs of water." Truly, we have witnessed a long drought here, even in the winter, not unaccompanied with blasts peculiar to the season, which have beat vehemently against the wall: and as there had been something of a rest experienced previously, I have thought some of our Friends might entertain fears, and perhaps not without reason, lest we should take our "flight either in the winter or on the sabbath-day." If so, perhaps it may not be amiss to mention, that some of us have recently given great offence to the "chief priests and rulers of the synagogue," by our obedience to what we believed to be required of us by Him who is "Lord even of the sabbath." . . . . We did, however, hear incidentally, just before thou wrote, that W. E. had advised thy father [J. Wilbur] to appeal. The information surprised us. . . . . I can see no other reason for their giving this advice, than a supposition that it may prevent us from going "out from among them,"—our adversaries,—by haste or by flight, which I rather expect they fear we shall; and being themselves in a strait, as they are somewhat committed to us, they are willing to put the evil day afar off, especially as they have but a small portion of the suffering to bear in the interim. It is indeed a momentous concern, an awful crisis! For the divisions of Reuben there *should* be great searchings of heart, that we may know what, and what manner of time the Holy Spirit shall signify, for the accomplishment of our deliverance from under bondage as cruel, and darkness as truly to be felt, as that which prevailed in the land of Egypt. I freely confess my inability to see what steps it may be proper for us to take ultimately. I am equally unable to see any good or any strength we are gaining by our connection with them. Still I must say, and I own that the remark bears with full force upon myself, that it is very important we should not take the cause into our own hands, or do anything rashly for the sake of ease and deliverance; lest we lose our own standing in the Lord's sight, be rejected of Him, and become ourselves monuments of His displeasure! Nevertheless, I mostly incline to the opinion that the injunction will go forth, "Come out from among them, and be ye separate." . . . .

The bottom of those people in Indiana is plainly seen, by their adopting the title of "Anti-slavery Friends." This is not Quaker ground: they have avowed a sectarian platform, have proved themselves sect-masters, though perhaps, in reality, they are not more so than those from whom they have seceded. But true Quakerism being "primitive Christianity revived," those who are in possession of it, having come, as George Fox said, "into that power where men shall agree," have got beyond sects and parties, and have attained to that which comprehends all minor principles of religious rectitude, of moral reformation, within itself. These stand upon a firm foundation,—aye, and a broad one, too, even as broad as the Truth itself, and are singularly quick of discernment respecting the branches from the same Root, and the motion of the same life, wherever it may appear; although such may be slow to identify themselves with that superfluous, spontaneous growth, which overtops the root, and oppresses the life of the true seed.

I have inadvertently and unexpectedly blundered upon these remarks, which can be of little interest to thee. They have been produced by a train of reflections upon the "anti-slavery cause" in general, into which I fell while penning that incidental notice of the separation in Indiana. And now I must say plainly, that while I wholly disapprove of the latter, there is much in the former, even looking at it aside from the interest and welfare of the slaves, which cannot fail to be deeply interesting to every true Quaker. I verily believe there is a motion of life among them, and that if they could but know the "mystery of the holy silence," and be brought into the experience of it, they would see a work to be performed, beyond the abolition of outward bonds; and not only so, but receive heavenly qualifications, availingly to plead the cause of the oppressed.

If there is anything here which thou thinkest likely to do harm, or hurt the feelings of any one, please exercise thy wonted care and prudence in the matter. I believe thou knowest how dearly I love, and how highly I esteem some dear Friends who have thought it right to take a more active part in these moral and benevolent works, than I ever found it my place to do. And what thinkest thou? Has it not been, in some of these instances, a sort of preparatory dispensation for a greater work? . . .

Thy sincere friend,

T. B. Gould.

To Joshua Maule.

Newport, 12th month, 13th, 1843.

. . . . Without the least desire to affix a high stamp upon anything which flows from my pen, as well knowing it does not merit it, and will not bear it; yet I freely own to thee, that in receiving communications of this kind, it seems very desirable that some degree of the savor of life should attend them; something of that which renders us like an "epistle written in the heart," which can "be known and read of all men" who have come to "the ministration of the Spirit." This, it must be confessed, is nothing less than "the hope of our calling;" and if we were but obedient to it, if we were but engaged to wait for it, even "until the Spirit be poured upon us from on high," how would it make the wilderness of this world like a fruitful field; and the desert—that which had been fruitful in nothing but briers and thorns—"to rejoice and blossom as the rose."

But this would be considered mysticism by the wise and prudent of this degenerate day; especially if the idea conveyed by the term *life*, and "the savor of life," were carried out to its full extent; seeing it is not supposed to be intelligible by them as applied to the ministry, much less then to matters of minor importance, such as, comparatively speaking, I admit this kind of communication to be. But I think thou, my dear brother, wilt agree with me, that we should be gainers by the experiment, if, while we profess to be led by the Spirit, we should apply that rule to the more ordinary concerns of life, so as to become acquainted with the motions of it; and having our spiritual faculties exercised by reason of use, we should be able to distinguish between the sweet savor of it, and the evil savor which is emitted whenever the "dead flies are mingled in the ointment of the apothecary."

. . . . I note what thou sayest respecting your trials, as well as that in relation to the disaffected persons among you. Truly *we* are neither exempt from the one nor the other; and doubtless these things are permitted for our refinement, both individually and conventionally. As it regards our poor Society, let us view it from what point we may, it does manifestly appear to be in a truly mournful condition; weakness and degeneracy have come over it generally, but of some places in particular it really seems as if the language of the prophet was verified: "That which the palmer worm hath left hath the locust eaten; and that which the locust hath left hath the canker worm eaten; and that which the canker worm hath left hath the caterpillar eaten." Yea, they have "laid the vine waste, and barked the fig-tree, making it clean bare," until there seems to be nothing left; not a "sherd to take fire from the hearth, or water withal out of the pit." And this is doubtless produced by individual unfaithfulness, together with an unsound and unsanctified ministry, the withering effects of which I think are plainly apparent where it has been exercised. Such have sown to the wind, and reaped the whirlwind. On the contrary, where a living stream of Gospel ministry has been mercifully kept open, more greenness, more strength, and more life appears; as in Philadelphia and Ohio yearly meetings:* but even these, it seems to me, come short of the primitive times, of the brightness in which those sons of the morning, those stars of the first magnitude in the firmament of the Lord's power, shone in their day. How far the circumstances of the times in which they lived, and the personal suffering which they endured, may have contributed to the wide difference which, I think, is apparent, between the early Friends and the best modern ones, in respect to zeal, vigilance, and success in the cause and work of the Lord, it is not my intention to venture an opinion now. Still the cause is the same, the principles are the same, for truth changeth not! And what they were in their day, they were by the power thereof.

Neither have I any doubt but that there are some, yea, many, scattered about here and there,—although I fear these are, in comparison with others, "like one in a family or two in a tribe,"—who stand in a measure of the same power in which the early Friends stood, are contending for the same principles, are walking by the same rule, and minding the same thing. But I am ready to conclude that the reason why so much difference appears, in regard to the success of modern laborers in the cause of truth, may be found in the darkness of the day and time in which we live. For, notwithstanding the loud boast of light and knowledge (and perhaps men never did, in any age, climb higher into the tree of *head*-knowledge), yet is it not, in respect to the true light and the living knowledge, a dark day, "a day of darkness and of gloominess, a day of clouds and thick darkness," wherein "judgment is turned away backward, and truth is fallen in the streets, and equity cannot enter?" Truly equity cannot enter in the high places of Israel, so called, where they cry aloud, "The temple of the Lord, the temple of the Lord are

* It is necessary to bear in mind the *date* of this remark.

these!" Judgment is turned away backward, and justice is excluded! He that departeth from iniquity is sure to make himself a prey, while they that tempt the Lord, by boasting of His authority, are even, to all human appearance, delivered! Surely the Lord will visit for these things, either sooner or later! Neither His justice nor His judgments will sleep forever! Whether it be in our day or not, I believe He will yet cause proclamation to be made, as among the Gentiles, to "prepare for war," to "wake up the mighty men;" that He will issue His injunction and commission to the men of war, to come up, "as in days of old, and as in former years," against the mighty; and that He will require them to beat their ploughshares into swords, and their pruning-hooks into spears, and enable the weak to say, "I am strong." . . .

Thy affectionate brother,
THOMAS B. GOULD.

CHAPTER IV.

The promoters of innovation continued for some time to cherish the hope of influencing Thomas B. Gould, by motives of "fear, favor, or affection," so as to induce him to forego his conscientious convictions in regard to the schism which he saw was imminent in the Society, and unite with them in their measures. But finding him not to be moved thereby, but increasingly firm and undaunted in opposition to the evil practices by which the new views were promoted in the Society, the leaders of the party in Newport proceeded, in 1843, to institute disciplinary proceedings against him, as *out of unity with the body.* This expression, about that time, was frequently perverted to the purpose of vilifying at an easy rate any against whom no tenable, direct, or specific charge could be produced, but whose steady adherence to their testimony against the removal of our ancient landmarks seriously obstructed these unhallowed advances towards change, and must be put out of the way.

The manner in which T. B. Gould was treated by those in authority at this time (no less than the treatment and disownment of John Wilbur by the same party, a short time before), was disgraceful to persons claiming to act for any professing Christian Church. They finally succeeded in disowning him, though not until, by the separation which their party had themselves already effected in Rhode Island Quarterly Meeting and its monthly meetings, they had cut off all their own rightful claim to act on behalf of the Society, or to be considered as constituting a portion of its true members. Several years afterwards, in compliance with the expressed desire of some for distinct information on the subject, T. B. Gould wrote a de-

16

tailed statement of these strangely irregular proceedings against him, which will be seen in the following letter to Y. W., and in one afterwards written to a friend in Ohio; some parts of the latter having been omitted, to avoid repetition of portions sufficiently elucidated in the former. These letters, though referring to events of 1843 and 1844, were written after his visit to Ohio, ten years afterwards, which will account for some allusions to matters appearing here out of the order of dates.

FROM T. B. GOULD TO Y. W——.

NEWPORT, 11th mo., 9th, 1854.

MY DEAR FRIEND:

Thy kind letter of the 6th inst. is just received, and although pressed for time and much indisposed, I hasten to answer thy inquiries respecting the time and manner of proceeding against me, in order to my disownment by those, who, before they had accomplished their avowed object in seeking to make me an offender, themselves went off in a body from Rhode Island Quarterly and Monthly Meetings, and, according to the decision of Philadelphia Yearly Meeting, set up separate meetings, in violation of the order, and contrary to the discipline of New England Yearly Meeting, and of the Society of Friends.

Thou askest: "With what offence wast thou charged, and when?"—which it is somewhat difficult for me to answer at this distance of time, as I kept no record at the time, and as the charges made by the overseers of Newport Preparative Meeting, during the only official visit which I ever received from them both, as such, were so indefinite, and so often changed, and went back during so long a period,—no less than six years (although during all that time I had never been so much as admonished by them, or, until very near the time of which I am now speaking, by any others, concerning any [alleged] misdemeanor); and for the additional reason, that they would neither tell me certainly whether they should carry a charge against me to the next preparative meeting, nor yet, in terms, what it was to be, if they carried one, which they said they "probably should do." But they did it not, and so I concluded it was given over for one month, as nothing was said about it in the preparative meeting, which I attended; and accordingly I set out with my wife to attend the next monthly meeting, then held about eight miles from Newport. But we were unable to reach there, by reason of our attempting to go in a sleigh; the sleighing being good in the town, but on getting a few miles out of town we found the snow so much drifted, and the roads so bare, that we could not reasonably proceed, and had to turn back; and before we could have changed our vehicle, &c., and have reached the meeting-house, it would have been so late in the day, and the meeting so nearly over, that I felt easiest, under the circumstances, not to make a second attempt. And so they availed themselves of my absence from the monthly meeting, and carried their complaint into it, without its ever having been laid before the preparative meeting in any shape. This manner of proceeding was strongly objected to, as irregular, by some of my strongest opposers; they said it would be taken advantage of by me; but the clerk, who was also one of the overseers of Newport, and bitterly opposed to me, insisted on its being entered on the minutes, alleging, as I was told, that it was a favorable time, and such as might not occur again, the individual being absent; and so it was done, and a joint committee of men and women appointed to labor with me. This was in the second month, 1844; and thou canst judge whether this manner of proceeding was regular or not. I had never known, and the oldest and most experienced members of this monthly meeting had never before known of a complaint or charge being carried to the monthly meeting, except through the medium of the preparative, until now!

The committee so appointed had repeated opportunities with me, during a period of nine months. The first and second time they visited me, I think they did not bring a copy of the charge with them; at any rate, they would not produce it, if they did, neither did they seem to know what the charge was. But as I insisted upon knowing distinctly what was charged against me, the next time they came, they brought what they said was a true copy of it; but they refused at the same time to let me see it! saying "It was sufficient for them to know what Friends had against me." I still urged my right to see it. One of them, who was scarcely capable of reading *printed* matter correctly, said he would read it to me. I asked him to let me read it myself. He said I might look over his shoulder and read it, but he could not let me have it in my hand. I asked, "Why not? did they suppose I would deface it, destroy it, or retain possession of it against their wishes?" He said, "No; they had entire confidence in my honor and integrity! but D. B." (the clerk of the monthly meeting, and the bitterest of the two overseers of Newport Preparative Meeting, and a very active member of the yearly meeting's committee also), "had told him not to let me have it by any means." And they treated me so unreasonably and unhandsomely in this interview, that I declined any further intercourse with them, as a committee, at that time, unless they would pursue a different course: and I did leave the parlor and shut the door after me when I went out, for it was cold weather; but I did not go out pettishly nor hastily, and I had also other good reasons for going out, which I did not think needful to mention to them. Neither did this end that interview, for they followed me into the back part of the house, where, for some reason or other, they had chosen to enter at first, and from whence I had invited them to go into the parlor, which they seemed reluctant to do, although my wife was sweeping when they came into the dining-room, and sat down, seeming resolved to stay there, though I told them I could not endure the dust, which was yet unsettled, and they all knew I was suffering with asthma. But this made no difference to them. Indeed they seemed throughout, to delight in causing me to suffer in every way in their power. After they came out of the parlor into the dining-room, I had occasion to remind one of them of something he had said, while we were together in the meeting-house yard, at a certain time; whereupon he promptly denied it, and, in a very irreverent manner, made use of the sacred name, appealing to his Maker vehemently and repeatedly, exclaiming, "God Almighty knows that I never said so!" He had told me that the greatest desire he had, was to have me disowned, on account of my intimacy and unity with J. Wilbur, and also on account of my disunity with and opposition to J. J. Gurney, whom he at the same time represented as a superior being! I now cautioned him against denying it, as I distinctly remembered what he had said; and let him know that his manner of doing it was equivalent to the taking of an oath; that it was a very wrong and inconsistent thing to swear at all, and that it was doubly so to swear falsely. He said he knew it, but that he would do so, and went on with his appeals to his Maker, in a way which was very painful and fearful to hear. There were two other men, and two females of the committee present. One of the latter was in the station of a minister. She and one of the other men, as well as this man, are all since deceased, and there is now but one member of the committee alive and in possession of her mental powers: she at that time had not long been a member of the Society, and was wholly silent throughout.

They had several interviews with me after this, pursuing me through a long and very severe attack of illness, which brought me near to the grave. Sometimes when they came, I said little or nothing to them, not feeling at liberty so to do; then they would report to the monthly meeting, "that the young man was somewhat *meliorated;* that they were in hopes his sickness would be of use to him, and that he would be induced to make an acknowledgment." And so they kept the case along during nine months, not disowning me until the day that the separation took place in this monthly meeting, and after it had taken place. During all this time, they refused to let me see the charge, unless I had consented to see it upon conditions and under circumstances which I did not feel easy to submit to. And yet one of the committee did in a roundabout way let my wife see a paper which he said was the charge, which was to this effect: "that the overseers of Newport Preparative Meeting had several times" (and this was untrue), "treated with T. B. Gould, for having manifested himself out of unity with Friends in all the meetings of discipline of which he is a member, and also for having charged the overseers of Newport with being actuated by a spirit of envy and malice." Now it availed me nothing, to be able to show that I had a right to express a different sentiment or judgment from those who bore rule in meetings for discipline, or that their doings were inconsistent in themselves, and with our principles and discipline. And in regard to the latter part of the charge, I had merely stated, as a reason why a charge which was brought against another Friend ought not to be entered on the minutes of the preparative meeting, or to be sent to the monthly meeting,—that one of the overseers who brought it had admitted to me, that the other overseer had been actuated by an envious and malicious spirit against the Friend complained of, and that being conscious of having the power to do it, he was resolved to have him disowned.

Thou askest whether I "ever felt or expressed to any Friend, uneasiness for that which was made the ground of their dealings with me?" To which I can answer, that according to the best recollection I have, I never did either feel or express any uneasiness with it. I never doubted its rectitude, or made anything like an acknowledgment to the overseers or the committee; although in conversation respecting these things I may possibly have admitted, some time or other, that it was probable I might have conducted the defense more wisely than I did, but I never thought it would have made the least difference as to the result. Indeed one of the overseers told me, that those who united with J. J. G. were determined that I should be disowned at all events! This overseer was rather a clever, but not a very shrewd man, and was, I believe, really unwilling that I should be disowned, although he seemed incapable of pursuing a straightforward course, or of understanding why I was unwilling to make an acknowledgment to them, or to the committee, for having done what I believed to have been required of me. He is not now living. He sought repeated opportunities with me, without the knowledge, as he said, of the other overseer of our preparative meeting, to try to induce me to satisfy his colleague; whom I knew I could not satisfy, unless I gave up the whole ground of my testimony against those wrong things, which he owned to me constituted the whole cause of their proceedings against me. For he told me plainly, that he was satisfied I had acted conscientiously; and not only so, but said he, "Thou hast been exemplary and consistent with thy profession from thy childhood to this day; everybody knows that; and I am willing to acknowledge it;" adding, "But thee knows that there are many Friends who are determined to have thee disowned; I am not one of them, but D. B." (the other overseer) "is, and they have the power to do it!" I asked him, "If they were convinced of my integrity, and if I had always been exemplary and consistent with our profession, what they were treating with me as an offender for?" "Why," said he, "they look upon thee as a main spoke in the wheel of opposition to J. J. Gurney, and as being likely to bring about a separation in the Society; and unless thee ceases to oppose his sentiments, and will make an acknowledgment, and satisfy Friends for what thee has said against him and his writings, they are determined to disown thee." I told him, "that so far from seeking to produce a separation, the object of my labor and concern had been to prevent it, by opposing the introduction and adoption of unsound sentiments, and the inconsistent and disorderly practices consequent upon their dissemination; knowing as I did that a *departure* from *first principles* would lead *those who departed* into a separation from the Society; which I had labored to prevent, in the ability received, being very sincerely desirous that Friends might continue to be united in the ancient faith and principles of the Society, and fully convinced that the adoption of *new principles* would produce a separation, provided any portion of the members stood faithful to the ancient standard." But he said, the great body of Society were united with J. J. Gurney, &c., and he would advise me "to stick to *the body*, right or wrong!" "Why," said he, "if Rowland Green, Thomas Anthony, and John Meader, were to advise me to do a thing which I *knew to be wrong*, I should do it! I like to pin my faith upon the sleeves of such men as they are. And why can't thee do it? I see a great many things done which I know are wrong; but I do as they tell me to do, and they must take the responsibility!" So much for this overseer: and the committee were not one whit sounder or more reasonable, and much less moderate and civil.

A short time before the overseers of Newport visited me, I received a visit from Edward Wing and Asa Sherman, who stood in the station of overseers of another preparative meeting; and upon their saying that they had come to have an opportunity with me, I asked in what capacity they had come? They said, "as overseers." Whereupon I queried whether they had not come too soon; adding, the overseers of Newport Preparative Meeting, to which I belong, have never yet so much as admonished me. They affected to express surprise at this, and Edward Wing immediately replied, "We came as members of the quarterly meeting's committee."—"But thou art not a member of that committee," said I. "Well then," said he, "we came as members of the yearly meeting's committee." To which I replied, "Asa Sherman is not a member of that,—but no matter: what is the occasion of your coming?"—(for I saw it was unavailing to stand upon technicalities, Edward having resumed, "We came as overseers, and as members of the quarterly and yearly meeting's committees, all three!")—To which Edward replied, "Friends were much dissatisfied with what thee said in the quarterly meeting the other day."—"What did I say, Edward, which gave Friends uneasiness?"—"Oh," said he, "I cannot tell what thee said; thee knows what thee said, and we want thee to make an acknowledgment for it. Thee said a great deal; thee used a great many words, and we know thy memory is good, and we can believe what thee says. Now we want thee to tell us what thee said, and to make an acknowledgment for it, and then we shall know!" I endeavored to show them the unreasonableness of their coming to treat with me as an offender, for something which I had said in our quarterly meeting (for business), without their knowing what it was, and then calling upon me to bear witness against myself, which I told them no man, not even a criminal, was bound to do. But Edward, not seeming to see the force of this in any respect, continued to urge me to tell them what I did say; gratuitously informing me how very candid and honest they considered me to be, and how implicitly they would rely upon my giving them the very words which had been used; and withal repeating the declaration, that I had said a great deal, had used a great many words, &c. Whereupon I appealed to Asa Sherman, who had been silent hitherto, to know whether he could say that I had said a great deal, or used many words, in the quarterly meeting at the time referred to. To which he replied, that he could not say that I used many words; but added, "Sometimes there is a great deal said in a few words;" and immediately added, "I must confess that I felt more dissatisfied with what thee said in the monthly meeting, than with what thee said in the quarterly meeting." I then asked what I said in the monthly meeting, which gave him uneasiness? "Why," said he, "thee used severe and violent language there."—"What was the language, Asa?"—"Why, thee said that Simeon and Levi were brethren, that instruments of cruelty were in their habitations, and thee went on and quoted the whole passage!"—"Did I quote it correctly, Asa?"—"Oh, yes, very correctly."—"And thou callest that severe and violent language, dost thou?"—"Yes," said he, "I do; we felt it very keenly." To which I merely answered, "It was the language of the patriarch Jacob, and by thy acknowledgment, correctly quoted; and if you felt the force of it, or deemed the language violent, I don't know that I am to be blamed for it." They immediately changed their plan of operations, and commenced fawning upon me, telling me how much they loved me and esteemed me, and that if I would only renounce J. Wilbur, and get out from under his clutches, and have unity with them and J. J. Gurney, what a fine Friend I should be, and how they would promote me to great honor, &c.; all which had no more effect to induce me to change my course than the other; and they soon after took their departure, with the assurance of abundance of love and good-will; not having brought anything against me, so far as I can recollect, except what I have here mentioned.

I had quoted the language of Jacob in the monthly meeting, upon the occasion of a minute of disownment having been made against a Friend, who, by the confession of one of the overseers, had been dealt with in a spirit of envy and malice. And the evidence of the truth of this assertion was most abundant, although I never so charged them at all: but they wrested the words which I had used, so as to bring it against me in such form as best suited them and their purposes.

About the same time that I received the above-mentioned visit from the overseers of Portsmouth Preparative Meeting, and before the overseers of Newport took up my case, it was brought up in the *Select* preparative meeting, and an attempt was made to enter my name, as a delinquent, upon their minutes, and to get a committee of that meeting (of which I was not a member) appointed, to labor with me, as I was informed; and they also tried to induce my father to serve on this committee. But he told them that as I was not a member of that meeting, they had no right to enter my name on their minutes as a delinquent; and steadily declining to have anything to do with the measure, which was no doubt intended as a double snare for *him*, they finally *seemed* to give it up, and the meeting broke up. But my father was no sooner well in his chaise, and gone out of the meeting-house yard, on his way home, than the rest of the select members returned into the meeting-house and resumed the subject; and having thus got rid of my father, they deputed a female elder, who was a relative of mine by marriage, and one of the shrewdest of their number, to take an opportunity with me. And she soon after sent me a message that she wanted to see me. I was very unwell when I received it, and scarcely able to walk; but suspecting what the nature of her concern was, I thought I would make an effort to go and see her at the time specified, as she was much my senior, and the ground so covered with ice that she could not come to me; and I feared, if I went not, however poorly I was, that I should be charged with omitting it from some unworthy motive. Upon my going in, she manifested some surprise, and confusion also; for she must have been sensible I was unfit to be out; and she seemed under considerable embarrassment in opening the subject; but finally told me that she had been appointed at their last select preparative meeting, to convey to me the feeling of the select Friends respecting myself. I inquired, "At the last meeting, cousin Hannah?" "Yes, at the last." "Why, my father was present, and informed me that there was no such committee appointed at that time." This increased her embarrassment, and she was fain to come out with an account of the informal manner in which it was done, as above related. However, she said that there was abundance of concern manifested for my advancement and encouragement in every good word and work; that the select Friends were unanimous in this desire; that they did not wish to throw the least obstruction in my way; but still they felt dissatisfied with what I had expressed in the public meeting, when a certain minister from a neighboring meeting was present; they thought it was not in harmony and unison with what he had expressed; and there had been one other occasion, in which my public communication had given concern to Friends; and that it was evident there was not that degree of love and unity, and harmony in exercise, and concern with *the body* of Society, in a general way, as would be very desirable: but that she was instructed to inform me, on behalf of the select members of this monthly meeting, that if I would be careful not to say anything in public which might seem to clash with what Moses H. Beede, John Meader, and such Friends said, and to cultivate more intercourse, and manifest more unity with them, that there was nothing stood in the way of my promotion to the extent of my desire! &c. But I told her, that I had never been seeking after honor or promotion from man; that if I were at liberty to seek for it, I was not ignorant what course would seem most likely to insure it; that I had done that only which I had been convinced was my duty to do, and therein had found peace; and could not shape my course, and unite with things which

I was convinced were wrong, for the sake either of ease or preferment, or to please any man, or body of men; being satisfied that those who sought to please men could not be the servants of Him whose kingdom is not of this world, &c. We had much plain talk upon the subject, but the above includes the whole of what was alleged against me; and it is not a little remarkable that, although I was raised up in a public testimony for the truth, in the very midst of great secret opposition at least, and of a powerful, persecuting spirit, yet those two occasions were the only ones of a public nature which were ever objected to, so far as I know, by any of those people, or indeed by any other. If there has been dissatisfaction felt, it has never been mentioned to me, or come to my knowledge; and I attended meeting constantly with those people five years after my first appearance in that line; although it is true that in that day such appearances were by no means frequent. On one of the occasions which she referred to, the minister who was at our meeting had been hammering at great length about love, and unity, and charity, seeming to make that all in all, although it was manifest that the "love of God" was not by any means "perfected" in him; and after he had been done a suitable time, I quoted the passage, "Except your righteousness shall exceed the righteousness of the Scribes and Pharisees, ye shall in nowise enter the kingdom of heaven," showing in what that kingdom consisted, where it was designed to be, and upon whose shoulders the government was to rest, and unto whom the gathering of the people was to be. But this offer of preferment seemed to be the last attempt to gain me over to them, by such as were initiated and understood the designs of the leaders; and was most probably made merely to reconcile some of the more moderate and less knowing ones to the measures which were very soon after instituted, to disown him whom they could not induce to bow even with the offer of "honors, offices, and places."

There is one question which thou hast put to me, which remains to be answered, to wit: "When was the testimony offered?" Now I do not exactly understand to what testimony thou alludest herein. If to a testimony of denial or disownment, I can only say that the first knowledge I had of such a testimony having been issued against me, even by the separatists, occurred in Ohio Yearly Meeting, the other day; when a man, Zadoc Street, held up a paper, and declared that it was a testimony of disownment against me; but no such thing was ever offered to me at any time! I was merely informed, by a person who chanced to meet me in the street in 1844, that I had been disowned by their last monthly meeting; to which I replied, that I had never been a member of their meeting; but that Rhode Island Monthly Meeting had fully exonerated me from the charges which some of those who had separated themselves from it, and set up a new meeting of their own, out of the order of the Society, had prepared against me; and had dismissed the case from the minutes, and restored me to my rights and privileges as a member, of which those who had now manifested themselves to be seceders had for a time been permitted to deprive me.

Although I felt bound to endeavor to maintain the ground upon which I stood, with firmness, yet I had also thought it right to submit to their requisitions, however unreasonable or unkind, except in such cases as I thought would involve a compromise of principle. I never refused a visit from them at any time, however inconvenient or unsuitable; though I believe my wife did refuse to let them see me once or twice, during my very severe illness, without my knowledge, she not judging it to be at all safe or proper, and she knew best what was proper for me at that time; yet, after I got somewhat better, I thought best to consent to see them before she thought it suitable for me; but I was made willing to suffer, and did endeavor to do so patiently; and I am confident that I was enabled to keep, in a good degree, both in the patience and in the faith also, even that faith which is victorious, though it be through suffering.

Now, having given thee this long account, I fear it may prove tedious to thee; but I could not in any other way have made thee so fully sensible of the nature of those spirits which I had to contend with. It was, however, frequently manifest that the power of truth came over them, and they could not gainsay what was uttered in its behalf; and they often seemed to be at their wits' end, not knowing well what to do or say next; but then they would fall back upon the power which they possessed, and to which they seemed resolved that every knee should bow.

28th of 11th mo.

Thou wilt see by the date of the previous sheet, that I commenced it immediately upon the reception of thine, although I was much unwell and unfit for writing, neither could I write much at a time; and so, what is before written was done at intervals, and was several days in hand. When reading it over, I could see the want of method, and that I had gone too much into detail; and fearing it would be as tedious to thee as it is unsatisfactory to myself, I thought I would let it lie by me, until I felt well enough to re-write and abridge it. But seeing no prospect of being able soon to do this, I have concluded to let thee have the perusal of it, and when thou hast made such corrections of misstatements with regard to the matter, as thou mayst see fit, I would thank thee to return these two sheets to me; and therefore enclose two postage stamps, to enable thee to do so without expense to thyself. This request is not founded upon any lack of confidence in thy integrity or prudence, but upon its being the only record of these things which I have; and since such record has been made, I would rather have it returned to me again, when the purpose for which thou so kindly requested it has been answered. And I would rather thou did not hand these sheets much about, on account of the bungling manner in which they are written, &c. My health has been very poor since my return; my throat and lungs are in a sad state. An almost incessant and distressing cough, great difficulty of breathing, reduction of strength, and very little appetite, so that I am mostly confined to the house and to my room; though I do sometimes get to meeting: but the prospect of better health in future looks discouraging, and when, if ever, I shall be able to accomplish what I had in prospect in the State of New York, seems doubtful. Still I have not as yet been able to feel a release from the burden of the concern. But when we had got through in Philadelphia and Jersey, my way closed up, as regarded proceeding to New York, and I thought best to return directly home, and attend our own quarterly meeting and meeting for sufferings; to which last I felt particularly drawn for divers reasons, one of which was my being clerk of that meeting. My dear companion too found it necessary for him to return home, on account of his own ill health and affairs at home, and I could not think of going on alone. I had also good reason to acknowledge the good hand of the Lord herein, as well as in previously leading us about and instructing us, from day to day, in the way wherein He would have us to go; so that I hope no harm was done to that good and glorious cause, which we really had at heart, however we may have been looked upon by those who judge only according to man's judgment. Although conscious of many weaknesses and shortcomings, yet the retrospect of our little, though in many respects painful embassy, has afforded a degree of solid satisfaction and peaceful quietness, perhaps greater than I had ever known before. Yet I think I have never experienced greater poverty, or more humbling baptisms, than at times since my return. . . . . . . And if thou shouldst feel any degree of satisfaction with my account of the manner in which I treated my committee, who certainly were not the most reasonable beings that I have seen, even in my short day, I would like to know it; neither would it be uninteresting to me to know, if it were proper, who it was that called the matter up? But I can leave this, with the rest, to thy better judgment, and remain thy sincere and affectionate friend,

THOMAS B. GOULD.

To Mary V. Doudna.

Newport, Rhode Island, 1st mo., 8th, 1855.

My dear Friend, Mary V. Doudna:

Thy truly acceptable and deeply interesting letter, of the second of eleventh month, was duly received; and I did consider very kind thy writing to me, and was particularly glad thou gavest me a copy of thy dear brother Caleb Gregg's entire letter. I have felt near sympathy with him, in his very close trials; and well I may, for he was treated by the Gurneyites in Iowa very much in the same way that I was myself in New England; neither do I suppose that latitude and longitude make much difference in the fruits and practices that proceed from the same spirit. . . . . . .

As there was so much said in Ohio about the matter of my disownment by the separatists, and as they continue to render me so notorious by repeatedly publishing my name in print as a disowned person, &c., I feel inclined to tell thee a little of the manner in which it was effected, and let thee judge for thyself of the similarity of the proceedings with those in thy brother's case: and if thou thinkest it would be of any service, or afford the least encouragement to him, thou mayst send it, or a copy of it, to him, with the assurance of my near sympathy and true love in the fellowship of suffering for the cause sake. Truly he is seldom out of my mind, although personally unknown; and I do sincerely and earnestly desire, that he and the dear Friends who have stood by him hitherto, may be enabled to stand and maintain the ground they have taken, and be preserved from making any unnecessary concessions to the Gurneyite power, or any compromises with it! . . . . Indiana Yearly Meeting was not only previously and entirely governed by a wholly arbitrary power, but has since fully identified itself with the separatists in Ohio!

But I will proceed to the account of my own case; and in the first place I will say, that from the time I openly manifested uneasiness with the unsound doctrines of J. J. Gurney, when he first came to this yearly meeting in 1838, his partisans gave out that I ought to be disowned for it, and sought secretly to prepare the way for it, and to have me treated with by the overseers. But it so happened that the overseers [at that time] of Newport Preparative Meeting, to which I belonged, had unity with me in my testimony against J. J. G., and would not do the bidding of the clerk of the monthly meeting, who was a strong Gurneyite and a member of the yearly meeting's committee, or take their advice to call in the aid of the overseers of Portsmouth Preparative, who were both Gurneyites; and so the clerk of the monthly meeting, whose name was D. B., no doubt under the advice, or with the concurrence of the yearly meeting's committee (who were all Gurneyites to a man), set himself to work to have the overseers of Newport removed, and to get himself and another man who would do their bidding, appointed in the place of the old overseers. But it took them several years to accomplish this their purpose, for Rhode Island Monthly Meeting at that time, according to the admission or declaration of the clerk, was about equally divided on the subject; and not only so, but in the mean time they took up John Wilbur's case, which kept them very busy for a long time, furnishing them full employment; and during this time also I asked for a certificate to proceed in marriage; which by our discipline tied their hands for a while; and after we were married, they tried for a while to see what effect they could have upon me, by changing their tactics, and showing much attention to my wife, in order as I suppose to gain her over to them. But finding her immovable, and having succeeded in removing the old overseers, and getting David Buffum, and Jethro F. Mitchell, appointed as such, and also in disposing of John Wilbur's case, and as they thought getting rid of him, they proceeded to lay a dear friend of mine, a member of this particular meeting, under dealing, upon a charge of unbecoming behavior in meeting; which being interpreted, was declared to be a want of unity with J. J. Gurney and Moses H. Beede, who was then a member of this meeting also. This was in 1842 and 1843, and from 1838 until this time, I had never, nor in the course of my whole life, been so much as admonished respecting any misdemeanor by any member, either officially or otherwise. Still, in an underhand way, and behind my back, D. B., and all the Gurneyites great and small, had been doing and saying everything in their power to lessen my influence and destroy my religious character; declaring, wherever and whenever they thought it would do, that I ought to be disowned; that the thing they most wished was to have me disowned, but that they did not see how to get hold of me, &c. So that in laying my friend, T. P. N., under dealing, I doubted not they expected, through my advocacy of his case, to get hold of me: and accordingly, soon after he was disowned, I was called on one day by Edward Wing and Asa Sherman, overseers of Portsmouth Preparative Meeting, a branch of R. I. Monthly Meeting. . . . [See letter to Y. W.]

Very soon after this assurance that nothing but obedience and harmonizing with that party, stood in the way of my promotion to great honor, I received an official visit from David Buffum and Jethro F. Mitchell, the [new] overseers of Newport, in good earnest. They would not specify what they had against me, except in the general declaration that "I was out of unity with the body;" neither did they make any effort in any way for my restoration; but David Buffum, who was the chief speaker, treated me in a very haughty and imperious manner, saying that they intended to carry a complaint against me to the next preparative meeting. He said so repeatedly, in great heat. I asked him what sort of a complaint they meant to carry; but he would not tell me, saying it was sufficient for them to know! I then asked, how I could be expected to answer to an unknown charge, or how they could know that I was unable to disprove it, or show it to be groundless? They said, or rather D. B. said, that they knew well enough, and so did I. I pressed my right to see and know distinctly what was charged against me, before they carried a complaint to the preparative meeting. They would not, while together, give me any assurance that they would let me see it; but D. B. finally said, that they would not say positively that they would carry one to the next meeting, but that it was probable they should do so; and so they left. But J. F. M., who was the more moderate of the two, and the mere tool of the other, came back alone, and told me that he would try to let me know, before the preparative meeting, whether they would carry a complaint to it, and also to let me see it. . . . . [See letter to Y. W., for the account of J. F. M.'s visits alone. Speaking of one of these, after defending himself from the charge of wishing to promote a separation, he goes on as follows]:

He said he did not doubt my sincerity, or that I believed it was my duty to do as I had done; but that I ought to submit to the judgment and take the advice of my friends. I asked him if such could be supposed to be my friends, who had been seeking underhandedly, for five years, to destroy my religious character, and to deprive me of my right as a member of the Society, and saying whenever and wherever they thought it would bear, that the thing they most desired was to have me disowned; and yet had never given me any advice upon the subject, all the time they had manifested such uneasiness with me behind my back? Was this friendly? Could such as these be my friends? What would I gain, save the loss of my own peace of mind, by condemning, according to his own acknowledgment, a conscientious and consistent course, for the sake of pleasing or satisfying such as himself had also acknowledged had neither acted conscientiously nor consistently; and such, too, as had certainly given their support and countenance to the introduction and promulgation of unsound doctrines and wrong practices? Why, he said, that I ought to pin my faith upon their sleeve, that he did so himself; that he knew there were many wrong things in the Society, there always had been; but that if the members of the yearly meeting's committee, such men as Rowland Green, John Meader, and others whom he named, were to advise him to do what he *knew to be wrong*, he would do it! and let them take the responsibility! But I let him know, that my faith in the power of any man, or body of men, to release me from responsibility and accountability for my own conduct, was not near so elastic or so blind as his appeared to be. And a great deal more of this sort passed between him and me, and the committee which was afterwards appointed to treat with me also. . . . . [See letter to Y. W., for an account of the case being brought before the monthly meeting.] . . . . Towards evening of the day on which their monthly meeting was held, I was standing in the door of my father's house, which opened on the street, as the mail-stage passed by into the town. In the stage was a man, who, I afterwards learned, had been that day appointed one of the committee to treat with me; and upon seeing me stand there, he threw up his hands, and cut up strange antics, calling out loudly, and apparently speaking to me, though I could not hear what he said as he rattled by in the stage, which was full of people, not members; but I understood by his actions that he was very much pleased!—and I told my wife that I had no doubt they had at length accomplished the design they had long entertained, of placing my name as an offender on the minutes of the monthly meeting. And sure enough, it was not long before this man came to my house, and said, the committee wished to have an opportunity with me that morning; which I consented to grant them; and he with the other two men, and two women, accordingly came. . . . . . [See letter to Y. W. for the details of the committee's visits.]

. . . . . . They had many opportunities with me during a period of several months that they kept my case along. In this time I was very ill indeed, and they did not hesitate to pursue me when I was too sick to see any company, and my life was despaired of by my friends and my physician. Some of their offers to visit me during this period my wife rejected, without my knowledge, for prudential reasons. But when I knew of their wish to see me, I always consented to it, as long as they pleased, after the first interview. Sometimes I said very little to them, not feeling raised up to do so, or, in other words, qualified for it. Then they would report to the monthly meeting, as I was told, that the young man was very much "*meliorated*," that his illness had been of service to him, and that they were in hopes he would make an acknowledgment! And so they had my case depending from month to month, and did not make a minute against me until after the separation had occurred in Swanzey Monthly Meeting, in Rhode Island Quarterly Meeting, and also in Rhode Island Monthly Meeting; which, as sustained by Friends, dismissed my case from the minutes, and restored me to my rights and privileges as a member in unity, at an adjournment of the monthly meeting, held that day. The separatists, on the same day, pretended to disown me from their meeting, although I had never been a member of it. . . . .

THOMAS B. GOULD.

TO JOHN WILBUR.

NEWPORT, 1st mo., 7th, 1844.

MY DEAR FRIEND:

. . . . I really hope that our correspondence may not cease, though if it should, I trust we shall continue to be as epistles written in each other's hearts; and then it matters little how things are as to the outward; for with the hidden fellowship and the inward life, outward signs bear small comparison, except as they proceed from and are produced by it; when indeed they are truly pleasant, and often prove "like apples of gold in pictures of silver."

We have heard with much concern of the illness of thy dear wife, and feel anxious to hear from thee more particularly of her state. Really it does seem as if we were likely to be tried on all hands; those who are dear to us, and to whom we have been accustomed to look for sympathy, and who have often ministered to our necessities, and also to our encouragement, are either removed or being taken from us, while the combat thickens, and the strife increases. But He, whose the cause is, and for whom we stand in jeopardy every hour, knoweth best what is best for us, and will doubtless cause all things to work together for our good, as our reliance is unreservedly placed upon Him. . . . .

. . . The difficulties in the Society have been so noised about in the town, and have produced such an excitement therein, that we have much work with the townspeople, who stop us at the corners of the streets, to inquire into the cause of it. When so inquired of, I have frequently thought fit to answer these sober inquiries, although I have not yet pursued the plan of our adversaries, to go round and drum people up, and hunt them down, in order to make interest with them and to proselyte them; nevertheless I can but trust and believe that the witness for truth in the hearts of some of these, who are found as in the highways and hedges, has sometimes been reached, and that they have been thereby convinced, "that He who is with us is more than is with them," notwithstanding all their loud boasting. A Baptist minister here lately took an opportunity with father, and afterwards with me, to express his sympathy with us. He told me that he very much desired to hit upon some plan of reconciliation between the parties, and that those who did remain upon the ancient foundation of true Quakerism should be relieved from their sufferings, and restored to their rights and privileges, and the others should forbear their tyranny and renounce their errors, that so we might be spared the reproach of an open schism. He thought a fair investigation, a reference to impartial arbiters, whose decision by mutual agreement should be binding,—and if such could not be found in the Society, to put it out to godly men of other persuasions—would be useful; and asked me if I was willing he should propose it to the other party, with whom he is acquainted, and to whom, he said, he had strongly recommended moderation! I could not help smiling at this, and told him I was quite willing he should make the proposition, provided he did it on his own responsibility; but that it would be in vain, that the breach could not be so healed, neither would such a measure be in accordance with our principles; that we were quite willing to suffer in this cause whatever they might be permitted to inflict, although it should extend to excommunication itself (for a time) from a Society which we dearly loved; relying upon Him, whose the cause is, for our final deliverance and justification, which, in His time, we were fully persuaded, He would show, &c. To which he emphatically replied, "You have not come to that experience but through deep suffering; *they* do not feel so!" I thought there was some life in this answer. "It really did me good to hear it," as John Roberts said of the old Bishop. What a pity it is, these goodly people keep up such a noise and bustle, as to be much strangers to the true silence, or, as William Penn said, to the "mystery of the holy silence;" and how much more passing strange, that "*my people* do not know, that Israel doth not consider!" I sometimes think, yea, often, that the former, who, in comparison with the latter, may not perhaps improperly be called "publicans," will enter the kingdom, will understand the mystery, before them! For the Lord can call (and will He not call?) those that are not, as those that are. . . . .

T. B. GOULD.

In writing to Ethan Foster, under date of 1st mo. 15th, 1844, he says:—

. . . In the immediate prospect before me, of being deprived of my rights and privileges in a Society which I dearly love, which are as precious as ever in the general, however they may be viewed in this particular section of it,—I can say, without boasting, that I feel much quietness and peace, am ready to count it all joy, and to be thankful that I am permitted to suffer in this cause, although it should extend to the final loss of all, which, as to the outward connection with the Society, I hold most dear.

Farewell.

FROM T. B. G. TO JOSEPH KITE.

NEWPORT, 2d mo. 11th, 1844.

MY DEAR FRIEND, JOSEPH KITE:

It is now a long time since I received a very acceptable communication from thee; and although I have often—yea, very often—thought of thee and it, in the interim, yet one thing or another has hitherto prevented me from giving thee this kind of assurance of my love and affectionate remembrance. But of latter time I have thought more particularly of addressing thee; and although it may be only as the voice of "one born out of due time," or as the communication of the disciples formerly, when they "walked by the way and were sad," yet I trust it may not be wholly unacceptable to thee, who, I doubt not, art often engaged in the consideration of those things which have happened in Jerusalem, being thyself no stranger to the afflictions of Joseph in this day of sore bondage, as in the land of Egypt. But, my endeared friend, whatever may be the trials and provings of our faith and patience, it is an unspeakable consolation to feel and know the arm of the Lord to be underneath, for our support; and that He will not suffer us to be tried beyond what He will enable us to endure, as the eye of the mind is kept singly upon Him; and that "there is none like unto the God of Jeshurun, who rideth upon the heavens in thy help, and in His excellency on the sky. The eternal God is thy refuge, and underneath are the everlasting arms." I may acknowledge that I was never so established and confirmed in these truths as in times of sore conflict, when all other help seemed to fail, and the poor mind was utterly shaken and broken off from reliance on any other power. Then it is that the arm and power of the Lord is revealed, as in days of old, as in the land of Egypt, and in the field of Zoan. And truly, much occasion indeed have some of the poorest and hindmost of the flock and family, to magnify and adore the right arm and power of the Lord, who has enabled them to say, "I am exceedingly joyful in all my tribulations:" for as these have abounded, the consolations of the Gospel have also abounded, to His praise who alone is worthy and transcendently glorious in holiness, fearful in praises, doing wonders. . . .

This case of —— is an aggravated one. But it is a consolation to us, as his crosses have increased, to see him bow submissively to the yoke; he having, in accordance with the experience of the faithful in all ages, found the Power under the cross; and we cannot doubt, if he continues faithful, that he will find the crown, beyond it. But this warfare against spiritual wickedness in high places is indeed grievous, and waxes hotter and hotter. Many there are who have fallen and are falling, both on the right hand and on the left; so that, amid the general desolation and gloom, it requires no small degree of faith to believe, without doubting, the ancient declaration, "The destruction shall not come nigh thee." Nevertheless, I have not the shadow of a doubt but the Lamb and His faithful followers will have the victory. . . .

I do not consider it of much importance what may become of me,—that is, of much importance to other people,—and I really feel considerable delicacy in speaking of it at all: nevertheless, in respect of the kind interest which thou hast been pleased to manifest in me, all unworthy of it as I feel, I will venture just to say, that all the male overseers of this monthly meeting have been engaged in laboring with me occasionally, for several months past; and as they are all members either of the quarterly or yearly meeting's committee, they have sometimes professed to labor in one of these capacities, and sometimes in all three, and that too in the same interview. . . .

One of them, in a subsequent interview, freely declared that I had been exemplary and consistent with my profession, from my childhood up to this time; but he said that they considered, that I had great influence over others, and that the good of the body required my disownment, notwithstanding; for I exercised that influence of which he had spoken, to draw Friends away from the body, and to oppose them in their prominent measures. I told him he was entirely mistaken with regard to my having exerted any influence which I might possess, adversely to the good and unity of the body; that, on the contrary, I had exerted it, as I felt bound to do, to prevent a breach of unity, by taking a firm stand against the introduction of unsound doctrines into the Society, which had ever been the source of schisms in the Church. He said, if I would only acknowledge my error in opposing that certificate [the returning certificate for Joseph John Gurney, in New England Yearly Meeting] and other measures in the yearly and quarterly meetings, and promise not to oppose them in future, they would not molest me further, and a very little would do. But I told him I could not do any such thing; and that while I valued my birthright very highly,—as, by his admission, my whole course through life had given evidence,—I would sooner be deprived of it than do violence to the testimony of the Spirit in my conscience, which bore witness against those doctrines, and the "prominent measures" which had been taken in consequence of their introduction and adoption.

They have sometimes appeared quite troubled in their own minds during these interviews, and in some measure to feel the force of Truth. And for their sakes it is, that I am made willing to meet them, wherever and whenever they choose to require it; although, as I have not spared to tell them, I do not consider that they have any right to treat me as an offender, and of this they themselves seem to be sensible. . . . .

With unfeigned love to thee and thine,

I am thy affectionate friend,

THOMAS B. GOULD.

TO JOHN WILBUR.

NEWPORT, 2d mo., 29th, 1844.

MY DEAR FRIEND:

I have been greatly disappointed, inasmuch as I have not heard a word from thee, or from my dear friends at Westerly, since the quarterly meeting. I have felt no little embarrassment and mortification in respect of my failing to reach Providence myself, after having written to C. Perry for the purpose, among some others, of encouraging him to be faithful in that particular. But I was really not a little sick, when the time came, and equally disappointed; for after all, in no ordinary degree, I did desire to "keep that passover;" albeit I knew that bonds and afflictions awaited me there, with a double portion of bitter herbs. But then the love of truth and Friends sometimes, through favor, casteth out fear, and maketh willing, yea, and more than willing, to suffer both for it and them. I know not why it is so (whether from our isolated, solitary condition, or otherwise), but I certainly never did experience so much of an enlargement of heart, and of the abounding of true and unfeigned love towards the whole household of faith, and to you, my dear friends, in particular, as of latter time. Truly this is what makes me so anxious to hear from you, as I cannot see you, which is more desirable, and, were it practicable on my part, would soon be realized. But prisoners must wait, if it may be, with patience, but not always or necessarily without hope. . . . . .

Having business in the neighborhood, I lately spent a night with our dear friends, Seth and Mary Davis. I found them more feeble in health than I had ever before seen them, though still about. They are, as might have been expected, greatly bowed down under a sense of their and the Church's great loss, in the removal of dear James Tucker. I passed W. G. S.'s door twice, and very much wished to have called there, but could not; and it was well I did not, for I broke down in Hilbourn Woods, about halfway from the head of Westport to the bridge, which made me very late home, and a very cold tedious time I had of it. W. S. has closed up his business there, and the prospect is that he will leave this yearly meeting, which I very much regret, and sincerely hope he will not himself suffer loss by it. Ah, it is a great point to know where our lot is cast, and to keep in it. I am more and more persuaded that if we, who are more immediately under bondage, suffering, and reproach, are but favored to keep the faith, and to abide in the patience, we shall "stand in our lot at the end of the days." Still, it is difficult to refrain from saying, the Lord hasten it in his time!

Jethro Mitchell has had another opportunity with me, of about two hours and a half, though he denied its being official; and I have also submitted to —— ——'s fallacious and unfruitful labors. She did try hard to convince me how dearly they all loved me, and how highly they esteemed me, desiring my progress in my calling, &c.; which her solemn asseverations, I was enabled to meet with direct evidence to the contrary. Some of the facts and circumstances thus adduced, she, as the shortest, easiest method, freely admitted were very improper in those who acted them; but still, she said their love and good will to me remained unchanged through all! She told me, I could not think how much the prospect of my disownment troubled her, she could not sleep at nights in consequence of it, could not bear to think of it, &c. To this I responded, that I neither doubted it troubled her, nor marvelled at it; and that I believed it would trouble her more yet, and be heavier and harder for her to bear, if it did not, with other things, prove more than she could bear. She said she wished the prospect was as hard to me as it was to her. I told her I would not have her think me insensible of the hardship and injustice of being deprived of my birthright without a cause; which I was not disposed to sell for a mess of pottage, nor at liberty to exchange, for another, the inheritance of my forefathers. But as I had labored after patience and resignation to whatever they might be permitted to do with me, I had found that which rendered hard things easy and bitter things sweet. This silenced her on this point, and she really seemed to feel it.

But the next day after I saw —— ——, being the day before the last preparative meeting, they hatched up a complaint; and Jethro having promised me a sight of it, but being ashamed to come with it himself, sent it by F. C.; but with a strict charge not to give or allow me to take a copy; though he informed me that it was to be presented the next day [which was not done], and expressed much surprise at the quietness and peace which I evinced on the occasion; saying that he thought, if they were all in as good a frame of mind, these things might be easily settled; and if the overseers could see me as he saw me, and hear what he had heard, he thought they would not be disposed to carry this thing any further. But I told him they had seen me under no other circumstances, neither had I manifested any different feelings; that I could truly say I felt no hardness towards any of them, nothing like revenge or retaliation, although they were disposed to persecute me and others to the very extent of their power, and were not therefore to be blamed for not going further; but on the contrary I really pitied them and deplored their condition (especially D. B.'s), believing they could do no other, in the spirit they were in; and that they were "like a troubled sea, which could not rest, but whose waters cast up mire and dirt" continually. . . . .

T. B. GOULD.

From Ezra Comfort to Thomas B. Gould.

Second month, 23d, 1844.

Dear Friend:

My mind is almost continually with you in your afflicted state, but I do not know what I can do more than to sympathize with you, which I think I can feelingly, having passed through a similar state of things.* When we are deeply engaged for the welfare of the Society and its members, then to be accounted as enemies to the truth, and evil-doers, dealt with and disowned from Society as such by those whom we have in time past taken sweet counsel with—very close are the conflicts and trials of such, especially when we see them trampling the order and testimonies of truth under their feet. Oh! this requires much patience, and deep indwelling upon the sure foundation,—but as this travail is kept to, and this ground maintained, clear I am that all things, that in Infinite Wisdom may be permitted or ordered to come upon us, will work together for good, not only for us, but for the cause of our dear Lord and Master; for He can control the destroyer and his evil designs, and turn them to His own glory, and bring a heavenly blessing upon us; for He worketh sometimes by ways as much higher than ours as the heavens are above the earth. This my soul knoweth right well, for He did open a way for my deliverance when or where I saw no way. So it will be with thee, and with all the rest of the Lord's faithful servants, as there is a keeping the word of his patience; for He will keep them in the hour of temptation, and glorious will be their crown of reward; while the enemies of truth will fret and weary themselves, and shall not prevail, but shall howl for very anguish of soul; which at times is the case with some of those who went from us, by the same outgoing spirit that is with you. It is the same spirit, though under a different covering, for the fruit that it brings forth is the very same. Oh! I saw it as clear as ever I saw the sun at noonday, those that are

* Ezra Comfort had suffered much persecution from the Hicksites, and been disowned by them in the early appearance of that schism.

led by it will fall, as they did with us, because they have no foundation. It is our grand enemy's delight, after he has exalted for a time, then to cast down,—thus great and grievous will be their fall!

I have often remembered our Saviour's testimony concerning the inhabitants of Jerusalem: "Oh! that thou hadst known, in this thy day, the things that belong to thy peace, but now they are hid from thine eyes." This being the case, such call evil good, and good evil. It is no marvel then that they persecute their Divine Master and His servants; nay, they cannot do otherwise but go on waxing worse and worse. I mourn for them, for they are in that state (the leaders of them) that the Apostle described, that have tasted and handled of the good Word of life, but have "fallen away." . . . . . .

I have heard they are about disowning thee. Heed it not,—keep near thy Divine Master, and He will enable thee to rejoice that thou art worthy to suffer for His name's sake; and He will enable thee to fill up thy measure of His sufferings which are left behind, for the body's sake, which is His Church. If they numbered Him among the transgressors, think it not strange if we are accounted as such. After the good Spirit departed from Saul because of transgressions, then it was that an evil spirit troubled him, and he sought to slay righteous David because his ways were upright, but he knew his were evil, and in his rage, Cain-like, slew the priests of the Most High without a cause, and in his jealousy and fury, hunted David to take his life, as a partridge is hunted in the mountains, even after he was convinced he had sinned and done wickedly. Ah! I have often thought of David's appeal to Saul, since I was in your land, when I have looked at the case of dear John Wilbur, and now at thine; for they are endeavoring to drive you from your "inheritance in the Lord," saying unto you by their conduct, "Go, serve other gods." As the end of Saul was, so will their spiritual end be, unless they repent; but as David trusted in the Lord, and kept His righteous law, He preserved him out of all evil, and set him on the throne, to reign over all Israel in Saul's stead. Thus it may be with you, my dear friends. The time may come, yes, I believe it will come, when, instead of their disowning you without a cause, you, or some of you, will have to disown them for their transgressions, as we had to do with those who went out from us, for they were not of us.

I have heard they have confirmed the judgment of the monthly meeting, by the quarter, in dear John Wilbur's case. I hope he will appeal to the yearly meeting, that all the members may get to know what an arbitrary spirit there is amongst you, and that all that may be unjustly disowned hereafter may likewise appeal. It is a duty these owe to the Society, and to the cause of Truth, let the result be what it may, and however humiliating and trying it may be. I hope the time will come when you may see the way (if that outgoing spirit continues to go on) to separate from them, and represent your situation to some other body. There is certainly a large number in the limits of your yearly meeting, who cannot unite with the course in which things are carried on amongst you; for the heavenly order which was established under divine direction by our early Friends, is totally laid waste in the yearly meeting, as well as in its subordinate branches. All is done or overruled by committees, and every one that cannot unite with such a course of procedure, and ventures to let his dissent be known, is accounted disorderly and out of unity. While this is the case—while these committees do all the business, first out of meetings, then in meetings—all concluded on out of meetings, and these conclusions carried through by the same persons in meetings, it is but a sham to hold such meetings! Such a state of things as there is in your yearly meeting, has never before been in any yearly meeting since we have been a people—a body wholly arbitrary, not governed by its own discipline, or its own decisions—which I was a witness to when in your meeting; but my desire is that all Friends, everywhere within your limits, may undauntedly and fearlessly (except the fear of the Lord, but in His fear, and in the authority which He gives) stand forth, and bear a faithful testimony against such an evil practice; for any one who has clear discernment must see that such a course of procedure, if pursued by that, and all other similar bodies, will ultimately destroy the Society; for no association can continue without order and government. Oh what a departure from Truth! For Truth always leads into a blessed order and heavenly government; but this outgoing spirit has always been a wrathful, turbulent, persecuting spirit. My very soul's desire is, that we who are favored to see these things, may be preserved in great watchfulness and fear, that we may be enabled to walk in uprightness amidst these accumulated trials, and show forth, by our meekness and humility, that we are following our meek, patient, and suffering Lord.

Please give my love to all our suffering friends as opportunity may offer. Tell them I am almost continually with them in spirit and in suffering. We are not exempt from trials here by the same restless spirit. I sometimes am ready to fear that our trials will be very heavy; but amidst these gloomy prospects, I am at times strengthened by a degree of living faith, that after this day of shaking is passed over—for I believe the time has come, and is coming, when not only the earth but the heavens also will be shaken—that there may not anything remain in Zion, the Church of Christ, but that which cannot be shaken. Oh, saith my soul, may the Lord hasten that glorious and happy day, when the mountain of his house shall be established on the top of the mountains! Then there will be again a flocking unto it, as there was in days that are past.

I have seen a letter written to Alice Knight by dear John Wilbur. I was renewedly comforted in hearing it read, being satisfied that he, amidst all the storms and tempests that have been permitted to beat against him, is still favored to keep on that sure, immovable, and eternal foundation, that never can be shaken by all the combined powers of darkness; and as he keeps on it, it will keep and preserve him unto the end, and after this scene of conflict is over, glorious will be his crown. And I desire to be his companion unto the end, even if it may be in bonds for the Gospel's sake. I shall always be glad to receive letters from him, thee, or any of my dear suffering friends that feel a freedom to write. . . . .

My love to R. Gardner, and all our dear suffering friends thereaway, has not abated from what it was when I mingled amongst them in person, but increased; and I hope it will increase, until we are bound up together in that bundle of life that will never be separated. And the tender feeling of love and life that I had in parting from thee and thy dear companion, I trust will never be erased from my memory whilst I remain in mutability.

Thy affectionate friend,

EZRA COMFORT.

FROM JOHN WILBUR TO T. B. G.

HOPKINTON, third month, 6th, 1844.

MY DEAR FRIEND, THOMAS B. GOULD:

. . . . How comforting, confirming, and strengthening, that truly patriarchal epistle, which thou hast copied from that man of God who has freely given himself up to be a fellow-sufferer with the suffering seed in this land! On my own part, I feel unworthy of the sympathies and fellowship of such a man; but more abundantly unworthy of the mercies and loving-kindness of Him, who not only visits His persecuted and suffering children with His own immediate manifestation of His peace-giving and life-giving presence, but also is pleased to raise up and prepare eminent servants and handmaidens, through an experimental partaking of the same cup of suffering, and by the constraining of His love and power, willingly to place themselves side by side with those who are placed as a mark for the archers, and to endure their part of the reproaches which have fallen on them. What shall we render?

Well, my dear Thomas, I found other comforting things on the sheet which thou sent me, besides the copy from our dear Ezra Comfort. I now allude to the account of thyself being so mercifully sustained and comforted, under the extreme pressure of persecution by false brethren. In this we mutually participate, and, as I trust, at times rejoice in the goodness of God, and give thanks to His blessed name, because He upholdeth and encampeth round about those whom He hath put forth in defence of the truth and His own exalted testimonies. May our faithfulness and obedience be commensurate, in some degree, with the greatness of His purposes, the glory of the cause, and the favors which He bestows! My almost constant prayer is, that He who hath called us to serve Him in the endurance of tribulations for His great name's sake, will be our keeper and our preserver through all; and that all may redound to His honor and to His own eternal glory. . . . .

J. WILBUR.

DRAFT OF A LETTER FROM T. B. G. TO ——.

NEWPORT, fourth month, 9th, 1844.

MY DEAR AND MUCH-ESTEEMED FRIEND:

. . . . It might not have been amiss if I had written ere they laid me under dealing, feeling as I did at different times, more particularly engaged to it, just previously to that circumstance, which may now render this unacceptable and improper; and if it should, it will only go into the scale with other weights and burdens which have nearly overbalanced thy poor correspondent, and which at times he is ready to fear will quite overbalance him.

I do not mean to complain, but if those who are hunting after my life, who are endeavoring to deprive me of my inheritance in the Lord and among His people, should be permitted so far to succeed as to change the feelings of the latter towards me, it would be grievous indeed; it would be cruel and doubly hard to bear; and I freely own to thee that I dread nothing more, except the loss of life itself. It seems a very serious matter to utter it, although it is strictly true, that in my extremity, I am sometimes ready to say: Even if my life is given me for a prey, what good shall it do me, or who shall show me any good? seeing "Israel" acknowledgeth me not! Ah! my life is bound up with my people! I was never more deeply and feelingly sensible of it than now, when on the very point of being outwardly separated from them. Oh! the bitterness of *their* anger, and the cruelty of their wrath, who would separate that which the Lord hath joined together! I am indeed, at times and seasons, when it pleaseth Him who is Lord of all, favored to see that they cannot effectually and permanently do it. Yet when He hideth Himself, and nothing can be seen but my grand enemy within, and his agents and servants without, how he does multiply and augment my fears in this and other respects! For he knoweth how tender I really am on this point; and my outward enemies know it too; and persuaded I am that they are not without hope that Friends will cast us off, as they have done and are doing.

But I will try to restrain this gush of personal feeling, though, until self be slain, it will frequently appear; and perhaps thou mayst excuse it, as I do not pretend to have conquered that foe; than which I often think and feel, we have, or I have, few greater or more formidable to overcome in this warfare. And I will venture to express a hope that you, at your approaching solemnity, may be enabled, not for the sake of the persons who suffer here, but for the cause' sake, for which, as I trust, they suffer, to do something, which may have a tendency to promote it, or at any rate to prevent its falling into disrepute. So far as we can see and judge, it is not gaining ground here. The timid, who have hoped against hope for some time, are falling back and joining the ranks of the aliens almost daily; and unless some decisive measures are taken soon, things will undoubtedly get worse and worse.

I find that many very choice Friends with you, have strong hope that the two appeal cases, coming before our next yearly meeting, will produce a powerful effect therein. But it does not appear probable, to those who have had perhaps a better understanding of the way in which things are managed here, than they could well have, unless they had been eye-witnesses from the beginning, and so had seen the "material," as one Friend said, of which this yearly meeting is composed. Many who have perhaps some sincerity left, are so terror-stricken, that it would seem to require almost if not quite a miracle, to enable them to rise above it, and miracles are not expected in these days. . . . . . .

My dear Martha and myself have, within a few days, returned from a visit to our mutually dear friend, John Wilbur. We spent about a week in Hopkinton and Westerly, to our great satisfaction; and Friends there are generally well. Dear J. Wilbur does not appear to have contracted even the smell of fire upon his garments; though so long in the furnace heated seven times hotter than it was wont to be heated. I thought I never saw him clothed with so much brightness before. In sitting with him, an expression of William Penn's concerning George Fox I think, was much in my mind: "That his very presence expressed a religious awe." And his gentleness, condescension, meekness, and humility, as well as his patience under suffering, and resignation to it, which is not in this day perhaps often exceeded, if it be equalled, are truly engaging, very instructive, and encouraging to those who have an eye open to see through the clouds of dust which have been raised against him. His precious wife has been quite ill this spring, but is now much better in health. His and her friends have been apprehensive, I believe, that he would be bereaved of his true help-meet, whose real worth is best known by those who are most intimately acquainted with her. . . . . . .

From T. B. G. to Ezra Comfort.

Newport, 14th of 4th month, 1844.

My endeared aged Friend, Ezra Comfort:

Twice, since I received thy very kind and acceptable letter, I have commenced writing to thee, and in both instances, covered no inconsiderable portion of my sheets; but meeting with unexpected hindrances in completing what I wished to say, they have been laid aside, like the writer, as useless and out of date. I now merely mention it to let thee see that I have not been unmindful of thy kindness and paternal care, of which, indeed, I feel wholly unworthy, and also of addressing thee in this way. Neither do I seem to have anything to say now, which can be interesting; and yet it does appear as if some acknowledgment was due to thee.

. . . . It is now more than a week since my dear wife and self returned from a visit to dear J. Wilbur and some others of our friends in Hopkinton and Westerly. We found them generally well in all respects; and I believe it was to our mutual satisfaction. It was truly instructive and edifying to be with J. W., and to behold his meekness and humility, patience under suffering, and resignation to it. The savor of life is to be felt in his company; and the expressions of David seem verified in him, "They that be planted in the house of the Lord shall flourish in the courts of our God; they shall still bring forth fruit in old age; they shall be fat and flourishing." For notwithstanding he hath refused the portion of the king's meat, and the polluted wine also, yet he hath thriven upon the pulse and water, yea, upon the bread of adversity and the water of affliction.

My mind is much with you, in this the time of your yearly meeting, not without some feeling like the prophet, when he said, "O Judah! keep thy solemn feasts, perform thy vows:" believing also, that "in Judah God is known, that His name is great in Israel, that His habitation is in Jacob, and His dwelling-place in Zion." And in the strength of Him who reigneth King in the midst of her, may you stand and abide; clearly manifesting to her and your enemies, that you "have a strong city," and that "salvation is appointed for walls and bulwarks." And so, a banner being given you because of the truth, you will appear terrible unto them, and they will flee before you as the chaff is driven by the wind from the threshing-floor. But lest I should exceed my bounds, I will forbear. Nevertheless my cup seems full; and is it strange that we should fix our eyes steadfastly upon you, and expect somewhat of you?

I have thought, if you could only address an epistle to this yearly meeting, clearly pointing out the ground and cause of things with us, and remonstrating against those things, that great benefit would result from it, if it were written in the power and authority of that Spirit which is as a sword; and which is not only "a discerner of the thoughts and intents of the heart," but is able to make a separation between that which is of the Lord, and that which is not of Him. For these people, however they may and do intrench themselves in their strongholds, are exceeding sore, and very jealous of their honor, as they esteem it. They despise correction, and will not bear reproof; both of which, as the regular correspondents of this yearly meeting, you have a right to give: and are you not bound, if the original object of a correspondence between different yearly meetings is carried out, to give it? It does seem as if there was never more necessity for the use of great plainness of speech. Great would be the relief to those who are suffering here, and apparently without a remedy, as it respects the members of this yearly meeting. For although I perceive that several valuable Friends amongst you have strong hope that those with us, who do not unite with the proceedings of our adversaries, will, when they get to be more fully informed, rise up and rebel against them, and put them down; yet those who have had perhaps a better opportunity of judging, do not see any reasonable ground for such a hope, unless there should be some very efficient help from abroad.

I believe it would be as easy for the Ethiopian to change his skin, as for the class of Friends referred to to rise above the fear of man, and the terror by which they are stricken down. Indeed, there seems to be, even among those of whom we had hoped better things, an increasing disposition to get over, swallow down, and reconcile, or rather, to be reconciled to, things which they at least have known to be wrong, and in direct violation of the truth. And is there not great reason to fear that such will remain servants forever? Oh, this desire for ease, together with the fear of man, is a snare into which many, very many, have fallen, and are falling—for the number is apparently increasing! And our adversaries are very busy, throwing dust continually into their eyes, and heaping reproaches upon us. No stone is left unturned by them: their engines are constantly at work, both day and night; yea, sea and land are encompassed to make one proselyte.

While, on our part, nothing is done, save what may be accomplished by an endeavor to suffer patiently; for, comparatively speaking, we open not our mouths, but rather lie in sackcloth and ashes, although, it may be, "unburied, in the streets of the great city, where also our Lord was (and is) crucified," as silent witnesses against them and their doings! Oh! the mockings, scoffings, and revilings which we meet with! Great, too, are their rejoicings over us, in our suffering state; shaking their heads at us as they pass, and saying, in a language well understood by some, "Ah, ha! so would we have it!"

But there is, through adorable mercy, much consolation in the assurance, that if they should be permitted to "kill the body" (which, in some instances, seems not wholly improbable), there is no more they can do, unless these things should unhappily have the effect to drive us off from the sure Foundation. And great indeed is the danger felt to be; for the grand enemy within is as busy as his servants and ministers without; and when his purpose is not effected by his roaring as a lion, then the form of a serpent is assumed, in its crooked windings and twinings round the poor and ofttimes beclouded traveller in a wilderness of woe, because of the absence of Him who alone can cause the "reeds and rushes" to spring up "in the habitation of dragons where each lay," and the desert to "rejoice and blossom as the rose." At such seasons, when He is thus pleased to appear in His own divine Light and Life, and to discover and make manifest the enemy by the light of His countenance, and to quicken, deliver, and save the soul from the power of the serpent by His life, then indeed we can be exceeding joyful in all our tribulations. But it is extremely difficult to keep the faith and patience, when left as it were to one's own; which does happen, or is permitted, while great darkness is felt over all the land, as from the sixth hour unto the ninth, and we are compelled to cry out in very anguish, "Why hast Thou forsaken me?" But, who is sufficient for these things? and, who shall be able to stand?—are queries almost continually arising in my mind; and truly I am often, yea, very often, greatly distressed with fear, lest the serpent who beguiled Eve may have beguiled me, and that I shall not be able to stand, but shall become a prey to my enemies.

Thou seest, my dear and truly honored friend, that I have written to thee in great freedom. Not that I consider it a light matter to address one so far above me, in every respect; but because, if I write at all, I must do it freely, and as things present; for I know not how to write a studied, formal letter. And as a kind father sometimes allows his little child to use freedom with him, and excuses it, if he goes too far, in respect of his youth and inexperience, so I hope thou mayst feel towards me; who am the least and hindmost of the flock, if indeed one of that number; and having, at any rate, no other claim than a feeling sense that I do love the brethren, and a true willingness, yea, a strong desire, to be in subjection to them, however stubborn and rebellious I may be accounted by those who say they are Jews, and are not. And if thou shouldst feel inclined to write to me, I beseech thee spare not any advice, reproof, or correction that thou mayst feel disposed to give, in any respect or as to any particular; for I could receive it from thee, and that too, as a great kindness: and I do wish thou wouldst write to me whenever and as often as thou mayst find freedom. Thy last was a greater comfort to me, than I have language to convey an adequate idea of. Having passed through a similar trial thyself, to that which I am now under, though not in so much weakness, thou canst understand the temptations peculiar to it: but it does seem as if none but those who have travelled in the same path, can fully realize the hair-breadth trials to which such are subjected. And I can truly say, that next to the loss of the Divine love and favor, comes in the fear of being estranged and separated from His people, cast out upon the wide world, without either house or home, in a visible church sense, and therefore exposed to greater dangers and manifold privations. Yet I dare not compromise or retract the ground which has given my adversaries so much offence; although, I doubt not, great weakness has been manifested, in my yet sincere endeavors to maintain that ground.

I cannot but hope that thou mayst be required to come back to this Boston government, although, in a manner, "banished upon pain of death." . . . . I do hope, if it should be laid upon thee, thou wilt give up to it, nothing doubting. But do not misunderstand me, as to the ground of my speaking of it. . . . .

My dear parents and sister unite in dear love to thee, in which my Martha and I would affectionately join them, and also to thy wife and every member of thy family, as if named. And so I conclude,

Thy unworthy but sincere friend,

T. B. Gould.

To Peleg Mitchell.

Newport, 5th mo., 12th, 1844.

My dear Friend:

. . . . Without having any doubt as to the legality of the will, or our proceedings under it [the Greene Trust], I do dread a lawsuit, even more than disownment by Rhode Island Monthly Meeting, which will probably be realized in the course of this month. But this prospect, &c., has cost me more than any one, I apprehend, can form a full idea of, unless they have travelled the rough and thorny path under similar weakness and infirmities. . . . . It would be well for all, who are in any wise concerned in that cause which requires unqualified decision, to consider, when they let manifest calls for it slip by without action, that a "more convenient season" may never occur. I cannot doubt, that if those who saw these evils creeping in, had been quite faithful in the onset, they never would have reached their present enormity. But I do not mean to be at all personal in these remarks; I merely throw out a general hint, in the great freedom which I have ever allowed myself to use when addressing thee.

We had not before heard of your afflicting bereavement, in which we have truly sympathized with you. But, ah! how little can be availingly said on this subject!—I have sometimes thought, the less the better. It was the remark of some one, and I think, of Thomas Clarkson, that the language of real grief was always short. And should not the language of sympathy and condolence, on occasions like the present, be short too? When I came to that part of thine, how involuntarily my heart throbbed for our darling little prattler, and I sought to make the case my own! . . . .

C. T. and D. K. attended this meeting, two weeks ago yesterday. Their communications were very striking, and David's remarkably so. He commenced with the decree of the king Nebuchadnezzar, and the published consequences of the lack of obedience; the faithfulness of the three children, their preservation, and the honor which resulted therefrom to their Almighty Preserver in the fiery trial to which they were subjected; dwelling upon it, as also on the destruction of the image which he saw in his dream, by the stone cut out of the mountain; saying, the day of the Lord was coming upon everything which was high and lifted up, upon all the high mountains and gilded towers; and that although the image was in part made of gold, yet even this, which was accounted the most precious of metals, was dashed in pieces and destroyed by that little stone, &c. He then spoke of Daniel, and his refusing to obey the king; that he still continued to call upon the name of his God in a public manner; but, he said, the king Darius had been unwittingly brought to sign this decree, through the influence which the presidents, governors, councillors, &c., had over him; and when he found how seriously it affected Daniel whom he loved, he set his heart upon him to deliver him; but then came in the presidents, the governors, the councillors, and the captains, with the argument that the laws of the Medes and Persians could not be changed; and so they prevailed with the king and over Daniel. Then he expatiated upon his deliverance, and the exaltation of the name and power of the Lord thereby, applying it, in a very remarkable manner, to some of us; who knew of states and circumstances existing in that meeting, of which most probably he was wholly ignorant, as to outward information; for he assorted altogether with our adversaries, on this Island,

and in Newport put up at M. H. B.'s. It did seem more like ministry than anything I had heard in a long while, and so did their communications in the afternoon, at Portsmouth, whither I went. . . . It is near one o'clock in the morning, after a laborious day in other respects; but it is really pleasant to converse with thee once more in this way. . . . Farewell.

T. B. GOULD.

TO ETHAN FOSTER.

NEWPORT, 10th month, 28th, 1844.

. . . . . I cannot divest myself of an impression that thou, my dear friend, hast had to tread in very low places, and to drink as of the bitter waters of Marah; and the language has sweetly arisen, "Let thy Urim and thy Thummim be with thy Holy One." If it be a season of conflict, of deep and painful conflict and strife, keep thy eye singly to Him who is both light and perfection. Do not, oh! do not cast away thy confidence and the shield of faith, lest thou find to thy cost (as I have done) that without faith it is impossible, either to please God, or to stand fast in the day of trial. Being, through the wiles of the grand enemy of all good, divested of the shield of faith, the poor way-worn and beclouded traveller is left exposed and defenceless to his every attack; then, many and grievous are the wounds which he inflicts with his barbed arrows and cruel darts, till one is ready to give all up as lost, and to listen to his teaching, and feed upon it, to the great loss and weakening of the soul! I do not throw out these hints as charges against thee, by any means; and I may be altogether mistaken in supposing thou art or hast been tried in this way; but having had some reason to know what a hard taskmaster he is, by the things which I have suffered at his hands, after he had got my attention fixed upon his temptations and snares (instead of keeping it to that, and upon that, which would have discovered them, and preserved from them), I felt inclined to encourage thee to press through the crowd of difficulties, dangers, and besetments, even to Him in whom the living virtue and the blessed healing and preserving power is; that so thou mayst not suffer as I have done for the want of it. It is a blessed and happy state, so to keep the watch in the Light, as to walk in the shining of it with great fulness of spirit, as S. Crisp said. Here the enemy cannot hurt or destroy. But I do not speak as having attained; far from it; nevertheless this is the mark, this is the prize of our high calling.

Last fourth-day evening I received, in all probability, the last visit from my committee, viz.: E. W. and wife, J. S., and F. C. They were extremely arbitrary in their behavior, and manifested much bitterness of feeling, with the exception of Elizabeth W. . . . . . On sitting down together, some time was passed in silence, which was at length broken by Edward saying they had come to see what I had to offer to the committee. But I told them I was waiting to see what they had to offer, and I was willing to hear what they might have to say, desiring them to speak freely. Their business, they said, was to get an acknowledgment from me; that was their business. I told them, I must first know my offence. They said, the overseers and the monthly meeting would require an acknowledgment, a written acknowledgment of what I said to it and them; that I knew what it was, well enough; there was no need of talking about it, or of my seeing the complaint—which I had called for, and which they said they had forgotten to bring with them. I asked them, if it was not necessary to exhibit their charges in writing, why it was necessary for me to make a written acknowledgment? They said, because the overseers and the monthly meeting would not be satisfied unless it was in writing; that they were not unwilling to show me the complaint, and never had been! "Why then did you refuse to do so?" Do please mark the answer given by J. S.: "Because David Buffum said thee had seen it!" I will not go into all that was said, pro and con; but I told them that I was the aggrieved party (going into many particulars which I need not name to thee, and which they were not very willing to hear, continually interrupting me), and might with more reason require an acknowledgment from them. They said that I had declared my disunity with Friends, that I had said I had no unity with the monthly meeting. This I denied, in language as moderate as I could, and to meet the case. They then undertook to justify the charge, by referring to my objections to particular subjects before the monthly meeting, &c.; this, they said, was what they founded the charge of disunity upon. But I told them that I could name many eminent disciplinarians who united in the sentiment, although I would confine myself to one—T. E.—a Friend who entertained very different views from myself with regard to Joseph John Gurney, but who told me that, to lay a Friend under dealing for having entertained or expressed different views from others with regard to the transaction of the affairs of the Church, or for having objected to particular things (which is the right of all to do), was unheard of in our Society. They did not like to hear this.

Edward said that J. J. G. had gone home; we had nothing to do with him, or he with it (which was more fully spoken to and explained by me); and he immediately changed ground, and charged me with having labored for many years, by writing and showing letters, and otherwise, to produce a schism in the Society. I told him, I was conscientiously clear of the charge; that the object and end of my labors had been to prevent a schism, &c.; but inquired if this was a part of the original complaint, and asked if he had ever seen anything which I had written, and called upon him to produce the letters he spoke of, that I might know what they were. He said they could be produced, in a manner which showed that they could not be by him, and that he merely did it to frighten me; but without producing that effect; and then, with rapid motion, he charged me with having planned the separation in Fall River, and advised and assisted in its accomplishment. But I told him, the first knowledge I had of that event was communicated to me in detail by one of their own number, Job Sherman, and of course I denied the charge. But he asked me, if I was not very intimate with Israel Buffinton? to which, regardless of consequences, I answered in the affirmative, adding, "He is a very particular friend of mine!" They continued repeatedly to press me to an acknowledgment; and I continued to show them wherein I had been aggrieved, and how zealously they had labored to ensnare me, and to make me an offender. After a great deal more, of this kind and similar, had passed, Edward proposed to go, and F. C. thought it was not edifying to stay; but Job wished Friends to sit a little in silence; for which, if thou hadst been present, thou wouldst not have suspected me of unwillingness, after what I had heard. And so, after a little while, E. tried to preach to me, which was I think the first time she had said anything after the first silence; and she now seemed to find hard work of it, although I must say she was moderate, respectful, and even tender, so far as words go. Another short pause succeeded, and they made another motion to leave; when I said, that I would be glad if they would sit a little longer; which they appeared to do willingly, and for some considerable length of time; until I was constrained to open my mouth amongst them, in much brokenness and fear, and in a few words; wherein an appeal was made to the Searcher of hearts, who knoweth what is in man, and needeth not that any should testify unto Him of man; with the expression of a fervent desire, that He would be pleased to furnish with wisdom to guide amidst the storm, and strength to endure and stand firm, that so His name might not be dishonored. The feeling which had spread, before and after this, was peculiarly solemn, and it did seem as if E. could not wholly resist it, and was constrained by it to respond to and endorse what I had said. But this was more than Edward could bear, even from her; and so he kicked right out, and said, that he had been looking for an evidence of the right thing, but he could not feel it. This was at parting; and I told him, as I had occasionally done before in the course of the evening, that it did require a right disposition of mind and a qualification in himself, to feel and appreciate the evidence of divine regard which the Great Master was pleased to afford. They urged me again, to send in an acknowledgment before the monthly meeting next fifth-day; when, they said, they should report according to their feelings. But I told them, I did not feel like writing one, that night, and so we parted. The select meeting passed the next day, without anything of note being done or attempted: but D. B. was very busy, that afternoon and the next morning, seeking interviews with my committee, in order, as I doubted not, to direct their movements and superintend their report. Most probably they will finish this part of the business on fifth-day. . . . . .

As respects a division in the quarterly meeting, I was intending to express to thee my fears, if it does take place, whether it can be carried out satisfactorily in the different monthly meetings. . . . . .

With dear love to thee and thine, and your cousins down town, farewell.

T. B. G.

The events at this time transpiring in the Society at large, and particularly developing in his section of it, pressed heavily on his mind, and at times greatly affected his bodily health; though it is evident from his letters, that through all he was graciously supported by that Arm of divine power and goodness on which he relied; and that his faith was from time to time mercifully renewed, when it was almost ready to fail. His wife, writing to their brother and sister in Ohio, in the eleventh month, 1844, thus described his condition, and briefly alluded to some of the causes of his sore trials.

. . . "I had wished my Thomas to write to you at this time; but he is so depressed on account of these things, that it is as much as I can do to keep him up at all. The burdens resting upon him of latter time, have been greater than he could bear. His case is still before this monthly meeting, and the committee keep coming from time to time; and have latterly been so abusive and insulting, that I could scarcely suffer them to continue in the house. But he treats them well, and abides in the everlasting patience. Truly, if ever 'patience had its perfect work,' I think it has in him." . . .

And about the same date, Thomas wrote to his brother-in-law, Joshua Maule, as follows:—

. . . "I would freely give thee an account of things as they transpire, if I had time and ability; but the former I am very much limited for, and the latter extremely deficient in, in every respect. Those things, referred to by my Martha, have a powerful effect upon my health, and writing is extremely irksome and very injurious to me. Sometimes, when I otherwise might do it, I cannot write at all, such is the rush of blood to my head, and the disordered state of my nervous system altogether. My liver also is much diseased, and although I have been hard at work all day, it has been very painful even to walk about. What the end will be, or when, I cannot tell; but I often think it will soon come. My great desire is, that the measure of suffering may be filled, and that the prize may be gained. But it is a great matter, so to walk as to obtain, in the midst of this crooked and perverse generation." . .

The separation of the innovating party from the true Society of Friends in New England, commenced in the autumn of 1844; a disorderly secession having been effected by them (through the interference of the committee of the yearly meeting), in Swanzey Monthly Meeting at Fall River, a branch of Rhode Island Quarterly Meeting, to which Thomas B. Gould belonged. This secession, the fruit of the determined efforts to support the cause of J. J. Gurney, spread through New England Yearly Meeting, sweeping large multitudes along in its headlong course; and T. B. Gould was brought into very deep concern and exercise of mind, that the remnant which had stood faithful to the ancient principles of the Society, and were now left much stripped and scattered, might be enabled to sustain their meetings to the honor of truth.

FROM T. B. G. TO ETHAN FOSTER.

NEWPORT, 11th mo., 19th, 1844.

MY DEAR FRIEND:

In these times of great and awful shaking, when it not

only *seems* as if everything that can be shaken will be shaken, but when it really is so,—and those who have stood hitherto have need of all the strength and encouragement which may be and is doubtless derived, in this day as it was formerly among those who feared the Lord, from a frequent speaking one unto another in His fear,—I thought it might not be amiss for one of the least and hindmost of the flock, again to call unto thee, and to inquire of thee in the language, but I trust not in the spirit, of those who stood upon the mount of Esau: "Watchman! what of the night?" It may however serve no other purpose, in the present instance, than to let thee know that I am looking for tidings, while I communicate a few. . . . .

. . . But if the quarterly meeting had only directed the monthly meetings to adjourn in such manner as to accommodate their committee, it would have covered and obviated many difficulties in regard to meeting, which will now undoubtedly occur, both in this monthly meeting and that of Providence, and, I fear, insurmountable difficulties, in our present weak, stripped, and scattered condition. But it does appear to me that you may, at Hopkinton, with propriety, after the separation shall have taken place in Greenwich Monthly Meeting, change the place of holding your meeting for worship there, and thus get rid of such heads as you now meet under; always provided that it shall appear best and right to do so, when met under the canopy of Divine Wisdom. In a general way, it strikes me that Friends had better patiently endure until after the yearly meeting. If I could believe that our women would endure the exposure of meeting in the open air at Portsmouth, at this inclement season of the year, I should think best that they do so patiently, and good might come of it; but I doubt their being able to do it, or to abide a contest for the house each time. Thou mayst think this a needless burdening of to-day with the weight of futurity; but I cannot help looking at the difficulties, as well as at the advantages of our present condition for some there, inasmuch as the day of our deliverance from them seems to have dawned,—"The morning cometh, and also the night." I want to know thy judgment of these things. It never was at any time, perhaps, more important that we should be guided in wisdom and by wisdom; whether we are owned by any other yearly meeting or not, which I much doubt will take place very soon, if ever. . . . .

With dear love to thee and thine, with those above named and their families, in which my dear M. unites, I must conclude, and remain thy sincere friend,

THOS. B. GOULD.

TO JOHN WILBUR.

NEWPORT, 19th of 12th month, 1844.

MY DEAR FRIEND:

. . . . We have felt much solid satisfaction and comfort in the attendance of our religious meetings; several of them have been mercifully owned in a remarkable manner, though held in silence until last first-day, when He, who openeth and none can shut, set before me an open door, and there was much brokenness apparent in several who were in attendance, in a particular manner. . . . . It was truly one of those seasons for which we have cause to be thankful, and from which we may take courage; notwithstanding the rage of our adversaries, and that increasingly, in order to stop that which is beyond them; for they, even they, are limited. . . . .

The weight of things, as thou must see, rests heavily upon a few, and the responsibility is great, which I would gladly divide, and more too. I can truly say, I find the cross as great as ever, and a deeply settled aversion and unwillingness to take it up; still there is something which compels, and it feels increasingly constraining and diffusive; but lest I go too far, I will not add, even to thee, whom I look upon as a father indeed; and in the scarcity of such, perhaps thou wilt excuse the simplicity and freedom of a little child; and believe me to be, in all sincerity, truly thine, with love unchanged.

T. B. GOULD.

To Peleg Mitchell.

Newport, 30th of 12th mo., 1844.

My very dear Friend:

Few letters have been more truly acceptable or deeply interesting, than one which I received from thee of the 8th ult.; and I fully intended to have written ere this; although I did purposely omit an immediate reply, on account of some little indecision for a time, as to whether it might not be proper for me to be in New Bedford at the time of your quarterly meeting, when I hoped to have met thee. And knowing that our dear, tried, but faithful friend, J. Wilbur, was intending a visit to your island [Nantucket] soon after our quarterly meeting, and that he could better inform thee and others there of the events of that eventful day, than I could by letter or otherwise, there did not seem to be so much necessity for me to speak of them. But as thou hast not probably had as good an opportunity to hear from the monthly meetings, I wished to have given thee some account of them; but have been so pressed with cares and concernments of different kinds, that I could not seem to do it when I wished and as I wished.

Thou mayst however have heard about the visits of the committee of the quarterly meeting as sustained by Friends, to the different monthly meetings. So, before I speak of that, I will say, that the separatists carried complaints against my Martha, my father, and cousin John Mitchell, into our preparative meeting immediately following the quarter, on account of their *having, as they said, attended a separate quarterly meeting;* and our Friends' endeavors to prevent these charges from being sent forward to the monthly meeting, having proved unavailing, both men and women remained in the house, after the others had gone through with their business (having declared their intention to do so, *upon their minuting these charges*), and held the preparative meeting in the order of the Society; but not without great opposition and much abuse, from those disorderly and intolerant people. . . . A separation also took place in Western and Hopkinton Preparative Meetings upon similar grounds, before the next monthly meeting occurred after the quarter, viz.: their persisting in entering and forwarding complaints against Othniel Foster and his wife (I think), in the one, and Thomas and Phebe Foster in the other, for having attended and sustained the quarterly meeting. I know not what you may think of this, but Friends here thought the time for effectual resistance had then come, and that otherwise they would certainly give up the ground which our Friends had taken in the quarterly meeting, by suffering them to be laid under dealing for sustaining the same.

The committee of the quarterly meeting first attended Providence Monthly Meeting, and were enabled to sustain it; although they encountered great abuse, and met with continual interruption from J. M., W. J., and many others; who, notwithstanding they adjourned their meeting, in consequence of the presence of the committee and others who, they said, were under dealing, yet they did not leave the house, but stayed there during the whole time that Friends were engaged in the transaction of their business (as I was told by several of the committee), warning them out of the house, in every character and office they could think of, and ridiculing and upbraiding them on account of the smallness of their number, the meanness of their appearance, and the diffidence, &c., of their clerk. And not only so, but the young men would, sometimes, hiss, groan, and laugh outright at them, looking up at J. M. for approbation; who would nod his assent and laugh with them, in true Hicksite style. Hicksite, did I say? Nay; this is worse than Hicksism; for *they* never did claim to be exclusively "the body," or that they were infallible! But how universal and lasting is the authorized criterion, notwithstanding it seems to be very generally overlooked or unheeded by those who, "having eyes, see not,"—"By their fruits ye shall know them!"

Rhode Island Monthly Meeting, which was held at Newport, occurred the next day after that of Providence, which occasioned our friends a hard drive to get here, but divers of them came. The men's monthly meeting, at this season of the year, is held in the committee-room over the little part of the house; and at the close of the public meeting, when our Friends attempted to ascend the stairs, they found a strong guard of the Gurneyites posted thereon, who told them, without exception, they could not go up; and they actually forbade those whom they did not even pretend to have laid under dealing! But there were some who argued the case with them until they were fain to admit that they had not power to keep them out, and, to cover their shame, finally told them they might go in; but reply was made that they should not be free to do so unless their friends too might be admitted. These went far enough to see that they had a pensioned naval officer, though of low degree, standing by the door at the top of the stairs, holding the hasp over it, and J. F. M. at his side, to give him the necessary information as to who might go in. . . .

. . . . Our men Friends, being thus excluded, sat down quietly in the large cold room below, where the men's yearly meeting is held; and having proceeded to appoint a clerk, and make a minute of the acceptable presence of the quarterly meeting's committee, as well as some others explanatory of their present situation and circumstances, they concluded to adjourn, to meet again at two o'clock that afternoon at my father's house; and having given the women this information, they adjourned accordingly.

The women were differently circumstanced; not being compelled to move, they could not be got rid of so easily; so after the clerk had opened the meeting, the quarterly meeting's committee laid the minute of their appointment on the table; which, as might have been expected, was not noticed; but they proceeded for some time with my Martha's case without noticing her presence, although they must have known she was there. At length, on the acceptance of the minute of the quarterly meeting being urged (I think), as well as objection being made to what they were doing in regard to Martha, they began with vehemence to request her to withdraw; and the clerk then said she did not know of her being present, which it required some of J. J. G.'s "simple faith,—mere credence" to believe! But sister Lydia now stood up and said, that as the clerk had refused to recognize the minute of the quarterly meeting, or the presence of its committee, and as she had persisted in entering a complaint on the minutes against an individual, on account of her having united with others in sustaining the quarterly meeting, after a portion of its members had separated themselves from it, she would inquire whether the time had not come for Friends to appoint a clerk who would serve the meeting in subordination to the quarterly meeting, according to discipline and good order (or words to this import), and proposed the appointment of Martha S. Gould; which being united with, she was accordingly appointed, when they proceeded in much the same manner as the men did (only both meetings were held in the same room at the same time), until they received information from the men of their conclusion to adjourn, when they also adjourned, to meet again at our house, at the same hour that the men met at father's.

At the adjournment, the men took my case into consideration (as it stood referred to this monthly meeting), and after full investigation and solid consideration, concluded to dismiss it, and to restore me to my rights; the women's meeting having been consulted and uniting therein; and both men and women made minutes, embracing the peculiar circumstances of the case, and the irregular and ill-founded manner in which it had been introduced into that meeting, and continued from month to month, by those who had now separated themselves from Friends.

After the women's meeting had concurred herein, and the minute had been completed, they called me into the meeting, and I took my seat once more among them; having lived to see fulfilled an impression made on my mind at the time of their laying me under dealing, and which I ventured to mention to our friends, Seth and Mary Davis, as well as some others (I think); that there would be some change in the posture of things ere they got through with me, so that I should not have to appeal; and I even went so far as to say to them, that I should not be disowned by the Society: howbeit those people made a minute against me that day. But it did seem to me not a little remarkable that they themselves should have produced a separation, and that it should, in the ordering or overruling of things, have extended as far as the quarterly meeting, ere they seemed to have power to do it; for the will was not wanting years ago. However, no tongue could utter, nor the pen of the most ready writer describe, what I have had to pass through, and more especially during the latter part of the time of their dealing with me.

Friends also took into solid consideration the state and condition of Newport Particular Meeting; and apprehending the time had fully come for it to be held apart from those people who have possession and entire control of our meeting-houses, concluded that it should be held, "until a different arrangement can be made," at our house, at the usual hours on first and fifth-days; which has been since done, to the great relief and comfort of Friends, as well as of some others who meet with us.

As the minute of the appointment of the quarterly meeting's committee to visit subordinate meetings authorized them to act therein on behalf of the quarter, in rendering them such "advice and assistance as circumstances might seem to require and way open for;" and Friends having been at this time forcibly excluded from their usual meeting-room, and having no reason to expect anything better at the next month, when the monthly meeting would in course be held at Portsmouth; and our friend William Boyd of that town, although not a member of our Society (though his wife is), having witnessed these and other their acts of intolerance, and having freely offered his house to hold the monthly meeting in, and thus opened the way for it; the quarterly meeting's committee were united in judgment that it would be best for us to adjourn to meet there at the usual time in the twelfth month, and to hold the public meeting there too, at the same time as heretofore; and a minute was accordingly and regularly made in both men's and women's meetings to this effect. And before I leave this subject, I must be allowed to say that I have seldom witnessed more weight and solemnity over a meeting, than during the time these two propositions were under consideration.

Greenwich Monthly Meeting did not occur until after

ours, and by this time the Gurneyites had laid nearly or quite all the members of the quarterly meeting's committee under dealing; nevertheless, they went through with all their business in their presence, without an adjournment, and so, according to their own confession, committed another violation of the discipline, which they seem to consider themselves at liberty to do, whenever they please. Upon the minute of the quarterly meeting being laid on the table in the men's meeting, and rejected, Friends proceeded to appoint a clerk and open the meeting, and then waited patiently till the others had got through; when they were enabled to transact their business to a good degree of satisfaction, and without much, if any, disturbance from their adversaries, although R. G. and several others stayed during the whole time; but for some reason they did not think fit to act as their brethren did at Providence. . . . . I believe the women did not appoint a clerk until the others had left the house. Thus thou seest, my dear friend, the monthly meetings in this quarter have all been sustained. . . . .

Speaking of the sanguine expectations of our friends there [in Philadelphia], of those people giving back and coming over to us, I am free to acknowledge that I am not so much looking for an increase that way, as from the highways and hedges. Several items in thy letter tended to revive the hope, and confirm the belief, which has been raised in my heart, and with irresistible force again and again, and from time to time, during the course of these years of deep trial and proving, yea, even at times of the deepest trial, and when things, as to all outward appearance, and humanly speaking, were at the worst; that there would be an increase of faithful standard-bearers and burden-bearers gathered into the true sheepfold of rest, and the green pastures of life, even to sit under the free and immediate teachings of Christ, the great Shepherd and Bishop of souls, every man under his own vine and fig-tree, where nothing could hurt them or make them afraid; for nothing can hurt or destroy in the Lord's holy mountain. And how sweetly and encouragingly has the language been sounded in my spiritual ear: "Strangers shall stand and feed your flocks, and the sons of the alien shall be your ploughmen and your vinedressers." But, in that day when the Lord of the harvest and of the vineyard shall accomplish this, His "strange work," and bring to pass "His strange act," and incomprehensible to the eye of man's wisdom, yet neither strange nor impossible to and with him who calleth them that are not as those that are, that no flesh may glory in His presence, or have the praise of His works,—well will it be if those who account themselves, and are too generally accounted, the children of the kingdom, are not cast out! . . .

Thy sincere friend,
THOMAS B. GOULD.

TO JOSHUA AND SARAH MAULE.

NEWPORT, 16th of third month, 1845.

MY DEAR BROTHER AND SISTER:

. . . . [One of you] inquired as to the progress of the separation. It has not yet extended beyond the limits of Rhode Island Quarterly Meeting, and probably will not until after the yearly meeting. This quarter, since the dissolution of South Kingstown Monthly Meeting, is composed of four monthly meetings, viz.: Rhode Island, Greenwich, Swanzey, and Providence. In Rhode Island Monthly Meeting only twenty adults remain with Friends decidedly, although several others decline attending either meeting, professing to be waiting for the action or decision of other yearly meetings. Only one member of old Greenwich Monthly Meeting remains with Friends; but there are at least fifty adults (including some very aged and infirm Friends) who were formerly members of South Kingstown Monthly Meeting: quite as many (and I believe more) in Swanzey Monthly Meeting, to which may be added several undecided yet: and in Providence Monthly Meeting only thirteen. Here, again, are several undecided persons, and from among these, now and then, one comes straggling over to us; but I have not yet heard of one who stood with us at the time of the division, that has since gone over to them. But there were, I think, seventy persons who signed the appeal against the dissolution of South Kingstown Monthly Meeting, some of whom did eventually go with the Gurneyites. In all these enumerations, both sexes are included. The four monthly meetings have all been sustained; some of the preparative meetings have not, their members, as well as of divers particular meetings, having all gone off in the separation. When the separation shall have taken place in the yearly meeting, &c., I think in all probability there will be as many left with Friends, in Salem and Sandwich Quarterly Meetings each, as in this; perhaps half the number in Dover Quarter; and it is feared that the remaining four quarters will go off. Still, divers have stayed with us whom we did not expect, and some who may not do us much good: in view of which, I sometimes think of the "mixed multitude," who went up with the children of Israel out of Egypt, though we cannot so well speak of a multitude. . . . The Gurneyites in Swanzey Monthly Meeting have come to actual force, to keep Friends out of their public meeting, when a meeting for business followed it, in divers instances; and in others, to seizing some by the collar, and otherwise, and dragging them out so: lest, these being seated in the house, *they* should have to adjourn! Are not these legitimate fruits of a spurious ministry and unsound principles? . . .

Farewell.

T. B. GOULD.

TO SETH AND MARY DAVIS.

NEWPORT, 25th of third month, 1845.

MY VERY DEAR FRIENDS, SETH AND MARY DAVIS:

Although a long time has elapsed since I have written, yet I have not been unmindful of you; but on the contrary you have been much and often in my affectionate remembrance, however opportunity has not presented for saying so in this way. As your quarterly meeting has approached, and under an apprehension that it may or will be a season of renewed or increased trial to you and other dear friends within its limits, I have felt inclined to address you, and if it may be, in the language of encouragement to endure and stand faithfully and firmly in the defence of the truth, in whatever way it may require your support and defence. And oh, my beloved elders therein, what nice attention it does require, what dedication of ourselves, and devotion of our all, if we do yield obedience in these trying times! I have sometimes feared that, on the part of some, there has been a withholding of that which would have been offered if there was less to be feared on account of the offering. So that through fear of suffering, or of the consequences, a sufficient degree of light and strength of motion to act in, has been lost, while waiting for clearness. But it does appear that there is no time to be lost, and that unless what little there is left be faithfully improved, not only particular states, but the Church will suffer great, and perhaps irreparable loss. . . . . .

But, friends, have we not encompassed a dark mountain in the wilderness long enough, and is it not time, high time, to journey forward? Is it not time for Zion to arise and shake herself, seeing the bands with which she has long been bound down are being loosed by Him who only can open the gates of brass, and burst asunder the bars of iron? Hath he not said to some, and is He not saying to other prisoners of hope,—*Go forth!*—and renewing his commandments, as of old to those who sat in darkness, to show themselves in the Light? Yea, I am persuaded that it is so—that what may be compared to the year of Jubilee—of release—has nearly come, wherein all who will, may go out free. But verily those who will not, must remain servants forever! And I greatly fear there are some (though among this number you will not suppose I reckon you), who will prefer servitude, with the enjoyment of the leeks and onions of Egypt, to deliverance therefrom, with the inconvenience and exposure of dwelling in tents, and the perils of continual warfare, until the old inhabitants of the land shall have been overcome and cast out. But the former need not expect any greater honor among the Egyptians, such of them at least as have had some sense of their bondage and the darkness which covers that land,—they need not expect any greater honor than being made hewers of wood, and drawers of water;—while the latter, in the Lord's due and appointed time, when the necessary portion of suffering is filled up, and the warfare is accomplished, will not only gain possession of the gates of their enemies;—but of the Land of Promise itself!

In looking at the state of some, who have had, in a good degree, a right sense of the state of things in this yearly meeting, and who, from their age, station, and experience, may have been fitly called masters in Israel, I have been often and forcibly reminded of good old Jacob's description of his son Issachar: "Issachar is a strong ass, crouching down between two burdens; and he saw that rest was good, and the land that it was pleasant, and he bowed his shoulder to bear, and became a servant unto tribute." And heavy, very heavy, I believe such will find their burdens to be, in the great day of account!—while those who choose rather to suffer affliction with the people of God, than to enjoy the pleasures of sin for a season, will not only receive a double portion of the "recompense of the reward" while here, but reap the fruition of joy unspeakable and full of glory in the presence of the Father—"the God of Abraham, of Isaac, and of Jacob"—in the world to come. May He preserve us all in faithfulness to Himself, whatever portion of suffering and reproaches may be involved therein!

Truly the difficulties which we in this quarterly meeting have met and are likely to meet with, in sustaining our meetings, are neither few nor small; but as these have abounded, the consolations of the Gospel of peace and reconciliation have also abounded, as some of us can say from, I trust, a good degree of living experience, and I think we might add, to His praise! And my fervent, heartfelt desire is, that whatever may transpire, the creature, and all that appertains thereunto, under whatever refinements it may exist, or however deceitfully the "treacherous dealer" may operate, may be continually reduced, and under every dispensation, whether of suffering hunger, or of abounding in the good things of the Kingdom, be laid in the dust forever.

I suppose you may have seen J. J. Gurney's letter to William F. Mott, which his admirers are now industriously circulating, in order to produce the impression that he is disposed to make satisfaction for his departures; but it is passing strange, that any who are at all aware of the extent of his defection in principle, should be so credulous as to take this letter for his and their justification: inasmuch as he therein again fully justifies and defends his writings, and declines any condemnation, by saying expressly that he has peace in the retrospect of his labors as an author, without making any exception. He places all his boasted submission of his writings, upon the ground of condescension, and not at all upon the defective character of the writings themselves. Moreover, his submission, if such it may be called, was, by his own account, to a few friends near London—to a few of his own personal friends,—and these, by other and independent accounts, were of his own selection, such as he knew would handle them very tenderly and carefully indeed, because they were in full unity with the innovations and modernizations of doctrine which they contain. And thus, as he doubtless foresaw, these new views would receive an additional sanction, without incurring the least danger of their being willing to spare any one of the passages which have given all sound Friends so much concern. It is plain enough to be seen at a glance, by all men who have read this celebrated letter, that the only error which he admits, or even supposes, or for which he expresses any regret or sorrow, is, that he printed the "Brief Remarks" without the sanction of the morning meeting. No allusion is made to any erroneous views in it, although he must know that when the views which it inculcates are once adopted, the whole foundation of Quakerism is removed as it respects those who imbibe his views therein expressed: and doubtless he thinks it a pity that they got into circulation so soon, as they were so glaringly inconsistent as to shock the minds of Friends, both in England and America. . . . .

But if he did regret the circulation of this book on

account of the principles it contains, would he not say so,—would he not come honestly forward and retract and condemn those principles, and would he not be forward to do this as publicly and as widely, as the books containing them have been circulated, without regard to the mode in which they obtained that circulation? Can any man suppose that such an author would be satisfied to do it by a private letter to an obscure individual? But he has been content to let these *principles* pass without any condemnation at all—he only thinks it was unwise to *print* it without the sanction of the morning meeting. . . . . .

I must bid you affectionately farewell, and remain very sincerely your friend,

THOMAS B. GOULD.

TO PELEG MITCHELL.

NEWPORT, 25th of 3d mo., 1845.

MY DEAR FRIEND:

. . . I fully intended writing to thee earlier, but have been much pressed for time, in consequence of the very severe illness of both my beloved parents at the time of our quarterly meeting in the second month (which prevented any of us from attending that meeting); and since they have partially recovered, my hands have been fully employed with other matters of importance. My dear wife and self attended the adjournment, which, as well as the other, was a very satisfactory good meeting, wherein Friends were favored to feel, in a good, and of latter times an uncommon degree, the preciousness and blessedness of brethren dwelling together in unity, and harmoniously laboring for Truth's honor, instead of the honor of man and the establishment of a confederacy for the subversion of truth and the right way of the Lord.

. . . [In reference to the prospect of a separation in the yearly meeting, and of the Gurneyites' probable attempt to prevent Sandwich Quarterly Meeting from being held on Nantucket, he says:] If they should make this attempt, and you should passively submit to it without objection, rely upon it, our adversaries will take advantage of it, and throw it in your teeth afterwards; as they have not failed to do repeatedly in other cases, notwithstanding their own unparalleled exertions to prevent Friends from giving expression to their feelings, and their own consciousness that it has been owing to a tender fear of being drawn out into an activity beyond the limitations of truth. But, my dear friend, I am, upon very serious consideration, abundantly convinced that our arch-adversary, the transforming angel, has been too successful in thus preventing the prompt and faithful exercise of our Christian testimony against wrong things and unsanctified manœuvring. As you are, on Nantucket, perhaps the most numerous and closely compacted body of experienced and solid Friends that we can hope for, within the limits of this yearly meeting, to strengthen our feeble and remotely stationed bands and ranks in resisting the hosts displayed and arrayed against us, it does appear to me that a proportionably greater degree of responsibility rests upon you, and others of similar character within the limits of Sandwich quarter. . . . .

And truly, as Stephen Crisp said, the weight of things comes daily more and more upon some, with an undoubted evidence as to the source from whence it springs. That this may be our individual experience, that we may be increasingly prepared and qualified, not only to feel for the afflictions of Joseph, but to labor for his deliverance out of bondage, that so Israel may serve the Lord in the line of divine appointment, and with the offerings of His own preparing, in the place which He shall choose, is what I greatly desire; and I believe the Lord "will hasten it in His time," whether few or more shall be found willing to accept of the way which He hath provided for their deliverance. For surely, He hath opened and is opening, as dear Ezra Comfort said, a way for our deliverance, where we could see no way, and at a time when we looked not for it. . . . .

Thy sincere friend,

THOMAS B. GOULD.

CHAPTER V.

THE separation which had been produced by the advocates and adherents of J. J. Gurney (members of the meeting for sufferings, and of the standing committee of the yearly meeting), in the Monthly Meeting of Swanzey, held at Fall River, and which, as we have seen, extended, in the eleventh month, 1844, to the Quarterly Meeting of Rhode Island, to which Swanzey Monthly Meeting belonged, was, in the course of events, the procuring cause of a similar division in the ensuing Yearly Meeting of New England in the summer of 1845. From the large portion of labor and exercise which consequently devolved on T. B. Gould, it is needful to record here the principal circumstances of that important crisis. This is the more necessary, as it has been followed by like separations from the true Society of Friends, on the part of the same modernizing class, in various portions of the Society, where their influence and power have been sufficiently great to bring about their own measures, and a remnant of faithful Friends has been endued with strength to stand firm to their ancient faith and discipline. In such cases, a due regard for the safety of the ark of the testimony, for the very existence of the Society on its original ground, and for the fulfilment of their own individual duty as members of it, has constrained the honest-hearted to unite together in withstanding the further inroads of error in principle and practice, and in refusing to be identified with the modified system, and with the schismatic course by which it was sustained. They have herein acted according to the principles clearly advocated by Robert Barclay, in unison with the Apostle Paul, that after due and ineffectual endeavors to convince and reclaim, they who stand faithful to the true doctrines originally accepted, not only have the power, but are under a solemn obligation, to "withdraw" from those who are introducing into the Church such innovations and disorderly practices as would be fundamentally inconsistent with its original character, and involve them in complicity with a departure from the true faith of the body.

After the separation in Rhode Island Quarterly Meeting, the leaders of the innovating party foresaw the conflict that would follow in the yearly meeting, and took prompt measures to provide for their own numerical success in the crisis. They issued from the meeting for sufferings an illusory representation of what had already occurred; assuming to themselves a high tone of religious authority, by which the minds of many were entangled, before they had an opportunity of knowing the truth or fallacy of statements so boldly and authoritatively asserted; and in several of the quarterly meetings, when representatives were to be appointed to the ensuing yearly meeting, they attempted, too successfully, to control the appointments, so as to secure a very large preponderance of their own adherents in the representative body. So that, when the yearly meeting assembled, the representatives, with few exceptions, were found to be a "packed" body, composed mainly of those who had been active in the persecution of sound Friends for their testimony against innovation, and of those who, they knew, from previous circumstances, would act according to their own bidding.

When the yearly meeting assembled, in the sixth month, as was expected, two sets of representatives appeared from Rhode Island, one from each of the meetings claiming to be the true Rhode Island Quarterly Meeting. If strict impartiality had been exercised between the two claimants, in ignorance of their respective merits, neither set of representatives would have been minuted as such, until the yearly meeting had concluded its judgment as to which represented the true body. But the clerk, who was one of the advocates of J. J. Gurney, read, among those from the other quarters, the report of the Gurney meeting, and minuted the names of its representatives at once, as being the representatives of that quarter, and afterwards the others merely as purporting to be such; thus forestalling the judgment of the meeting, and placing the latter in a disadvantageous position. It was now proposed that the question should be referred to the decision of all the representatives, except those of both parties from Rhode Island. This would have insured a result favorable to the Gurney party, and with a knowledge of the certainty of such a result, they pressed it. Sound Friends could not submit to its reference to a body so made up beforehand. They represented to the meeting, that several of the representatives were members of the yearly meeting's standing committee, already implicated in this very question, and active participants in the measures which had produced it; that unfair and proscriptive measures had, in some of the quarters, been resorted to in the appointments; that the impartial character of the body of representatives was thus greatly vitiated, and a fair adjudication rendered entirely improbable, if not impossible, inasmuch as the sufferings of faithful Friends, in their endeavors to stand for the cause of truth, and the sad difficulties in which the yearly meeting was now involved, were mainly attributable to the proceedings of those very men who, in the body of representatives, would have the entire control of the decision. They therefore urged that the yearly meeting itself should deliberate on the matter, that all the members present might have an opportunity of hearing and judging on the merits of the case. There was considerable expression in favor of this proposal, by Friends from different quarterly meetings; but many continued to urge the reference to the representatives. The sound portion from Rhode Island informed the meeting that they could not consent to such a reference under the circumstances. But the clerk made a minute, giving it that direction. He then made a truly extraordinary proposition to the meeting,—no less than the suspension (for the accomplishment of the purpose then in view) of an organic rule of their own printed discipline,—a proceeding probably never heard of before in the Society of Friends. He proposed to suspend that rule of the discipline of New England Yearly Meeting (in the language of the world, their *constitutional law*), which requires the representatives to meet at the conclusion of the sitting on second-day morning, and agree upon a clerk for the year, and report the same to the adjournment. This was a very important feature in the discipline of New England Yearly Meeting, founded upon the long-established sentiment among Friends, of the necessity of a judicious selection in the nomination to a service of such weight and responsibility. Although this proposal was objected to on the part of the sound representatives from Rhode Island, and the yearly meeting was reminded that its adoption would be a departure from the injunction of the discipline, yet a minute was made in accordance with the clerk's suggestion,—thereby displaying a sorrowful example to its members, of a body professing to be a yearly meeting of Friends, breaking one of its own laws to suit a temporary, needless, and factious purpose. The meeting, after this, adjourned to four o'clock in the afternoon. Before the adjournment took place, in view of the condition into which the yearly meeting was now brought, Friends desirous of maintaining the ancient principles and practices of the Society, and anxious that the yearly meeting should be sustained on its original foundation, were invited to take a solid opportunity of conferring together, to endeavor unitedly to see, under the guidance of Divine Wisdom, what step might appear right for them to take in this very peculiar and trying state of things. Many Friends accordingly remained in the house after the conclusion of the sitting; but finding it impracticable to confer together there without interruption, they agreed upon another place of meeting, and then quietly withdrew. Arrived at this stage in their proceedings, it may be best to quote their own statement of the subsequent transactions:

"Friends were introduced into deep exercise and travail of spirit, wherein living desires were raised in the hearts of many, for best help and direction; and when they again assembled, free from interruption, under an awful sense of the importance of moving only in the line of Divine appointment, they were united in judgment that it would not be right to appear with their case, before the representatives then sitting in our meeting-house; who were immediately informed of this conclusion. It was also the united sense and judgment of Friends, that in order to sustain the yearly meeting in conformity with its long-established Discipline, and upon its original ground, with the ancient doctrines and testimonies of the Society unimpaired, it was indispensable that the representatives should meet, and agree upon and propose a Clerk to the next sitting, as by discipline and former usage is required.

"The yearly meeting having again convened in the afternoon, soon after the opening minute was read, Prince Gardner [of Nantucket], on behalf of the representatives who met on Clerks (which included all those from Rhode Island [sound Friends] and some from Sandwich Quarterly Meeting), reported that they were united in proposing the names of Thomas B. Gould for Clerk, and Charles Perry for Assistant Clerk, for the ensuing year. This proposal was united with by many, but a large number opposed it, and the former Clerks continued to sit at the table. Whereupon, those agreed to and proposed by the representatives, were requested to take their seats at a table in a part of the house where most of the Friends who had united in their appointment were sitting. [This was a part of the meeting-house at one side of the portion occupied by the bulk of the assembly, and divided from it by a sliding partition, but which was at this time left open above the level of the benches.] After making a minute of the appointment of Clerks, &c., the names of the representatives from Rhode Island Quarterly Meeting of Friends were called, and all responded thereto. The Clerk then proceeded to read the report from that meeting, in which he was greatly interrupted by many in different parts of the house. Abraham Shearman, Jr. (the former Clerk), left his seat, and passing along the ministers' gallery towards that part of it where the Clerk was standing, called upon him to desist; but after a short pause, the reading was calmly proceeded in, until finished. After appointing a committee to prepare and produce to a future sitting, a more extended minute, to be entered on our records, embracing the very trying circumstances in which we were placed, with the ground and cause thereof, it did not appear proper, on account of the great interruption Friends met with, to introduce any further business at that sitting. The yearly meeting concluded to adjourn, to meet on third-day morning at the tenth hour, of which the women's meeting was informed, and adjourned accordingly. This fact being reported to the separate [Gurney] meeting by their messengers, they adjourned, to meet at the same place, at the ninth hour.

. . . . "Friends assembled on third-day morning, and found our meeting-house already occupied by the separate meeting, — whereupon the yearly meeting gathered and was opened in the yard, the men's meeting near one end of the house, and the women's at the other. Each meeting appointed a committee to apply to those in the house for the vacation of the Clerks' tables for the use of the yearly meeting and its Clerks, and also for the transfer of the books and papers thereof; which application having been made and unconditionally refused, we were deprived of the reports from all our quarterly meetings, except Rhode Island. One representative from Salem and three from Sandwich Quarterly Meetings, uniting with us, were recognized as such by the meeting; which, with those from Rhode Island, made thirteen representatives to the men's meeting who have remained with Friends.

"After being thus obliged to hold our meeting, both of men and women Friends, *standing in the open air* for nearly two hours, it was concluded to adjourn the yearly meeting to the Baptist meeting-house in Clarke Street, which was kindly opened for that purpose. Friends having removed from our meeting-house yard in a body, convened again immediately at the place proposed; and sitting for a time together, our hearts were tendered and united under the cementing influence of the Great Head of the Church, who, as we feel bound reverently to acknowledge, has been pleased in His unmerited mercy, and in a remarkable manner, to own us in the way which we go, to manifest Himself among us by His Spirit, to uphold and preserve us by His power, amid the varied conflicts which we have had to pass through, for His great name's sake. Under feelings of deep sorrow and concern for those who have been drawn aside from the truth, and of thankfulness to the Lord our Preserver, such was the solemnity and the preciousness of the covering which, in adorable mercy, was spread over us, that it was concluded to adjourn without introducing any business at that time.

"The subsequent sittings of the yearly meeting have been regularly held at the same place; and although greatly reduced in numbers, Friends have been mercifully favored during these several sittings, to experience renewed and abundant evidence, that He who leadeth the blind by a way which they know not, and in paths which they have not seen, is not unmindful of His people,—and that, while, in the counsels of His own will, He hath permitted them to be thus sifted and very closely tried, yet that He will, in His own good time, gather the outcasts of Israel and the dispersed of Judah, raising up judges as at the first, and counsellors as at the beginning, who shall not err in vision or stumble in judgment, but who shall be enabled, by His holy help, to lay judgment to the line, and righteousness to the plummet: for Zion was to be redeemed through judgment, and her converts with righteousness; and we are persuaded that He who reigneth King in the midst of Zion, will verify His ancient promise, 'I will restore health unto thee, and I will heal thee of thy wounds, saith the Lord, because they called thee an outcast, saying, This is Zion whom no man seeketh after.' 'Behold, I will bring again the captivity of Jacob's tents, and have mercy on his dwelling-places; and the city shall be builded upon her own heap, and the palace shall remain after the manner thereof. And out of them shall proceed thanksgiving, and the voice of them that make merry: and I will multiply them, and they shall not be few; I will also glorify them, and they shall not be small. Their children also shall be as aforetime, and their congregation shall be established before me, and I will punish all that oppress them.'"

. . . . . . "Furthermore, we are engaged to testify and declare, that while we have the fullest unity with the ancient established principles, doctrines, testimonies, and discipline of the Religious Society of Friends, as held and supported from the beginning, and as published authoritatively to the world in Robert Barclay's "Apology for the true Christian Divinity," his "Catechism and Confession of Faith," and his treatise on "Church Government;" also by George Fox, William Penn, Isaac Penington, George Whitehead, and all those bright sons of the morning in unity with them;—yet we have no unity or fellowship with those adverse principles and doctrines of Joseph John Gurney, as exhibited in the following extracts from his published works, and illustrated by the disorderly practices and proceedings of his adherents; those principles and doctrines being, as the extracts from the writings of some of our early Friends, which we have contrasted therewith, will show, plainly inconsistent with the doctrines of the Gospel of our Lord and Saviour Jesus Christ and His Apostles, as recorded in the Holy Scriptures of truth, which are of divine authority, being given by inspiration of God, and written by holy men of old, as they were moved by the Holy Ghost.

"We therefore entreat and exhort our dear friends, everywhere, to be on their guard against receiving or imbibing any principles or doctrines that are not in accordance with those held and promulgated by the early approved writers and ministers of our Society, which we have herein referred to; and who were made in their day eminent instruments in the Divine Hand, of reviving primitive Christianity, exalting the standard of truth, and of gathering a distinct and peculiar people unto Him who was the foundation of the prophets and apostles, Jesus Christ himself—the Rock of Ages—being the chief cornerstone."

. . . . . . "In conclusion, we feel concerned affectionately and earnestly to invite all those who make a profession of the truth under our name, in this time of great commotion, to centre more and more to the unflattering witness, and gift of divine light and grace within themselves, which never will deceive those that faithfully follow its leadings. Thus shall we know more and more of an establishment on that Rock on which the true Church of Christ is builded, and against which the gates of hell shall never be suffered to prevail. May none of our dear friends be discouraged in view of the great sufferings which a faithful adherence to the truth may bring upon them; but remembering the glorious reward promised by our Holy Redeemer to those who are willing joyfully to suffer for His sake, and to sacrifice near and dear things for His cause, may we all look to Him who remains to be the Helper of His people, with earnest desires for preservation.

"And as, in the integrity of our hearts, this is the case, although in His inscrutable wisdom, He may permit us to be sorely tried, even to an hair's breadth, both for our furtherance in the ever-blessed truth, and the advancement of His own glorious cause in the earth, yet as we abide in the everlasting patience, we shall know the angel of His presence to go with us, and be permitted to enjoy the reward of that inward peace and satisfaction, which the mere dweller in the outward court may talk of, but never can possess."

An undue confidence in certain leaders of the people, and desire to stand well with the rulers, had taken possession of many minds, even among those who at first had seen more or less clearly the discordance between our ancient principles and those of the modern school. The arch enemy of all truth, who is ever ready to take advantage of our weakness, easily persuaded these, that it was very comfortable to take the words and deeds of those in whom they had placed their confidence, as unquestionably correct and safe for them to follow, instead of submitting to the arduous engagement of entering individually into close religious travail and exercise of spirit, by which they might have been qualified to discern between the voice of the stranger, and the still small voice of Him who would have led them safely by the footsteps of the flock, in the green pastures of life. Thus lending a willing ear to the "charmer," they became more and more bewildered, till they stumbled in judgment, and were carried away in multitudes by the delusive representations now set afloat: so that in some quarters very few were found prepared to unite in supporting the true standard, in opposition to the powerful influences brought to bear upon them from within and from without.

The yearly meeting, in view of the distracted condition into which the Society in New England was now thrown, by the disorderly and factious proceedings of the Gurney party, the fallacious representations spread abroad by them of the separation which had taken place, and the almost overwhelming prevalency of defection in influential quarters, believed that great difficulties would attend the honest endeavors of Friends to sustain their meetings in accordance with the ancient principles and practices of the Society. A committee was therefore appointed, to visit the quarterly, monthly, and other meetings, as way might open for it, and extend aid, as enabled, in the support of the testimonies of truth as always professed by us. T. B. Gould being one of this committee, an interesting view of some features of the visits may be gathered from several of the following letters.

He received, about this time, an encouraging letter, among others, from a Friend in the ministry, then residing in New Jersey.

From William Scattergood to T. B. G.

Millville, 7th mo. 21st, 1845.

Dear Friend, T. B. Gould:

My thoughts have been so often turned towards thee, with some others in your parts, during the past few weeks, that I seem to see no other way than to endeavor to impart somewhat of the sympathy that attends my mind towards thee, in this way. It is not in the sense of abounding, nor of having much to communicate; but as a trying period has overtaken some of you, who are engaged to stand for the law and the testimony, it cannot but tend to affect all such as love the Lord Jesus in sincerity, with feelings of lively and tender interest. "When one member suffers, all the members suffer with it," is the language of the experienced apostle, and is witnessed by such as are alive in the Lord down to this day; and as there is a patient abiding with the seed which is under suffering, there is something known of being one another's helpers as well as joy in the Lord.

We are happily thus far placed in a situation in which we are not immediately involved in the confusion caused by unruly and unsettled spirits, who, having lost ground in themselves, are seeking to keep up an outward profession, and more than that, are seeking pre-eminence over others and in the church. But I apprehend we shall not long witness immunity from the desolating effects of this unhappy defection from the cross of Christ, which is the groundwork of all schism and contention in the church.

Well, I think I can say, in looking at the wave that is rolling towards us, and which is no doubt to overwhelm many in its progress, may our dependence and foundation be upon the everlasting Rock which cannot be moved, and against which the winds and waves will beat in vain. How important, in those who are engaged to stand against the innovations of the present day, that they be found with their loins girded about and their lights burning; that they should witness a fresh and fervent engagement, day by day, to have on the whole armor of light, that so they may stand against the wiles of the devil! I have felt, in looking at the prospect before us, of having again to enter as it were into warfare with unruly spirits, as though it was an awful one; and having been a participator in a degree in a former separation, the thought of this has affected me, with more than ordinary desires that my own dependence and strength might be alone in Him who is mighty to save. It is only as we are thus brought in true humility to depend upon Him, that we can hope for safety as regards ourselves, or victory, in a church capacity, over the enemies of the cross of Christ. May our abiding then, my dear friend, be here, and may we be more concerned that truth and righteousness may prevail, than any other thing. Truth is truth, though all men forsake it; and as we hold fast to it, He who is said to be the Way, the Truth, and the Life, will maintain his own cause, and we shall witness true exaltation in His way and time, which is not to be hastened or promoted by any contrivance or device of the natural mind or will. Oh! it is good to dwell low with Him, in his holy fear!

We have had accounts of your late yearly meeting; and while we mourn with you over the defection of so many, yet I look forward with hope, that those who remain attached to our religious principles and testimonies may be so afresh engaged to know their abiding to be in the Vine, that heavenly and blessed fruit may be more eminently manifest among us than for the time that is past. If this is not the case, if love, joy, peace, long-suffering, meekness, goodness, faith, are not more eminently to be seen among us, what profit shall this separation be to us? Our unity and fellowship is not so much in the belief of opinions and notions about religion, as in that holy and blessed Spirit whereinto all the living members of Christ's spiritual body are truly baptized, whereby they are made one body, even as we are called in one hope of our calling. May this be more and more our experience as a religious body, and may this sifting, shaking season, tend to drive us home to the impregnable fortress, where the Lord's presence dwells! My heart is enlarged in feelings of tender solicitude for those of my own age and younger, that we may be preserved in the hollow of the Lord's holy hand, and that, in our engagements in the church, we may be preserved from doing anything to hinder or mar the Lord's work. As we are thus preserved patient and watchful before Him, he will at seasons clothe with his divine power, so that one shall chase a thousand, and two put ten thousand to flight.

I could enlarge much upon this weighty and solemn occasion; but as I have no desire to multiply words, have only to commend thee, with other of our dear friends in your parts, to the keeping and guidance of the Shepherd of Israel. May He be your bow and battle-axe, your shield and exceeding great reward. If this is the case, though Israel be not gathered, though there may be little left of us as a religious society, yet will you be precious in the eyes of the Lord, and He will afford the sweet consolation, of which He is the only Source and Fountain.

My love to thy wife, in which my Elizabeth joins; also to such as I may have some acquaintance with in your quarterly meeting, &c.; and with the salutation of near affection, I remain thy friend and brother,

WILLIAM SCATTERGOOD.

FROM T. B. G. TO JOSHUA MAULE.

NORTH BERWICK, MAINE, 26th of 8th mo., 1845.

MY VERY DEAR BROTHER, JOSHUA MAULE:

. . . Such has been the press of business growing out of our peculiar situation in New England, that I have been able to pay scarcely any attention to my own affairs, since I parted with thy Sarah. I am now here, with others of our yearly meeting's committee, waiting for Dover Quarterly Meeting, which is to be held at this place to-morrow and the day following. . . . We sat nearly eight hours in Salem Quarterly Meeting, held last fifth-day at Lynn, before the Gurneyites got ready to adjourn and leave Friends in possession of the house. About fifty men remained, including the committee of the yearly meeting; there were, however, but six or seven women, the rest clinging to the skirts of a distinguished female minister there, who is not yet prepared to take a stand herself with us, although she advised her husband and children to do so, and they did. Oh, the baneful effects of the love of popularity! How few there are that are willing to be of no reputation, for His sake who left us an example that we should follow Him!

North Berwick Monthly Meeting occurred the same day as Salem Quarterly Meeting; and the Gurneyites here, with J. D. L. at their head, separated themselves therefrom, in consequence of the old Clerk being in unity with Friends; and the time of his appointment having expired, they sought to effect a change, much in the same way they did in Swanzey Monthly Meeting, as told in the Address. But failing to do so in the regular way, they persisted in the appointment of a new one, organized a new meeting, adjourned it, and left Friends with the regular Clerk in the house, on the men's side, and he also retained the books and papers. But the women's Clerk went off, and took the books and papers with her. Fifteen men and as many women remained in the house. In Salem, it appeared the leaders had previously agreed to make no reply to anything we might say. To many of their members, (so much have they been kept in the dark), the state of things was comparatively new and unheard of: they accordingly made many inquiries as to the ground and cause of things, which were very fully answered by Friends, embracing what our opposers no doubt considered high charges against themselves in regard to doctrine, discipline, and so forth. But they never disputed one single word which we uttered, during the six hours we remained together; and thus very fully manifested the extreme weakness of their cause, especially as they were requested to do so, if we had in any respect misrepresented them. And some of their yearly meeting's committee were present, both old and new; for they have, it seems, disbanded their standing committee, and have now merely got one similar to ours, to sustain their meetings, &c.

Thou hast doubtless heard, that in Sandwich Quarterly Meeting, held on Nantucket, there were as many men left as attended our yearly meeting; and more women, there being very nearly, if not quite, one hundred women. Truly, in our passing along under many difficulties and heavy burdens, we do find some bright spots, even such as we had not thought or heard of; even such as have been fitted and prepared as in the mountains, for the rebuilding of the temple: which I have no doubt will yet, as faithfulness is abode in, be beautified and made glorious, as in days of old and as in former years. Nevertheless, the work is great, the burdens are heavy, and the faithful laborers few. . . . . .

Friends are very anxious to hear how it will go in Ohio. Nevertheless, they have seen enough to convince the most doubtful of those who endured the test at the yearly meeting, that it was done in the ordering of Best Wisdom, and that a way was wonderfully opened for us, beyond what we could have asked, or thought of, or believed. That New York committee, which was designed to assist in and complete our overthrow, together with the English people, proved the means of our being safely and honorably delivered; the counsel of Ahithophel being turned into foolishness.

Truly thine,
THOMAS B. GOULD.

TO MARTHA S. GOULD.

NORTH BERWICK, MAINE, 26th of 8th mo., 1845.

MY DEAR MARTHA:

. . . We had a tedious time at Lynn; yet I did not suffer as much during the six hours we waited upon our opposers, after the shutters were closed, before they got ready to adjourn, and leave Friends in the house, as I did on Nantucket. In this time we had a fine opportunity to open up the ground and cause of things; and J. W. did it very fully, without one word of reply from any of them, although he charged them boldly. When they at length got ready to adjourn, they left about fifty men in the house, including the yearly meeting's committee. But among the members of Salem Quarterly Meeting who remained, there are some very choice Friends, who have been fitted and prepared, as in the mountains, for this day. . . . .

THOMAS B. GOULD.

TO MARTHA S. GOULD.

WESTBROOK, MAINE, 9th mo., 5th, 1845.

MY DEAR MARTHA:

I wrote home from the house of Timothy Varney, of Kennebunk; and the next evening received thy note, at the house of J. H., in the town of Gorham, about five miles the other side of Windham meeting-house, where the quarterly meeting was held yesterday. We got to J. H.'s house about sunset (twenty-five miles from Kennebunk), that is, J. Wilbur, I. Buffinton, and myself, and were very kindly received and comfortably entertained; they being farmers, and very clever sort of people, although they go with "the body." William and Elizabeth Hill, and Mary Davis joined us there in about an hour after; the two former having returned from Kennebunk, in order to meet and bring dear Mary Davis; she having been home since the quarterly meeting at Berwick, and returned again to bear us company in this painful service, to the conclusion thereof.

Perhaps this was the largest quarterly meeting ever held here. It not being known that we were in the neighborhood (by the rulers), until we drove up to the meeting-house, it produced great excitement among them; and Stephen Jones, his brother Thomas, and Nathan Pope, an elder, joined by Edward Wing, took an opportunity with John Wilbur before meeting, and charged him to leave after the first meeting closed. I, seeing they had J. W., joined them; I. B. followed; when Edward Wing told them he supposed they knew we had all been disowned! which however did not frighten any of us. We took commodious seats in the meeting; and soon after, a young upstart, whose name is J——, delivered one of their broadsides, and a little after A. R. poured out another, which last was quite ingeniously done. She alluded to Balaam's being hired to curse Israel, his seeking for and using divinations and enchantments, Israel's abiding in their tents, and his curse being turned into blessing, &c. But J. Wilbur stood up shortly, and turned it all back upon her and them in a most workmanlike manner; showing that that people were no longer safe than while they did *truly* abide in their tent, dwelt alone, &c.; and that even Balaam taught Balak to lay a stumbling-block before the children of Israel; how they stumbled and fell upon it, and eventually became scattered and mixed among the people, for want of truly and really abiding in Him who had led them and preserved them while they stood in obedience to and dependence upon Him. This stirred up a silly woman who has lately been recommended here. The burden of her song was love, love, love!—everything that occasioned strife, she said, was Anti-Christ, and so might be known, &c. Here I could scarcely refrain from reviving the query: "Think ye that I came to send peace on earth?

I tell you nay, but a sword," and "to set the son against the father, and the daughter-in-law against her mother-in-law;"—and "the greatest enemies a man hath shall be they of his own household." But before I thought it seasonable to stand up, J. H., who is very deaf, and probably did not hear anything that had been said, rose up, speaking comfortably to those who were oppressed; but he did expose the nakedness and shame of the rulers. He uttered much sound doctrine and many home-truths; but I could not feel easy to *follow him.* He is a thorough "come-outer," of whom there are many in these parts, who serve to rebuke those degenerated professors; as it is written, "I will rebuke them by them that are no people, and by a foolish nation will I anger you;" but as they would gladly join hands with us if we would have them, it makes our path the more difficult. Young J—— however again stood up, and said something more; when they shook hands; after which Stephen Jones requested "*Friends,*" both men and women, to keep their seats, and those who were *not*, to withdraw. Many left the house,—all, I suppose, who were desired to leave, except ourselves. After sitting for some time, we were formally requested to leave. John Wilbur attempted to make reply, on which he was several times interrupted by Stephen and Thomas Jones; for whom he stopped till they had done, and then went on again, they crying out, "We have no unity with thee or thy company." But John proceeded till Stephen Jones requested men Friends to go into the women's apartment (the house being in two parts), which they seemed to understand, and acted accordingly, going out in confusion, while John Warren cried aloud, "We have no fellowship with the unfruitful works of darkness!"

On getting out of the door, we found a strong guard placed at that into which "*the body*" were entering. One of the sentinels was calling out, "Friends, walk in—walk in, Friends!" So I stepped up towards the door; upon which he said, "Thee can't go in, thee can't go in!" I inquired, "Is this the way you entertain strangers?"—he being a man whom I had often seen at Newport. He said, "It is the way we entertain such as come here to impose upon us and disturb us."—"How have I imposed upon or disturbed you?"—"Thee has been disowned!"—"Not by the Society of Friends."—"Well," said he, "thee is not a member of our Society; thee can't go in: we can't be disturbed." I told him, I should not press it any further than to clear myself; it was a relief to me that they had themselves prohibited us; we were clear, and the burden must rest upon themselves. There were but two male members of this quarterly meeting, who stayed out with us. Poor Mary Davis and Elizabeth Hill had it to bear alone in the women's meeting, except dear E. A., who is a sweet-spirited woman. After waiting about an hour, and finding they would not even open the meeting until they left, and that nothing could be done further than the relief of their own minds, these three Friends came out and left them. And having ridden seven miles, we have found a place of rest and safety at this house, where we expect to remain to-night also, as John Wilbur has an appointed meeting here this afternoon. . . . . .

T. B. GOULD.

TO MARTHA S. GOULD.

VASSALBORO', ninth month, 9th, 1845.

MY DEAREST MARTHA:

I wrote last at the house of Ebenezer Austin, on sixth-day I think. The next morning we left in their company for Durham, a distance of twenty-four miles; but John Wilbur feeling a concern to appoint a meeting at the village of Freeport, six miles short, we stopped there at a public house, and stayed the night. Although the notice was short, the meeting was large, the landlord kindly interesting himself to notify the people. Neither himself nor wife seemed to know anything of Friends, nor to have attended their meetings, although so near to Durham, which is a very large one. But I suppose our early Friends would have said she was convinced. She was truly tender and broken; could not do enough for us, apparently; and was very reluctant to part with us. However, we set out on first-day morning, and rode six miles to Durham Meeting, in a hard rain: but we went dry and comfortable before it. Here live S. and T. J., and they have poor N. D. for their chief preacher, whom they have converted into a hewer of wood and a drawer of water for them. But on this occasion they had B. J., of whom I have before spoken, to do their drudgery for them: and although we said never a word, yet our presence was sufficient to call forth their bitterest ire; and the said Benjamin did preach at us, and "call on the name of his God" to deliver them, vehemently. Thou canst imagine the worst, and not exceed the reality perhaps: yet we could bear it very patiently. . . . .

While we were in meeting, they turned our horse and carriage out of the shed under which, as we came early, we had hitched it; and much ado we had to find it, among the great number of carriages. No one invited us to dine, so we rode on, about four miles, crossed the great Androscoggin River, and stopped to dine at a tavern on this side, and in full view of it. It is the most rapid river I ever saw, running violently over a rocky bed, much of which is exposed at this season, as the river is low. When high, it must be terrific, even here, yet more so at Brunswick, about five miles below this bridge. . . . . Being kindly entertained, and having had a comfortable night, we rode on, about eleven or twelve miles, to Augusta, the seat of government in the State of Maine. . . . Here we stopped at a tavern to dine and have our carriage mended; for when within a mile or so of Lot Goddard's house, down came the back bar of our carriage. . . . . After dinner, our carriage being ready, we once more set forward towards the north, crossed the Kennebec, by the great bridge of Augusta, and rode up its east bank (through the southerly part of the town of Vassalboro'), about ten miles, close by the river side all the way. Then turning east about one mile, we came to the house of David Howland, who, with his wife and aged mother, gave us a hearty welcome. They were expecting us, as William Hill had written, and it was truly grateful to our feelings, once more to meet with those who could sympathize with us and joyfully receive us. . . . Vassalboro' Quarterly Meeting is held on sixth-day, about a mile from this house. . . . . . I have felt very anxious lately: yet I have sometimes thought, that He who calls for dedication to His cause, can keep those who are so very dear to me, and whom I have left for its sake alone, if it please Him, whether I am present or absent. My dear love to father and mother, sisters L. and M., and to thyself more than can be written or uttered.

Thy own,
T. B. GOULD.

FROM T. B. G. TO —— ——.

NEWPORT, 19th of ninth month, 1845.

MY DEAR ——:

. . . . . What do they make of us? Do they really think that we are so bad that we are not fit for social, for relative intercourse? Truly I have had many, very many bitter cups to take at the hands of the Gurneyites, but none were half so bitter as some such as these being administered by those who have professed to be our friends. Nevertheless I have once more ventured to write freely, and as I used to do, respecting our affairs. If it is burdensome, I shall regret it sincerely, as I love thee and all thine; under which conviction I conclude, and am as ever thy affectionate

THOMAS B. GOULD.

When we were coming home from the East, we met dear Mary Macey, with Benjamin and Rachel Gardner, going down to visit the families of such as would receive them, in those Eastern quarters. She had visited many families in Lynn, who did not go with us at the time of the separation there; and there were others whom she expected to visit on her return. I was at Lynn Meeting, both morning and afternoon, last first-day, and had good reason to be glad I was there, although it cost dear. But I was received beyond all expectation, and very differently from what I met with East, even by Gurneyites.

FROM ZENO CARPENTER TO T. B. G.

The 11th of 7th mo, 1845.

MY MUCH BELOVED FRIEND:

I salute thee in the love of the Gospel, fellow-traveller and fellow-soldier, bound to the land and city of God. My mind hath been drawn in much sympathy toward thee at times, since I saw thee in the city of Philadelphia. I wish thy preservation and prosperity every way; that thou mayst stand firm and immovable in the living and eternal truth. Let thy whole trust and confidence be in the holy Rock of Ages, Christ Jesus our Lord. He is the same as ever he was, strong and mighty, Lord of heaven and of the whole earth. I believe thou hast had many trials to pass through, many oppositions from those thou once travailed in spirit with: may thou be preserved, is the fervent prayer and supplication of thy friend, thy brother and companion in tribulation. It is beyond the expression of pen or tongue to set forth the mercy, the goodness, and loving-kindness of the "Ancient of days," to His poor dependent creature man. How humbly thankful ought we to be for His many mercies and kind favors conferred upon us! He is infinite in goodness; He is often pleased to look down from His excellent glory to bless, and favor, and strengthen, and confirm the poor weary traveller, that is on the way to the land of eternal rest. Well, dear friend, be not discouraged nor dismayed: if the Lord is on thy side, who can be against thee? Though all the powers of death and darkness, and even hell itself, should combine together, yet they will never be able to dismount or overthrow a servant of the living God, mounted upon the King's horse, and arrayed in royal apparel. No, verily; He is omnipotent and omnipresent; He ruleth in the army of heaven, and in the kingdom of men!

I trust it is in Gospel love that I felt thus to address thee. It has not been for thyself only, but thy dear companion, that I never saw that I know of: I felt that love to flow towards you, that is without bounds. May you join heart to heart, and travel hand in hand, in the glorious cause; and keep to the law and testimony, and to the sentiments of the Society of Friends, though many may deviate therefrom. I beseech it of you, dear friends and fellow-travellers, that you would stand firm and immovable, always abounding in the work of the Lord. You will often witness the love of God, and His glory, to shine in and fill the soul. What can be named more precious and comfortable? Oh, matchless goodness and marvellous loving-kindness, that a Being, altogether complete without us, should thus condescend to bless and to favor! It is cause of humility and self-abasement, and to bow in awful reverence before the Most High, for such dignified favors from the great and holy Head of the Church, whose mercies are innumerable, and still continue to be over all His works, new every morning, from generation to generation. May we, dear friends, serve, reverence, and adore, and love Him, in preference to all sublunary attainments!

I feel for you in that part of the land: trials, and deep ones, await you. Give not back; maintain your ground, your station and standing in truth; and keep on the watch-tower, a place of safety, under the sanctuary of our Lord, and out of the reach of the enemy of souls, who is continually on the alert, going to and fro in the earth, and walking up and down in it. His power is a limited one. The power of the Lord is above and over all, almighty, eternal, and incomprehensible. Therefore let us trust in the Lord, and lean not upon a hollow reed, nor trust in man, whose breath is in his nostrils, for therein is no safety. Let us pray fervently that the Lord from on high will be pleased, in unmerited mercy, to remember us, poor, frail, and finite creatures. There is nothing that we can do of ourselves, as men and creatures, that will in the least redound to the honor and dignity of the great and holy Head of the Church. May the "Ancient of days" keep and preserve you, and poor me, in His holy fear and counsel; that we may be strengthened to pursue the high and holy way that leads to the land of everlasting rest, and out of the reach of all trouble and temptation, to join the celestial family, and the spirits of just men made perfect, to sing the holy song of redeeming love, where God reigns triumphantly with His saints!

From your affectionate friend and well-wisher,

ZENO CARPENTER.

FROM T. B. G. TO JOSHUA AND SARAH MAULE.

NEWPORT, 1st month, 6th, 1846.

MY DEAR BROTHER AND SISTER:

. . . . As you may not have heard how we poor pilgrims fared after we left Berwick, where, I think I stated in my last, Dover Quarterly Meeting was to be held, I will just say that no quarter below Dover was sustained, although we went down to Fairfield, which is the lowest. It appeared that the Gurneyites came to a conclusion, after Dover Quarter, not to allow us to sit in the meetings for discipline; thus laying aside their resolutions to be quiet and bear with us, which they made so much boast of at Lynn. And at Dover, J. D. L. and his partisans nearly raised a mob while so earnestly recommending quietness and patience under their sufferings; sufferings produced only by our presence and pleading with them not to sell their birthrights for a mess of pottage, nor to exchange the inheritance of their forefathers for another. But they found, to their great chagrin and vexation, that while they allowed us to sit and state our case, as way opened for it, we gained the ears of some in every quarter, who had before been kept in ignorance of the true ground of the controversy: that they were losing ground, and we were gaining it, and that it would not do any longer to "suffer patiently," even such as it was, and *as* they suffered. But they must resort next to stratagem, and then to force. So, at Falmouth Quarter, which followed Dover, they did allow us to enter the public meeting; not, however, without vainly attempting to extort a promise of silence therein, and of leaving at the close. And at the close, they first requested those who were not members to withdraw, and so got rid of spectators. Then, as we did not leave, they singled us out, and formally requested us to do so, but not very civilly. We did not comply; and they then requested the men to withdraw into the women's apartment, and hurried them, first out of that part of the meeting-house, and then into the other, while a strong guard at the door prevented us from entering; which, however, we made no other attempt to do in any case, than just to advance towards it in a peaceable and becoming manner. But if we had advanced with the same determination to enter, which they manifested to keep us out, we should soon have brought them to blows! It was, however, no way flattering to the intellects of those assembled, to witness how submissively they suffered themselves to be dragged into the assemblies of a professedly non-resisting people. However, at Fairfield Quarter (the next in point of time), they would not allow any of us, either male or female, to enter the public meeting for worship (so called): our women Friends had not been reached by the manœuvre which excluded the male members of the committee from Falmouth Quarter, and had had some effective service in the women's meeting; although they were of course not able to sustain it. They would not even open that meeting during *their* presence, under a pretence they had no right to sit; yet neither of them had even been treated with at that time. So, after clearing themselves, they quietly withdrew, and joined the men Friends, who were standing in the yard, hard by the meeting-house; into which the poor Gurney people were crammed and *locked*, for very fear that any one should even feel a curiosity to speak with us outside! Truly we were made spectacles to men at least; but we did not envy them their condition, or covet their feelings; and I confess, theirs seemed to me a truly pitiful case.

But to return to Fairfield. We reached the meeting-house early, and found the doors locked, and a guard close by, watching. Our dear friend, Mary Davis, first ascended the steps, which were several feet above the ground, and tried the door in vain; upon which she took her stand on one side of it, against the side-light of the door, from which she did not move, after, till we left; as when the people began to muster, the guards stood between her and the door, to prevent her entrance. Many people collected and stood around, wondering; they not seeming as willing—other persuasions I mean—to be dragged or driven in, as our former Friends at Falmouth. It produced quite a sensation among the bystanders. And one of the guard, named D. D., in the station of an elder, treated Mary Davis very rudely, pushing, and crowding, and elbowing her, to get her off the platform of the steps endwise, whence she must have fallen several feet to the ground. But standing as she did between the posts, and against the side-light of the door, she was enabled, without any unseemly effort, to keep her feet; and during this time she had a remarkable testimony to bear to these doorkeepers; in which she spoke in a singular manner, which I could not then exactly comprehend, of the shortness of time, and how very dangerous it was to do anything, under excitement, and a false, blind zeal, which would militate against us, and prove our burden, at the day of righteous retribution! She did not speak loud, or so as to disturb those in the house, and moreover she was outside of the porch door. But David made a deal of noise, crying out against her for speaking, and trying to push her down while under that exercise. However, she did speak several times particularly to them, and before she had done, he gave over pushing.

A. W., another of their elders, and late superintendent of the yearly meeting school, peremptorily commanded us to leave the premises, and declared, if we did not, they would make us; for, said he, in a very boisterous manner (which, however, did not seem to disturb those in the house), "we will have none of your preaching here." After a while, the doorkeepers having succeeded, by great efforts, in getting all but ourselves into the house, and our friends feeling easy to do so, we got into our carriages, and joyfully turned our faces homewards. However, we still had another such scene to pass through, the same week, at Vassalboro' Quarter; only here the guard failed to drive, or —— —— to call, and invite, and persuade, and entreat all present to enter the house. Quite a company remained outside with us. We withdrew a convenient space from the house; the young men brought logs from the woods; and it proved one of the most solid and remarkable meetings which I ever attended. Yet those members of this quarter who stayed with us, did not think they could sustain the quarterly meeting; which I regretted, as there was quite a sufficient number, if they had had a little more faith.

. . . . . . On looking over this letter, I find that I omitted to state, while speaking of the very remarkable communication which dear Mary Davis delivered to the doorkeepers on the steps of Fairfield Meeting-house, how her communication, which seemed singular to me, although I had at the time no doubt of her authority, was explained. Two days afterwards, we heard that a noted Gurneyite minister, who went down, on the other side, to visit these quarterly meetings (and who had been extremely severe and abusive on John Wilbur and Mary Davis, both in the public and business meetings at Falmouth Quarter, the week before), had died very suddenly, and apparently insensible, while on her way to Fairfield; and her husband was then on his way home with her corpse; of which neither Mary Davis nor any of our company had then heard, or had the least outward hint; but which was well known to these people, and when we afterwards heard of it, served to explain some of their conduct otherwise not easily accounted for, any more than Mary's preaching. What puzzled me, was her speaking to them of such a thing having occurred among their ranks, as she did, and warning them therefrom, dwelling upon it, enforcing it; when I could not think of any case to which what she said was applicable, in the sense in which it was uttered. But they doubtless thought she knew all about it, and so shifted it off; although I know she was entirely uninformed of the fact, until two days afterwards. And to me it afforded a fresh and instructive evidence, that the spirit of prophecy is still bestowed even upon some of those who are accounted as the outcasts of Israel. . . .

Truly and affectionately yours,

THOMAS B. GOULD.

To Ethan Foster.

Newport, 22d of first month, 1846.

My dear Friend:

. . . . As for —— ——, I have not heard from him since I saw thee. I have never written to him since the yearly meeting, when I did reply to his notice of the famous committee of their meeting for sufferings coming here; which letter I believe he never received. I very much regret he should have acted as he did, according to the account in thy letter. But when I see the course pursued by some in Philadelphia, of whom we have had more reason to expect different things (for —— —— has always treated us and our cause more or less in a business-like, counting-house, or political manner), I am the less disposed to marvel at *him*, this time, although I wholly disapprove of it. We certainly have seen something of the same thing at head-quarters, though manifested perhaps in a somewhat different and more refined way: and how they are going to extricate themselves from the dilemma in which, as I view it, they are becoming more and more involved, I am wholly at a loss to determine. Poor —— is in a very delicate and critical situation, between two fires, and hard work I think he finds it, to reconcile and explain matters.

. . . . . . If our Philadelphia "Friend" had taken high, and truly Christian, or Quaker ground, with what additional weight would they have been enabled to rally to the standard of truth, which they still profess a strong desire to adhere to; but it is mournfully evident, that it must nevertheless be in their own way and time. They do not like at all, for us to suppose that there is any change amongst them adverse to us; and yet it requires but little discernment, to see that there is, and in prominent places too. There certainly, as R. Wardlaw said, in another case, has been an amazing falling off;—a sorrowful disposition "to do the Jews a pleasure," at our expense. There is a deal of working, manœuvring, and contrivance, to avoid the conflict, all neatly done up under the convenient plea of waiting for the right time to come.

Nevertheless, we have some firm Friends left there yet, but evidently themselves under bondage to those, who, as John Barclay once said, in a letter to thy father Wilbur, "stand high and bear rule, but whose feet have well-nigh slipped, the dragon having nearly swept them down with those who have fallen." However, I am not without an impression that all these manœuvrings will be overruled for good in the end. I should not be surprised if it should result in Philadelphia as it did here; if the very plans, which are laid with the utmost caution in the power of man (whose wisest counsels are often foolishness), should prove the means of helping us, and of the escape of such among themselves as are bound with a heavy yoke. . . . .

It seems they have already granted certificates to enable their members to marry on the other side; within the limits of their yearly meeting, which is "never going to own the Gurneyites!"—and it turns out, in the conclusion of the whole matter, that it is only "pretty much understood that there shall be no obstruction thrown in the way of marriage, until [that] yearly meeting decides the question!" We may guess when this is to be done, by a hint or two thrown out, that they are anxious to obtain *all the information* they can; so that, if way should open for it, they may prepare and publish a statement of the rise and progress of this heresy, beginning with Beaconism, bringing in Henry Bewley's book, and so beating about the bush, and *prolonging* the thing, as "to allow time" for their members to consider and understand the matter, before they are called upon to decide upon our epistle; or rather, before they do decide to receive it! Why, we have been gravely informed, that there is no doubt but we shall *in time* be owned by Philadelphia Yearly Meeting, "if"—mark—"*if* we are careful to keep up our yearly meeting!" Now, my dear friend, how long dost thou think we shall have to keep it up, according to this rule, before that material event takes place? I could give names, but I forbear. . . . .

Thy sincere friend,

THOMAS B. GOULD.

From Zeno Carpenter to T. B. and M. S. Gould.

Utica, the 7th of 9th mo., 1846.

Dearly beloved Friends:

I received your very acceptable letter the day before I left New York, about the time the yearly meeting ended. You have at times been brought very fresh to my memory, and near to my best life, fellow-travellers, bound to Zion, the city of the Living God; be not discouraged nor dismayed, though trials may await you. It's through great tribulation that the righteous enter the kingdom, and the seed is under suffering. Well, my dear friends, I feel myself poor and dependent, stripped and destitute, with nothing to rely on but the mercies and merits of Jesus Christ, often having to go as into the stripping-room, sometimes concluding I am one of the least of all the family; and have been of late under many discouragements on account of the situation of this poor Society. How I have most fervently desired that we might unite and harmonize together! I have heard nothing from you in that land since your yearly meeting, how you fare, whether you still are encouraged to believe you have pursued a right course. I have fervently desired for you, that in your solemn assemblies you may find Him, of whom Moses in the law and the prophets did write, Jesus of Nazareth, to strengthen you to pursue the heavenly journey towards the land of promise. I have prayed fervently for the preservation of the "smaller body" in New England, shall I say, the little flock and royal family. May the "Ancient of days" keep and preserve you in His fear and counsel, that you may stand firm and inflexible in the glorious cause of Truth and Righteousness! Keep low and humble, in humiliation and self-abasedness, and to sound orthodox Quaker doctrine. Let us harbor no new views, nor newfangled sentiments, but those laid down by our forefathers and predecessors in the truth—never a more consistent chain of religious sentiments; let us keep firm thereto, and be careful of imbibing these new floating doctrines in our land, of those who say they are in accordance with ancient Friends. I believe there will be a small number who will stand through all the storms and tempests, and through all the trials that await us;—that this Society will never be extinct. There will be, I firmly believe, a remnant preserved that will serve the Lord with fidelity and uprightness. These will be more and more strengthened to combat every difficulty, every trial and temptation of the enemy of souls, who is continually on the alert to draw aside from the narrow road. If these stand firm, Satan with all his combined forces, never will be able to surmount nor overcome these dedicated servants and handmaidens, that put their whole trust in the Omnipotent Arm of divine power, who is God over all and blessed forever!

It is a day of days, a day of mourning and lamentation, as it was anciently, "Rachel weeping for her children, and would not be comforted because they are not." The ways of Zion do truly mourn, because so few come up to her solemn feasts, so few are concerned to come up to the help of the Lord, against the mighty, that old, hateful and potent enemy. I am a secret mourner, I go mourning on the way, not only for my own short-coming, but for the declension of the Church from her ancient and primitive simplicity and purity. "Call the husbandman to mourning, and those that are skilful of lamentation to wailing; for in all streets shall be wailing!" Oh! my friends! how I do sincerely pray that this little flock and family may be preserved, her stakes lengthened, and cords strengthened, that there may still continue to be a succession of living standard and testimony bearers, that will stand firm for the cause and testimony, and through divine assistance stand immovable against all the powers of death and darkness. This is the fervent desire of one that wisheth health and salvation to the whole human race and family, and especially to the household of faith.

I should have liked to have heard how you got along in your yearly meeting; whether you were favored with the owning presence of kind Providence, and to feel His holy and sweet influence to the soul. What more precious than when we can feel the love of God and his glory to shine in and fill the soul? I am enamoured with it—it is worth more than a thousand of this world in a day that is fast approaching, when we must appear before the Lord and Judge of all the earth, to receive a reward for the deeds done in the body. And may we, dear friends, be prepared for it, having oil in our vessels, and lamps burning, that we may have a welcome admittance into the joys of our Lord! I feel comforted this morning, while I am writing, and am humbly thankful if I can be favored to feel a quiet mind. Oh, matchless goodness and marvellous loving-kindness, that He is still mindful of us, and has not forgotten to be gracious,—that a Being altogether complete without us, should thus condescend from His excellent glory, to bless and to favor with His sweet and sanctifying presence!

I should like to know, if thou wast willing to inform me, how you got along in your yearly meeting. There are many reports, and many hard sayings, concerning the "small body," as that there are "only a few stragglers gone off." I wish you in that part of the land to pay heed to this holy Teacher and Guide into all truth. Then no doubt you will advance in piety and virtue, and increase in number. There are comparatively few in this yearly meeting but what are Gurneyites; some meetings about all.

I now conclude, hoping I have written nothing that will be disagreeable to read; and may we, dear friends, if we never meet again in mutability, meet in the royal palace of God, to sing the song of redeeming love!

Your sure friend,

ZENO CARPENTER.

DRAFT OF A LETTER FROM T. B. G. TO ZENO CARPENTER.

NEWPORT, 9th mo. 11th, 1846.

MY ENDEARED FATHERLY FRIEND:

. . . . It is truly pleasant and strengthening to my dear wife and to myself, to get thy sweet and lively epistles, exhibiting a greenness in old age, and that "thine eye is not dim," in a spiritual sense, nor thy "natural force abated," that thy sword is bright and thy harness on. But oh! how few are left, compared with the "thousands of Israel" who once quickly responded to the sound of the trumpet, and were "prepared for war" when its well-known and certain sound "waked up the mighty men!" These things, the present state of things in our now poor and tempest-tossed, but once highly favored and firmly anchored Society, as thou very justly remarkest, call for mourning and lamentation, and not only so, but for those who are "skilful" therein. Yet how few there are who are truly skilful in this day, in discerning the signs of the times! How should those be able to discern and distinguish clearly, who have not only turned their backs upon the light which maketh manifest, but are even disposed to deny its existence? Still I am comforted in the belief, that there is a living remnant preserved, up and down, who go sorrowing on their way, "weeping day and night for the slain of the daughter of my people;" and that, for the sighing of these poor and the crying of the needy, who have none in heaven or in all the earth to look unto, but Him who is mighty to save and able to deliver even unto the uttermost, the Lord Almighty, in His own due and appointed time, will arise. Even when the days of mourning are ended, and the time is fulfilled, then He will give unto these the oil of joy for mourning, and the garment of praise for the spirit of heaviness; then will Zion arise and shine, because her light is come, and the glory of the Lord hath arisen upon her.

Thou inquirest about our yearly meeting, and whether Friends are still encouraged to believe they have pursued a right course; also in regard to our numbers. Now, it is true we are few in number, compared with those who have gone out from us because they were not of us, and because they were seeking an easier way than that of the cross. Still, our yearly meeting this year was much larger than last, there being between eighty and ninety men, and more than a hundred women in attendance; which, if I am rightly informed, is larger than Baltimore has ever been since the Hicksite separation. But if we had *ever* supposed that the right and wrong of the matter depended on the relative numbers, we have been favored to witness enough of the presence of Him whose promise is as good to the "two or three" who meet in His name, and are gathered to His power, as to the multitude,—to convince us of the contrary. So far as I know or can judge, Friends are still encouraged, and I think more and more so, to believe that they did pursue a right course. Nothing which has since transpired has ever shaken my faith herein. Indeed it is cause of humble thankfulness, that we have been favored to receive so many confirmations of the rectitude of the course, which, under an extremity, we pursued, but not without "great searching of heart," and fervent and united aspirations for Best Help and Direction; which, through adorable mercy, was not withheld, as we humbly trust, either then or since. Surely the Lord is good to them that wait upon Him, to the soul that seeketh Him; and as in the individual, so in the collective capacity. I think I never sat in a more solid yearly meeting, or more favored with the overshadowing of good. Still we feel very weak, and we are so. Much, very much, needs to be done, to bring things into the good order of the Gospel, which has been so long disturbed by the imposition of unsanctified hands. . . . .

From T. B. G. to John Wilbur.

Newport, 10th mo. 11th, 1846.

My dear Friend, John Wilbur:

I have not been unmindful of having given thee encouragement at parting, that I would write on my return from Nantucket. But as I stayed there over first-day, I did not reach home until last third-day, and have been very closely and necessarily engaged ever since. . . . Nathan Page and wife, and Lois Ives, were there. The former had an appointed meeting on fourth-day evening, which was large, and very solid, although it held considerably more than two hours: I marvelled at the patience of the people. The meeting held one hour before Nathan said anything; he stood an hour the first time, and about twenty minutes the second, with some pause between, and more after. But although he was thought to be favored, I did not consider him to be as much so as in the select meeting that morning, or the public quarterly meeting the next day. On both these occasions, he seemed to me and others to be eminently favored. The shutters also were opened on his account, after the business was concluded, and the service on this occasion devolved wholly upon him. He had, I understood, a public meeting at Padan Aram (or some such place), in the neighborhood of New Bedford, on first-day morning, and public notice given of his attendance at New Bedford in the afternoon. I was told, their new house was nearly or quite filled, and that he stood about an hour and a half at each place. . . . On sixth and seventh-days, I went with Prince Gardner and Peleg Mitchell, to see a few sick and afflicted people,—some six or eight families,—without seeing much more than a compliance with Friends' desire, that they should be noticed, except in two or three cases, where I felt particularly drawn. These last were to me times of favor, not soon to be forgotten; and as for the others, I suppose the purpose was answered merely by our calling. . . . I felt well satisfied with sitting with Friends there, in their meetings on first-day, without any notice being given. There appeared to be over two hundred persons present, both fore and afternoon. The meetings were mostly silent. . . . .

By a letter recently received from Philadelphia, it appears there are others there who entertain the same views as dear old E. C. The letter says, we "need not expect much from those who stand high and bear rule in the city;" that if they can only get matters settled without a separation, they will care but little what becomes of us! In order to effect this, the writer thinks that they will write again to London, complaining of J. J. G., and that he will eventually be induced to take back some things and smooth down others, and so the whole thing will be hushed up and quieted down, without being probed to the bottom! To prepare the way for this, she says, the doctrine of quietness, charity, forbearance, &c., is being preached now by some who have been themselves subjected to this kind of censure, formerly, on account of the same kind of "imprudence," by plain-speaking and straightforward conduct, which, in their turn, they now bestow upon others not yet remodelled. She speaks of B. H. W. and many other honest friends, as having been brought under this quieting influence, so as to be made willing to wait "five years," for those not yet prepared to take a stand in our favor, without being aware of the nature and design of it at all. She says, this kind of feeling prevails most, where the man, whom we all most deeply lament and deplore, as a standard-bearer having fainted, has most influence. The letter gives rather a discouraging view of things, both as it respects their standing and our prospects, so far as it relates to our being owned by them as a yearly meeting. The writer, however, seems to think we are as well off as any other yearly meeting; and of this, so far as it relates to Gurneyism, under one phase or other, there seems to be little doubt. . . . .

Thy sincere friend,

T. B. GOULD.

TO JOHN WILBUR.

NORTH BERWICK, ME., 19th of 10th mo., 1846.

MY DEAR FRIEND, JOHN WILBUR:

. . . .

Salem Quarterly Meeting was attended by about five-and-twenty men; and about half that number of women stayed through the meeting, some having left at the close of the public meeting, which was long silent, and laborious indeed to me; although, after Nathan Page had spoken, the clouds seemed to disperse. The meetings for business, both men's and women's, seemed to be times of more openness and favor, and I trust it ended pretty well. The next evening we had an appointed meeting at a pretty village, about a mile northeast of Nathan Page's house; which was well attended, the house being nearly filled; among the rest, one of Governor Endicott's descendants, bearing his name, was present. The people seemed raw enough, and scarcely to know anything of Friends' principles, some of which were opened to them; and eventually the way was made for the declaration of the Gospel to them, in, I humbly trust, a good degree of the spirit and power of it. After which, Nathan preached to them a pretty long while; when, having expressed satisfaction with the company of such as had given attendance, the meeting separated under a covering of much solemnity.

Yesterday, being first-day, we sat with Friends of North Berwick in the morning, and in the evening attended a meeting previously appointed for us at Great Falls. I went to it under a feeling of inexpressible discouragement. The whole day and evening was very wet, dark, and uncomfortable; but I was surprised, on entering the Town Hall, a very large and beautiful building, in which it was held, to find many people already assembled, notwithstanding the inclemency of the weather; and I can truly say, that I rejoiced in the conviction that the Master was with them. Others soon came in, to the number, as Friends thought, of seven or eight hundred; and I thought I was never made more feelingly sensible of the flowing and abounding of Gospel love towards any people, than to them; of which I soon apprehended it to be my duty to inform them.

A door of utterance and of entrance was mercifully and largely opened. Many literally said, Amen, to the Gospel truths declared; and, having taken my seat, a Methodist minister present, who, it seems, had been previously prepared to believe and to practise upon that divine precept, "Freely ye have received, freely give," stood up and expressed his great joy at having been not only permitted to hear the word of the Lord, but to feel the power, life, and substance of the things spoken of; adding, that he also could say, that he was not ashamed of the Gospel of Christ, because it is the power of God unto salvation to them that believe,—that, as long as he could remember, Friends had borne testimony to the power of the Gospel, to vital, practical, inward religion, to the substance of things, and against the form and shadow,—that his heart's desire and prayer was, that they might never lower this standard; but, on the contrary, might go on and prosper, and be enabled to exalt it, until others should be induced to rally to it, and to fight under it,—adding, there never was more need, &c. He stood, I thought, a little too long, yet the solemnity continued; and believing it right for me to add a very few words, by way of acknowledgment of their company and good behavior, and earnestly and affectionately commending them unto God and the word of His grace, as to that which was able to build them up, and to give them an inheritance among all those who are sanctified, the meeting was concluded, under a feeling of unutterable thankfulness to the God and Father of all our sure mercies, who had been pleased to send us help from the sanctuary, and to strengthen us out of Zion. Thou seest I have written freely to thee, believing it was thy due to know a little how we have got along. . . . . .

Do please write to me; and when it is well with thee, remember one of the poorest and weakest children (if I may be called one) that was ever sent out on such an errand. Farewell.

Thine as ever,
THOMAS B. GOULD.

TO MARTHA S. GOULD.

SALEM, 24th of 10th month, 1846.

MY DEAR MARTHA:

. . . . We reached William Hill's about nine o'clock, and the next day went, in company with William and Elizabeth, down to Kennebunk, where the Baptist meeting-house was well filled with people; who, although much unacquainted with Friends, came in very orderly at a quarter before eight o'clock, and behaved solidly and well through a pretty long silence; and how much longer it would have remained so I do not know, if Mary Varney had not "opened a door" for me, which I found it my place to enter, and things were opened which perhaps they never thought or heard of before. After which, dear Elizabeth Hill did preach most sweetly to them. She rather exceeds my expectations; still I had expected much of her. After she sat down, I found it my place to show from Joel, as quoted and applied by the Apostle Peter, that the Spirit was to be poured out on daughters as well as sons, &c. I felt great openness, both in regard to the call and qualification for the ministry, and the nature of Divine worship; as also of the necessity for all ministers of Christ implicitly to obey His injunction: "Freely ye have received, freely give."

We returned the same night to William Hill's, and reached there about twelve o'clock. But there was one thing I forgot to mention. Soon after we got to Timothy Varney's, at Kennebunk, J. M. and his wife, who live some thirty miles below, came there, on their way home, to stay all night, not knowing of our presence. They were Gurneyites, old people, and the woman had abused John Wilbur shamefully, when he was lately in their country. Before meeting, W. Hill and I. Buffinton accosted her pretty smartly about it. She shrunk back, as much as I ever saw one, but they drew her forth; and when I saw this fairly done, I thought I would try a little to help; and opening things somewhat as though I did it not, the old man began to fall in with what was said, and own it to be truth; which he did more and more, till he was not a little convinced, and I thought it well to leave the subject. But not thinking for all this, that they would dare to go to meeting, when we were about to go, Israel said I had better take leave of them, as they would most likely retire before we came back from meeting; so I shook hands with the woman, but offering my hand to her husband, he said he thought he should go with us. His wife made some objection, but he seemed determined to go, feeble as he was, and he went; after which he expressed to Israel his satisfaction with the meeting. We returned to William Hill's that night, a distance of fifteen miles, and reached there about twelve o'clock.

The next day I was down sick, not having been far from it for some days before. Fourth and fifth-days, quarterly meeting at Berwick; about sixty Friends present; both meetings times of favor. An appointed meeting on fourth-day evening, at North Berwick village, although Joshua Meader and others thought well of it, did not seem to me to be quite so well. I had to move very slowly and cautiously to find the stepping-stones, and to keep on them. Sixth-day, after quarterly meeting, we went to Lowell, William Hill in company; and had an appointed meeting there the same evening. But there were not more than sixty or seventy people present, the notice being short, as it was late before we could find a place to hold it in; and those who did come were not exactly the persons I had wished to see. . . . . . There were some plain and close things delivered. We lodged at a great hotel; and in the morning (seventh-day) went, before breakfast, to Boston, some twenty miles, after which we proceeded to Roxbury. . . . . .

We went back to Salem that night, where I commenced and wrote the first two sides of this sheet. Attended Salem meeting in the morning, and Lynn in the afternoon of first-day. After meeting, went over to Boston and lodged, in order to reach Fall River (where I am now writing) in time to attend their monthly meeting yesterday, which I did. I go to Freetown, about eight miles north of this, to an appointed meeting this evening, and to-morrow to Luther Lincoln's, twenty-two miles, where there is another meeting appointed for to-morrow evening. . . .

Thy own,
T. B. Gould.

To Rebecca Walton.

Newport, 11th mo., 10th, 1846.

My dear Friend, Rebecca Walton:

. . . . I have wanted and intended writing to thee, almost ever since thou left; but was either too unwell, or too busy to do it, before I left home for my eastern journey. When I started, I provided myself with writing apparatus for this very purpose, and I think I can truly say that I never lost sight of it for a day: but I suffered so much with asthma the whole time, that all I could do was now and then to write to my dear Martha.

In respect both to bodily suffering and exercise of mind, this journey has, indeed, cost me dear; but, through unmerited mercy, I have had no reason to doubt the rectitude of the concern. On the contrary, I have been confirmed in it day by day; and way has been made for me to get along, to my humbling admiration, unspeakable relief, and apparently to the satisfaction of Friends wherever I have been. But it has seemed much my lot to go forth into the highways and hedges, having meetings in divers places where, so far as was known to me or Friends, none were ever held before. And although the service was laborious, many of the people seeming quite strangers to our principles, and alike ignorant of "the mystery which has been hid for ages and generations," yet many of these, on being turned to Christ within, as the Way, the Truth, and the Life, the all-sufficient Teacher of His people, and the sure hope of the saints' glory,—received the word with "gladness," and acknowledged that these things were so,—some of them in a very remarkable manner. Divers, even of the ministers of other societies, Episcopalian, Baptist, and Methodist, who not only freely opened their meeting-houses to us, but themselves attended the meeting—(although I am very sure *their* principles were not advocated),—acknowledged what was delivered was the word of faith which the apostles preached; and in many instances, feelingly, I thought, bade us God speed. But among the people more especially, there evidently was a precious seed to be visited, and, I have no doubt, to be yet gathered; for it did and does still seem to me, that in many places the fields are already white unto the harvest. But, alas! the faithful laborers are few, very few indeed! Would that the Lord of the harvest would send such into the field: and if such as have been raised up, and qualified and concerned to go forth, are unfaithful, I am more and more persuaded and convinced, that, as it were, the very stones will cry out.

At Great Falls, New Hampshire, we had a meeting on a first-day evening, in the Town Hall. The day and evening were as wet, cold, and uncomfortable as a severe northeaster in that cold country could well make it; and I did not suppose that there would be more than fifty or sixty people out. (There is but one family of Friends in the town, and this family is with us.) But to my great surprise, when we reached the house, there were four or five hundred already assembled; and I thought, as I entered and took my seat, that the Master Himself was with them of a truth. Nearly as many more soon after came in, and it proved to be, through Holy Help, a time long to be remembered. . . . . At another place, a woman having walked five miles to the village of Westport in the morning, about her own business, saw the notice there of our meeting at three o'clock the same afternoon, and felt a strong desire to attend it, but could not without returning home; which she did on foot, and returned in the same way, making,—if she walked home again, which she expected to do,—twenty miles in all, that day. She seemed a feeble woman, too, but did not apparently regret coming. She said, it was ten years since she had attended a Friends' meeting. In our passing up and down, now and then we fell in with some of the Gurney side, who came to meeting, and afterwards went from one meeting to another: but these were young people, who probably did not care much about the matter.

Having appointed a meeting at Kennebunk, a small town in Maine, about fifteen miles east of North Berwick, we went thither, and stopped at the house of Timothy Varney, the only Friends' family in the place, of any description. . . . . . .

Believe me to be sincerely,
Thy affectionate friend.

To Rebecca Walton.

Newport, 23d of 12th mo., 1846.

My dear Friend:

. . . . . In one of thy letters thou asked me to give thee that anecdote of Isaac Lawton and the little negro boy, which I related to thee when thou wast here. I quite forgot it when I wrote. It is as follows, as nearly as I remember:

During the war of the Revolution, the British army took possession of the island of Rhode Island, and kept it for some time—I think one or two years. A company of these troops was stationed in Friends' meeting-house, at Portsmouth. One day, while Friends were thus deprived of the use of it, Isaac Lawton, a minister in good esteem, who belonged to that meeting, felt his mind drawn to go to the meeting-house, from which he lived about two miles distant. He went; and after some time, commenced preaching to the soldiers present. The opening on his mind was large, the concern weighty, and he expected to have much to say: but he had not proceeded far, when his way seemed entirely closed, he felt a full stop, and sat down abruptly. This surprised him, after so large an opening, and having, as he thought, clearly seen how he was to treat the subject. He had, however, scarcely taken his seat, when a little negro boy (I think about twelve years of age), who was present in attendance upon one of the officers, stood up with the same subject, commencing where Isaac had left off, and treating it as he had expected to do. He went on with such clearness and authority, and kept so close to what had been opened to Isaac's view, that the latter fully expected to be released from further labor on that occasion. But the little boy, after having spoken at some length, sat down as suddenly and unexpectedly to Isaac, as his appearance had been unexpected and striking. Isaac Lawton took up the subject where the boy left it, and continued to speak until he had relieved his own mind. Such is the account of this remarkable incident, as nearly as I can remember, in the language of Abigail Robinson and Stephen Gould, both of whom related it to me in their day, and they both knew I. Lawton well. I have also, some time since, seen it substantially the same in print—I think, in the "Irish Friend." Abigail Robinson was an eminent minister of this meeting, and Stephen Gould was a valuable elder, who collected an abundance of remarkable anecdotes. . .

Brother George and sister paid us a visit, the first of this month, on their way home from Sandwich Quarterly Meeting, held at New Bedford. They reported a good meeting, and well attended, although the day was very stormy. Seth and Mary Davis, and several Nantucket

Friends of their quarterly meeting's committee, had been down on the Cape, to visit Sandwich Monthly Meeting, a day or two previous. They were not very kindly received, nor allowed to enter the public meeting! The committee reported accordingly, and the quarterly meeting, having come to the judgment that that monthly meeting ought to be laid down, unless it would conform, &c.,—made a minute to that effect; which they directed to the monthly meeting, in order that if their advice and judgment be not regarded, they may dissolve it at their next quarter, and attach their members to New Bedford Monthly Meeting. I was glad to hear this, as there were some suffering cases among the members of that monthly meeting, who did not, in effect, belong anywhere. . . . . .

Thy sincere friend,
THOMAS B. GOULD.

FROM PRINCE GARDNER TO T. B. G.

NANTUCKET, seventh month, 6th, 1847.

MY DEAR FRIEND, THOMAS B. GOULD:

Thy acceptable letter of the 28th was received in due time. It was truly a satisfaction to hear from thee and thy dear Martha, who has an affectionate abiding-place in my mind, having been long since, I trust, brought into the unity of the Spirit in the bond of peace. What a precious favor, to be thus united into that oneness with our dear friends, whereby we may be enabled to rejoice with those that do rejoice, and to mourn with them that mourn! I think I may say, that thou art at times brought to feel as bone of my bone and flesh of my flesh, with living desires that the dear Redeemer may be round about, in every proving, trying dispensation that may be meted out for the accomplishment of His great and sovereign will; that we may be enabled often to say, thy rod and thy staff they comfort me.

Sensible we are, dear friend, of the truth of the declaration, that as gold and silver are tried in the fire, so are acceptable men and women in the furnace of affliction. I often feel desirous for myself, that patience may have its perfect work; being fully sensible, as this is abode in, deliverance will be wrought, by and through Him who was "a man of sorrows and acquainted with grief." And we have much to be thankful for; many are our blessings. I was ready to say, why do these things arise, to write to one who knows them well; but perhaps for our mutual encouragement, to be enabled to bear all and suffer all that may be dispensed in unerring wisdom, and to lay our mouths as in the dust, trusting in the encouraging promise of Him who said, "I will never leave thee nor forsake thee." May this be our individual experience, saith my soul.

. . . . . . I was pleased to hear of your particular meeting, that thou felt satisfied, and I have no doubt thou wilt; and it seems to me as though there might be an increase. But be that as it may, if we can feel something of the dear Redeemer near, who is often pleased to meet with those who have to sit in low and solitary places, what more can be asked or desired? To feel something of that solemn, quiet covering, which is not at our command, is cause of a little renewal of strength; though I believe every rightly exercised mind will feel the awful responsibility to hold all our meetings in the power of the Lord.

. . . . Our love is affectionately to —— —— and wife, I think I can say, with fervent desires for their encouragement, in this day of close trial and proving of our faith and allegiance to the great Head of the Church; as waymarks to honest inquirers for the truth as it is in Jesus, the great Preserver of men; speaking the language, in the line of conduct and intercourse with the world, Come follow us, as we are endeavoring to follow the great Head of the Church. How often are such made preachers of righteousness in their daily walks in life! Thou wilt please give our love to thy dear parents, who are often in my remembrance, with desires that they, in the decline of life, may know a being supported by that supporting arm of power, which can cause their setting sun to go down in peace. My love is to all who love the unchangeable truth. Now I must close, with saying that a letter from thee at any time will be very acceptable. Thou hast not got to learn, that I am neither a scholar nor much of a letter-writer; but in love I do feel at times to address my dear friends. My dear Mary joins in affectionate love to thee and thy dear Martha. Farewell for this time.

From thy attached friend,
PRINCE GARDNER.

FROM T. B. G. TO JOHN WILBUR.

NEWPORT, 20th of ninth month, 1847.

MY DEAR FRIEND, JOHN WILBUR:

. . . . A friend, who visited Ezra Comfort a short time before his death, told me recently, that such was Ezra's concern to come here, that he then said, if he had strength of body sufficient, he should make the attempt, notwithstanding the objections and opposition of those who bear rule in the city. . . . . .

How long will these things have to be? How long will they be permitted to rule, both at home and abroad?—hindering some from going, and others from coming; neither entering heartily into the work, nor suffering others? I have been ready to query sometimes, whether the cause of truth was not likely to suffer as much from some who stand high and bear rule in that city, as from those whom some of themselves used to denominate the "Providence Clique." And it would seem, from the effects and extent of their operations, that they are not less strongly "combined together," to weary us out, and rid themselves of us; however zealously they may exert themselves to put forth testimonies against unsound doctrine in the abstract. May they not expect to dispose of our rights and interest in the case, the easier, on account of having issued these testimonies, as it relates to our sincere but unsuspecting friends in that and other yearly meetings? . . . . .

Thy sincere friend,
THOMAS B. GOULD.

To Joshua Maule.

Newport, 1st mo. 27th, 1848.

My dear Brother:

Thine of the 20th was duly received yesterday, and we were truly glad to get it, having heard nothing from you since your last letter, giving an account of your very close trials, although we have felt very anxious to hear.

. . . Thy account of the pause to which your adversaries seemed to have come, reminded me of the proceedings of ours, before the separation. They often seemed to come to their "wits' end," and would sometimes cease all visible action for several months together; but we generally found the old adage verified in them, "after a calm there comes a storm;" for they never lost sight of their work, and would fall upon it again with redoubled vigor; and it frequently appeared that they had been diligently engaged, all the while, maturing their plans, and preparing materials in secret, so as to advance with more certainty and effect. But I have sometimes thought, and especially since I read thy letter at Greenwich, that the worse they act, the better for you, provided always that Friends are vigilant and firm. After such a calm time, when they started again, we generally found they had gained one or more, sometimes several, who had previously travelled with us; and in this way our sufferings were greatly increased, until we were so reduced in strength and numbers, that there seemed to be literally nothing left to cling to or rely upon, but the Helper of His people; when all men seemed to forsake us, as they did and still generally do, forsake Him. Well, my dear brother and sister, for very near and very dear you both are to my best feelings (as well as natural), whatever conflicts of spirit and trials of faith may be your portion, and however great the perils to which you may be exposed, among false brethren; may your bow abide in strength, and the arms of your hands be made strong by the power of the mighty God of Jacob, who remains to be both the Shepherd and the stone of Israel! He is the Good Shepherd who laid down His life, his most precious life, for the sheep; He gathers the lambs in his arms, and carries them in his bosom, and sweetly strengthens their faith, animates their hope, and encourages them to bear up and press forward, with his own divine injunction and promise: "Fear not, little flock, for it is your Father's good pleasure to give you the kingdom." Oh! I am persuaded that as you and other Friends there abide faithful unto Him, amidst all that has been or may be suffered to come upon you, He will more and more lead you into the green pastures of life, and cause you to lie down beside the still waters thereof, where nothing can hurt you or make you afraid! Even when it shall hail, coming down with destructive effect upon the forest (the tall cedars of Lebanon and the sturdy oaks of Bashan), "the city shall be low, in a low place." The city which the Lord hath chosen, to place His name there, to manifest His power there, shall be low, in a low place; and so it, as well as all the inhabitants thereof (who have been gathered into it by the power of Him who reigneth King in the midst thereof, for it is the city of the saints' solemnities, where their spiritual sacrifices and offerings are daily offered up);—it with its inhabitants shall be preserved by Him, who remains to be a shadow from the heat, and a covert from the tempest and from the storm, even when the blast of the terrible one shall beat against the wall. This is the city which hath foundations, whose builder and maker the Lord alone is. Here the Stone of Israel is found. "Behold I lay in Zion, for a foundation, a stone, a tried stone, a sure foundation;" whosoever believeth therein and buildeth thereon shall neither make haste nor be confounded. Every tongue that riseth up in judgment against these, they shall condemn, because they are not to be judged by man's judgment, any more than the apostle was. For he that is spiritual judgeth all things by the spirit of judgment and of a sound mind, which has been bestowed upon him and restored to him, yet he himself is judged of no man. Such are not to subject themselves, or rather, subject the Lord's work and service, to man's judgment; but they are to keep a single eye to Him, and to the support of His testimonies, and the honor of his worthy name, and of the blessed unchangeable truth. "To whom we gave place by subjection," said the faithful and experienced apostle, when some who seemed to be somewhat, withstood and opposed him, "no, not for an hour, that the truth of the Gospel might continue with you!" And when the truth of the Gospel is involved and at stake, there is nothing gained by yielding, time-serving, and political manœuvring; but on the contrary, the cause is given or thrown away by it, and our own habitations in the truth are not "kept," but are always greatly endangered, if not ultimately and wholly lost. . . . . I conclude, and remain with sincerity, your affectionate brother,

THOMAS B. GOULD.

FROM PRINCE GARDNER TO T. B. G.

NANTUCKET, 2d mo. 21st, 1848.

MY DEAR FRIEND, THOMAS B. GOULD:

I have at times thought to address thee in a few lines, I trust from near unity of spirit which binds together the whole household of faith, extending over sea and land; if nothing more, than to serve as a token of my remembrance of thee and thine, and of the many hours spent together, in sweet communion; knowing at times what it is to suffer together, and favored at seasons to be permitted to rejoice together, so that we have cause to number our blessings, under all our privations. And what a mercy, from Him who knows what is best for us, that a little evidence is at times vouchsafed, that we have so merciful a High Priest, touched with the feeling of our infirmities, and knowing how to succor all those that put their trust and confidence in Him!

Thou knowest well, dear friend, what it is to have deep afflictions and many discouragements, when at times almost ready to say, "Carest thou not that we perish?" But, through adorable Mercy, thou hast at seasons felt the lifting up of His countenance upon thee, and the Sun of righteousness to shine on thy path, and been ready to say, "What shall I render unto thee, oh, Lord, for all thy benefits!" Then is there not cause to lift up the head in hope, trusting in the Lord, journeying forward in the way

He is pleased to lead? My mind is engaged for thy encouragement, so that, in the final completion of His great and sovereign will, thou, with all the faithful, mayst know a being gathered into that rest prepared for the people of God. . . . . .

When we take a view over our tried Society, and see so many who have stood as bright and shining lights, and now their brightness is eclipsed, a veil drawn over their brightness, is it not enough to make the faithful tremble for themselves, saying, "Who is sufficient for these things?" —having cause to fear that too many, from not dwelling low and humble before the Lord, have been dandled as on the lap of Delilah; and strong men have fallen asleep, until she has taken the seven locks of their strength, as it respects their best interest; and then, in this situation, when attempting to move in a sphere they once were enabled rightly to move in, behold their strength is gone! Yet, unwilling their loss should be discovered and their nakedness appear, they must be doing something, lest they lose their reputation. Thus they join with the great, the popular, the worldly and high-minded, or follow in their tracks, and fall an easy prey to speculative opinions and traditions of men; tossed to and fro, carried about with every wind of doctrine—almost anything rather than lose their great name! Well, surely, such do not produce the peaceable fruits of righteousness, but on the contrary, disorder and confusion.

I have long believed, as Friends remain faithful, keeping their ranks in righteousness, they need not be over anxious as to the future. I have an unshaken belief that the Lord will ever have a living remnant, whom he will be pleased to set His name amongst: so that I feel desirous that Friends making so high a profession may be more and more bringing forth fruits agreeable thereto; and I hope and trust it is so. And now, in drawing to a close, dear friend, I can say we are favored with health, our friends generally so. . . . Mary unites with me in affectionate love to thee, to Martha, and your dear children, to thy dear parents and their family, to all our friends as though named, in thy freedom. I can truly say I love all who love the unchangeable truth. Farewell. From thy attached friend,

PRINCE GARDNER.

FROM T. B. G. TO JOHN L. KITE.

NEWPORT, 3d mo. 17th, 1848.

MY DEAR FRIEND:

Thy letter was duly received, and we were truly glad to hear from thee, although the remembrance of thee and of thy timely visit had not passed away. We have often recurred to it, as one of the pleasant things permitted for our encouragement, in the course of our solitary pilgrimage through a wilderness country, where but few travellers are met with who are willing to pursue the same course, and to give us the right hand of fellowship.

Thou mayst suppose that I have been unmindful of thy request, to give thee an account of James Scribbens; but notwithstanding the delay, it has not been forgotten; although, being compelled to rely upon tradition, after taking some pains, I find myself wholly unable to tell thee even where he was born, or when he died. The anecdotes which I have heard of him, were chiefly related to me by several worthy Friends, since deceased, and independently of each other, but all substantially agreeing: That he was a man of very small natural talents indeed, not having common sense, or being capable of procuring his own livelihood, or even of knowing when he had eaten or drunken sufficiently; but that he had a very striking, convincing, and remarkable gift in the ministry conferred upon him, under the exercise of which it was no unusual occurrence for him to bring tears from the eyes of the audience, to such a degree, that there would be wet spots upon the floor between the benches on which the people sat; although, on his first rising, his appearance was so contemptible, and his matter so incoherent, and sometimes [apparently] so nonsensical, that it produced laughter among those who were assembled. But the old man would pull the cap which he wore upon his head, one way and another, and say to such as made themselves merry, "My good Master has not come yet. When He does come, you will laugh on the other side of your mouths!"—which was generally verified, as the Life and Power arose into dominion; the excellency of the Power being rendered more fully apparent, by the manifest weakness of the instrument made use of, that no flesh should glory in the Master's presence. Abigail Robinson (Mary R. Morton's sister), a very superior woman, and an excellent minister, who lived and died in this town, told me, many years ago, that when James Scribbens had a concern to travel as a minister, Peter Davis (of whom Joseph Oxley makes honorable mention in his Journal, and who, by the way, was John Wilbur's grandfather), generally, if not always, went with him, to take care of him; for, she added, he was not capable of taking care of himself out of meeting. And I have heard J. Wilbur say, that his grandfather Davis found it particularly necessary to watch over him at the table, it being customary in those days to put cider and other strong drink upon it; and when James took up the tankard, Peter would say, "Take care, James; that's strong cider." When they came to Newport, to attend the yearly meeting, A. Robinson informed me, they were wont to lodge at the house of her maternal grandparents, Thomas and Mary Richardson, which, as I am passing, I will say was at that time *the* house for Friends of note to lodge at: T. and M. Richardson being truly honorable elders; and he was for a long time Clerk of the yearly meeting. Their house was thronged with company of the best and most discerning kind. Yet it had been handed down from them to Abigail Robinson, that (I think on more than one occasion) after James had been powerfully engaged in testimony in the large public meetings during yearly meeting week, on returning to his lodgings, before a room full of company, he boasted that *he* preached, and that he preached excellently, too. "No, James," said Mary Richardson, "thou art greatly mistaken; *thou* hast not preached this day."—Why, he was sure he had, and that he did it well.—"No, James, it was thy *Gift* that preached," said Mary Richardson.

On one occasion of his being in Newport, I think, it so

happened that he got into the street alone, and being met by an envious priest, who was aware of his proverbial* weakness, the priest challenged him to a public dispute in relation to Friends' principles and doctrines, which he readily accepted. A time and place were fixed, upon the spot, and James ran home to his lodgings, and reported it to his friends; who, not a little alarmed at the intelligence, told him it would never do; that the priest was a man of sense and learning, and would certainly get an advantage over him, and that he must consider his own infirmities, and the honor of Truth. But James was inflexible, and quite confident of success; said that he had accepted the challenge, and it would be dishonorable to flinch; and not only so, but that "his good Master would stand by him, and support His own cause." Friends finally yielded, and bore him company, and, in the language of my informant, he came off "entirely victorious!" I think I had this from John Wilbur.

James Scribbens belonged to South Kingston Monthly Meeting, and lived sometimes with one Friend, and sometimes with another, in different parts of the Narragansett country. He was usually employed in some way which did not require much skill or thought; and at one time, while residing in the family of a Friend who lived near to one Doctor MacSparran (an Episcopalian missionary, who was sent over from England by "The Society for the Propagation of the Gospel in Foreign Parts," and settled in Narragansett, in 1727, I think, and appears to have been a learned and eloquent man), and being engaged in repairing a breach in a stone wall (or fence), by the roadside, the Doctor, who entertained a most contemptible opinion of the Quakers in general, and of James Scribbens in particular, in passing by on horseback, reined up his horse, and thus accosted him: "Well, James, how many tons of pudding and milk will it take, to make forty rods

* When I was a child, and before one of these anecdotes was related to me, or I had otherwise heard his name, I frequently heard persons who were not connected with Friends, use the proverb, "As weak as Scribbens." I have no doubt it had relation to him. I have also heard it since that time. It is a common saying here.

of stone wall?" Whereupon James dropped the stone which he held in his hand, and looking at the self-sufficient Doctor, said, "Just as many as it will take, of hireling priests, to make a Gospel minister!"

. . . . It so happened, that a man of note and learning, whose name I have forgotten, although I think he was a lawyer and a statesman, and eminent in both respects, attended a meeting in which James Scribbens preached; and was so affected by what he heard, that at the close of the meeting, he requested some Friend with whom he was acquainted, to introduce him to the speaker; commending the sermon in strong terms, and remarking that so great a preacher *must* be a very sensible and learned man, and that he wished to have some religious conversation with him, and to ask him some questions. The Friend (whose name I have also forgotten), endeavored to divert him from his purpose, by explaining the nature of our principles with regard to the ministry; that it was neither natural nor acquired abilities, but the reception of a heavenly gift, and the renewed extension of Divine favor, which rendered the labors of our ministers so weighty and powerful: that they were not however always alike favored; that this gift was sometimes bestowed in a remarkable manner, not only upon illiterate men, but upon those of small natural understanding; so that if he were introduced to such in private, after witnessing their public services, he would be at once surprised and disappointed. It was difficult to put the inquirer by; but the Friend at length succeeded, telling him withal that J. S. would probably attend a meeting at another place the next day, I think. To that meeting, however, the interested man followed James Scribbens; who was again engaged in testimony, in such a way as to increase the desire he felt to be introduced to and converse with him; of which he failed not to inform the Friend, who had invited him to attend it, and who found it still more difficult at this time to prevent their coming in contact with each other, than before. But he finally succeeded, and also gave similar information of another meeting at some distance, to which J. Scribbens was bound.

This meeting proved to be a time of more eminent favor than either of the others; and at the close of it a determination was manifested to converse with James, which the Friend could no longer resist. He accordingly introduced the parties to each other at another Friend's house (where I think they all dined); but the man whose feelings had been so wrought upon, and whose expectations had been raised to such a height, manifested his surprise and disappointment, upon attempting to enter into religious conversation with J. S., by exclaiming to the Friend who had done his best to prevent it, "He *is* a fool!"—and instead of putting difficult theological questions to this weak but sometimes highly favored instrument, for solution, he simply asked him the meaning of some ordinary words in the English language; to which James with great simplicity replied, that he did not know.—"But," said the inquirer, "you made use of those words in your preaching today." —"Very well," said J. Scribbens, "I knew *then!*" In the conclusion, this man confessed that he had read many books upon the subject, but that his acquaintance with James Scribbens had furnished the most conclusive evidence of the truth of the Quaker doctrine of divine immediate revelation, that he had ever met with.

It is said, there is but a step from the sublime to the ridiculous; and so it is related of James Scribbens, that while riding in the woods, he was sorely afflicted with toothache; and verily thinking he should not live, he dismounted, tied his horse to one tree, and lay down under another to die. Directly it occurred to him, that if he should die there, people would say that he died drunk, and what a reproach it would be! So he got up, and with a piece of chalk which he took from his pocket, wrote upon the tree, "*James Scribbens died with the toothache*,"—and lay down again to die. By-and-bye his tooth became easier; he mounted his horse and rode off, leaving the notice of his death, and the cause of it, plainly inscribed upon the tree.

Now, although I have, in a bungling way, and without regard to order and method, put down the chief of what I have heard respecting J. S., yet I want thee distinctly to understand, that even if thou should think it worth while to print any part of it, I shall expect thee to put it into better shape than this for the press. The last anecdote, and several other particulars, I have merely noticed, to give thee as full an idea of the man as I well could, with the scanty materials at command. I intended to have written to John Wilbur for information respecting him, but owing to my many engagements, have omitted it, until it was too late, if thou get this in any reasonable time. I should think he would be as likely to know about him as anybody now living, if not more so. Christopher Healy once lived in the same neighborhood, and may probably have some knowledge of him. . . . . . .

Fourth mo., 2d.—I am just in that nervous, depressed state of mind, that I seem ready to doubt of "any good;" and almost everything—even those comparable to grasshoppers—have become burdensome. Not but that I am still truly glad to receive letters from my friends, and the reading of thine again, yesterday, was momentarily refreshing, in the feeling of life and Gospel fellowship in which it was evidently written. But it has not dissipated the gloom with which I am surrounded, almost overwhelmed, so that I had almost come to the conclusion to write no more letters; hoping thus to escape the commission of some folly; which I am quite sure I should commit, were I either to undertake to set forth by number the clouds which appear in the horizon, according to my apprehension, or to frame an image of the good things of which thou speakest, and of which, I doubt not thou wast authorized to speak. To one who can feel for those who are in bonds, as bound with them,—to a member of that body in which, if one member suffers, all the living members suffer with it,—what I have written will be sufficient, if not too much. And so, with unfeigned love to thee, and a sincere desire to be remembered for good, in the nearest approaches of all saints to the Lord,

I conclude, and am thy friend,

THOMAS B. GOULD.

To William Hodgson.

Elmside, Newport, 26th of ninth month, 1850.

My dear Friend, William Hodgson, Jr.:

. . . If I should undertake to teach thee, as Job's comforters did him, how to conduct thyself under affliction, thou might justly reply to me as he did to one of them: "Lo, mine eye hath seen all this, mine ear hath heard and understood it." Still I cannot doubt thou hast very close trials and exercises to pass through, by the permission, if not in the ordering, of Him "who setteth the solitary in families," and who hath unquestionably clothed some with the spirit of mourning and lamentation, and made them skilful therein. And surely the day in which we live calls for it; for it is a day of treading down and perplexity, wherein the wayfaring man ceaseth, and many of the standard-bearers have fainted: even such as seemed strong for the work; but they have seen that "rest is good, and the land that it is pleasant;" and so they have deserted the standard of truth, and bowed their shoulders to bear another yoke than the cross of Christ, and so become servants unto him who always was an enemy thereto.

In times of great trial and difficulty, when some of those upon whom we had been accustomed in some sort to lean, (or of whom we had expected that they would lead forward in the work of rebuilding the wall which has been broken down, or in setting up the gates of that city, which have been burnt as with fire,) have been removed by death, and taken from the evil to come, and others have been wounded by the archers in the enemy's camp, and have fainted and fallen on the right hand and on the left; how much harder work it makes for such as are left, for those who dare not desert their posts and flinch in the day of battle, because they prefer the welfare of Jerusalem and the prosperity of Zion above their chiefest joy. And thus it frequently happens that such as did consider themselves in the rear, are constrained to move forward and to stand in the breach, although by so doing for Zion's sake, they are still more exposed, as a mark for every archer. Neither can these lay down their defensive weapons, put off their clothes, or take that rest, which is as natural and desirable to them as to others; only for Zion's sake they will not seek for it, or avail themselves of it, when it is offered to them, on condition of their surrendering the city to the ravages of the destroyer.

. . . I have often secretly desired that thy bow might abide in strength, and that the arms of thy hands might continue to be made strong by the power of the mighty God of Jacob, who is both the Shepherd and the Stone of Israel. How consoling is the promise, "Behold, I lay in Zion, for a foundation, a stone, a tried stone, a sure foundation;" and it is equally true, that whosoever buildeth thereon shall not make haste nor be confounded: they shall neither flee away before their enemies, nor be confounded by them. But the Good Shepherd, who laid down His life for the sheep, Himself shall defend them, covering their heads in the day of battle, and giving them the victory; and not only so, but he will lead them into the green pastures of life, and cause them to lie down beside the still waters, where nothing can hurt them or make them afraid. He will hide them in his pavilion from the strife of tongues; He will be their battle-axe, their sword and their shield, and their exceeding great reward. "These things will I do unto them, and not forsake them, saith the Lord Almighty." Suffer, then, my dear friend, the word of exhortation and encouragement (although it may come from or through a mean instrument and a weak brother), to hold fast that which thou hast, and let no man take thy crown; nothing doubting but that He who has been with thee in six troubles, will deliver thee from the seventh also.

I am persuaded that His purpose is to put some, who have abode in faithfulness and devotion to Him and His cause through all, into the very places of such as did run well and do valiantly for a season, but have been captivated by the honors, and the offices, and the places which were offered unto them, if they would only bow a little, and yield a little of the ground which they had taken against that spirit which is at "war with the woman and with the remnant of her seed." Which spirit is indeed splendidly delusive, and the image which is raised up and presented by it to the mind, is, as Isaac Penington said, "painted just like Zion, and looks like Zion, but it is Babylon still;" although it contains the *form* of sound words, and is able to contend, in its own way and time, for sound doctrine too, and is also exceedingly zealous for the *order* of the Gospel; but yet it may be detected by those in whom the true anointing abideth, because it denieth the *power* thereof. And from such we have apostolic authority for turning away, for coming out from among them and being separate from them; and not only so, but is not the gracious promise added, "I will receive you, saith the Lord?"

I had no expectation of writing thus when I commenced, and it will doubtless seem strange to thee that I have thus written; but as things have been presented to my mind, under a feeling of much sympathy and near unity with thee, as also, I believe, under some sense of the state of things among you, I have put them down in great freedom, and greater confidence in thy discretion, as to the reception or rejection thereof. And if it may serve to convince thee how glad I should have been to have communed a little with thee, face to face, when thou wast here, or be of the least encouragement to thee, when thou walkest by the way and art sad (for I do believe that, according to my small measure, I have had some experimental knowledge of similar trials to some of those which have fallen, and may yet fall, to thy lot), my object in writing will be, at least in some part, answered. And so, with the salutation of love unfeigned,

I remain thy affectionate friend,

THOMAS B. GOULD.

To CHARLES PERRY.

NEWPORT, 16th of 3d mo., 1852.

MY DEAR FRIEND:

Thine of the 10th inst. was duly received, and from that time to the present, I have been wanting to tell thee how truly acceptable and deeply interesting it was to me and my dear M. . . . We had heard nothing of our dear friend J. Wilbur's getting along, except his arrival at New Hope (I think it was), and of his expecting to attend Bucks Quarter the next day. . . . .

What the result of this visit may be, I suppose the wisest amongst us, or even among them, can scarcely foresee: but one of the weakest and hindermost of the flock, like myself, may possibly be permitted to hazard the expression of a belief, that our dear aged friend's head will continue to be covered in the day of battle, and that He, who hath evidently called him forth and gone before him, will "deliver him from the people and from the Gentiles;" inasmuch as it is evident, that they are not all Israelites who have been accounted such, or who still doubtless consider themselves "masters in Israel." How strange and unaccountable it seems, that poor —— —— should have been apparently so ready to go on his errand, and so prompt to deliver his message at Damascus! For I suppose there is little room to doubt, that he was sent by authority of the chief priests and rulers of the synagogue. But if the utmost stretch of that popular (shall I use the expression?) Christian virtue, charity, will not admit of the supposition that he did it ignorantly, yet is it not possible that even one who has been as eminently favored as he has doubtless been, may, by letting in the reasoner, and adopting the doctrine of expediency, become so blinded as to think that he was doing the truth a service?

Notwithstanding, so far as thou hast informed me, there seems to have been, considering all the circumstances, a remarkably "open door" set before our dear friend, yet I cannot doubt but he has also been "in deaths oft;" for it is an awful thing "to be baptized for the dead;" and I am ready to say, still more so, to have to stand, as it were, between the living and the dead; and if I am not mistaken in my own feelings in regard to the nature of his service, it has been somewhat in this line. Oh! may the plague be stayed! He is almost constantly in my mind. I have thought of writing to him, just to let him know that much; but really am so very poor as to feel myself unable, totally unable and unworthy even to hand a cup of cold water in the name of a disciple. But I do nevertheless still love the brethren; and when thou art writing, if it be not too much trouble, thou mayest let him know that I love the fathers and the elders also. And when thou seest that mother in Israel, his wife, whom I have ever loved sincerely, and desired to honor in the truth, do please tell her, if thou judgest it meet for me to say so, that I have thought much of her in her loneliness, and under her portion of the burden of this weighty and (is it not?) rather peculiar work and service; and that I have felt for her too, according to my small measure; just querying of her withal, whether David's men, who stayed by the stuff, did not share the spoil with those who went forth to battle?

But I did not expect to have run on thus when I commenced, or to have written many lines, being also pressed for time. Thou must, dear Charles, excuse the haste, &c., and so I conclude, with dear love to thee and thine, and the rest of our dear friends there, as if named.

Thy sincere friend,
THOMAS B. GOULD.

TO WILLIAM HODGSON.

ELMSIDE, NEWPORT, 15th of 4th month, 1852.

MY DEAR FRIEND, WILLIAM HODGSON, JR.:

. . . . . It may seem strange that I should inflict one of my poor scrawls upon thee, just at the commencement of your yearly meeting, when thy time and attention will no doubt be fully and more profitably employed. And yet it did seem right, even for me, to send thee a salutation of love, and to bid thee "good speed" and "good cheer" just at this time.

Is there not such a scripture as this: "Go thy way, eat thy bread with gladness, and drink thy wine with a merry heart, for now thy work is accepted?" I may not quote it correctly, for it is long since I have read it, or even thought of it, till since I have been writing these last few lines. But really, my dear friend, is there not cause for thee, and perhaps others, to be encouraged? I am not indeed looking for or expecting great things (and hope I shall not be so understood), or for any great and remarkable change to take place immediately; although it may be so, as all things are possible with Him whose power is omnipotent, and whose name is Wonderful; and we know that He can, if He pleases, change the hearts of the children of men, as a man changes the water-course in his field; and will He not overturn, overturn, overturn, until He comes to reign, whose only right it is to reign in His Church and among His professing people? Yea, and is it not manifest that He hath arisen already, and commenced the work, going, as of old, before His disciples into Galilee?

. . . . I cannot doubt that the company and services of our dear aged friend, John Wilbur, have been truly acceptable and encouraging to thee and many more; while to many among you who do not pass for Gurneyites, I suppose the fact of his being there has produced similar sensations to what those unsound professors formerly experienced, when they were wont to exclaim, upon the arrival of G. Fox amongst them, "The man in leather breeches has come!" I think no one could have gone thither, whose visit would have been less acceptable to such as these, or so difficult for them to escape from the effects of it; nor so likely to be really and extensively useful in the promotion of the great and good cause which even these still profess to have in view and at heart; although the singleness and uprightness of their purposes, and the usefulness and acceptability of their services, seem to be rendered exceedingly doubtful, by the continual "bleating of sheep, and lowing of oxen," and an evident intention of saving the best of these, with the king, alive, however great the necessity, or positive the injunction, utterly to destroy Amalek. Well, those things which oppose and resist the progress of this people, and hinder them from following their Leader, and supporting, in their ancient purity, the doctrines of the Gospel, and the testimonies of truth, which have been given us to bear, will continue to oppose and resist, as they did Israel of old, until they are overcome and removed out of the way. And when we shall have been emptied from vessel to vessel, and sifted as from sieve to sieve, so as to be brought out of the mixtures, wherewith even Ephraim hath mixed and is mixing himself among the people, until he hath lost his strength, although he seemeth not to know it; then, may we not hope that, as a people, in some places at least, there may be a renewal of strength, and of a degree of ancient zeal for the Lord's honor, and that the truth may again prosper, and shine forth with its wonted brightness? But with regard to some, who appear to have sadly failed, and stopped short of the mark, turning back in the day of battle, although they had been eminently favored and eminently useful, apparently, having been manifestly preferred to Manasseh, art thou not often ready to adopt, in relation to them, the mournful language, "How shall I give thee up, O! Ephraim? how shall I deliver thee, O! Israel? How shall I make thee as Admah? how shall I set thee as Zeboim?" I cannot doubt that thou art often greatly distressed for such as these, and that thy soul is in bitterness on their account, as for thy first-born. But the measure of suffering must be filled up; and it is required of some, not only to stand in jeopardy every hour, but in the gap also, as a mark for every archer, while they are deserted by many who have stood for a time exceedingly near. To witness the desertion and the fall of these, and to be baptized for them, is very close, hard work, sufficiently so to make us of all men most miserable, if it were not for the consolations of the Gospel communicated, with the promise, I will stand by thee and deliver thee; I will never leave thee, nor forsake thee. Be thou faithful unto death, and I will give thee a crown of life! And is there not also consolation in the belief, that He who hath promised, is able to raise those up also who may have fallen, to heal those who have been wounded, and even to breathe again upon, re-animate, and bring together, such as have been scattered hither and thither, and become exceeding dry, like the dry bones of the valley; causing them again to stand upon their feet firmly, and even to fight His battles? I may acknowledge, perhaps, with safety and in confidence to thee, that, even at this distance, and without having ever stood, like thyself, in very close connection with some among you, whom I have nevertheless "esteemed very highly in love for the work's sake," my spirit has been often, and is, clothed with mourning for them, earnestly desiring, if it be possible, that they may be induced to come down, that they may be made willing to be of as little account as the truth is, and to continue to follow in the footsteps of the flock of the companions of Christ, let who will turn aside, and although such as were accounted members of Israel, and of the family, should be lacking in their tribes, having chosen to remain in Egypt, "where also our Lord is crucified." When I have considered how valiant some of these were in contending for the faith, and how much better they seemed qualified for it than any of us (only excepting that able and veteran soldier, J. W.), and moreover, that like the men of Ephraim formerly, they seemed almost ready to chide with us if they were not called to the battle, and placed in the forefront of it too,—which place, for one, I have ever been more than willing they should occupy, having always esteemed "the gleaning of the grapes of Ephraim," in a certain sense, as being "better than the vintage of Abi-ezer"—when I have considered these things, it has seemed not only very sad, but very strange and unnatural also, that there should be any cause to fear that David's description of the death of Abner might in any event be applied justly to any of them. And yet it does *not* seem probable, though their hands are not bound, nor their feet put into fetters, that they will be slain *while fighting the Lord's battles*, in whose victorious army they were *wont to be* ranked among the "first three mighty men." But how true it is, that the race is not always to the swift, nor the battle to the strong; nor durable riches and righteousness to men of great natural understanding, or even of uncommon spiritual gifts and large experience of the goodness and mercy of the Lord in the land of the living; unless there is an abiding in humility and in the Vine of life! How many stars, apparently of the first magnitude, the dragon seems to have obtained power, nearly or quite to sweep down in these days, and in this time of times upon which we have fallen; wherein it does seem as if everything that can be shaken or removed, would be shaken and moved out of the way;

not the earth only, but heaven also; that that which cannot be shaken may remain; even the new heaven and the new earth, wherein righteousness shall dwell! For I do believe that there are those now living, who will afresh receive the injunction, to "be glad and rejoice forever in that which I create;" forasmuch as He whose promises are unfailing will, in His own due time, "create Jerusalem a rejoicing, and her people a joy." . . . . .

Thou wilt not, I trust, suppose that I have had anything in view, more than what is included in, or conveyed by the declaration, that "they who feared the Lord spake often one unto another;" and however thou may receive this my *occasional* writing, it has been done under a sense of much weakness, and in fear.

I shall feel quite anxious to hear how J. W. fares next week; as also how you are getting along with the committees set apart for your especial benefit and restoration to the body of *modified* Quakerism; which at best is but as cankered gold, or as wine mixed with water, in comparison with ancient Quakerism, with primitive and vital Christianity. . . . .

It is late, and I must bid thee farewell; although I feel almost reluctant to part with thee even so; for thou hast been brought very near.

THOMAS B. GOULD.

TO PELEG MITCHELL.

NEWPORT, 18th of 5th mo., 1852.

MY DEAR FRIEND:

At Greenwich, in the public quarterly meeting —— was largely opened, upon the nature and qualification for the performance of true worship under the Gospel dispensation. He was lively and skilful in administering and dividing "the word of the truth of the Gospel;" showing, with clearness and effect, how, as individuals and meetings are gathered to that spirit, and truth, and power, in which alone true and acceptable worship can be performed, all forward spirits and unsanctified offerings would be kept down, and *that* would rise into dominion and prevail over all, which remains to be the crown of glory and diadem of beauty in every rightly gathered assembly. As I sat beside him, and listened with admiration and joy at the excellence of the gift, not wholly without feelings of thankfulness to the divine Author and heavenly Giver thereof, I could not repress the *fervent* though *secret petition*, that neither one thing nor another might be permitted to tarnish its lustre, that the gold might not become dim, nor the most fine gold changed! * . . . .

I must conclude, with dear love to thee and thine, in which my dear M. unites.

THOMAS B. GOULD.

To MARTHA S. GOULD.

NEW BEDFORD, 10th month, 11th, 1852.

MY DEAR MARTHA:

. . . . The kindness of Friends everywhere could not be exceeded; and I have also got along in other respects to my humbling admiration, and even to my astonishment; the doctrines of the Gospel, and the mysteries of the kingdom, having never been so largely opened to me or through me before. Dear cousin Francis Taber is very feeble, and was, before he went to Nantucket; but he told me after the select meeting last fourth-day, that he felt better, adding emphatically, "for it has been a good meeting!" And it was so, indeed, and a truly remarkable one, of which, dear Mary Macey, Mary Davis, and others, bore public testimony in the meeting. On sixth-day evening, I had an appointed meeting at Siasconset: the house was filled, and the people were remarkably attentive and quiet throughout. . . . .

On first-day, the afternoon meeting was put off till four o'clock. Public notice was given, and the house was very nearly filled. The morning meeting was not a small one. And in the evening a meeting of the colored population, at one of their own meeting-houses, which was filled, and

* The secret impression of danger implied above, as prompting the petition in the mind of T. B. G., for the safety of this individual, was sorrowfully verified a few years afterwards.

was to the satisfaction of Friends at least. The only remaining native Indian left upon the island [Nantucket] happened also to be, or was present; of which, when I heard of it, I was glad. It was an interesting meeting. In the midst of a large opening (for me), I felt a full stop and sat down, though not apparently so abruptly as to be particularly noticed; whereupon dear C—— arose, and had a lively and striking testimony, in harmony with my own feelings. Dear —— followed him, after which I was favored in a few words to obtain relief, and the meeting closed, in as hard a rain and as dark a night, I reckon, as ever poor dear Mary Barnard and Sarah Paddack, and Thaddeus and Eliza Coffin were out in; for we literally waded home, through sand and water, and they seemed almost like quicksands to me, when I thought of the women, and the first two especially. We had an exceedingly rough passage, the first half of it, today. . . .

I expect to have an appointed meeting at Fair Haven, the village opposite to this place, to-morrow evening; to attend Dartmouth meeting on fourth-day morning, and an appointed meeting at Padanaram in the evening; North Dartmouth meeting on fifth-day; an appointed meeting in Slocum's Neck fifth-day evening or sixth-day; possibly one at the head of Westport River on seventh-day, and probably both meetings at this place on first-day next; to go to Fall River on second-day, and to return home the same evening. . . . . . .

Know assuredly that I am thine affectionately,

T. B. GOULD.

CHAPTER VI.

On the 7th day of eleventh month, 1852, Thomas B. Gould attended a public meeting for divine worship in Friends' meeting-house near Little Compton, a village on the eastern passage into Narragansett Bay. An individual present, not a member of the Society of Friends, attempted to take down in writing what was delivered by Thomas on that occasion; probably not being then aware of the strong objections held by the speaker, in common with Friends generally, against the practice of writing down, in a religious meeting, communications of that kind. This person afterwards sent a transcript of it to the Friend who had accompanied Thomas to the meeting, and the following copy is believed to be substantially correct, as far as it goes. It may safely be inserted in these pages (since the decease of the speaker), as affording an interesting and instructive view of his doctrine and expression in preaching the Gospel; and without any intention of introducing, or sanctioning, the practice of publishing the communications of our ministers, in a general way.

After sitting for some time in silent waiting on the Lord, he arose and declared as follows: "I believe that it is quite possible for men and women, while they continue to observe forms which have been abrogated, to aim sincerely at the substance; and also, that it is equally possible for those who reject the use of forms, to fail of attaining to an experimental knowledge of the substance; and yet it is exceedingly important that all men and all women should be really and truly qualified and prepared to worship and serve Him who created them, and who not only created them, but created them for the very purpose of worshipping, and praising, and glorifying Him, and in order to this end, hath not been wanting in bestowing upon His rational, accountable creation, the means of attaining to the knowledge of Himself, and of the way and the manner in which we should come before the Lord, and bow ourselves before the most high God, in such a manner as will find acceptance with Him who has been declared to be the God of knowledge, and that by Him the actions of all creatures are weighed in the even scales of divine justice, of divine wisdom, of divine knowledge; and His judgment is just, for just and true are all His ways. And yet it is or may be matter, and should be matter of great encouragement to us, and of thankfulness by us, that mercy still covers the judgment-seat, that God is indeed merciful and long-suffering unto the children of men, and that, although they may pass a great part of their lives in a state of lamentable forgetfulness of Him, and want of right qualification to worship and serve Him; yet in His unutterable mercy and unbounded love, He is not slack concerning His promises, but is faithful toward us; not willing that any should perish, but that all should come to the knowledge of Him and of His truth, and so be prepared to worship and serve Him in spirit and in truth, and finally be saved with an everlasting salvation.

"I may acknowledge that my feelings, since taking my seat in this meeting, have been of a rather peculiar and truly exercising nature; under a consideration, an humbling consideration of the great need there is among the children of men, of greater dedication of heart unto the Lord, of a more serious and earnest engagement of spirit, to know for ourselves, how we shall come before Him in the manner that will find acceptance with him; for it is indeed our reasonable service. An experienced apostle made use of strikingly earnest and persuasive language, when he said, 'I beseech you, brethren, by the mercies of God, that ye present your bodies a living sacrifice, holy and acceptable unto Him, which is your reasonable service.' I may not quote the language precisely as it stands recorded in the Holy Scriptures of the New Testament; for it so happens that I have not recently read the passage; neither have I at all studied, or so much as considered, what I should say, or what I should speak unto you, previously to my entering under this roof. For it is not in accordance with the principles which the Society of Friends hold and most assuredly believe in, to premeditate what they shall say, or what they shall speak, on such occasions as this; neither is it, or ever was it, my practice. I am not ashamed to acknowledge it; nay, verily, but on the contrary, for some reason or other,—I know not, neither am I curious to know,—I believe it to be incumbent upon me thus publicly to acknowledge it. It is not the practice of any authorized minister of this Society, when they assemble with their brethren for the purpose of performing worship unto God;—it is not their practice to sit down in a meeting and consider what they shall speak unto the people; but rather, to turn their minds inward unto Him, unto that God who is a Spirit, and who is to be worshipped in spirit and in truth; to get themselves unto the watch-tower in the secret of their own souls, and there to hearken what the Lord shall say unto them by the manifestation of His own Spirit and of His own power; and not only so, but what they shall answer when they are themselves reproved—for men and women, although they may have received a gift of the ministry from our Lord and Saviour Jesus Christ, yet they are men and women of like passions, and subject to like infirmities as others, and I have sometimes thought are permitted to be assailed by greater temptations.

"And yet there are assuredly no idlers in the Lord's house, or amongst his people; and it is indeed a great mistake for any to suppose, when they assemble themselves together for the worship of God, that any man, however eminently gifted, can possibly be enabled to perform, *for them*, divine service, divine worship: but it does indeed sometimes, and it may frequently happen, that among such as are gathered together for the worship of God, into a state of solemn, awful, reverential silence before Him, that some one or other among these inward spiritual worshippers may be renewedly qualified and raised up to speak a word in due season unto such as are weary, to give forth a word of exhortation or reproof, according as the Lord's Spirit shall give them utterance and qualify them so to do; and such an engagement may indeed be blessed both to such as are exercised in it, and to such as hear them. But it is not worship, merely to assemble together for no other purpose than to listen to the words of ministers. There must be a preparation in the hearts of those who hear even the Gospel itself, or else we shall not be edified at all thereby. For we have the testimony and authority of the Holy Scriptures for declaring, that except the word preached be mixed with faith in those who hear, it shall not profit the people. And faith is a heavenly gift. It is the gift of God. It is not a mere notion; it is not a mere assent of the understanding to the truths of the Gospel as they stand recorded in the Holy Scriptures; it is something beyond this, more excellent, more heavenly, and more powerful; for it was by faith that the elders obtained a good report, and if we are ever so happy as to obtain a good report, it will be by faith also. 'Faith is the substance of things hoped for, and the evidence of things not seen.' 'And this,' said an experienced apostle, 'is the victory which overcometh the world, even our faith.' Now that which can enable any man or any woman to overcome the world, must be something more than a wind of doctrine, something more than an assent of the understanding to certain principles and doctrines, however excellent. It must be something practical, inward, and powerful in its nature, which shall enable them to renounce the pomps and vanities of this wicked world.

"Such was the nature of the saints' faith. They possessed a living, efficacious faith, which was able to save their souls. It was a shield unto them, whereby they were preserved from the temptations and the snares with which he assailed them, even as he assaileth us. For who of us are free from the temptations and snares of the enemy? Are we not some of us made experimentally certain, that the adversary goeth about as a roaring lion seeking whom he may devour; and not only so, but as a cunning, crafty serpent, seeking whom he may deceive, and whom he may betray, whom he may induce to turn from the worship and service of that God who created them, unto the worship and service of the enemy, the adversary, the evil one? It remains an undeniable truth, that his servants we are unto whom we yield our members to obey.

"It is in and by Jesus Christ alone, that we may find acceptance with God the Father, who is a pure and holy Spirit, and requireth pure offerings and sacrifices to be offered unto Him. Neither is there any other name or power given under heaven, whereby we can be qualified to offer acceptable offerings unto God the Father, but by and through the name of His only-begotten, well-beloved Son, our Lord and Saviour Jesus Christ. All divine worship and service is to be performed and offered up in His name and by His power; for there is no such thing as salvation in any other, or acceptance with God the Father by any other. Men have sought to climb other ways into heaven, and to perform divine service in strength which came not by our Lord and Saviour Jesus Christ; but such have not therein found acceptance, such have offered an impure and unholy offering; because they were not acquainted with the ministry of the sanctuary, and of the true tabernacle, which the Lord hath pitched, and not man. They have offered in the time and the way which they have devised in their own hearts. They have warmed themselves at a fire of their own kindling, and lain down in sorrow at the end; because there is none other than the fire of God's own altar which can enable us to *worship God in spirit*, and to *have no confidence in the flesh*. These are the true worshippers in the temple, whoever they are and wherever they are. If they are not yet completely redeemed from some observance of forms and ceremonies, yet are they the true worshippers in the temple, the living members of the church and body of Christ. These are all in some measure gathered unto that which is within the veil, whither Christ Jesus, our forerunner, hath entered. These are made partakers of the hidden manna, which cometh down from heaven, and giveth life unto the world. These do not merely make a profession of performing divine service; but they have known what it is to sanctify the Lord in their hearts, and He has become their hope, and their aid, and their souls are bowed in awful reverence before Him, saying, 'Lord, what wilt thou have me to do, and how shall I appear before thee, in order that I may receive a little strength renewedly from Thee?' And so they are gathered into a state of silent, patient waiting upon Him. Their expectations are from Him, and from Him alone; and such do at times and seasons joyfully experience the truth of that Scripture, that 'they that wait upon the Lord shall renew their strength.' They shall, and do, and are enabled to renew their spiritual strength in and by Him, and by the assistance which He, of His goodness and mercy, is pleased to afford unto them, whether it be immediately or instrumentally communicated. For as God is a spirit, the soul of man is a spirit, and it doth not require the intervention of words, in order that He may communicate substantial good to our souls. He can cause us to hear His voice, even the voice of His only-begotten and well-beloved Son, although no words should be vocally and literally sounded in our ears.

"What great encouragement there is then, for such as may be much removed from the opportunity of participating in the many helps which are provided in His church and amongst His people. They cannot be excluded from the instruction which comes from Him, or from the high and holy privilege of waiting upon Him and worshipping Him. Jacob worshipped, leaning upon the top of his staff, and we have no account that he had any company save the presence of that God whom he worshipped. Well now, if we are favored to feel and know something of His presence with us, something of instruction from Him how we shall worship and serve Him, then we may rest assured that we are in His house, even in the house of God, whether we have any other than a stone for our pillow, yea or nay. Remember how it was with the patriarch Jacob, when he saw the heavens opened, and a ladder which reached unto heaven, and angels of God ascending and descending thereon. Why, he said, 'This is none other than the house of God!' And that is none other than the house of God, in which we are made sensible of His presence, of the manifestation of His Spirit and of His power: and it doth indeed become such as are so made sensible of it, to put off their shoes from off their feet, for the place whereon they stand is indeed holy ground; and as they are thus prepared by the Lord Himself to stand in awful reverence before Him, He will open their ears to hear His voice, and will teach them and instruct them as man never taught or could teach them. They shall find their souls sustained by the bread of life, by the Word of God Himself. For it is declared, that man shall not live by bread alone,—that is, by outward, elementary bread,—but by every word that proceedeth out of the mouth of God and of the Lamb. And so they will joyfully and happily experience, as David did, that it is good for them, both patiently to wait and quietly to hope for their God; and thus they shall renew their spiritual strength, so that they shall be enabled to run in the way of His divine and holy commandments without being weary, and to walk therein, even in the way of life and salvation, without fainting.

"And Christ Himself, the Son and sent of God, is the way of life: 'I am the way, the truth, and the life; no man cometh unto the Father but by Me.' And if any man attempt to climb up any other way, or offer up any sacrifices and offerings, except it be by and through Him, the great High Priest of our profession, by whom all offerings are to be offered up, such will not find acceptance; they will but offer the sacrifice of fools, considering not that they do evil when they pretend to draw nigh unto God, and to make mention of His glorious, holy name, while their hearts are far from Him! Oh! He will be sanctified in those that come nigh Him; and 'let him that nameth the name of Christ depart from iniquity,' is a divine injunction which will stand true to the end of time. Oh! have we, some of us, ever been made justly sensible of the holiness, the wisdom, the mercy, and the power of God? Most men, when they are brought, or about to be brought, into the presence of the great ones of this earth, the great men of this lower world, feel more or less of awe pervade their minds. Well now, He is King of kings, and

Lord of lords, the blessed and only Potentate. His name is high and holy. It is above every other name that can possibly be named, 'and His name is called the Word of God;' and He hath caused His name to be proclaimed before Him, and at the name of God and of Christ, even at the name of Jesus, 'every knee shall bow, and every tongue confess that Jesus Christ is Lord, to the glory of God the Father.' Oh! how serious, how solemn a thing it is, for us to feel and know that we stand every moment in His presence! And how necessary it is for us, that we should live and walk in His fear! For the fear of the Lord is the very beginning of wisdom, and to depart from evil is understanding; and if we are brought under a true sense of His fear, and sufficiently humbled before Him, He will, I am persuaded, teach us of His ways, and how we may appear before Him. So that, if any lack wisdom as to this matter, if they lack wisdom as to how they shall appear before the Lord, and bow themselves before the Most High God, let them ask of Him who giveth liberally and upbraideth not. Let them hearken unto Him, and He will instruct them, when they listen to the inspiring word of His own divine Spirit and power, as it is proclaimed in their souls; and so they shall be livingly instructed in the way and the manner by which they shall be qualified and enabled to worship and serve Him with their spirits, in the Gospel of His Son."

FROM T. B. G. TO CHARLES PERRY.

NEWPORT, third month, 30th, 1853.

MY DEAR FRIEND, C. PERRY:

. . . . I am not insensible how forcibly, though briefly, thou hast commented upon the many remarkable passages and incidents of thy grandfather's letters and journey. But it is not just now, and has not been this long while, either a new moon or a Sabbath-day with me; and yet I have not felt like venturing out to "gather sticks," or even like attempting to kindle a fire with such as I have on hand, however dry and combustible they may be. Still there seems to be need enough of fire, for it is a cold, wintry season; but artificial heat seems unlikely to do any good, and the query often recurs, "Who shall show us any good?" For "I am a worm, and no man;" I am like a dead man out of mind, or like a broken vessel; the chief, if not the only sign of life being the still continued sense of the love of the brethren, and especially of the fathers and the elders, the faithful, valiant, and truly honorable laborers in the great and arduous field of the Lord's harvest; although I do not feel worthy or able to express it to them; and yet, according to my small ability, I think I have travailed and sympathized with them, or some of them, often sincerely desiring that He would be pleased to raise up, and qualify, and send forth more laborers into His harvest; for such as are rightly qualified, and willing, and faithful, are indeed very few. While on the other hand, there are so many busybodies, who have not tarried at Jerusalem until they were endued with power from on high; whose time is always ready, and who either run while there is a tumult, and consequently have no certain tidings, sowing to the wind, and reaping the whirlwind; or speak great swelling words of vanity, prophesying falsely; the people all the while being so bewitched with their sorceries and enchantments, that they love to have it so, and therefore multiply their teachers to tickle their itching ears for them.

All these things operate as a discouragement; and unless there is a double portion of faith, long experience, and I am ready to add, a threefold commission, how shall the query be surmounted, "Who is sufficient for these things?" who shall be able to endure the perils which all must encounter, who venture out in these perilous times, times of peril by sea and peril by land, and even greater than all these combined, perils among false brethren? Oh! how I do feel for him [J. W.], in going again as into the very mouth of the lion! For it is mournfully evident that there is that which is of the same nature, even among those where, as I suppose, his lot is now cast (notwithstanding their professions of love, and unity, and harmony); in opposition to everything that has a tendency to rend the veil, and to make a distinction and separation between the precious and the vile, between that which is of the Lord, and so in the divine harmony, and that which is not of Him, and consequently in the enmity, discord, and confusion. This will, sooner or later, be manifested by such as have not gotten the victory over the mark of "the beast, and over the number of his name;" which they surely have not obtained who take counsel of man, and undertake to rule by man's fallen wisdom. But their ships may be broken as at Ezion-geber, and the mouths of the lions may be stopped. For the Lord is still able to stop the mouths of lions, and to quench the violence of fire, although it may burn never so vehemently or hiddenly; and to bring forth such as are faithful, unhurt by the one, and without even the smell of the other upon them. . . . .

With love as ever, thy sincere friend,

T. B. Gould.

To William Hodgson.

Newport, 5th month, 15th, 1853.

My dear Friend:

Thou hast been so much and so often in my remembrance for a month or two past, that I have been upon the point of writing to thee, again and again; and I certainly think I should have done so ere this, had I been in possession of as many and as large opportunities of leisure as some people. . . . .

It is probable thou hast heard, that the quarterly meeting united with the concern of our dear, aged, and devoted friend, J. Wilbur, and endorsed the certificate of South Kingstown Monthly Meeting, by which he was liberated (so far as Friends there could do it) to pay a visit in Gospel love to Friends and others in Great Britain and Ireland. . . . I doubt not, that there are many amongst you, and such too, as "seem to be," not only "somewhat," but *very* wise in such matters, who have already come to a judgment, and decided against the concern, as not in the truth, or in the order of Society, or of the Gospel, if not as being either childish, or wilful and presumptuous in him, and also as manifesting weakness and folly in those bodies who have officially sanctioned it. There is, however, to me some cause for encouragement, when I am favored to see and to feel that different meetings of Friends, or even solitary individuals amongst them, have so sanctified the Lord in their hearts, as to let Him truly become their fear and their dread; in whose fear the beginning of true wisdom, as well as the increase and perfection of it, and of holiness also, most surely is. For *out* of this fear, and without a degree of that holiness which can only be known and perfected therein, no man can see the Lord, or expect to receive a true answer from Him, however frequently, from his position or station in the professing church, he may seem called upon to judge of such important concerns as relate to His service and the affairs of His Church. What a dangerous snare "the fear of man" often becometh, to those who are governed by no higher rule or criterion than man's fallen wisdom! How frequently they become entangled in the consequences and contingencies which they have vainly, if not presumptuously and of themselves, sought to avoid; not seeing the end from the beginning with the eye of faith, which the Lord alone can open, and which He will not suffer to "wax dim" while any continue to be pure in heart.

Thou mayst well ask why I should write thus to thee. I can only say that it has come of my reflections or impressions of the state of things, I am ready to add, even with some of you. Yet I truly and comfortably, and, as I think, upon good ground, hope better things of thee, even such as accompany salvation and deliverance from the wiles, and baits, and refined delusions, in which great men, and rich men, and wise men have been ensnared—yea, and women also,—who have received precious gifts and had long experience, attaining to such eminence and high stations in the church, as to have become unduly elated; and who love to bear rule over those whom they may consider of less note and importance than themselves; but who, having kept their own habitations in the truth, and in the valley of humility, where the dew of heaven resteth long, the fatness and blessing of the earth also which lieth under, has been given to them; and their bows have abode in strength, and the arms of their hands have been made strong by the power of the mighty God of Jacob. But the dragon hath really been permitted to "sweep" others somewhat "down," although, through the power of his delusions, and their own self-sufficiency and self-confidence, they are not fully and rightly sensible of it; yet the sweetness, the tenderness, and the true zeal and heavenly divine life are mostly gone; and in the room thereof another thing has come up, merely in the image and likeness of that which was and is divine, and ought to be so confessed and owned, in whomsoever and wheresoever it may appear. And oh, what an abundance of creaturely activity this leads into, in one way or another! How excellent and desirable it seems, to those who look only upon the surface! What an abundance of love and devotion! What zeal for the outward order! How careful to preserve the *form* of godliness; and alas! how ready to *deny* the *power* and the *life*, when it seems likely to be set over the form and the letter!

Now, whatever any may think of our dear friend J. W.'s concern, and however it may result, when it comes to be laid before our yearly meeting of ministers and elders; I have no doubt, nor the shadow of a doubt, that it has been right that he and Friends should be brought under it thus far. He may indeed be released from it: the resignation of his mind to perform the visit, may be accepted instead of the deed. But I think clearer and stronger evidence of its being in the ordering of Divine Wisdom, than was afforded at the time of our quarterly meeting, could hardly be expected or desired in any similar case: and I should not be at all surprised if he be eventually liberated. . . .

To Joshua Maule.

24th of sixth month, 1853.

. . . . He [Francis Taber] is in a very declining state, and not likely to last long, with an affection of the heart and dropsy combined, I believe. But he, as well as my own dear mother, has lost none of his interest in the cause; and although we greatly missed him during yearly meeting week, with other worthies who have been removed since you were here; yet our meeting was, I believe, acknowledged by all, to have been the largest held here since the separation, and I think not less satisfactory than any other. The children and young people, of whom there were scarcely any present for several years, have grown in years and stature, and I hope, as regards some of them at least, in the truth also; yet I regret to say that many of them are not, either in appearance or in fact, as plain and consistent Friends as could be desired. Then again, although many of the elders have been removed and are removing, I think that others of a younger class have really deepened in the root of life, and consequently become more skilful in the management of the affairs of truth and of the Church. There were three sittings of the select yearly meeting, one more than usual, in consequence of the opening of our dear aged and devoted friend, J. W.'s weighty and important concern, and the preparation and approval of his certificate. . . . .

The public meetings were large, and I think on the whole ended well and satisfactorily; although there were some appearances in two of them, which added nothing to the weight, however much to the measure. In that on first-day morning, our dear friend, N. P., was largely opened and eminently favored. . . . . In the afternoon, but one voice was vocally heard, and that Friend was not very lengthy; the rest of the time being spent in solemn silence; and although the earlier portion of the meeting was sufficiently exercising, yet truth rose into dominion, and crowned all in the end, as was believed by many Friends, as well as some others who were prepared to acknowledge it. On fifth-day, dear Mary Macey opened the public meeting with the injunction, "Keep silence before me, oh, ye islands, and let the people renew their strength;" being largely, though not lengthily, but closely and weightily engaged in a searching testimony against those things which stand opposed to an increase of spiritual strength. Dear J. W. followed, in much the same line of labor; not long: and Elizabeth Hill, who is a sweet and lively minister, much deepened and enlarged in her gift since you were here, followed him in an acceptable and weighty manner.* Then, I am sorry to say, the ark of truth's testimony was twice considerably jostled, however unintentionally so, by inexperienced hands being unadvisedly set to it. After which there was an apparent necessity for the solemn injunction first uttered in that meeting to be again revived; and the attention of the people was recalled to that Power, which was and is able to say, "Peace, be still," and to produce a great calm. The instructive circumstance of Simon's wife's mother lying sick of a fever, when the Master himself came and laid His soothing and cooling hand upon her, with the notable, strengthening, and calming effect immediately produced, even such that she arose and ministered unto those who were present, was also briefly adverted to; and the meeting ended solidly, and, I think, pretty well. . . . .

Farewell, in every way.

THOMAS B. GOULD.

TO WILLIAM HODGSON.

ELMSIDE, NEWPORT, 7th mo., 26th, 1853.

MY VERY DEAR FRIEND, WILLIAM HODGSON, JR.:

. . . . . . Poor, and stripped, and weak, and short-sighted as we are, and even likely, in some respects at least, to be still further stripped and weakened; yet we are, in great and unmerited mercy, sometimes helped and strengthened with a sight and sense of things which many prophets and wise men have desired to see, and have not seen them. So that we are a little encouraged and re-animated to hold on, and to press on, even to that which is not visible to any eye, save the inward eye, which the Lord opens and re-opens by the repeated application of the eye-salve of His kingdom. And oh! what fulness there is in that heavenly expression, "My kingdom is not

* Since deceased.

of this world;" and what consolation all the patient sufferers for it will find, in the continued verification of this truth, however tribulated their way through this world may be! How repeatedly, as their eyes are kept single to the mark for the prize of their high and holy calling, will they be confirmed in the truth, "But now,"—even now, in the midst of their afflictions, arising from the mixtures and impurities of such as are really striving to become heirs of both kingdoms, whatever their pretensions, or even their hopes may be,—"But now is my kingdom not from hence!" Neither is it very remarkable, that such as are preserved in singleness of heart and eye unto the Lord and His honor, and the coming and establishment of His kingdom, and that alone, in themselves and others, should be favored to see beyond others, whose eyes the god of this world hath really blinded, lamentably blinded, and in some cases, it is to be feared, not in part only; although they may, with great self-complacency, account themselves much wiser in their generation than the children of light. . . . .

J. W. came here a week ago last sixth-day, and stayed the night at father's, and the day following I took him to Fall River. A very pleasant visit and precious time we had together; though he seemed, as it is natural he should be, much bowed under the weight of his prospect. . .

27th. Being at Fall River a week ago last first-day, and so far on my way, after meeting I rode over to New Bedford to see our dear friend, Francis Taber. Israel Buffinton went with me. He seemed overjoyed to see us, and rather more comfortable in body than we had expected to find him, though much changed since I saw him in the fourth month: but still clear as a bell in his understanding, lively and fervent in spirit, manifesting a continued and earnest engagement for the welfare and faithful maintenance of the cause and testimony of truth. We felt well repaid for our ride in the dust and heat.

What sad work they have made in England with poor L. M. H.! . . . . . Neither does the Philadelphia "Friend" seem to hesitate copying from the "British Friend," that mixed account of the yearly meeting in

London, including (whatever else they may have eschewed), that part in which we are spoken of as separatists or seceders. Do the managers of the American "Friend" wish their readers by degrees to become accustomed to hear us spoken of in that opprobrious manner, and so to be gradually reconciled to it? In this and similar ways, I do consider the good cause, which we have feebly endeavored to espouse, has been much injured, and the hands of our adversaries and the adversaries of truth greatly strengthened: neither do they fail to see it, and to take advantage of it, however reluctant any may be to have the real tendency, if not the design, of their conduct detected. . . .

I remain as ever thy sincere friend,

THOMAS B. GOULD.

DRAFT OF A LETTER FROM T. B. G. TO CALEB HAWORTH.

ELMSIDE, NEWPORT, 24th of 9th mo., 1853.

MY DEAR COUSIN, CALEB HAWORTH:

. . . . . I have at times felt, and continue to feel not unfrequently, a good degree of that precious unity and fellowship with thee in spirit, which is beyond words or letters; and which, while it is mercifully and preciously continued, precludes the idea of any change in those who are the subjects or the objects of it, except such as is consistent with the truth, and that growth in the same which must necessarily, in some good degree, be experienced by as many as do keep their habitations therein. But, my dear cousin, while I can in truth and sincerity address thee with full confidence in thy integrity, and steadfast abiding in the truth and in the faith; although I am and have been for a long time wholly destitute of any outward information or clue to thy standing whatever; yet I am not insensible to the changes, the great, if not the radical changes, which time and circumstances have manifested in many, who seemed formerly to stand as firmly as thyself. In this respect, we of the "smaller body" in New England, continue to have much to suffer, many and close trials of our faith and patience to pass through, beside those which are common to others, if I may be allowed the expression.

For our situation is peculiar, and very clearly distinguishable, so that we seem to furnish a ready mark for every archer. And when those who, for a long time, stood with us fearlessly in the breach, desert their posts, and go over to the ranks of the enemy openly, or by directing their arrows secretly at us, endeavor to wound and weaken us, and really increase their ranks and strengthen their hands, it is very discouraging, and causes close looking to the Foundation, and feeling after the cause; that we may know the one to sustain us, and be enabled to support the other according to the ability received, and to what may be required at our hands. However, I do not wish to be understood to say that any of our members here in New England have turned back, or given up the ground which we were compelled to take, at the time of the separation (for *we* did not make the division: our adversaries, and the adversaries of truth made it, and drove us into the position which we now occupy; there being no alternative, unless we had proved derelict from our duty and our principles); but there are many in other places, especially in Philadelphia and Ohio, who, to save themselves trouble, and under the plausible delusion (as we believe), of keeping the outward order and unity of the Society unbroken, are striving with all their own strength and the strength of their influential stations, to patch up and smooth over that which is wrong in the root, as well as in the branches and fruit; not appearing to care what becomes of the testimony, nor of such as have been made willing to part with all, reputation, and ease, and in some instances almost life itself, rather than to compromise that testimony. All this is repeatedly sacrificed by such as still claim to be the champions of sound doctrine, and to have no unity with innovations or innovators; though they tolerate, and wink at, and give more and more encouragement to both, while they increase the burdens, and augment the reproaches, of such as they themselves acknowledge to have suffered faithfully in opposing the same. But, they say, it is very important that Friends should continue a united body, and show an undivided front to the world: as if the *numbers*, who still meet in one house and constitute one yearly meeting, could give credit to our testimonies in the sight of the world; which is quite keen enough to discover that the harmony *is* interrupted, and the power in which Friends once stood and acted is very much lost. There are some of us in this country, and I doubt not there are such with you, who go bowed down under a sense of these things, not knowing what will be the end of the inconsistencies and confusion of tongues, which appear and are heard in the camp.

But of one thing I feel confident, that in the end it will be made manifest, that no good has been gained by seeking to save that alive which has been and is appointed for destruction; although it may be done under the specious pretence of offering it in sacrifice. Everything which opposes the progress of the children of Israel, of the true seed, ought to be removed from the camp, ought to be faithfully testified against; the idols, both of silver and of gold, ought to be "put away" from amongst us; and when the trumpet shall be blown again in Zion, with that certain sound which is still able to awaken such as have fallen asleep, and to prepare them to fight the Lord's battle, there is much that will be slain, which passes now for the best of the sheep and the oxen. Then a solemn assembly will be called, and a fast sanctified; and the priests, the ministers of the Lord, will be clothed with the spirit of true mourning, and be made skilful in lamentation; and there will then be hope that the Lord will be jealous for His land, and pity His people, and cause them to arise and shine, because their light has come, and the glory of the Lord has arisen upon them. How different from glorying in our shame, while our confusion covers us, even to that degree that we cannot see ourselves as we really are; vainly supposing that we are rich, and increased with goods, and have need of nothing, while we are really poor, and blind, and naked, and stand in need of everything! Oh! what an apprehension of fulness and safety appears in the printed account of London Yearly Meeting! Such sufficiency to act; and what an abundance of activity! And amidst all this, the one thing needful seems to be almost wholly wanting. "Oh, my people! they which lead thee cause thee to err, and destroy the way of thy paths!"

But I had no intention of writing at such length when I took up my pen; merely thinking I would say to thee, as dear John Wilbur is going over, that I hope thou wilt meet with him (for I trust thou canst receive him, notwithstanding his bonds); for if his life should be spared, with our own lives, to see him again, it would be so pleasant to my dear wife and to me to have some account of thee by him. I have no doubt it will be considered as a very presumptuous, or a very foolish act in him, to attempt to cross the ocean again at his time of life, and under existing circumstances, both with you and us. But I have no doubt myself of the rectitude of the concern, however it may terminate; whether he lives to get there or not, and whether way is made for him publicly or not; and surely, with any man of his capacity and sensibility, nothing less than the most imperative sense of religious obligation could have induced such a sacrifice. Neither can I doubt there are some, scattered up and down, who will be prepared to receive him, and to receive him with open arms, although it may cause them some, perhaps much, suffering.

Oh! that there was more of a willingness, both with you and us, to suffer! And will not Friends have to come to this before they get back, or can get back to primitive ground? The mode of suffering, to be sure, has changed: formerly it was from without; now it is from those with whom we have peradventure been accustomed to take sweet counsel, and to go up to the Lord's house in their company. After all, I have sometimes doubted, whether we could take the spoiling of our goods, or endure long imprisonments, any easier than we can risk our rights in religious society, and the loss of a good name therein. I know, by experience, that the last mode of suffering is not easy to be endured. I remember my affliction, the wormwood, and the gall. But I was sometimes permitted to feel a consoling assurance that my life would be given me for a prey; and that nothing would be permitted to harm me, if I faithfully followed that which I was favored to see was right and good. And I have had no cause to repent having done so. But if I had consulted expediency, and looked at the consequences, I believe what little I had would have been taken from me; yea, that I should have suffered loss of all! Many, very many, have split upon this rock, not looking at the mark for the prize of the high and holy calling, with a single eye.

It remains to be as true, that "he that receiveth whomsoever I send receiveth me," as that Christ's sheep hear His voice and follow Him, but will neither receive nor follow the voice of the stranger. How unsafe it is to depart from this ground, even in what may be considered little things, the multitudes who have recently fallen in this way, both on the right hand and on the left, bear mournful witness. . . . . .

FROM T. B. G. TO WILLIAM HODGSON.

NEWPORT, 10th mo., 13th, 1853.

MY DEAR FRIEND, WILLIAM HODGSON, JR.:

. . . . . . It seems to me that there is great delusion somewhere; that this spirit of amalgamation is splendidly delusive; and the tendency of it is glossed over with a very smooth and exceedingly fine-looking varnish; but, after all, a slight knock often proves sufficient to crack the varnish, and to show that all is not glorious or harmonious within; that the boasted patience is not exactly the patience of the saints; neither is the unity talked of, like the unity of the one true and living faith which they kept and possessed, and by which they obtained the victory over its enemies and theirs, instead of being obliged to surrender to them, and being overcome by them.

I understand that B. H. said, in their select yearly meeting, that neither body in New England received your "Report" in the spirit in which it was written; and that both bodies had done violence to the discipline and order of the Society. Dost thou take him to be an *original* character? I should much like to know wherein *we* have violated the discipline; and should scarcely fear to ask him who *invented* the slander, whether we did not receive the Report of your meeting for sufferings, in as creditable a spirit (not to speak of common civility, or Christianity either), as our acknowledgment of its reception was received, by the power which ruled in your yearly meeting? How much religious good can be reasonably expected to be gained by anybody, from continuing to meet, year after year, in the present disjointed and unsound state of Ohio Yearly Meeting (and perhaps some others), is scarcely a question in my mind. On the whole, I think, whatever of good remains among them there, is quite as likely to be increasingly tinctured with the leaven of the Pharisees (thou knowest what that was declared to be), as it is, to be instrumental "in restoring that which has gone astray, and gathering them into the true sheepfold." But time will undoubtedly make manifest what the real object is. The tree will be known by its fruit.

Thou art doubtless aware ere this, that our dear friend, J. Wilbur, sailed on the 28th of last month, in the ship Niagara, with his son Amos for a care-taker. I hope ere this they have safely landed on the shores of that once eminently favored isle. I spent a day or two with him at Fall River, and took leave of him there, the evening before he sailed. He seemed fresh and lively in his spirit, and increasingly bound to the service; expected to proceed directly to London, and to remain for a time about there. I was glad to find that L. A. Barclay heartily united with him in this prospect. I was reluctant to leave him short of the ship, and I know it was some disappointment to him; but my dear mother was so poorly, I could not feel easy to go further from home. Except, however, a very ill turn during my absence, she has continued much in the same state as when I last wrote to thee. . . . . .

T. B. GOULD.

TO WILLIAM HODGSON.

ELMSIDE, 2d mo. 8th, 1854.

MY DEAR FRIEND, WILLIAM HODGSON, JR.:

. . . I have almost daily thought of writing to thee, and truly I have much wished to do so; but for several weeks after I received thy letter, my precious, lamented mother lay so very ill, and in such a suffering condition, that I could not do it; and during the last week of her life, by constant watching, both day and night, at her bed-side, and exposure to strong currents of air (which were indispensable to her), I contracted a very severe cold, or a succession of them, which settled on my lungs, and which, a few days after the funeral, laid me upon my own bed, and confined me there for many weeks, in great suffering, and danger of my life also; and I have been since, until yesterday, wholly confined to the house, when I went over to father's for the first time, it being very pleasant. But I have already found that I could not even do that with impunity, though with great caution; my lungs, or bronchial tubes, being yet in such a weak and disordered condition; although I am in hopes, when the weather gets finer, that I may once more get about again, nearly as I have been accustomed to do.

Speaking of my beloved mother, I think she was the greatest sufferer that I ever saw; and it has been my lot to witness a good deal of suffering. But her mind was preserved in the most perfect calmness and peace to the last; and there was even a heavenly expression of humility, tranquillity, and resignation, resting upon her countenance, which attracted the attention, and elicited expressions of admiration, from transient beholders. One giddy young woman, who happened to go into her room, remarked to my wife, on leaving it, "What a feeling of peace and quietness pervades even the rooms of such as are prepared for death! I was very much affected by it, all the while I stayed there. She must be very good!" This seemed striking to me, and the more so, as nothing had been said by any one, to lead to it. Indeed, dear mother would not allow anything of the kind to be said to her. She very seldom alluded to herself in any way, during her sickness; and when she did so, it was always with the most unaffected humility and abasedness of self, that I ever witnessed. A few hours before she was released, she desired me to give her dear love to Friends in Philadelphia whom she knew, and she mentioned thee by name. This last I have felt bound to say, and the rest thou must excuse, if thou canst. Her memory is precious to me beyond what I can express, even if it were desirable. . . . .

How silent and cautious "The Friend" continues to be! Truly, if Friends had only been as "wise and prudent" previous to the Hicksite separation, the errors of Hicksism would not have been exposed; every man would not only have been allowed to enjoy, but also to promulgate his own opinions; and what an edifying degree of love, and unity, and harmony might now have been enjoyed, by those who professed to hold to sound principles, with such as had adopted the infidel sentiments of Elias Hicks! Well, this *may* be in the ordering of Divine Wisdom, but I doubt it. I have no confidence whatever in the modern doctrine and practice of expediency. This prudential wisdom, I cannot away with it. . . . There are many articles in "The Friend," that are neither wholly clear, nor wholly dark to me; a kind of mongrel, apocryphal production. It would be very desirable to have things made so plain, that there could be no mistake about them. And there is some consolation in believing, that there remains to be a beautiful simplicity in the truth; although judgment seems to be often "turned away backward, and truth to have fallen in the streets, so that equity cannot enter." But it was (was it not?) when the Lord "saw that there was no man," no faithful, unflinching advocate for truth, and "wondered that there was no intercessor," that "His own arm brought salvation, and His righteousness it sustained Him," and the truth of His cause. May it be so now!

Second month, 11th. I have had an ill turn since I commenced this letter, by reason of which it has been delayed longer than I intended. I am too weak and nervous to write, now; but I thought I would try to add, that a Friend from Vermont has recently visited nearly or quite all of the meetings, and many of the families, in this yearly meeting, and also appointed a number of meetings amongst other people, to very good satisfaction. I had never so much as heard his name mentioned, until I heard of his being in Ohio at the time of their last yearly meeting, and that he was not allowed, or rather advised not to attend it. I have never heard him myself in the exercise of his gift, except in a private opportunity in my own room, while I lay ill in bed. That opportunity occurred wholly unexpectedly and remarkably to me, just before he left, after having spent several days and nights (on and off) at our house. A very precious solemnity spread over us, and continued for some time before a word was uttered; under which our hearts were contrited, and united in a good degree of that heavenly fellowship which is sometimes preciously experienced; and to the apostolic description of which, he added, "Truly, our fellowship is with the Father, and with his Son, Jesus Christ." He certainly reached and spoke to my condition, in a manner very striking to me, and he could have had no outward clue to it whatever.

There is nothing in the appearance, or perhaps in the natural talents of the man, aside from his gift, which seems very likely to produce a sensation; but as I have previously been quite as much edified and encouraged by the manifestation of "the Lord's power through a ploughman," as by "the wisdom of the north, or the eloquence of the south," there is a satisfaction to me in recording this fresh instance of it. And moreover, I thought it might possibly be interesting and somewhat encouraging to thee, to hear a report of good things coming again, as it were, out of Nazareth; of one, whom many would consider as an alien, a separatist, and an outcast, being shod with the preparation of the Gospel of peace, so that his feet appeared "beautiful upon the mountain" of the Lord's house and holiness; although this beauty can only be discerned by such whose eyes have been opened, and are kept open, by the repeated application of the eye-salve of the Kingdom. In being with, and thinking of, this Friend, I could not divest myself of painful reflections and impressions, with regard to that state of things which had excluded him from even a seat in Ohio Yearly Meeting. . . . .

Farewell.

T. B. Gould.

To Peleg Mitchell.

Elmside, Newport, 27th of 2d mo., 1854.

My dear Friend, Peleg Mitchell:

. . . . —— —— went up to see my precious mother, a few weeks before she was gathered to her everlasting rest, and it was to their mutual satisfaction. Oh! my dear friend, it had never been my lot to lose so near and dear a relative before, and the stroke was unutterably severe. Sometimes I think I could have borne it easier, if she had not been so great a sufferer; and at others, that all she suffered was necessary, to enable us to give her up. I am satisfied that her sufferings were not on her own account; and neither these nor her virtues can ever be forgotten while memory lasts. Greater humility, stronger and more prevailing faith in the Divine goodness and mercy, or better evidence that all would be and is well with her, I never witnessed.

There was an unusually large attendance at her funeral, notwithstanding the day was wet and lowering; and just before the hour, it came on to be very cold and blustering, the wind having changed. An unusual covering of solemnity spread over the company, and seemed to pervade the whole house, which was full of people. Not a word was uttered; no sound was heard but that of the wind outside; all was peace and quietness within; and just before the close of the opportunity, the sun, which had been hitherto obscured, broke through the clouds, and penetrating through the cracks between the window-shutters, filled the house with a mild, subdued, and mellow, yet glorious autumnal light; and I could not help thinking that it was a fit emblem of that more glorious, heavenly light, in the full fruition of which her purified spirit was, without doubt, everlastingly centred; notwithstanding the boisterous winds and tempests through which her gentle spirit had had to pass, in the course of her journey through this bleak, unfeeling world, and which had been permitted to beat against her, in her passage through the dark valley of the shadow of death; although, before the close, there was a great, a perfect calm, and she was permitted to pass sweetly, quietly, and so gently away, that we could not define the precise moment of our unutterable loss, or her eternal gain. . . . .

I suppose we may look for him [J. Wilbur] home again very soon, if he has not already embarked. I should not be surprised if he should be at the meeting for sufferings, in the fourth month, at New Bedford. But even if he should be, what a blank there is there! How little a while those two worthies, Francis Taber and Job Eddy, were separated! In how short a time, we who are left behind, were bereaved of them both! "Lovely and pleasant in their lives, in their deaths they were scarcely divided." But where shall we look for their equals, and who shall arise to fill their places? Truly, the prospect of a succession of such standard-bearers looks gloomy to me. The old people have gone and are going into the earth, and the young ones into the air. I often feel exceedingly discouraged; and in this respect, I suppose I am not entirely alone.

Dost thou see the "British Friend?" In their twelfth month number, they came nobly and boldly out in defence of the truth. In that of first month, they did pretty well, although they showed signs of faltering; and in the second month number, they seem nearly to have nullified all the good they had done, by far-fetched and needless encomiums upon the abundance of the labors of their numerous delegations, and missions to the uttermost parts of the earth; as if one fountain could send forth bitter water and sweet, at one and the same time! . . . .

As ever, thine,

T. B. Gould.

To Charles Perry and Ethan Foster.

Elmside, third month, 2d, 1854.

My dear Friends:

. . . . . . I unite fully with Ethan in the fear which he expressed in his letter to me, and I am almost ready to say, in the belief, that on account of the great degeneracy and corruption, both in church and state, a day is approaching, and almost at the door, which will try the faith and foundations of men, in a nearer and more personal manner than what has long been known, or is at all expected by many. And I am often ready to query, notwithstanding

I thus write, Who will be able to stand? Who, even amongst us, will be able to endure the devouring fire of persecution for righteousness' sake, when it shall extend to our persons and our estates, and even our lives also? I can by no means say that I feel able to endure it; I have no strength nor confidence in myself to speak of or to boast of; but I think I feel more and more, the necessity of endeavoring to cleave fast to that which is able to sustain all those who do put their whole trust and confidence therein, even the unchangeable, immovable Rock. But when I look out, upon the prospect and condition of things in the Church and in the world, I am often rendered entirely disconsolate; so that I am, as it were, compelled to flee to the Rock, and to get under the shadow and shelter of it, for protection and defence. . . . . .

As ever your friend,
THOMAS B. GOULD.

DRAFT OF A LETTER FROM T. B. G. TO JOSEPH BRINTON.

ELMSIDE, 23d of fourth month, 1854.

DEAR JOSEPH:

. . . . . . The deep interest which I have long felt in the proceedings of Philadelphia Yearly Meeting,—as that which, according to my sense of feeling, embraces within its limits the largest and soundest body of old-fashioned Friends,—has by no means abated; and I do earnestly desire that the time may be hastened, when the Lord shall arise for the help and deliverance of these from that which so grievously oppresses and afflicts them. But, whether it may be for "a time, times, or half a time"—whether the time may be shortened for the elect seed's sake, or He may seem to tarry long, and suffer the contradictions of sinners against Himself, yet I am persuaded that, in His own time, He will come, and will not tarry beyond it! Then will such as have continued with Him in temptation and through suffering, inherit the kingdom prepared for such, and for such only, from the foundation of the world. Then will they be permitted to return to the place of true rest, to return and come to Zion, the city of the saints' solemnities, and the tabernacle which shall not be taken down, which in itself remains to be an "eternal excellency," and will, no doubt, yet become the joy and the praise of the whole earth; although it may seem to be forsaken, and those who prefer its prosperity above their chiefest joy, may be deemed as aliens, and spoken of as outcasts, whom few men seek after, or seem to care for. But such as these, wherever scattered by the overwhelming flood which the dragon has been permitted to pour out of his mouth, do nevertheless experience a fellowship in suffering, one with another, and with the Captain of their salvation (who was Himself made perfect through sufferings); so that at times they can adopt the language of the experienced Apostle, when he said, "I am exceeding joyful in all my tribulations;" and again, "Although no affliction for the present may seem to be joyous, but grievous, nevertheless it yieldeth the peaceful fruits of righteousness to those who are exercised thereby." So that all depends upon our being rightly exercised by that dispensation we may be called to pass through, and on our continued faithfulness unto Him who hath called us, whether it be in suffering or rejoicing; there being danger on every hand, both right-hand errors and left-hand errors; and such as the enemy cannot destroy in one way, he may betray in another, where they less expect his attacks. But help, all-sufficient help, is laid upon One who is able to keep us from falling, and to present us faultless before the presence of His glory with exceeding joy.

. . . . . I have no hesitation in confessing my entire conviction that in true unity there is strength, and whatever does have a tendency to separate true Friends more widely from each other, certainly does weaken them; and a desire to promote or maintain this unity, is widely different from a combination or confederacy against the truth. I think the great pains which have been taken by some in Philadelphia to keep their members, who felt some sympathy and unity with us, away from us, has already done us great harm, and perhaps little good to them; for certainly, in a general way at least, those who have taken the pains to come and see for themselves, have not, I believe, gone away feeling less interested (shall I say unity?) with us, than before they came. . . . .

Thy sincere and affectionate friend,

T. B. Gould.

CHAPTER VII.

A RELIGIOUS engagement had been gradually maturing in the mind of Thomas B. Gould, to pay a visit in the love of the Gospel, to Friends in some parts beyond the limits of his own yearly meeting. This prospect of service at a greater distance from his own home than it had ever before fallen to his lot to travel, was attended with circumstances of peculiar trial. He was at this time greatly enfeebled by illness; and the sad reports which were spread abroad, of the prevalence of cholera in some places which he felt himself led to visit, were sufficient to cast down his particularly sensitive feelings. This formidable disease attacked his native city of Newport at this juncture; and very near the time fixed for his departure to Ohio, his own home was invaded, and four of his children were prostrated by it, two of them being reduced very near to the gates of death. He was brought into a great strait. He had been afraid of meeting the disease abroad, and discouraged about going, on that account; though not to such a degree as to cast away the shield of faith, or actually to shrink from complying with what he believed was really required of him. But now the trial was changed, and his nature was almost ready to recoil at the thought of leaving home, in the condition into which his beloved family were brought. Yet even here, and when the query was put by the good Remembrancer, "Lovest thou me more than these?" He that knoweth the secrets of all hearts was pleased to accept the acknowledgment, "Lord, thou knowest all things; thou knowest that I love thee;" and waiting faithfully on the all-merciful Hand of Him who afflicts in mercy and loving-kindness to His poor servants, he was permitted to feel the arm of the Almighty extended for his help, and for the confirmation of his faith and confidence in Him; and enabled to acknowledge, that "day unto day uttereth speech, and night unto night showeth knowledge" of His mercy and of His goodness. His children were all favored to recover, he regained his own health very considerably, and was made remarkably serviceable, by personal attentions, in relieving the distresses of many poor destitute persons in the cholera hospital of Newport, who had been shamefully neglected by some having charge of them. Thus all the home discouragements were taken away; and all fear was banished from his mind, in respect to the prevalence of the complaint in the places to which his sense of religious duty was about to lead him; and he bade farewell to his family and friends, in due time to accomplish what he had in view.

Another cause of discouragement attending this prospect of distant service, was one connected with the distracted state into which the great prevalency of the Gurney schism had thrown the Society of Friends. The temporizing and compromising system, which had sprung up within Philadelphia Yearly Meeting a few years before, had spread into Ohio, and had, in both those yearly meetings as well as elsewhere, greatly broken the ranks of those who had at first stood firmly against the innovations of the modern school. A "middle party" was the result of this new defection, more plausible and far more difficult to contend against, than open Gurneyism itself, inasmuch as its aim was more hidden and insidious, and its mode of procedure more illusory, slippery, and uncandid. But the tendency of this system of policy was, and still is, to lead into confusion, to destroy the vitality of the testimony of those who became entangled in it, and gradually—though of late rapidly—to carry them within the power of that very vortex which they once saw, understood, and abhorred. Many of its positions were untenable by right reason, and distinguished by great inconsistencies, such as have rarely been met with in the Society of Friends; in whose history, hitherto, the plan of temporizing and compromising with that which was opposing the pure truth, and rending the body from its foundation on the immutable Rock, had been unknown.

This spirit was characterized by a constant tendency to make concessions to the Gurney party, and a connivance at many of their irregular transactions, notwithstanding its high and unfounded charges against those who could not unite with it herein, of departure from the order and discipline of the Society. These concessions and connivances, including an inordinate deference to London Yearly Meeting, and desire to cling to it even in its present position of sanctioning error and schism, were with the vain hope of producing a reconciliation between elements essentially opposed to each other. But this system—not standing upon the ground of the unchangeable truth, but on that of policy and supposed expediency, and the alleged duty of "submission to the body" (or, in other words, to the *majority*),—had no convincing efficacy. Most of its power was attributable to the influence of certain members active in its promotion, to the great numbers naturally pleased with a way so much easier to the flesh, than that of "earnestly contending for the faith once delivered to the saints," and to its possession of the pen, in the two yearly meetings in America especially affected by it, and of an influential press in the one, the echoes of which were heard among the hills of the other.

There might certainly have been something amiable and attractive in the position of attempting to soothe the troubled waters, had this position been carried out consistently with a firm and unflinching maintenance of the Truth as it is in Jesus,—from which no church of Christ can safely abate one jot or tittle. But this system, while it professed to disapprove of the innovations in doctrine, and lamented the changes of discipline and practice which have been made in some places, soon showed its proclivity for the *popular* side of the question, began to hush up the further exposure of the doctrinal errors of Gurneyism, and manifested a settled aversion and hostility to the "smaller bodies;" alleging that they (not the Gurney party, who were in the majority), were the separatists from the Society; refusing the reception and publication of their documents, and denying them the right to have their members and ministers recognized, in the meetings where it had the power to prevent the reading of their certificates, or the appointing of meetings at their request. Thus, though still professing *a degree* of unity with them as *individuals*, and fallaciously conceding to them *in words*, the right of such recognition as was needful to *secure* them in the enjoyment of their rights as members, by a strange inconsistency, it refused them the very means by which that membership could be placed beyond doubt or cavil; as Thomas B. Gould soon found exemplified, in his own case, in Ohio Yearly Meeting. In short, it may be truly said, that this system (very similar to that which in England, in 1836, frittered away and frustrated the issuing of a clear testimony against Beaconism), has for more than ten years, in Ohio and Philadelphia Yearly Meetings, kept the Society in perpetual distraction (instead of the hollow harmony which it aimed to promote), by its too successful attempts to turn aside the living sense and solid judgment of the church; which would otherwise have carried the testimony of truth over the heads of opposers, would have convinced many honest but entangled minds, and would have prevented much of the defection, and many grievous departures, which have taken place in several yearly meetings; and thus the Society might have been enabled to go forward in true harmony and peace, as in years gone by, under the guidance, care, and help of its holy Head and High Priest, the Immanuel, God with us, the Way, the Truth, and the Life.

Such was the spirit and system which T. B. Gould foresaw that he must encounter, as well as original Gurneyism, in visiting Ohio Yearly Meeting; and such was the spirit which rendered the separation that occurred there at that time, so defective in its results.

The reader may, by the foregoing remarks, be prepared to understand certain allusions and circumstances, mentioned in his letters during that journey, which might otherwise be obscure or almost unintelligible.

Although only forty-one years of age, he had now been in the exercise of the public ministry of the Gospel, for fourteen years. Having faithfully occupied the gift received, he had been made ruler over more, had grown from a stripling to the stature of a man in the Lord's service, and was made "an ambassador for Christ," a "steward of the mysteries" of the Kingdom, and, we humbly believe, "a pillar in the temple of the Lord, that should go no more out." His ministry was sound in doctrine, weighty in substance, earnest and dignified in aspect, full and clear in expression, watchful and calm in delivery, beautiful in the elucidation and confirmation of the great truths of religion by that which "was written aforetime for our learning;" reaching the witness in the hearts of the hearers by a wonderful sweetness to the spiritual ear, and by the baptizing power which accompanied it, and demonstrating to the candid mind, beyond a doubt, that its spring was from the living fountain, which issues from under the altar of the Lord. Yet "this treasure" was in an "earthen vessel," and was all of Grace, no glory belonging to the instrument.

FROM T. B. G. TO WILLIAM. HODGSON.

ELMSIDE, 13th of 7th month, 1854.

MY DEARLY BELOVED ELDER BROTHER:

. . . . I never remember to have felt more peaceful; quiet satisfaction, at the close of any yearly meeting, or for a longer period thereafter, than since the last. But to or for everything there is a season, if not an end; and so I have found it in regard to what I may perhaps be allowed to term that sabbath of rest; for oh! what plungings have been my portion since, and continue so to be; in and under which, thy very seasonable and salutary acknowledgment of fellowship therein, was so far truly comforting and encouraging. . . . . . .

With what perspicuity and fulness hast thou reached and covered the whole ground occupied by that "plant," which I greatly fear has become like a "degenerate plant of a strange vine" unto Him, who designed to make it a plant of true excellence and high renown! It certainly did, for a while, shine forth with great brilliancy; the fruit was exceedingly sweet to the taste, the form thereof was beautiful and comely, and its smell delightful. But for want of keeping close enough to That from which it derived all its excellence and comeliness, I greatly fear that the "harvest will be an heap" of trouble "in the day of grief and of desperate sorrow." In addition to what I have lately had to suffer on my own account, I have felt much of the "bitterness of death," on account of such as seem evidently to have forgotten the God of their salvation, and to have become unmindful of the Rock of their strength. When last in that locality, I had publicly to proclaim, in the hearing of such as vainly supposed so, that the bitterness of death was by no means past; seeing Agag was yet alive, and that wicked woman Jezebel, who calleth herself a prophetess, was still suffered to teach, and seduce, and to bring into spiritual Sodom and Egypt, where our dear Lord was and is crucified: yea, it seemed to me as if there had been an inscription afresh written, comparable to that in Hebrew, and Greek, and Latin, and set over His head.* And yet I have lately had reason to fear, that I am not myself entirely clear of blood-guiltiness, because of my having let some know how dearly I loved them; but the full amount of esteem which I felt for, and expectation which I had of them, I never did disclose to the party referred to. Oh! how necessary and how profitable wisdom is to direct in all things, if it were only sufficiently sought after and abode in! . . .

30th.—I wrote the foregoing on the day of its date, being at the time in a very suffering condition from an attack of asthma, dyspepsia, and bronchitis combined; and unable either to lie down, or to take sufficient nourishment of any kind to prevent great suffering from hunger, besides the difficulty of breathing. The last symptom was somewhat relieved in about ten days from the commencement of the attack, by repeated discharges of blood from the bronchial membrane, as my physician said, and of which I have no doubt. By this, with the remedies used, I have been and am greatly weakened, being scarcely able

* This has since been sorrowfully verified.

to write these lines; neither have I attempted to write one line before, since the former date. . . Notwithstanding my weak and suffering state many ways, I got to monthly meeting last fifth-day; and therein was constrained (not willingly), to lay before Friends a concern which has ripened and settled upon me, to visit the meetings of Friends in some parts of New York, Philadelphia, Baltimore and Ohio Yearly Meetings, and if way should open for it, to attend the last-named yearly meeting; and also in the course of the visit to appoint some meetings among those not of our Society, as Best Wisdom may direct. I did and still do believe, the time had fully come for me to lay this burden before Friends. I had a secret hope they would take it upon themselves; but they did not. It was united with feelingly, and a committee of four Friends, two men and two women, appointed to prepare a certificate, and bring it before an adjournment of the monthly meeting, which was held yesterday; when the certificate was passed. It remains to be seen, what the quarterly meeting, which occurs next fifth-day, will do with it. Thou mayst rest assured, that it has not been without very close conflicts, and the exercise of some faith, which has been mercifully a little renewed at times, that I have ventured thus far. Few persons, I apprehend, have greater natural reluctance to such work, and to leaving home, even when in tolerable health, than myself. And in my present weak and suffering condition, along with the circumstances of the times in the Society, and the prevalence of cholera in many places, it seems to me very doubtful whether I shall, if indeed I am able to set out, ever reach my home again: neither do I know of any companion. But my dear Martha, although she says she could not consent to my going *now*, if I were in other respects ready, on account of my feebleness, still feels confident that I shall begin to improve after quarterly meeting, and continue to gain strength as I proceed on the journey. Last night I got no rest at all, being unable to lie down, or to sleep in my chair, till after six o'clock this morning; when I was favored to get a choice nap, only wakening up in time to get to meeting.

Eighth month, 4th.

Yesterday was our quarterly meeting. It was much larger than was expected, and considerably larger than has been usual when held here, although few beside our own members were present; and it proved a season not soon to be forgotten, both as regards the public and also the last meeting. In the former, after a time of great famine and strippedness, dear J. Wilbur was raised up with a small opening, and in great bowedness evidently; but the waters gradually arose, until they could not be passed over, by reason of the breadth and length, as well as the depth thereof; and they seemed to be of a renewedly healing quality, comparable to the river of the water of life, afresh set in motion for the especial benefit of the careless sons and daughters present, some of whom I trust were mercifully baptized therein. Dear Elizabeth Hill followed him, in a lively manner; and Phebe Foster followed her, in a sweet and touching communication, though short. She was evidently clothed with a garment of humility; and when she sat down, the meeting was remarkably covered with the spirit of prayer and thanksgiving.

. . . . After the ordinary business had been gone through, thy poor correspondent opened his concern, and laid the certificate of the monthly meeting on the table: whereupon J. Wilbur said, that although it was the province of the quarterly meeting to judge of such concerns upon their own merits, yet he thought it best that the certificate of the monthly meeting should be then read; which was done; and the whole meeting seemed to be dipped into much feeling, and a longer than usual, and very profound silence prevailed; during which my own mind was mercifully brought, as I humbly trust, into entire resignation, either to go or stay; although up to this time I had tried to hope, that by some means or other the thing might be stopped in the quarterly meeting, and the burden thereby transferred from mine to other shoulders. At length dear J. W. stood up, and remarked, that his mind had been very forcibly turned back to the time, and impressed with the declaration of the Saviour, when he sent the primitive disciples forth, and told them that they should bear witness of Him and for Him, at Jerusalem, in Samaria, and unto the uttermost parts of the earth; how he not only sent them forth, but gave them their message, even the word of the Lord to deliver, going before them, and abiding with them, their sure protection and all-sufficient Helper. He had been renewedly comforted in believing that this thing was of the Lord; that He was about to send forth a messenger, and that Himself would give the message; that He, as He was relied upon in singleness of heart, would be mouth and wisdom, tongue and utterance. He then feelingly alluded to the straits and baptisms that must needs have been passed through (as well as what might be expected to come), before such a prospect could have been yielded to in these perilous times; but he did believe that a few standard-bearers had been preserved, and would be preserved, even amongst us, and that the law would continue to be sent forth out of Zion, and the word of the Lord from Jerusalem. This is the substance of a part; but there was much more which I could not properly put down, and perhaps I have related too much already. However, while I felt none the less sensible of the awful responsibility, or of my own utter weakness, nothingness, and insufficiency, it was truly strengthening and encouraging to me. There was another long and solemn pause, during which many hearts were tendered and affected even to tears, and all present who could have been expected to do so, in due time expressed their unity. Dear J. W. went with me into the women's meeting, where it met with a very similar reception; although here, as in the men's part, it took many, if not most present, entirely by surprise: and after the female members of our own quarter had expressed themselves, Elizabeth Hill seemed constrained to acknowledge her near unity and sympathy, with considerable more, somewhat after the manner of J. W. in the other meeting; and there was a fuller endorsement prepared and placed upon my certificate, than I could have had any expectation of. . . . .

And now, my dear friend, let me add, that my health

has improved, my appetite is better, though still poor, and I am still suffering a good deal with asthma, but nothing to be compared with what I did two weeks ago; and with what diligence I can, I am making ready to set out; not knowing what will befall me on my journey, saving that "the Holy Ghost witnesseth, that bonds and afflictions await me," and, it may be, of no ordinary kind; although I am not prepared to say how it may be as to "every city," neither am I looking for great things in any respect, or to make an extensive visit within the limits of any yearly meeting; and if I can but be favored to do what my hands may find to do, whether it be in silent suffering or in active labor, and to do no harm, it will be all that I can expect, and in that case I may not lose a sufficient reward. My dear friend, Israel Buffinton, expects to bear me company, and with him I am fully satisfied.

J. J. Gurney, when here, seemed to be under some guard, while attending the yearly meeting; and I could not say much more about his ministrations at that time, than that the whole course and tendency thereof was wrong-end-foremost and out of joint; not one ray of light, life, or Gospel authority. After the yearly meeting, he had an appointed meeting here in Newport. He was long silent therein, which I believe was unusual with him; and when he did at length speak, he still seemed rather guarded. But he did nevertheless say, in the course of his communication, that "simple faith—*mere credence*,—formed a *fundamental* link in the great chain of Christian doctrine, in the Gospel of life and salvation." This I consider unsound doctrine. In a neighboring meeting, he declared, that the best of men before the flood had but a very little light, or a glimmering ray of light; that the light which they had, even the best of them, was not to be compared with what was or might be now enjoyed by the weakest Christian. An old elder who was present, said to me afterwards, that, although Joseph John might consider himself one of the best and strongest of Christians, he doubted much whether he had quite as much light as Enoch! . . . Farewell.

T. B. G.

FROM MARY DAVIS TO T. B. G.

DARTMOUTH, eighth month, 20th, 1854.

MY BELOVED FRIEND, T. B. GOULD:

I know not the cause why I have felt my mind unexpectedly drawn to write a few words to thee. When thou wast brought to my mind, thou appeared rather poor and low in spirit, a condition that has been the clothing of my mind as with a garment for a long season; so that I have scarcely been able to look up: yet I desire not to complain, but to acknowledge my unworthiness.

I believe it right for me to say, that when I heard of thy concern to visit the suffering seed in different parts of the Lord's heritage, I felt in my heart to bid thee God speed; and the language that our valued friend, James Tucker, adopted, on taking leave of my dear husband and me, when we were going out on such a mission, was revived: he said, "Go, and the Lord be with you. Be ye wise as serpents, and harmless as doves." I desire this may be thy experience; and I believe, dear friend, thou knowest, without my telling thee, that the Blessed Master will not be wanting on His part; but will, as our trust and confidence is in Him, be ever near such as He is pleased to call and send on His service, will string their bow, and cover their head, as in the day of battle; while such as are disposed to run unsent, and when there are no tidings ready, although they may overrun the true messengers, and arrive at the very place where the message is to be delivered, yet they are to be set aside as useless. I could add much, of my own true love and regard, but I feel a care lest I should exceed, and burden thy mind. . . . .

Thy friend sincerely,
MARY DAVIS.

FROM T. B. G. TO JOHN WILBUR.

NEWPORT, 25th of eighth month, 1854.

MY ENDEARED FRIEND, J. WILBUR:

It was truly kind in thee to write to me from Fall River, and ever since I received thy letter I have wanted to tell thee so; but a variety of causes, and some severe afflictions—bringing into fresh conflicts of spirit, and very close trials of the little grain of faith—have hitherto unavoidably prevented me.

One week ago last seventh-day, I took our two oldest boys with me to Fall River, intending to be there over first-day, and to bring the girls home too on second-day; which I did, reaching home about four o'clock P.M., safely and well. But about one o'clock, third-day morning, Harry was taken alarmingly ill; and about four o'clock P.M. of the same day, Ecroyd was even more alarmingly attacked with the same disease; which Doctor King positively pronounced to be cholera, neither is there any doubt of the fact. In the short space of three and a half hours from the time Ecroyd was taken, all apparent pulsation ceased, he became cold all over, and had every appearance of the very near approach of death; and this, notwithstanding we used every means in our power or knowledge to cause a reaction, before the Doctor came. He continued in this state, sinking lower and lower, full four hours and a half. We put mustard on his feet, and rubbed him with warm mustard-water and cayenne, wrung cloths out of hot mustard-water, &c., but nothing would do. His eyeballs were fixed and turned up, with the lids half closed; and although he could speak, yet towards the last he could not see. We considered him nearly gone, and so did the physician; when I proposed putting him bodily into a tub of warm mustard-water, which we did; and although at first it seemed as if he would not live to be put into the tub, yet in a few moments he began to show signs of sensibility; and the Doctor, who sat feeling for his pulse, looked up joyfully, and announced that he could now feel them at intervals, and added, "They get better and better; now I believe he will rally and do well." Thou canst judge of our feelings when, on putting him into warm blankets, we found him gradually becoming naturally warm, and his pulse quite regular, and also restored to sight.

When dear little Ecroyd had thus revived, I turned towards poor Harry, who (though he was first taken with much more apparent severity, and fifteen hours before his younger brother), had seemed to be better, and, we had thought, was doing well; but our attention was somewhat diverted from him by the very alarming state of Ecroyd. Harry had very much changed for the worse, and was now rapidly sinking into the same state of collapse; but on putting him in a warm mustard-bath, he also pretty soon revived, and they are now both doing well. The next seventh-day morning, our two youngest children were taken with the same disease, and both very severely; but having provided ourselves with proper medicines, and also obtained some sad experience, the means employed were blessed in such a manner as to arrest its progress; and although the little babe is still far enough from being well, we are in hopes he will continue to improve.

It is now first-day, the 27th. I had expected to leave home last sixth-day evening, but the dispensation of an all-wise Providence, herein adverted to, rendered it impracticable and apparently improper for me to set out at that time. Israel Buffinton was here yesterday, and we expect to go to New York to-morrow evening; although by constant watching and anxiety, as well as having my hands alternately in hot water and ice, I have contracted such a cold that I am quite a cripple from extreme lameness and pain in my back. How I shall do I know not; but through it all, my concern has not abated; neither has the grain of faith, previously vouchsafed and continued, been lost sight of or diminished; although I am not looking for any mighty work to be called for, or to be done by me. But if I can only be preserved from doing any harm, and from bringing reproach to the precious cause, I think I can say that I feel willing to suffer and to be reproached; for I do know that the cause is good and worth suffering for. And hard as it has been and is for me to leave my beloved family and Friends here, yet I feel anxious to be on my way, not knowing how long time and opportunity for the accomplishment of my work, or rather, for the filling up of my small measure of suffering, may be lengthened out to me. But, whether longer or shorter, I do earnestly desire that it may be accomplished, that so a place of rest may be obtained at last, through unmerited mercy and redeeming love. And oh! my dear, fatherly friend, mine eyes have been opened to see the hand of the Lord in this afflictive dispensation of His divine providence and inscrutable wisdom; so that I can say, day unto day has uttered speech, and night unto night has shown knowledge.

The manner in which my humble prospect was received and approved by our quarterly meeting, has been very confirming and comforting to me, although it has also increased, if possible, my sense of awful responsibility. Dear Mary Davis has since written to me in the same way, and Mary Macey has sent me a sweet message of unity and encouragement, and so has Mary Barnard.

. . . . . It is very sickly here; more so than I have ever known in my time. There have been more than fifty cases of cholera which have proved fatal,—many of them in the course of a few hours,—in this small town, within the last four weeks. Most of these have been among the poorer class of natives and foreigners; yet several very sudden deaths have occurred among the middle and upper classes of society, and many, very many, more of these have been attacked with cholera and other diseases which follow in its train, which have been controlled or arrested.

The cholera hospital, to which the poor Irish and others have been carried,—eight or ten cases sometimes in one day,—is right east of our house, in those red buildings just beyond our premises. As many as four corpses have been taken from there alone in one day, several times in the last two weeks, and buried immediately after death, without the least ceremony. I have been much at the hospital since our boys got better, from a sense of duty; and have done what I could to relieve the sufferings of the poor dying creatures, with some little success, although more has been made of it by the people of the town than I wished or merited. But they have been wholly forsaken by the Catholic priest, and by the self-styled Sisters of Charity, of which last, through the prevalence of Romanism, we have a number here. But my going to the hospital has at least had the effect to arouse the sympathies, and to call up the action, of others, who kept at a very safe distance before. I found them not only shamefully neglected, but actually abused by the nurses, who were paid no less than ten dollars per day for their worse than useless attendance. They—the nurses—ordered me out, when I first went, although I said not a word; and when I refused to go, they threatened *to keep me there*, alleging that such were the mayor's orders. But I told them I would report myself to the mayor, and take the consequences. I did so immediately, who thanked me for my attention, and said, that no other person, except the physicians, had interested themselves at all; and that himself was worn down with the claims upon his time and attention, caused by the prevalence of the disease. He freely issued a written order for my admission, whenever I saw fit to go, and required the keepers or nurses to treat my suggestions with attention. The next morning, I went up there again, without showing my order; when they sought to drive me out, telling me that it was in violation of the mayor's orders, and that they did not want me there; to which last I assented, but the first I denied. Pretty soon one of them asked me if I had got liberty of the mayor. I told him I had, and more than that also. . . . . . . The result was their discharge, and the obtaining of better men, and more skilful and conscientious nurses, at a more reasonable price. But the mayor was not to be blamed; for at the first the panic was so great, that none but the most reckless and worthless could be got. . . . . . .

Farewell; and do remember me for good, in your nearest approaches to the Lord.

THOS. B. GOULD.

TO MARTHA S. GOULD.

BALTIMORE, 30th of 8th mo., 1854.

MY DEAR WIFE AND CHILDREN:

. . . Dear Robert Scotton came in [to Philadelphia] from Frankford early in the day, on purpose to meet us, and had just left W. H.'s, when we reached there. We passed him in the street, and I pointed him out to Israel, although I did not know who he was, and still less thought of his coming to the city to meet us. Yet, like Paul at the Three Taverns, it furnished a fresh occasion to thank the Lord and take fresh courage. He came to William's early this morning, and freely went with us to the Western meeting; which was large and very quiet, not a dog moving his tongue, although some in that nature were there; and Robert Scotton spoke of the meeting as being to his entire satisfaction, and also, in his judgment, a remarkably favored one, notwithstanding very close things indeed were given me to deliver.

. . . . [Alluding to an individual who had been reached by his testimony on that occasion, he says:] So thou seest, my Master was pleased to give me favor in the heart of one stranger at least; and not only so, but He surely did fulfil His promise to me, which I received before I asked for my certificate, namely: "I will show thee a token for good, that thine enemies may see it and be ashamed;" and also, "I will go along with thee, and help thee, and make thy way for thee." . . . .

I enjoyed the ride through the country here very much, especially as my mind was clothed with a feeling of precious quietness, peace, and thankfulness, beyond what I have ever known; and in the desires raised for my own preservation, thou, my dear heart, and all at home, were sweetly included. Farewell!

Thine entirely,
T. B. Gould.

To William Hodgson.

Colerain, Belmont Co., Ohio, 9th mo., 2d, 1854.

My very dear Brother:

Thy letter to brother Joshua did not get here until some time after we did; so we hired a two-horse carriage, and came up from Wheeling, getting here about ten o'clock yesterday morning, weary and dirty enough, I can assure thee; but my heart was filled with thankfulness, inasmuch as my good and gracious Master was not only pleased to renew His promise to me (when, as we commenced going up the mountains, my faith began to fail as to our living to get over them), that we should be preserved, so that no evil or accident should befall us, but also to fulfil it, at least as to the outward. This morning, brother Joshua thought best to take us to the boarding-school before meeting; where we met with a cordial welcome from the superintendent, N. P. H., and his wife. The extreme heat of the weather exceeds anything I have ever before known, both day and night; and it has been so, all the way and all the time, since we left Baltimore, except just on the top of the Alleghany Mountains.

. . . . Joseph Hobson was truly kind and open, saying he was right glad to see me here; and so was dear honest old Robert Holloway, who is a lively, old-fashioned minister, though very much despised. They two went with me unflinchingly to [the select] meeting.

. . . . Not a word was uttered by any one, until W. Kennard proposed that the clerk should open the meeting; which he did, and proceeded to read the minutes of several of the strangers present; after which he added, "There is also on the table a minute or certificate from New England, and I am ready to query whether the meeting will not pursue the same course with regard to it, which has been taken in former years." . . . . [After the usual minute was made, in regard to the certificates, which had been read] J. Kenworthy inquired whether the *other* minute [or certificate] which the clerk had referred to, was from a branch of New England Yearly Meeting with which this yearly meeting formerly corresponded, or whether it came from the "Smaller Body," &c. The clerk did not condescend an explanation. Ann Taylor, Esther French, Edith Griffith, and many others, male and female, broke out into a continuous string of abuse against the "Smaller Body," and the presumptuous but apparently unknown individual who had *intruded* himself upon that meeting; making use repeatedly of very opprobrious epithets, some of them vehemently calling for the *name* of the intruder; which, however, neither the clerk nor any other person present thought fit to give them. . . . I plainly saw that, under the circumstances, silence would be decidedly my best *policy*: yet I felt called upon to say, "that inasmuch as the question had been asked, whether the certificate referred to came from a branch of New England Yearly Meeting, with which this meeting formerly corresponded, I thought it right that both the meeting and the individual should know that it did, and that moreover the certificate was endorsed by a quarterly meeting, which, after a careful and apparently impartial examination of the whole subject, of the unhappy separation which had taken place in New England, including the ground and cause of it, the yearly meeting of Friends in Philadelphia had solemnly decided to be the ancient and regularly established quarterly meeting of Rhode Island;" and I added, that "this decision was duly authenticated, and had also been printed and published" [as J. K. expressed that he had not before been aware of the fact]. . . . I saw how it was with some, who really, I have no doubt, felt much sympathy for me, but for fear of adding fuel to the fire which the Gurneyites kept up, let them have it their own way without a word in my favor—making a sacrifice of me, rather than prolong the discussion, or further endanger the quiet and peace of the meeting. But my good Master stood by me and helped me, bearing up my head above the billows; so that I could even hold up my head, and sit very quietly and patiently through it all, not feeling in the least moved or disheartened by it, because He had, measurably at least, prepared me for it before I left my home. . . . The vituperation of the Gurneyites was [at length] diverted from my shoulders considerably, and turned upon Philadelphia Yearly Meeting; at which I was not sorry, as it afforded me some relief: and all opposition to my sitting, finally ceasing, the clerk proceeded with the ordinary business. This seemed to me to exhibit a very low, weak state of things. . . . .

The meeting for sufferings was held in the afternoon, at three o'clock; which, after all, and under the circumstances, I thought it best for us to attend, being also advised to do so, by several Friends. . . . .

After meeting many Friends gathered around us, and seemed right glad to see us. . . . .

First-day. I have been here at Mount Pleasant all day, sitting in silence and astonishment at the captivity of this people. In the morning meeting, E. P. G. stood up early —proceeded to denounce one—guilty of unforgiven sins of the deepest dye, warned him of the danger of his being suddenly cut off, &c. . . . . . [See letter to J. W., E. F., and C. P., of 9th mo., 9th.]

Second-day evening. There was no attempt made to keep us out of the meeting, as was expected, this morning.

. . . . B. Hoyle opened the meeting, and the assistant-clerk read the reports of the quarterly meetings, and, with the clerk, the minutes of all the strangers present, except my own and that of I. Buffinton. Benjamin even called for such minutes as Israel Buffinton's, that is, for such as not being for members of the select meeting, had not been laid on the table by the clerk thereof; and in such a way as to render our sitting there, unaccredited, likely to straiten us additionally, and to be noticed by others. Then opened such a tirade of abuse, as never fell to my lot before; there was a deal of it, intermixed with some little censure of the clerk, for having proceeded so far with the business as he had done, while I was present;—all which I bore in silence, until they began to reflect darkly on me, for not only having produced no certificate, but also for not having explained the reason why I had not. I then thought it was time for me to speak; and accordingly stated, in substance, that I not only had yielded to come here under a deep sense and clear conviction of religious duty, after having turned the fleece, and proved it, both wet and dry, but that I had also received the full unity and concurrence of the monthly and quarterly meetings of Rhode Island; that these had been duly laid before the first sitting of the select yearly meeting; but that, owing to the manifestation of a similar feeling there, to what had been shown here, and the regard which the clerk of the select meeting paid, as I supposed, to the feelings of those of opposite sentiments, and in order to prevent such an exhibition there as had been made of opposing sentiments here, they had not been produced; notwithstanding they came from a quarterly meeting which had been decided to be the true Rhode Island Quarterly Meeting, after careful and impartial investigation of the whole subject, by a yearly meeting which has been considered to be one of the most solid and weighty yearly meetings in the world.* I also declared that my companion, Israel Buffinton, was duly furnished with a minute of concurrence from Swanzey Monthly Meeting; and how the separation took place there; who were the separatists; and as for what had been charged respecting my disownment, that it had only been done by a body of separatists; for I had always been a member of Rhode Island Monthly Meeting of Friends, and therefore was not an intruder, but had a *right* to a seat. I said considerable, and was on my feet three times I think; which I found necessary to do, as they called some of my statements in question. But as I further explained and proved my statements, they soon began to call on their own partisans to give over; and finally dropped me almost entirely, and turned upon the clerk; who, to save himself or the meeting, lowered the ground too much, I thought, for his own safety or that of the cause; telling them they might make the meeting as select as they chose, provided they did it consistently with our principles or discipline, and did not appeal to the civil authority;—and I, said he, will not object to it. He repeated this several times: but it did him no good, for they would not let him go on with the business while we sat there, which he was evidently disposed to do: and so, after sitting four hours in this way, the meeting adjourned. The representatives met after dinner, and had a very stormy time, some being determined that B. Hoyle should not be clerk any longer; and so fourteen representatives, out of forty-two, determined to carry in the name of Jonathan Binns for clerk, and James Bruff for assistant-clerk. The question was asked by some "middle" man, whether, if T. B. G. and I. B. were excluded, they would then consent to have Benjamin Hoyle's name carried forward;

* Philadelphia. See its "Report on the Division in New England."

but they answered, No!—he had done enough, beside this, to disqualify him, and it would make no difference at all.

Third-day. This morning I went to the second and last sitting of the select yearly meeting. There was not the least sign or word of dissatisfaction with my sitting therein, shown by any one. E. P. G. however delivered another loud and pointed call to repentance for unutterable sins. The yearly meeting convened at eleven o'clock. . . . . It was again supposed that they would forcibly keep us out of this, the second sitting of the yearly meeting; but no such thing was done or attempted. As soon as the meeting was opened, one Jabez Coulson said he was directed by a large part of the representatives to propose the name of Jonathan Binns for clerk; which was directly united with by many, in quick succession; when Nathan Hall said, he was requested to inform the meeting, that the representatives had been together, but were unable to agree upon any names to offer for clerk and assistant. The usual minute for the continuance of the old clerks was proposed to be made, and strongly urged by Friends. . . . . . . But there were some not disposed to be put down at all, although many of their own party halted long. It was, I should think, nearly two hours, after they began to urge them to go, before they could get their new clerks to the table, and it was some time after this, before he ventured to make and to read the minute of their appointment.

After a deal of time had been wasted in listening to them, and their many and high charges against B. Hoyle (who has gained nothing in any way by his weak endeavors to compromise matters with them), and Philadelphia Yearly Meeting, and myself, Friends finally adjourned to ten o'clock to-morrow (fourth-day morning), and left them sitting in the house, where they remained two hours longer, making six in all. I never uttered a word during either this or the select meeting to-day; but it seemed more than they could well bear (or indeed some others either), even to see me sitting there, though clothed in sackcloth and ashes. . . . . .

And so they have gone. I have never yet had quite so trying a service as this to pass through; and yet I have not been permitted to doubt the rectitude of my coming. . . . . . . As we passed out of the meeting-house, and I perceived only about one-fourth of the whole number left behind, it did feel to me as if "the people were still too many." . . . . B. Hoyle plainly declared to the separatists to-day, that New England Yearly Meeting *had a right* to suspend the article of our discipline respecting the appointment of clerks, and fully admitted the *larger body* to be the yearly meeting! When he saw that it did no good, but much harm every way, he declared that he had repeatedly done violence to his own feelings to please them; but this helped him no more than the other; and it is possible he may in time learn that honesty is the *best policy* after all.

. . . . . All this, and much, very much more, we have seen, felt, and suffered in silence. But my Master told me this morning, that He would fight for us, and we should hold our peace; and I have obeyed Him herein, although many Friends evidently wonder at my silence, and others, I believe, are equally afraid of me. . . . . .

T. B. GOULD.

FROM NATHAN HALL TO WILLIAM HODGSON.

HARRISVILLE, HARRISON CO., OHIO,
9th month, 11th, 1854.

DEAR FRIEND:

I have just returned from a meeting at Harrisville, appointed by our mutually beloved friend, Thomas B. Gould; who requested that I should give thee some account of his getting along in these parts, his engagements and present indisposition preventing him from writing to as many of his dear friends as he would wish to.

I know not whether thou hast had a letter from him since his arrival here, or not; but suppose thou hast had some account of him, in connection with the separation that has recently taken place in our yearly meeting. Information so received may give an unfair statement of existing facts, as it is reported, even in this vicinity, that he was the cause of the separation; and some hard things are said of him, both in public and private, relative thereto. I am not about to give an account of the separation (as thou hast doubtless had divers more full relations of it than my present purpose or limits will permit), further than relates to our friend, T. B. Gould. His certificate, with a number of others, was produced to our select meeting on seventh-day. The meeting pursued its usual course, which is, to read no such documents from any portion of the Society in New England. Of course it was not produced to the yearly meeting on second-day morning; but it being known that he and companion were present, it was strongly urged by the Gurneyites, that no business should be done till the meeting was made select.. This they made the principal bone of contention during most of that sitting. But it was several times distinctly stated by a part of the representatives, who met in the evening to propose the names of Friends for clerk and assistant, that they would not agree to the name of B. H. for clerk; that he had "disqualified himself for that service years ago;" and that, rejecting T. B. G. and companion, would not change their intention of offering other names, which they then proposed. So that it would be doing injustice to New England Friends, to say that they were the cause of the separation. And even if it were so, surely it would have been a very frivolous excuse for such a desperate course as was pursued.

. . . . W. and C. Evans, and our New England Friends, were of course all the strangers that remained with us. The latter had not much vocal service in the meeting, no doubt very sensibly feeling somewhat trammelled by the circumstance of their not being fully acknowledged. They were at meeting at Concord yesterday. I thought Thomas was favored, and very much so at the one appointed in our meeting-house to-day. It was composed partly of non-professors, and professors of various kinds, some that seldom attend any of our meetings; and being nearly all entire strangers to him, he had no outward means of knowing their condition; yet I think it was as appropriately spoken to, as I remember to have heard on any occasion. I think I never heard the coming, suffering, and crucifixion of our Saviour, with His mediatorial offices, more clearly brought to view at any time; declaring what He had done for us without us, and showing the necessity of receiving Him in his second coming, or spiritual appearance; and that the first was unavailing without the last. He seemed fearfully and awfully impressed with the state of some present, and labored earnestly, and may it be effectively, for their restoration. This is more than prudence would dictate to say *to* a minister, but I have only said it *of* him, and thou wilt see that he is not hurt by it. . . . . . . He has a meeting to-morrow at Flushing, and next day at Guernsey. . . . . .

I am, with love, thy friend,
NATHAN HALL.

FROM T. B. G. TO JOHN WILBUR, E. FOSTER, AND C. PERRY.

COLERAIN, BELMONT CO., OHIO,
9th to 19th of 9th mo., 1854.

MY DEAR FRIENDS:

The yearly meeting concluded about eleven, A.M., and we have been allowed to sit without any one (except those who have seceded) objecting thereto; although it has been very manifest that our presence was quite as galling to some that remained behind, as to those who left. We have had a most trying week of it indeed. However, no objection whatever was made to our sitting in the meeting for sufferings. . . . The same morning I went to the select meeting. . . . There were many strangers present with minutes, who all went with the seceders except W. E.; but their certificates were all read, and minuted as being satisfactory, and their company acceptable.

. . . . . . Dear J. H., who kindly took me into the meeting and into the upper gallery, did speak once or twice, to express his desire that the meeting might be allowed to proceed quietly with its business; which it was finally allowed to do in my presence, although I was singled out, and preached to, and prayed for, in the most pointed manner imaginable. The next day [first-day] in the great public meeting, in the morning, E. P. G., very early, and before the meeting was near gathered, commenced speaking, in what seemed for a time to be a most loving and peaceable manner; but after having sufficiently daubed her own partisans with untempered mortar, and cried "peace, peace," where there was no peace, she singled out *an individual* then present, who was "going about sowing discord among brethren." She was *sure* there was *one*, and thought there might possibly be more than one; but one there was of this description, who was guilty of the most "abominable and unforgiven sins;" describing them, or attempting to do so, but in a vague and indefinite manner. However, they were of an unpardonable nature, and she asserted that she was divinely commissioned to pronounce woes and judgments upon the devoted head of this "poor, miserable sinner," and to say that unless very speedily repented of, it would be forever too late, this being the *very last call*, and she the favored instrument of its delivery, and also of the malediction, which was this: that they "would sink his guilty soul down, down, down, to the lowest hell, where the worm dieth not, and the fire is not quenched," &c.! This she repeated three several times, and then referred to Ezekiel's vision of the image of jealousy, and the chambers of imagery, with the abominations committed therein by the ancients of Israel, repeating in the course of this division of her subject, nearly the whole of the eighth chapter of Ezekiel. Her appearance was splendidly delusive, seeming very like her who sat "as a queen and no widow," vainly and wantonly supposing that she should see no sorrow. . . . But I never felt or sat a meeting myself more quietly or peacefully in my whole life, feeling an evidence in myself that these things were all false as applied to me; and my good and gracious Master standing by me, and strengthening and comforting me, yea, and upholding me also by His Spirit, in a manner altogether beyond what I can express. . . . As for me I had nothing to do, but to set an example of silence.

. . . In the last sitting of the select meeting, no objection was made to my sitting, nor any allusion whatever made to me, except by E. P. G., who declared that the day of my visitation, or of mercy and grace to me (as I understood her) was extended beyond what she had previously thought or seen, although it was nevertheless extremely doubtful whether I would repent; and if not, down, down, down, I must speedily go! The answers to the queries in the select yearly meeting, and the summary thereof, were managed (with one exception), so as to represent that things were in harmony and unity; of which —— took special and most satirical notice. J. Kenworthy and others had, in the former sitting asked B. H. &c., if they really thought that the "smaller body" and its members were in the right, why they did not say so, and openly acknowledge us; for, said he, and with great effect upon them, too, "Friends, there is but a right and a wrong; there is but truth and error!" I sat among them in the select meeting with my lips wholly sealed, except as previously stated, but beholding with my inward eye, how the potsherds of the earth dashed one against another, and the abominations committed by the elders of Israel in their secret chambers of imagery, even such as have been accounted as the ancients of them! . . . The division immediately followed this sitting of the select meeting.

On second-day morning, ... B. H. had encouraged such as were there without minutes (such minutes as had been introduced and read from the select meeting), to explain the ground or cause of their presence; and —— had accordingly done so, and several others; Israel Buffinton's minute had also been laid on the table, and no notice taken of it whatever; when the Gurneyites, having previously said abundance against our sitting in the meeting, without any notice having been taken of it (except that when they requested all such as were not members to withdraw, and insisted on our doing so, dear old Robert Holloway said he did not know of any not members, or who had not a right to sit, being present), commenced calling directly upon us, to know, if we had certificates, why we had not produced them; and if we had no credentials, they requested us to make a verbal statement of the occasion and circumstances of our coming and being there, &c. I now felt the time had come for me to say, "that I had come amongst them under a solemn and convincing sense of religious duty; the concern having long rested with much weight upon my mind, and this time having been clearly pointed out, as the proper one to come here in, after turning the fleece again and again, and proving the religious rectitude of the concern, both wet and dry. And not only so, but my concern was fully united with by Rhode Island Monthly Meeting of Friends, of which I had always been a member, and I was furnished with its certificate, and the endorsement of Rhode Island Quarterly Meeting, duly signed by its clerks; which quarterly meeting, after a careful investigation of the whole subject, had been decided by Philadelphia Yearly Meeting to be the true and regularly established Rhode Island Quarterly Meeting. These certificates were duly presented to the select yearly meeting held here the day before yesterday; but owing to the manifestation of a similar spirit of opposition, to what we have seen here, and from a feeling of tenderness in the clerk (as I suppose) towards those of opposing sentiments, they were neither read there nor introduced here. However, Friends, you may rely upon it, that, after what has been said here, I would not remain in this house another moment, if I had not felt it my duty in the first place to come, and in the next place to remain in this meeting, and if I did not also know that I have a right so to do. So that I wish it to be distinctly understood, that I do not consider myself as an intruder, neither did I ever intrude myself into any place where I had not a right to go. I do not ask for the privilege of sitting here as a favor, I claim it as a right." I said considerably more in regard to Israel Buffinton and his certificate, and its having come "from the ancient Monthly Meeting of Swanzey, from which those who now constitute the larger body in New England first separated themselves, leaving the regular clerk at the table, and the Monthly Meeting of Friends of Swanzey in the house, in the regular transaction of its business: that the same class of persons afterwards separated themselves from Rhode Island Quarterly Meeting, received the reports from the new and spurious Monthly Meeting of Swanzey, and fully identified themselves therewith. It was so, as regards the yearly meeting called the 'larger body,' of which so much has been said. But, Friends, they are a body of separatists from the order and discipline, as well as from the principles and doctrines, of Friends. By these I freely acknowledge that I have been disowned; but I never was, in any manner, out of unity with or disowned by Friends, as so often stated in this meeting, nor until after the separation had occurred from Rhode Island Quarterly Meeting; which a yearly meeting, that has been considered one of the most solid and weighty yearly meetings in the world (that of London not excepted), has clearly, and fully, and unequivocally decided to be the ancient and regularly established Quarterly Meeting of Friends in Rhode Island." Hereupon the most violent Gurneyites, even those who had stated that they were able to prove my disownment, and held up the written documents which they had in their hands, making a flourish of them, began to say, in different parts of the house, that they were fully satisfied that it would never do to discuss this question in that public manner, although they were willing to meet me in private! "But," said they, "Friends, we are losing ground; let us say less, and act more firmly." And dropping me, they called upon the clerk to make the meeting select, saying they were satisfied he had it in his power to do so; and that if he had not given us his countenance, and manifested a disposition to go on with the business in our presence (blaming him, and rebuking him sharply for having gone as far with the business in our presence as he had), we would neither have been there, nor persisted in our resolution to sit there, after all that had been said against it by them. Whereupon the clerk began to clear himself from the charge of accountability, clearly showing them that he did not want us there; which had a tendency to manifest what spirit he was of, to some honest Friends who had been greatly blinded and deceived. But the Gurneyites would not accept it, and cried out the more vehemently against him, saying he had wholly and previously disqualified himself for acting as clerk. B. H. then tried more fully to clear himself of us, and threw us more completely into the hands of the Gurneyites, who gnashed upon us with their teeth, almost or quite literally, and seemed ready to destroy us. But B. H. said again and again, "Friends, you may make the meeting as select as you please, and I will not object to it, provided you do so consistently with our principles, and do not appeal to the civil magistrate." But they paid no attention to his earnest efforts to save himself, no matter at what cost, and charged him with treachery, &c., more vehemently than ever, clearly showing that they had no confidence whatever in him; and who could wonder? I then purposely said, that the clerk was in no way responsible for our presence; that he had been scrupulously careful not to give us the least encouragement; and that it would be great injustice to him to charge him therewith; that, as regarded myself, I had no wish to deceive any one; I meant to be an honest man, and was willing that every tub should stand upon its own bottom. This evidently displeased the clerk; but he showed his duplicity still further by saying, "Friends, you must see how that the individual has assumed the whole responsibility of his being here to himself." This was not true: I had done no such thing; but I clearly saw and understood his design to make me appear ridiculous, and presumptuous also. But an adjournment being proposed, in order to give them an opportunity to make the meeting select, I let it pass, biding my time. Between this and the next sitting, no one attempted any private labor with us, as had been proposed, to keep us out; neither was the least impediment thrown in the way of our going into the house. At the next sitting the separation occurred. . .

On fourth-day, a committee was appointed to prepare a statement of the facts of the separation. On fifth-day afternoon, a paper was brought in and laid on the table, purporting to have been prepared by the committee. . . . This narrative of facts was read early in the meeting, and united with, without much, if any, objection by any one; but it brought me under great distress, as I foresaw, when B. H. wrested my words (when I had merely exonerated him from all responsibility touching our presence) into a presumptuous assumption of the responsibility myself; which I had neither thought, said, nor intended, but, on the contrary, had expressly referred the responsibility to Him who brought me under the concern to come, and who required me to stay, and had made me willing to suffer for His name and cause' sake; whose name and cause I, at the same time, declared to be exceeding precious to me, even more so than any other consideration whatever; which declaration was also mercifully attended with a convincing evidence of its truth, which not even the Gurneyites could gainsay or wholly resist, and some of them openly acknowledged it at the time. But I said not a word now, until after they had gone through all the queries and answers, and we had had abundance of what is called preaching, from ——, ——, ——, and others. Near the close of the meeting, I stood up, and said, in substance, that I had never considered it a light matter to utter a word, or to occupy a moment of time, in such an assembly as that; but under a serious consideration of the nature of the document which had been read early in that sitting, I felt a necessity laid upon me to say, that if that part of it which stated that I had assumed the whole responsibility of my presence in that meeting, could be so altered as to say, that the individual referred to had fully exonerated the clerk from all responsibility respecting his presence, it would be truly relieving to my feelings, and also in accordance with the truth. I also appealed to them with some effect, in the language, "All things whatsoever ye would that men should do to you, do ye even so to them," &c.; and added a doubt, as this circular was to be appended to all their epistles, whether that part of it which stated that the clerk had repeatedly expressed his entire willingness that those who objected to our sitting in the yearly meeting should make it as select as they pleased, provided they did it in accordance with our principles, and did not appeal to the civil magistrate,—I meekly expressed a fear, whether the retaining of this part of the statement would be *of any service to the Clerk*, and that it might injure his reputation and lower his standing with the only class of Friends, in the different yearly meetings, who could be expected to advocate the reading of the epistles which were to be sent forth, bearing his signature as the Clerk of Ohio Yearly Meeting; and so it might seriously affect the decision which would have to be made between the reception of their epistles and those of the separatists; and also the cause and reputation of truth, which I plainly declared was of far more value than any personal considerations whatever; and that I could truly say, that I was quite willing, so far as I was personally concerned, to be of no reputation, either here or elsewhere; or, in other words, "I am willing to suffer for His name and cause' sake, who is everlastingly worthy: I have no desire, Friends, to be in any better repute than the truth is, amongst you!" This brought great solemnity over the meeting; very many Friends wept much. . . . The document was referred back to the committee for alteration and amendment. . . . . This paper was brought into the last sitting of the yearly meeting. . . . It appeared to have been very materially altered throughout: the most objectionable passage, respecting myself, was altered in conformity with my suggestion or request, so as to say that I fully exonerated the clerk from the responsibility of our presence. In other parts of this paper, too, where we had, in the first essay, been spoken of merely as individuals, we were now spoken of as Friends, members of the Society, &c.—and in other respects, too, with more consideration and respect. It was then sent into the women's meeting, to be entered on their minutes; but they were unwilling to have it go upon their records, by reason of the expressions of B. H. being still retained therein, respecting his willingness that we should be excluded from the meeting, &c. Very general and decided objections were made by the women Friends to this part of the document, and it resulted in their sending two of their number into the men's meeting, to inform it how very unsatisfactory it was to them. . . . They both spoke with great effect, in the men's meeting, in our favor, and against those actions and expressions, respecting us; saying that women Friends were deeply grieved, that the clerk should have so spoken respecting the two Friends from New England; that he had no right so to have spoken, and ought not to have done so, &c. B. H. made some little effort to defend himself, by saying, that one of the individuals had expressed himself satisfied with it. Others said, it was merely a statement of facts, and could not now be altered. Finally, dear Israel Buffinton said, that, although he deeply regretted the clerk's having said so, at the time, yet, as he did repeatedly so express himself, it could not now be helped, and he felt satisfied, or willing, it should stand as it did. This was the first and last time that Israel said anything in the yearly meeting, and it was well-timed indeed; he also had discernment to see that the retaining of this part would do B. H. and his party far more harm than it would do us. And I was, I confess, astonished at the blindness which must have overtaken poor ——, or otherwise he must have seen it.

What Israel said, seemed to satisfy the women, and they returned directly to the women's meeting. The essays of epistles to the other yearly meetings had all been read before the women came in; and after they were agreed to, I let Friends know, "that I thought it right for me to acknowledge, that I had listened to the reading of them with much interest, and had truly considered it a privilege to be present: but that I had also been led to consider, that if these epistles were really and truly the language of the Spirit to the several churches to which they were addressed, the matter of their reception or rejection was in such case a very serious one; inasmuch as they who refuse to receive whatsoever and whomsoever the Lord sends, refuse to receive Him, and they that refuse to receive Him, refuse to receive Him that sent Him." After somewhat more in this line, I let Friends know my own firm and renewed belief, however it might be, as to the matter of their reception, "that there would be no necessary cause of discouragement, if they should not be received and acknowledged by some of the yearly meetings with which this yearly meeting had heretofore corresponded; that we were living in a dark and cloudy day; that the spirit of the world and of the age had so blinded the eyes and hardened the hearts of many up and down amongst Friends as a people, that it seemed as if they would not or could not believe, although a man should declare the truth unto them; that this was a spirit of unbelief in and departure from the truth; that such was the blindness which had happened unto Israel, that it seemed to me there was great need, even for some who *had* been eminently gifted and deeply experienced, to be so humbled under the mighty hand of the Lord, as to availingly put up the petition for an increase of faith; that so they might be able to adopt the language, Lord, I believe, help thou mine unbelief; and that their eyes might be opened to see the way and work of the Lord in this our day and time, which was a dark and stormy time; but the darkness and the light were, in a sense, alike unto Him; He had His way in the sea, and His path in deep waters, and his footsteps were not known, except to such as were made willing to follow Him even to prison and to judgment; that clouds and darkness were round about Him, but righteousness and judgment were the habitation of His throne. That I did verily believe it was at least by His permission, that things were being so shaken; and that, if I was not mistaken in my feelings, the language was applicable, 'Yet once more I shake not the earth only, but also heaven,' and that everything that could be shaken would be shaken, that that which was immovable might remain: yea, that He would 'overturn, overturn, overturn,' until He came whose right it was to rule and to reign over all, whose power was in itself over all the powers of darkness, and who would yet, I firmly and renewedly believed, be magnified in the sight of those who had in different degrees become forgetful and distrustful of his power. But it was better to trust in the name and power of the Lord, than to put confidence in princes; for the Lamb and His believing followers would have the victory in the end, and such as rejected Him, and turned back from following Him, would be confounded and brought to nought." But I cannot attempt to give even the substance of what was spoken, any further. . . . A solemn pause ensued, during which, Ann Branson and P. Fisher came in; and I did rejoice that my gracious Master had raised me up before they came, and showed me a token for good, which mine enemies had seen and felt also, being, as I do believe, somewhat ashamed.

W. Kennard, on taking my hand at the close of this, the last sitting of the yearly meeting, told me emphatically, that he had near and good unity with me and my testimony in that meeting, and also in the public meeting on fifth-day. But notwithstanding the unity and near fellowship of very many Friends, B. H. undertook to lay an injunction upon them, not to appoint meetings for me at all. He professed a willingness that I should attend them as they came in course, but declared that it would be going beyond the yearly meeting, to appoint meetings, seeing my certificate had not been read therein nor received thereby. But dear Robert Holloway, a sound, old-fashioned minister, who with Joseph Hobson, a valuable elder, had stood unflinchingly by me the whole week, told them this would not do; and so called the ministers and elders together at the School (after we had left for brother Joshua's), and said to them, "Friends, if that dear Friend from New England feels a concern to appoint a meeting in any place, and calls the select members and overseers together, and lays it before them, and they unite with it, who has power to say no, seeing they are the proper authority, according to our discipline, to decide upon such a concern?" All present acknowledged it was so, but B. H. and J. E., neither of whom said anything. Robert then said, "There is no question, then, but Thomas can appoint meetings, if the select members and overseers agree to it:" and he was answered in the affirmative, except by the two who remained silent. Robert then rode several miles out of his way, to brother Joshua's, to inform us hereof, and to encourage me to attend to my prospect faithfully, as very many other Friends all over the yearly meeting had done before. . . . .

The meeting at Harrisville, on second-day, was large and much favored, people flocking to it the more, I suppose, on account of the unwonted notoriety which the Gurneyites, and some others not *known* by that name, have given us. At the conclusion, N. H. expressed to me his full unity and entire satisfaction; and encouraged me to keep steadily to my prospect, regardless of gainsayers. Indeed there were many tears shed at this meeting: one great, stout-looking man, not a member, (for general notice was given) was so broken, and shed so many tears, through the melting power of Truth, which did mercifully overshadow us in a remarkable manner, that they literally ran down his cheeks and dropped in such profusion as to make a large wet spot on the floor of the house where he sat. But I relate it only by way of acknowledgment of the goodness and mercy of my good and gracious Master, who has hitherto fulfilled the promise which He made to me, before I left my own habitation, that He would stand by me and help me; and He hath performed His promise to me, in a manner that has been marvellous in my own eyes, and as I humbly trust to the strengthening of many, and to the promotion of His own praise and glory; which, with the cause of truth and righteousness, was what I singly had in view in coming hither, and have been made truly willing to suffer for.

. . . . We went to Guernsey Preparative Meeting on fourth-day, lodging the previous night with our dear faithful friend, Robert Holloway. The meeting was large; and I was pretty soon raised up in it, having very clear doctrine to deliver, and feeling, I believe, somewhat as Paul did, when he spoke of fighting with wild beasts at Ephesus. But they sat silently and very quietly until I had done, when both a man and an English woman spoke somewhat by way of censuring me and excusing themselves, or trying to turn off what they clearly showed they had felt keenly; for my testimony had been to the good old way, and against new notions, calling the attention of such as had turned aside out of the way, unto Him who remains to be the only Way of life and salvation, as well as the Healer of breaches, and the Restorer of paths for the lame to walk in. The man said, it was not the first time the old adversary had transformed himself into the appearance of an angel of light, and sought to deceive the very elect by preaching sound doctrine! But it neither moved nor harmed us. . . . After this meeting, we rode over to Robert Smith's, at Stillwater. . . . . As we rode away towards

Ridge Meeting, —— and wife walked along by the side of our carriage, urging us to go to their house. But as we had eaten at the same table for nearly a week, and often side by side, and as at the close of the yearly meeting he had bidden me most emphatically "farewell," without saying one word about it till now, although he knew of my prospect of visiting some of their meetings; I did not incline to go, or to take other notice of what he said, about our coming back and lodging there, and seeing if he did not treat us kindly, &c., than to say, that I should like just to see his house. He finally asked me, if he had not treated me generously?—acknowledging, withal, that he had been most kindly treated at my house; to which I replied, in the hearing of his wife, for whose ear, as well as for his own, I intended it, "B——, I am greatly concerned for thee! I am afraid, if the Philistines press thee much further, or much harder, thou wilt fall upon thy own sword, as Saul did!" He replied, "I am obliged to thee, Thomas;" and so we parted, without my seeing his house, which he said was near, but hidden by the forest trees.

. . . I was silent therein [Ridge Meeting], until near the close; when I found an engagement to stand up, and was mercifully favored in so doing, to my great relief, and, for me, with much clearness and demonstration, though not lengthy. While I was on my feet, —— wept like a child. . . . He seemed as if he could not do enough for us; and well he might, for he had not had strength to stand firmly in the presence of B. H. and W. E. But I had perceived some change in his feelings, before the week was out, and he expressed satisfaction with our visit. . . . . We returned to Robert Smith's, and lodged there, feeling my mind drawn towards that family; with whom we had a precious opportunity in the morning, before we set out for Plainfield; wherein I had to open the mystery of iniquity, and the manner of its working in this our day; and to show them, that it is sometimes necessary to contend *earnestly* for that faith which was once delivered to the saints, or else we shall certainly make shipwreck of faith and a good conscience, and lose that goodly inheritance received from our forefathers, and which ought neither to be sold, nor exchanged for another. . . . . . .

After the meeting at Plainfield, we went to visit an aged Friend, by the name of Aaron Roberts, who was very low with dysentery. On sitting down by his bedside, he soon said, before a word had been uttered, "I feel sweet unity with your spirits." I was just ready to say the same thing in reference to him. There was no need of many words here, and I merely expressed the sense given me, of his having fought the good fight, and kept the faith, and of there being a crown of righteousness laid up for him in heaven, whether an entrance into the heavenly kingdom should be sooner or later granted to him. I was afterwards informed, by his family, of his having frequently expressed the full assurance thereof. . . . . . .

We returned to brother Joshua's last evening [the 18th of the month], and intended resting here to-day; for although I scarcely ever felt so well during a whole week, as I did during the week of yearly meeting, when I had so much to bear in all other respects, yet no sooner was my way opened amongst Friends, and all other things seemed to be much more favorable, than I became very unwell, and have travelled over a great deal of bad roads in much physical suffering; and attending a meeting every day for a week (except one), was of itself wearisome to both body and mind. But a severe attack of asthma, first-day night, prevented me from getting much sleep, or lying down; and it continued through second-day so badly that I could not write. . . . . . .

Yours sincerely,

T. B. GOULD.

TO MARTHA S. GOULD.

SOMERTON, BELMONT CO., OHIO, 15th of ninth mo., 1854.

MY DEAR MARTHA:

I received thy letter, giving me the first account of dear little Mattie's having had the cholera, last seventh-day afternoon, on returning to brother Joshua's after the close of yearly meeting. It affected me deeply, but I was enabled, after close conflict, afresh to resign you all into the hands of Him who doeth all things well; who did unquestionably call me forth, and hath gone before me in a marvellous manner, making darkness light before me and crooked paths straight; also literally opening a way where there seemed to be, and was, no way until He opened it; even giving me favor in the sight of the Egyptians, causing the wrath of man to praise Him, and restraining the remainder thereof!

B. H. and others manifested no more disposition to show us any favor, after the separation, than they did before; and our certificates were not only not read, but everything which he had said against our sitting was incorporated or included in the Account of the Separation, prepared nominally by a committee, but written by ——
——. . . . . .

I felt drawn to attend Concord Meeting on first-day. Public notice was given in the immediate neighborhood, and the house was filled; many Friends, elders, and overseers coming thither from neighboring meetings, and attending the meeting; in which my gracious Master showed me a manifest token for good. After meeting, about twenty of these Friends from a distance went to brother Joshua's to dinner, and a precious time we had! To some of these I opened my prospect of appointing a meeting at Harrisville the next day, and at Flushing on third-day; which was fully united with, and they were appointed and held accordingly, to the satisfaction of Friends, the meetings being large, and the houses filled.

From Flushing we went to Guernsey, and attended their meeting, on fourth-day, which was large; stopped at Stillwater, where B. Hoyle lives, and lodged at Robert Smith's. Here we called the ministers and elders together, and I laid my prospect before them, to attend the Ridge Meeting, which lay beyond Stillwater, yesterday; to have an appointed meeting here at Somerton to-day; to return to Stillwater, and have an appointed meeting there to-morrow; and then proceed to Plainfield, the next first-day. They sat long upon it, and finally decided not to appoint a meeting for us at Stillwater, although Elizabeth Smith and others had full unity with it. B. H.'s friends urged us to alter our course, and attend Stillwater Meeting next first-day: but I let them know that my prospect as to time and place, &c., was clear, and that if they were unwilling to meet us on seventh-day, we should go on directly to Plainfield, which we expect to do. We then went to the meeting at the Ridge, and in this meeting —— —— was broken to pieces, and was as kind and tender as possible, and rode over to this place with us, where William Kennard resides. William had told me, at the close of the yearly meeting, that he had unity with my service in their great public meeting at Mount Pleasant on fifth-day (the Gurneyites were all present); notwithstanding my service therein had been very close and searching, commencing with the passage: "By the rivers of Babylon, there we sat down," &c.; being also led to speak to the children of the captivity, in the land of their captivity.

Sixth-day evening. The meeting at Somerton this morning was a favored one, and after it we went to dine with Anne Conrow. Many other Friends dined with us; and after dinner, falling into silence, dear R. P. had a lively testimony to bear, expressive of heavenly fellowship. William Kennard followed her in a remarkable manner, expressive of full Gospel fellowship with us, and of a clear and undeniable evidence that our coming was of the Lord; "who had called and qualified a minister and messenger of the unchangeable Gospel, and sent him forth to raise the ancient standard of truth in its purity;" also a belief that some had been gathered to it by means of a faithful suffering for and testimony to it, and that many more would yet, by such means, be induced to rally to this standard, &c. I was wholly silent. William Kennard rode this morning several miles, to labor with —— ——, who had been previously notified thereof, to induce him to come to our meeting; but he would not. He said, with great inconsistency, that he had full unity with me as a true Gospel minister, but this matter of appointing meetings was going beyond the yearly meeting, &c.

. . . . . . In the last sitting of the yearly meeting, I had a close, searching testimony given me to bear, relative to the state of the Church in general, and of this yearly meeting in particular; and also to the state of deeply experienced and eminently gifted persons present, which —— and others fully understood and could not gainsay, and with which W. K. expressed full unity. . . . . .

To W. Hodgson.

Richmond, Ohio, 20th of 9th mo., 1854.

My dear Brother, W. Hodgson, Jr.:

. . . We took leave of each other in great unity and tenderness of spirit, and went on our way rejoicing, towards Plainfield Meeting, which we attended on first-day last; and public notice being freely given, the house was very closely filled, and a precious meeting we had. For here, as in all other places where I had requested such public notice, the hearts of the people seemed to have been previously prepared for it. . . . In the meeting at the Ridge I was long silent, not expecting to have anything to say; but as the time to break the meeting drew near, my Master raised me up in a short testimony to His own power, and the sufficiency of it for the accomplishment of His own work, without the help of man's contrivance, and against his will and working. . . . We attended Short Creek Monthly Meeting yesterday, in which I was silent until after the shutters were closed; and so also were all others present, and there were many.

I am leaving this part of Ohio with a very quiet, peaceful mind, for which I desire to be thankful. It is near two o'clock, fifth-day morning, and I have not been able to sleep at all, since a short nap about this time yesterday morning. My general health is better than for the next week after yearly meeting, when I was very poorly, although we had a meeting every day except one; and yesterday, at Short Creek, was a most trying time; yet, for the last three or four days and nights, I have been so very asthmatic, as not to admit of my lying down, except for a very short time. I have been writing now, in addition to a hard day's travel, six hours and more, alone in the parlor at this tavern, my kind companions having been in bed during the whole of this time; and we are to start at half-past six in the morning.

Love to thee and thine, even much more than I can speak or write adequately of. Farewell, till we meet.

THOMAS B. GOULD.

To MARTHA S. GOULD.

RICHMOND, OHIO, 20th of 9th mo., 1854.

MY DEAR MARTHA:

We left brother Joshua's this morning about nine o'clock, and have stopped for the night at a tavern in this place, on our way to Salem, which we expect to reach to-morrow evening. Brother Joshua and his son Jacob, and Nathan Cook and wife, came with us. Joshua has hitherto taken us through the country, wherever we have been, in his own carriage, and expects to continue with us until we reach Philadelphia; which has been and is a great comfort and help to us. . . . .

. . . I was not able to walk thither, having, for the last three days and nights, suffered extremely with asthma, except just while we were sitting in Short Creek Monthly Meeting, held at Short Creek yesterday; in which I was wholly silent, except a short testimony in the meeting for business, partly in reply to the objections made by the Gurney people against our sitting, or being allowed to sit there, and partly by way of a call upon them to give over their disorderly proceedings, and return to first principles, as the only way whereby they could be restored to the unity of the faith, and the peace and harmony of the Society could be restored, while they remained members of it, &c.; which had such effect upon some of the more moderate among them, that I. L., as I suppose, perceiving it, and fearing the consequences, turned angrily round, looked up in my face, and told me to sit down! I paused a moment, looked at him, and he turned away his face and was silent; when I proceeded with what I had to say, without altering my position, or the tone of my voice;

neither was I conscious of being in the least affected by it, in any way. But this is the first time that any of those people have manifested public opposition to me, or have failed to listen with respectful attention, while I was speaking; excepting the uneasiness of E. P. Gurney and Ann Taylor, during part of the time I was on my feet in the great public meeting at Mount Pleasant, during yearly meeting. At Short Creek yesterday, which is a very large monthly meeting, and a majority of them Gurneyites, J. S., an elder, compelled us to take the head of the meeting: but I had no commission to draw the bow, or to shoot a single arrow there, in the public meeting. Several of these people have at different times borne apparently an involuntary testimony to my sincerity, and also to my being a Gospel minister; and yet they say that I cannot consistently be received as such, because I am a member of the "smaller body," and have only been acknowledged by it, and since the separation. On the other hand, some of the more moderate, but wavering ones among them have, as I am informed, been convinced of the rectitude of our position, and have freely acknowledged that their states and condition have been spoken to in a manner which they could not gainsay or resist. And I do know that our visit has been to the comfort and strengthening of many Friends; which, with the incomes, and, at times, the abounding of peace and consolation, amidst all our trials, affords a merciful and abundant reward; for all which I desire to be thankful. . . . .

In the last number of "Friends' Review," there is a pretty full and pretty fair account of the separation. What they say was expressed by me, is very just, so far as it goes; and what they say about the relative numbers, is quite as near the truth as the account in "The Friend." I judged that about one-third went off with the Gurneyites; many stayed with them, when Friends first left the house, at the time of the separation, merely from curiosity, and to see what they would do; and a sorry time they had to keep their own men together.

The meeting at Plainfield, last first-day, was very large, the house being exceedingly crowded. It was also an eminently favored meeting; my good and gracious Helper enabling me to speak to the states of that mixed multitude, in a manner which was to my own humbling admiration, and to the satisfaction of Friends. This is the meeting where, many years ago, they refused to appoint a meeting for Jonathan Backhouse, of which I have often heard thee speak. . . . . . A. P. said that my coming here at this time was in answer to prayer; for she had prayed that the Good Shepherd would send one of his anointed messengers, from among the "smaller body," to visit this land; and that, when she heard I was coming, it rejoiced her heart, and she could hardly wait to see me. They were all united in giving public notice of the meeting. . . . . Before we left ———, we had a very solemn parting opportunity together. Many other Friends were present, but my gracious Helper enabled me so to divide the word of life among them, as to reach their several conditions without giving any offence. There was not, I believe, one dry eye in the room, and some, not of the family, wept aloud during the whole time, and for some time after. As for poor ——, her eyes were not dry much if any of the time after she sat down in the meeting at Plainfield, while we stayed in the neighborhood. In the public meeting, it fell to my lot to show the difference between the true Gospel worship and the true Christian ministry, and a mere profession of it and of religion without coming to the experimental heart-work, and knowing the power of it revealed in our souls. I was afterwards told that there were many of other persuasions present, beside those of no profession, and Hicksites; none of whom escaped, and some were very plainly reached.

With love unfeigned, I am thine,
T. B. Gould.

To Lydia Ann Gould.

Alliance Station, 21st of 9th month, 1854.

My dear Sister:

Thy truly acceptable letter was duly received last second-day. . . . . .

. . . . The whole country through which we have travelled, since crossing the Ohio River, is one succession of hills and dales; in comparison with the former of which, Tammany (Miantonomi) hill would sink into insignificance. They are generally either cultivated to the very tops, or covered with timber; many of the trees being more than one hundred feet high, and three or four feet through at the butt; and often running up to the height of fifty or sixty feet without a single branch, though of solid oak. . .

We crossed the Ohio River on a wire bridge, nearly one hundred feet above the level of the stream. . . . . Our first business, after crossing the bridge, was to go up one of what they call the "river hills;" but I should think it might safely be called a mountain, for it was six hundred feet high, and the distance to the top of it by the road, nearly three miles; but we had, in this case, a plank road nearly all the way up, and to brother Joshua's door. . . .

At Harrisville [appointed meeting], while on my feet, I noticed a great, strong, fine-looking man in the meeting, who seemed to have much to do to hold up against what was said; by-and-bye he began to weep, and continued to do so until the tears rolled down his cheeks, and dropped on the floor to such a degree as I had not before seen in any case; for, when I passed by where he had sat, there was a spot on the floor literally wet with his tears. There was another man at their meeting, a Friend (which the former was not), who had been very undecided in regard to the great question which is dividing the Society; who told Nathan Hall that he was now convinced where the strength lay, for his state had been so spoken to in this meeting at Harrisville, that he had no doubt remaining.

At Flushing we lodged at Isaac Mitchell's, who, with his wife, was as kind as could be to us. They live in a most outlandish place to get to, through the woods and up and down the hills; but when once there, it is really very pleasant, until one has to get away again. They live, too, in the midst of a thickly-settled neighborhood of nice Friends, their nearest neighbor being one of the clearest-sighted ministers in this yearly meeting. She, with many other Friends, came in in the evening, and a time of silence occurring, she had weighty encouragement to offer. . . . . .

From Flushing we went to Guernsey, and attended their preparative meeting as it came in course. There the most active and violent leaders of the separatists live; two of whom, after I sat down, undertook to clear themselves from what had been expressed, by denying that they had departed from the truth and faith of Friends; but it amounted to nothing; neither did they any greater harm to us, than to cut one of the straps of brother Joshua's carriage, that which held the trunk-rack up, which we discovered before we put the trunk upon it. We lodged here at dear old Robert Holloway's, a valuable minister. . . .

Farewell.

T. B. GOULD.

TO MARTHA S. GOULD.

FRANKFORD, PA., 29th of 9th month, 1854.

MY DEAR MARTHA:

My last letter to thee was written at Richmond. We went the next day to Salem, where we arrived about sunset, and were most kindly received by W. and P. F., who heartily agreed to have public notice given of our intention of being present at Salem Meeting the next first-day. The day following we went to Middletown, about twelve miles off; Samuel Street taking us in his carriage. . . . The elders and overseers, being called together, freely and unitedly agreed to appoint a public meeting there for us the next day, and to call the members of two other meetings, further off, to our meeting at Middletown; which I was quite willing they should do, although I told them I did not think it would be required of me to visit those two meetings. However, a considerable number of their members came to Middletown, and it proved to be a large and satisfactory meeting; and after dining with a large company of solid, agreeable and clear-sighted Friends at the house of W. H., . . . and having had a remarkable parting opportunity with them, we returned to Salem, lodged at W. Fisher's, and attended their meeting next day; which was very large, and eminently favored. . . . . . . That afternoon we rode several miles to an appointed meeting at New Garden, to which the sound Friends of Springfield and one other meeting, I think, were also invited; and divers of them came. The meeting was very large; some twenty Friends went out to it from Salem; many more were there than could get into the house; and yet it was a solid, favored time, strength being given me for the labors of the day, in a sufficient and abundant portion. This closed my public service in Ohio. We returned to Salem the same evening, with dear Robert French. . . . . Robert has been, from the time of our first meeting with him, on seventh-day of yearly meeting week, like a dear brother and father to me. We lodged that night at his house most pleasantly, and spent second-day in taking leave of Friends in Salem; taking tea at William Fisher's, where upwards of forty Friends came also, to take leave of us; and a solemn and affecting parting opportunity we had, which will not, I trust, soon be forgotten. . . .

We took the cars for Pittsburg about sunset, arriving in that smoky city about nine o'clock the same evening; which we passed through in an omnibus, and it was a gloomy ride; for, in addition to the ordinary smoke, they had fires burning in the streets, all over the city, on account of the cholera; which had raged there just previously, to the extent of one hundred deaths per day, as we were told, and no doubt it was so. But we passed safely through it, through favor; as we did, the next day, through Columbia, where it had been quite as bad. Many of the inhabitants had deserted it, and we were told that it was impossible to get graves dug fast enough for the dead; and so the poor bodies were taken to the graveyard, and left above ground whole nights, until graves could be dug for them. We got some sleep aboard the car; . . . and were favored to reach Philadelphia at nine o'clock on third-day evening; where I joyfully received and read thy letter, it being the first line I had received from thee, dear heart, since the day Ohio Yearly Meeting closed.

We attended the Southern District Monthly Meeting on fourth-day. . . . It passed off without opposition:

H. C. and J. E. expressed unity with my testimony; although it was very close; and at Arch Street yesterday much the same. We have an appointed meeting here to-day, to which I now must go. . . .

T. B. GOULD.

To M. S. GOULD.

AT THE HOUSE OF JAMES MOON, 12th of 10th mo., 1854.

MY ENDEARED MARTHA:

My last was written at Frankford, since which I have not been able to write one word, although I have thought of it, and wished to do it, much oftener than the returning morning, I can assure thee. But we have been so constantly engaged, a meeting almost every day, and several times two meetings daily, with long rides between them, and much company wherever we have been, that I could not do it; and so thou wilt have to excuse me, as I trust thou canst and wilt do.

The meeting at Frankford was well attended, and satisfactory to all, I believe. E. Pitfield, without knowing of my concern, was drawn thither; and attending the meeting, labored quite extensively in it before I said a word; neither did I know of her being there at all, until I heard her voice. We dined together at William Kinsey's, went back to the city, took tea at B. Albertson's, lodged at William Hodgson's, and the next morning left for Westtown, in company with dear brother Joshua. Brother Joseph met us at Westchester, and took us to Westtown. At the depot there [several other Friends] met us; and laying before them my expectation of being at Westchester meeting the next morning (which was first-day), and that I wished public notice given, and also wished a meeting appointed on second-day at Whiteland, they cordially assented to my propositions. We went the next day to Westtown, where we passed the afternoon pleasantly with J. and H. S., &c., and the next morning, brothers Joseph and Joshua went with us to Westchester. The meeting was large and favored, though my line of labor was rather close, commencing with the passage, "There is no king saved by the multitude of an host, neither is a mighty man delivered by much strength. An horse is a vain thing for safety; neither can he deliver any by his great strength. But the eye of the Lord is upon them that fear Him, to deliver their soul from death, and to keep them alive in famine." . . . . . . Soon after dinner we went back to Westtown, and attended that meeting in the afternoon. . . . . . Here we parted with dear brother Joshua; we had been daily together for a month, I think, in great nearness and sweet fellowship.

We had a pleasant ride with David Cope, and passed the night at his house in like manner; had a good meeting the next day at Whiteland, which Samuel Cope attended, and afterwards took us in his carriage to his own house to tea, and to dear Moses Baily's to lodge; who, with his wife, and their only son, was truly glad to see us. . . . . . The next day we attended Sadsbury Monthly Meeting; where our certificates were read, and our services publicly approved in the monthly meeting, both men's and women's; though not minuted, or endorsed, it not being, as they said, their practice in any case. . . .

The next day, Bradford Monthly Meeting was large, notice having been given of our coming; and a time of great enlargement and much favor. After this we went to Morris Cope's, and met with a cordial reception from him and his wife. We attended London Grove Monthly Meeting the next day, in which, as at Bradford, our certificates were read in both men's and women's meetings, and our services approved unreservedly. . . . . Morris Cope went with us, the next morning, to Nottingham Monthly Meeting, within the limits of Baltimore Yearly Meeting. There we were not only received joyfully, but our certificates were read in both meetings, and our services approved. . . . . .

At Little Britain we had a good meeting; M. C. having a testimony early therein, which opened my way to great enlargement, both doctrinally and practically. And truly, in this respect, the favors vouchsafed in every meeting, except that of Short Creek, in Ohio, have been marvellous in my eyes. . . . . Although I have been so frequently and continually engaged, yet fresh matter has been abundantly supplied in every meeting; so that those who have followed us from meeting to meeting have not been wearied by a thrice-told tale; for which favor I have been truly thankful, as for many others which I cannot mention. But I think I may say that my strippings and plungings have been commensurate, or at least correspondent, to the favors vouchsafed.

Little Britain is twelve miles from Nottingham; at both which places there is an interesting company of Friends, and they have nice new and commodious meeting-houses. . . . . . . After dinner at Little Britain, we rode about twenty-five miles, crossing the Susquehanna River near Port Deposit, and lodging at Gideon Smith's, at Deer Creek. Attended that meeting on first-day morning, which was large, some notice having been given. Here were many clever Friends, who were truly glad to see us, and some Gurneyites, even some from the city of Baltimore, who were very civil and quiet. After meeting we dined at an inn, there being no Friend's house near enough, or on our way to West Grove, in Pennsylvania; which we reached about seven o'clock in the evening, having again crossed the Susquehanna River. We lodged at the house of Levi Wickersham; and word having been previously sent on, we attended an appointed meeting at West Grove on second-day morning at eleven o'clock; and another at New Garden at four o'clock the same afternoon. Both of these meetings were large and favored. The former place was the residence and meeting in which dear old William Jackson lived. We saw his grave and that of his wife, and also the house and room in which they both lived and breathed their last. It is of logs, and very plain and old, but large. We saw the house where John Churchman lived, and passed the meeting-house which he attended; a large old building, one half of brick, the other of stone. It is now, with the ground in which he was buried, in the possession of the Hicksites, who are quite numerous, but scarcely a Friend in the neighborhood. We parted with Morris Cope in unity and brotherly feeling; and Thomas Whitson and Thomas Harvey took us to New

Garden, where we met with Hannah C. Haines; and after meeting there that afternoon, we took tea and lodged at Thomas Lamborn's. . . . . . Thomas took us the next morning twelve miles, to an appointed meeting at Birmingham; where, to my surprise, I saw seated in the gallery, when I entered the meeting, William Scattergood, Nathan Sharples, and Edith Kite, who had come over from Concord to meet us. . . . . The next morning, William Scattergood brought us in his carriage twenty-three miles to Philadelphia, dined with us at William Hodgson's, and came also with us on the boat to Bristol; where we parted with him, he returning to Philadelphia. . . . . . .

Farewell; thy own,
T. B. Gould.

From Wm. Scattergood to M. S. Gould.

Concordville, Pa., 10th mo., 13th, 1854.

Esteemed Friend, Martha Gould:

Having had within a few days an acceptable visit from thy beloved husband, I feel inclined to drop thee a line or two, by way of information as to his getting along in this neighborhood. Not that I doubt thy receiving from other sources, and also from himself, similar accounts; but believing that thou wilt be glad to have the tidings of his success confirmed, I am not afraid of the repetition, if so it should prove. He signified, himself, that he found it somewhat difficult to find suitable opportunities for writing; and thus, unless volunteers are found, thou mayst not know how to follow him in what has appeared to some who have looked at his present engagement, as a perilous encounter with the spirit of the world. I can truly say I have sympathized with thee in thy anxious thoughts about him, under the circumstances in which he has gone forth in the present concern; but so far as I have been able to perceive and to learn, he has witnessed the truth of the declaration to one of the tribes in Israel of old: "As thy day, so shall thy strength be;" and I trust also that his shoes will have been found to be as iron and brass, not wearing out to the end. We received notice here on second-day evening last, of his intention or prospect of having a meeting at this place the next day in the afternoon: and the way appearing clear, it was accordingly appointed for three o'clock on third-day; and was attended by a larger number than is commonly found at any of our meetings, whether appointed or otherwise. The service in it, both in testimony and prayer, was, as far as I can understand, satisfactory, and to my own feelings was attended with that calming, settling influence, which I believe should attend the ministry of the Gospel of peace.

In looking over Thomas's movements, both within the limits of our yearly meeting and in other places, I have thought it might be compared to the circumstance of Haman being compelled to lead the king's horse, while Mordecai rode: for truly the spirit of Haman has been largely found among us hereaway, even in those who have been largely confided in by the King of kings; who have thereby been led to exalt themselves, and to despise and contemn those who would not bow to the glory which, though not of themselves, they were determined should be regarded as their own. This spirit, emanating from individuals in high standing, and spreading hither and thither, has affected many who were afraid to think for themselves, and drawn them aside from the simplicity of the truth; but on the present occasion, has been made to bow at the clearly heard command of the King of kings, in favor of those who have spoken good for Him, and discovered the treachery of His pretended friends. I would that the comparison might be carried out, and that the King would in His wisdom, and in mercy to His Church, command that this unrighteous, overbearing spirit might be hung upon that gallows upon which it has been intended that the humble pleaders for the truth should be exposed. I have seen and felt (I think) that nothing but the command of the Lord of all, could have carried thy dear Thomas through the various exercises to which he has been exposed since his leaving home, giving him wisdom and understanding, and a ready answer to those who, though making high professions, are secretly enemies to the cross of Christ.

And now I desire to encourage thee, and to strengthen thy hands to take thy share of the labors of the day; believing as I do, that those who "stay by the stuff," in patient endurance, will be favored to partake with those that go forth, of the spoil of the enemy; and that both of you, when favored to meet again, will be enabled "to rejoice in the Lord, and joy in the God of your salvation." I can truly say I long for dear T., whom I can truly call my brother, that he may be enabled, when reduced again to his station at the King's gate, which may yet again be his place and portion, to maintain his faith and patience, till the King, having put down this proud spirit that is among us, shall call for him, and give him the seals of the kingdom, and that authority without which we are truly but empty and unprofitable vessels.

It seems likely by what he said, that his tarriance here will not be much longer. He left Philadelphia now about two weeks since, attended the West Chester Meeting on first-day morning, the first of the month, Westtown in the afternoon, Whiteland (appointed) second-day; on third, fourth, and fifth-days was at Sadsbury, Bradford, and Fallowfield or London Grove Monthly Meetings; on sixth-day at Nottingham Monthly Meeting, within the bounds of Baltimore Yearly Meeting; and in all these monthly meetings his certificate was read, and satisfaction felt with his company. On seventh-day last, I understand he had an appointed meeting at Little Britain, a branch of Nottingham Monthly Meeting; to Deer Creek on first-day, then returned back into Chester County, and on second-day had a meeting at Westgrove in the morning, and at New Garden in the afternoon. Then on third-day came to Birmingham to a meeting in the morning, and as I mentioned before, to Concord in the afternoon. I may acknowledge that I have been struck, stranger as he must have been very much among Friends here, at the wisdom which has guided him in his movements so far, within the limits of our yearly meeting;

and I may also say, I am thankful thus to perceive that the goodness and mercy of our Holy Head and High Priest are not taken away from us; but that, as He is sought unto and followed in simplicity, he still condescends to guide by His counsel, and strengthen for the work of the day.

I ought perhaps to say, that on fourth-day Thomas had no meeting. I took him and his companion to Philadelphia, and accompanied them in the steamer to Bristol, where I left him in charge of a son of James Moon, to be at the wedding yesterday. So far as I could understand his prospects, I did not see that he would be kept from home longer than next week out; and I humbly trust he may be soon restored to thee, with sheaves of peace, and with his faith renewed and strengthened in that Arm of Power which has been the support of the righteous in all generations.

I have left my writing till so near the closing of our mail, that I have written in haste; and might say much more, but this may perhaps suffice to let thee know that He that puts forth hath gone before, preparing the way in the hearts of the people and their *rulers;* so that I trust this visit will be a sealing stroke to the prevalence of that temporizing spirit, which has so abundantly prevailed within our limits, as well as elsewhere; and if so be, we are permitted to see the church once more rising out of obscurity and out of darkness, let us be engaged to give the glory to Him to whom alone it belongeth; who hath preserved us in His mercy from the snare of the enemy, and whose gracious design it is that we should live to His glory, and be instrumental in promoting His cause in the earth.

With love to thyself and thy children (with whom Thomas has made us a little acquainted), in which my wife and daughter unite,

I am affectionately,
thy friend,
WM. SCATTERGOOD.

From T. B. G. to Joshua Maule.

Medford, N. J., 16th of 10th mo., 1854.

My dear Brother, J. Maule:

. . . . . The meetings, both at Birmingham and Concord, were solid, favored seasons, and the latter eminently so, both in testimony and supplication. At Birmingham it fell more to my lot to open the mystery of iniquity, as well as of godliness, which was done somewhat closely in divers important respects and particulars, which made the service trying; but a good degree of resignation was witnessed, and I trust of faithfulness also. I afterwards understood there were several Gurney people present, and some of them were from the city; to which William Scattergood very kindly took us the next day in his carriage. . . . The day after, which was the twelfth of the month and fifth of the week, we attended meeting at the Falls, or Fallsington, which was large, and very solemn from first to last. Jonathan Chace and Jane Moon were married at this meeting; after which my mouth was opened in testimony, in a manner very unusual for me, both as regarded the copiousness of the subjects spoken of, and the demonstration and power attendant. However, the effect produced by my feeble labors in all these meetings has manifestly appeared to be, to bring the minds of Friends into an increasing unity and heavenly fellowship with us, and one with another, in Him who remains to be Head over all things to his Church and people. Blessed forever be the name of our all-sufficient and adorable Helper, and Preserver hitherto! . . . . On the 14th we had a meeting, and a very remarkable one too, through the renewings of Holy Help, at Byberry. The day was wet, but notice having been extended also to the Hicksites, many of them came, and afterwards seemed kind and tender, several of them inviting us to their houses to dinner, and showing us many other attentions; insomuch that I supposed they were really Friends who did so, though no harm came of my mistake in any way, I believe. Indeed the house was so small, when I came to see it, in comparison with the old meeting-house, which they are, it is said, sufficiently numerous nearly to fill, that I doubted whether they would condescend to come to it; Friends being very few in number here, I was told, and much despised by many of the Hicksites. But after meeting, I found Friends were really much fewer than I had expected. However, this judging, in a sort, or for a time, according to appearances, and after the manner of men, did no harm; for I had at last to stand up with these singular expressions: "Who art thou, who queriest, 'what good can be expected, by coming here and sitting down with a small and despised company, who are no better than I am? Indeed I did not expect to gain any good by coming here. I am a moral man; quite as good or better than my neighbors who profess a more orthodox faith: but it is a rainy day, and I might as well spend my time here as elsewhere; I have nothing else to do!'" Having said this much, I saw a smile play over the features of a hard-looking old man, who was dressed somewhat plainly, and at the same time I felt inwardly convinced that he was the very man, the thoughts of whose heart had been made manifest. I was told afterwards, that this man was a real Hicksite, that is to say, an infidel; and that, on being notified of the meeting, he said he did not know whether he would come to it or not; that he was willing to be preached *to*, but did not like to be preached *at!* The mysteries which these poor deluded people have stumbled at, and refused to believe in, were largely opened, and the necessity of true faith and obedience weightily enforced; which would enable them to accept the plan of salvation, and the means provided for them, in the Gospel of peace and reconciliation. Although I did not at all suppose the number of those present, who had imbibed this spirit of unbelief, was near so large as must have been the case if all the Hicksites present were really unbelievers, yet I was mercifully preserved from saying anything which could have limited the application to a few individuals, except, as above stated, in the very commencement of what was uttered. . . . .

Farewell. Thy loving brother,

T. B. GOULD.

To Joshua and Sarah Maule.

Elmside, Newport, 30th of 10th month, 1854.

My dear Brother and Sister:

I think it will be two weeks to-morrow, since I wrote to you from the house of our dear friends, J. R. and M. S. Reeve, of Medford, New Jersey; and believing you will be glad to know that I was favored to reach my own home in peace and safety, and to find my dear M. and the children well, I have taken up my pen to give you the information; which I should have done sooner, but have been so asthmatic, and otherwise indisposed since my return, that I could not well write more than I have been absolutely compelled to do.

I think I told you in my last, that I attended Medford meeting on first-day. . . . The meeting was large, and, I believe, satisfactory to Friends, but trying and laborious to me. I lodged at J. R. Reeve's that night; divers Friends met us there. The day following we had an appointed meeting at Rancocas, which was large and well; many great and heavenly mysteries being opened, as I trust, in the life and power of truth. Here dear Rachel Roberts, the widow of Ebenezer Roberts, met us, and, with divers other Friends, dined with us at the house of Ezra and Phebe Haines; and, after visiting a family in the neighborhood, we returned the same night with J. and M. Reeve to their house; and they and their children went with us the next morning to an appointed meeting at Cropwell, and to another in the afternoon at Lower Evesham; both of which were large, divers Friends from neighboring meetings coming in, and some of them such as I did not expect to see. But it did appear that He who sent us forth, opened the way for us, and gave us favor in the sight of the people, filling my heart with faith, and opening a door of utterance, and, I trust, of entrance also, in a manner which was wonderful to me, and, I believe, to many more, considering what a poor weak vessel I am, and where I came from. For some who had evidently been disposed to doubt whether any good thing could come out of Nazareth, were induced to "come and see" where the

Master dwells; even with such as have no might of their own, with such as are poor and of a contrite spirit, and who tremble at His Word; and not only so, but I do humbly trust that, through the gathering influence of His heavenly love, some of these will be enabled to abide with Him, even as in the day of His temptation; and that He will appoint unto them a kingdom, "as My Father hath appointed unto Me."

The meeting at Lower Evesham was long silent; perhaps my faith, or that of others, has seldom been reduced to a lower ebb. But water came at length, by the way of the wilderness, so that they who had been brought together did not perish with thirst, as some, I believe, had supposed; and when the day dawned, the sun shone gloriously upon the water, and the armies of Israel were given to drink, and the Moabites were discomfited, and the victory was great in the end, the shout of a King being heard in the camp; and the voice of thanksgiving and praise was uttered by dear —— —— in such a manner that, if it had been called for, I could audibly have said, Amen! We went the same evening to Moorestown, lodged at the widow Rachel Roberts's, and attended their meeting the next day, where Josiah and Maria Reeve again joined us. In this meeting the door was unlatched for me; but it was only to open up to view the mystery of iniquity, Mystery Babylon the Great; though "built like Zion, painted just like Zion, and made to look" as nearly as possible "like Zion," yet it was Babylon still; and I had to tell them that there was nothing to be found in Zion, but the image and likeness thereof might be found in Babylon. Hard work and close work I had of it here, to my great surprise, for I had expected different things. But finding Babylon begin to totter, as a token of its fall, after a while I stood up a second time, having the mystery of godliness to open, and the everlasting Gospel to preach to them that dwell on the earth, &c.; and the meeting ended with solemn supplication for the children of the captivity, for the lost sheep of the house of Israel, and the dispersed and scattered of Judah; that they might be mercifully restored to their own land, and brought back to David, their rightful King, within the walls of Jerusalem, "whose walls are salvation, and her gates praise."

We dined at Samuel Matlack's, with Hannah Warrington and many other Friends. Chancing to ask Hannah, what was the matter at Moorestown? she quickly answered, "Thou hast answered the question thyself in meeting this day: if thou hadst prophesied smooth to us, I should have doubted thy authority: but there is a cause for all thy exercises amongst us, and I had near unity with thee therein." Soon after tea, we returned to the widow Rachel Roberts's to lodge. . . . The next morning, S. Matlack took us in his carriage to the city. We dined at W. H.'s, and spent the remainder of the day and evening in visiting divers Friends. . . . .

William Kinsey took us the next morning [first-day] to Germantown meeting, which was large, notice having been given of our coming: the house was very nearly full, and much labor fell to my lot. . . . I stood up with the words, "Suppose ye that those men upon whom the tower in Siloam fell, and slew them, were sinners above all men who dwelt in Jerusalem? I tell you, nay: but except ye repent, ye shall all likewise perish:" and proceeded to show that, all men who had not received the gift of repentance towards God and of faith in our Lord Jesus Christ, nor been enabled to bring forth fruits meet for the same, stood in need of repentance and amendment of life; and such were accordingly called upon to repent and believe the Gospel, even that Gospel which is not a mere theory, but the power of God unto salvation, and deliverance from the power and dominion of sin and Satan. They were called upon to repent and believe the Gospel, because the time was at hand in which every man's faith, and works, and buildings would be tried, and the nature thereof discovered; and so it was absolutely necessary for all to examine themselves, and try themselves, whether they were in possession of the true faith, which works by love to the purifying of the heart, and giveth the victory over the world, the flesh, and the devil; or whether they were merely in possession of a literal, historical, manufactured faith, which they had framed to suit themselves and to serve their turn, while they were conscious of being led captive by their soul's enemy at his will, or being subjects of the prince of the power of the air, the spirit which now ruleth in the children of disobedience. Hard, close work I had with the high professors of a merely notional religion; but was enabled to obtain some relief, and sat down a while; during the former part of which the solemnity was great, and prevalent apparently over even the strongest of the city Gurneyites, many of whom were present, beside several Friends, who had come out from the city. But I did not feel clear; and eventually had to stand up the second time, with the account of ten of the tribes of Israel being rent from the house of David, on account of the unfaithfulness of David's sons, who had reigned in his stead, or after him, &c.,—how Jeroboam was raised up and chosen in a remarkable manner, to reign over the house of Israel in Samaria; and how jealous he became of the men of Israel going up to Jerusalem to worship, lest their hearts should return to David their king; and so he set up a separate altar in Bethel, and another in Dan;—that he became so far degenerate, as to set up an idol calf worship, saying, "These be thy gods, oh Israel, which brought thee up out of the land of Egypt;" which became a great snare unto Israel, and they departed not from the sin of Jeroboam, who caused Israel to sin, for many generations. But there was a prophet of the Lord, sent out of Judah, to cry against the separate altar which had been set up in Bethel: and he cried against it in the word of the Lord, saying, "Oh, altar! altar! thus saith the Lord, thou shalt be rent, and thy ashes shall be poured out! A child shall be born unto the house of Judah, Josiah by name, and upon thee shall he offer the priests of the high places, which burn incense upon thee, and men's bones shall be burnt upon thee!" They were told how Jeroboam stood by the altar to burn incense, when this cry was uttered against his idol worship and separate altar; and how he stretched forth his hand against the Lord's prophet, saying, "Lay hold on him!"—that the hand which he put forth against the prophet was withered, so that he could not draw it back to him again, and he was fain to appeal to the Lord's prophet for help, saying, "Entreat now the face of the Lord thy God for me, that my hand may be restored to me again;" which request being complied with, it was restored, &c. Now all this was opened and applied to the state of individuals and things, in a manner so close that it was hard for me to utter, and for those concerned to bear; and I did not know but some from the city, and one in particular, would have gone out of the house. Dear —— —— noticed this man's uneasiness also, and was rather expecting that he would leave; but he did not, and the meeting soon after closed solidly.

. . . . We got to the North Meeting in good season, which was large, the seats on the ground floor on the women's side being closely filled, and nearly so on the men's side. . . . It was more than an hour silent, and I was in hope it might have ended so; but was eventually raised up with the language, "Woe unto them that go down into Egypt for ships, that stay on horses and trust in chariots, and fear not me, saith the Lord!"—querying very closely of some, in the language of the prophet to some of old: "What hast thou to do in the way of Egypt, to drink of the waters of Sihor; or what hast thou to do in the way of the land of Assyria, to drink of the waters of the river?"—and also declaring, "Thou shalt be ashamed of Egypt, even as thou wast ashamed of Assyria:" reminding them, some of them especially, that the Lord's people went down aforetime into Egypt, and the Assyrian oppressed them without a cause; and that, as was the case formerly, so it would be now; the Lord would bring down the stout heart of the proud king of Assyria, and humble the pride of his high looks: yea, although some might exalt themselves as the eagle, and seem to "make their nests in the rocks, and in the very top of the ragged rocks," yet "from thence will I bring them down, saith the Lord!" For that the day of the Lord would come "upon every high tower, and upon every fenced wall, and upon all pleasant pictures, and upon all the ships of Tarshish; and the haughtiness of men shall be humbled, and the loftiness of men be laid low," &c. But "unto you that fear my name, shall the Sun of righteousness arise with healing in his wings; and ye shall go forth and grow up as calves of the stall:"—ye shall tread down the wicked, who shall lie as ashes under the soles of your feet. Therefore "say not, a confederacy, unto all those who would say, a confederacy, but sanctify the Lord God of hosts in your hearts,"—even Him who can save by many or by few: and "let Him be your fear, and let Him be your dread;" yea, I say unto you, fear Him! Such was the substance of the earlier portion of what was expressed in the North Meeting; but there was much more both of a doctrinal, practical, and encouraging nature, addressed also to particular states and conditions; some of whom I trust were a little helped and strengthened. The meeting closed with solemn supplication, poured forth by Elizabeth Pitfield. With her we took tea and spent the evening. . . . Many Friends came in to see us and take leave of us; among whom S. Hillman came early, and stayed till nine o'clock. E. Pitfield ministered to us, in the language addressed to the primitive disciples and messengers of the Gospel: "When I sent you forth without purse, or scrip, or a change of raiment, lacked ye anything?—and they said unto Him, Nothing, Lord!" &c., and the opportunity closed with the language of supplication, for the blessing of preservation in the remaining portion of labor and suffering which may be allotted in this probationary state, as well as of thanksgiving and praise for the unmerited blessings and favors which had been received at the hand of the Lord, and manifested for the help and encouragement of His poor and afflicted people, who have none to look to or trust in, but His worthy name and power alone.

I called and spent an hour with aunt S., and returned to our lodgings at W. H.'s. Divers Friends met us at the boat the next morning, when we took our leave of them, and proceeded to New York. Here we took the steamer for home, where I arrived about four o'clock the next morning, and found my dear Martha and the children overjoyed to welcome me home again.

. . . . My visit both there and in Ohio affords me solid

satisfaction. . . . Still I have nothing to boast of, or to glory in, save my infirmities, which form a very poor ground and cause of glorying. And truly I can say, that although I was brought very low, before I was made willing to go, yet it has been my lot to have been brought lower since; and at this moment it seems very doubtful, how and when I shall be able to accomplish what remains of my prospect, respecting the meetings in New York. My health has been very poor since my return; I have lost my appetite, and some pounds of flesh, and am so weak and sick, that the writing of these sheets has been a work of time and labor to me. . . .

It is now the 8th of eleventh month. I wrote the first two pages of the other sheet, the day before leaving home to attend our meeting for sufferings and quarterly meeting, held on the first and second of this month at Fall River. My dear Martha went with me. . . . . The weather, which had been very fine and warm since my return, until last seventh-day, then suddenly changed to quite cold, and I took a very severe cold riding home; which has so seriously affected my throat and lungs, that it would not be at all surprising if I should be laid up for this winter, as I was the last, and as I have been since my return. . . . . I do hope you got my letter from Jersey, and that you will write soon, and tell me of Friends in Ohio; to whom my heart is strongly bound, many of them in the fellowship of suffering for the cause' sake. . . . . . .

T. B. Gould.

To Joshua Maule.

Elmside, 11th of 11th month, 1851.

My dear Brother, J. Maule:

. . . . . I never once thought of thy giving any copy of the former letter, though it did occur to me that thou might feel inclined to read either the whole or some parts of it, as thou might think suitable, to some of those dear Friends at Harrisville; which I could not object to, if thou thought it might be in any way encouraging to them. In this respect I have long since been made willing to sacrifice my own feelings, which would certainly lead me to seek seclusion and retirement, and by no means notoriety. Few can imagine what my naturally very sensitive feelings have caused me to suffer in this respect. Now my object in giving thee, in my last letter, some account of the manner in which I was led, was to commemorate the mercy and goodness of my all-sufficient Helper, in furnishing me, even to the last, with new matter, with matter adapted to the varied condition of those to whom I was called to minister, stranger as I certainly was, as to the outward, both to their persons and states. In this respect (and I knew thou wouldst both understand it and rejoice in it) I have great cause for thankfulness; and many more had reason to rejoice, and did rejoice, that the Great Head of the Church had regard not only to the low estate of His poor messenger, who went forth, and from meeting to meeting, without either purse or scrip, but also to the state of His professing, but degenerate, Church and people, and so caused the secrets of many hearts to be revealed! One striking instance of this kind has come to my knowledge since my return home, by a letter to Nancy Buffinton from Lydia Reeve, in which she gave an account of the meeting at Frankford. I was a total stranger there, and I told them so, except to a very few Friends who sat near me. But I had to speak to Hicksites, and Gurneyites, and Friends, to some of different sorts and grades of infidelity and unbelief, and even to such as wished to disbelieve even in the existence of a God, or any divine revelation whatever. And in treating of the divine testimony and authority of the Holy Scriptures in general, and also with regard to the coming and offices of the Saviour of men, His miraculous conception, holy life, suffering death, and propitiatory sacrifice for the sins of the whole world,—I stopped there, not feeling led to go further therein; and proceeded with other matter and doctrine, as it was opened to my view in that which I knew could only lead me aright; and sat down, after proceeding to considerable length, and speaking to a variety of states and conditions. But I had not long resumed my seat, when I had to stand up again, and say, in substance, that, unless

I was wholly mistaken in my feelings—adding emphatically, and I think I am not—there is at least one person present, who has taken exception to what has been expressed, as if there had not been, in terms of sufficient fulness, an acknowledgment of all the offices of Christ; because His being raised from the dead on the third day, and His ascending into heaven (and being seen in His ascending) and sitting down on the right hand of the throne of the Majesty on high, as our Mediator and Advocate with the Father, where He ever liveth, making intercession for us, had not been fully and distinctly adverted to; and so proceeded to open these heavenly mysteries more fully. Now L. R., in giving N. B. a very full account of this meeting at the time, or very soon afterwards, remarked that, at the close of this meeting, a Gurney woman (who, it seems, was present, although it was an appointed meeting, and judging after the manner of men, I should not have supposed such were likely to be present) — this Gurney woman remarked, in reference to the very singular manner in which I was led to stand up and speak the second time, "that she did not understand how T. B. G. came to know just what she was thinking of!" However, in thinking of these things (and there were many such instances), I have had cause to remember this scripture, in substance, at least, "Rejoice not that the spirits are made subject unto you" (even although it were only through the renewed manifestation and revelation of the Lord's own name and power), "but rather rejoice that your names are written in heaven!" . . . . .

Affectionately,

THOMAS B. GOULD.

To WILLIAM SCATTERGOOD.

NEWPORT, 30th of 11th month, 1854.

MY DEAR FRIEND, WILLIAM SCATTERGOOD:

I was favored to reach my own home on the 24th of last month, and from that time to the present have frequently felt inclined to address a few lines to thee; not that I have much to say, more than that thou and thine have been often in my affectionate remembrance, since I was so kindly cared for under your hospitable roof. Yet this is not all which I have wanted to acknowledge: thy great kindness in taking my dear companion and myself into the city, and also in going with us to Bristol, has not been forgotten; and even more than this, I have wished to acknowledge thy truly acceptable, and very kind and considerate letter to my dear Martha during my absence. . . . . .

And truly, in this journey, I have had frequent occasions reverently to acknowledge, that He who remains to be Lord of all, and Head over all things to His Church and people, even the least and hindermost of them, still leadeth the blind by a way which they know not, except as He is pleased to open it before them, and in paths which they have not previously seen; yea, He maketh darkness light before them, and crooked paths straight.

Many of those people [Hicksites at Byberry] seemed much tendered, and were very kind after meeting; and if Friends, such as are called orthodox, stood more in the life and power of truth, I should not wonder if there was yet a gathering to the Power and the Life, even from amongst those who have long wandered from the Father's house, "feeding upon the husks which the swine do eat," "spending their money for that which is not bread," and wasting their substance for that which satisfieth not. May the Lord hasten it in His time! . . . . .

At S. Matlack's, soon after meeting [Moorestown,—see letter to J. Maule], our certificates were read, which brought a feeling of solemnity over the company; during which divers testimonies were borne to the excellency of that Power which is one in all the living, and by which they are baptized into one body, and enabled to drink of one cup, even the cup of the New Testament in His blood, whose blood is the life, and the body is of Christ; of whom all the living do know what it is to feed upon it; and that, except they eat the flesh and drink the blood of the Son of Man, they can have no spiritual life in them; neither is this an imaginary eating or drinking, but a real participation in His body and blood.

. . . . . . And yet it does not appear as if those who

bear rule among Friends in Ohio were yet prepared to extend the right hand of fellowship to us in New England, as a yearly meeting. Well may we query, When will the wound which the daughter of my people has received, be healed, and the breaches made in the walls of Zion, be repaired? Yet I trust that we are as well prepared, by the things which we have already suffered, to endure this hardness and standing aloof, as those are, who are virtually saying to us, "Stand by yourselves; for if we are not more holy, we are more *regularly organized* than you." And I shall be mistaken, if the shaking that has already commenced does not continue, until the honest-hearted are brought to their senses; so as to see that it is not in the outward order, but the inward life and power, that the true succession stands; and that the *form without the power* is even to be "turned away from;" and so become prepared to acknowledge those who come in the name, and stand in a measure of the power of the Lord; who can save by many or by few, and who has not ordinarily manifested His arm of power and strength, while there was an undue reliance upon the "multitude of an host." . . . . . My dear wife desires to be affectionately remembered to thee and thine, in which I do fully unite, and remain

Thy sincere friend,
THOMAS B. GOULD.

To WILLIAM HODGSON.

ELMSIDE, 14th of 12th mo., 1854.

MY DEAR FRIEND,

. . . . I think there is much allowance to be made for different temperaments, even natural temperaments; for it often happens, that it is long before all the old inhabitants of the land are driven out: and there certainly is great allowance to be made for different degrees of religious experience and growth in the truth. But according to my little measure and sense of feeling, there is scarcely a more discouraging or trying feature in the besetments of the present day and time, than the great diversity of sentiment which really does exist, in regard to what may be called minor matters—I am ready to say "technicalities,"—even among Friends of pretty good and perhaps nearly equal experience. I was constantly reminded of it, and struck or impressed with it, in my late journey; and nearly,—shall I say?—overwhelmed with it, on my return home, or soon after. I can look upon it in no other light than as a sad evidence of the strong desire which Satan has, to have those, who may peradventure be said to have endured perhaps the first and second shaking; that he may sift them as wheat is sifted in a sieve, even again, and again, and again, until everything that can be shaken or sifted out is removed. But surely the watchmen *will* see eye to eye, when the Lord does bring again Zion: and some signs of it I thought I could discover, at times, while in your yearly meeting, and also in Ohio. At least there was a shaking of another sort from what I have been above speaking of, even as among the dry bones of the valley, and a coming together of bone to his bone, and sinews came upon them, and flesh covered them; and they arose and stood upon their feet, by the power and quickening virtue of the breath of life which came from the Lord, and which cometh and can come from Him only. And if we were only sufficiently concerned to feel this, to wait for it, to go not, as dear William Leddra said, one step without it, without feeling it, without knowing it to be "our life," then we should know Him who is the resurrection and the life; and not only so, but also witness the precious unity, fellowship, and oneness which remains to be in Him. He would not heal the wounds of the daughter of Zion deceitfully; but he would *heal* them, and build up the breaches in her walls, and restore paths for the lame to walk in. And there would be a blessed experience of the truth and fulfilment of that gracious promise, "My people shall dwell upon Mount Zion in Jerusalem; they shall dwell in sure dwellings and in quiet resting-places, when it shall hail, coming down upon the forest, and the city shall be low, in a low place."

But why should I write thus to thee? I am sure I had

no such expectation or intention when I began. Thou must try to excuse me for "pouring out" some of my impressions to thee, my dear elder brother. But it seems, even that great good woman, Lydia A. Barclay, found consolation in so doing: and truly, I have very often thought and felt what a privilege it is, to have a friend one can feel freedom with; and what a consolation to receive letters from such! How just and forcible her remarks are! What a precious letter! The reading of it did me good. I fear her day of active usefulness in the church militant is over, but she will leave behind her a bright example of primitive faithfulness and consistency. . . . .

15th of the month. [Speaking of A. B., then ill, he says:] In the prospect of her and dear L. A. Barclay's removal, one cannot help remarking how the choicest and most faithful and useful instruments are being, in all probability, released from further service in the church militant, at a time when both Gog and Magog seem to be gathered together to battle against the Lord and His little despised army of lappers. But the sword of the Lord's mouth is able to put to flight the hosts of the aliens' armies, and to manifest openly and renewedly, that there is "no king saved by the multitude of an host, neither is a mighty man delivered by much strength; that an horse is a vain thing for safety, neither can he deliver any by his great strength: but that the eye of the Lord is upon them that fear Him, upon them that hope in His mercy, to deliver their souls from death, and to keep them alive in famine." And, as thou remarked in thy last letter, I hope He may be pleased to arise for the help of His poor and afflicted people, and accomplish His purposes respecting them in His own time and way. . . . .

Farewell.

T. B. GOULD.

CHAPTER VIII.

From T. B. G. to William Hodgson.

Newport, 1st mo. 9th, 1855.

My dear Friend,

. . . I recollect distinctly, having quoted, in the meeting at Germantown, the sixth verse of the ninth chapter of Isaiah, and that, after quoting the language, "His name shall be called Wonderful Counsellor," I went on to say, "I purposely avoid distinguishing between the terms." I intended to guard against such a distinction. Since I came to age, I have always regretted the comma between the words "Wonderful" and "Counsellor." Of latter years, I have been frequently pained by hearing them quoted in the gallery, with a long pause between them. It did not use to be so: the early Friends, ordinarily at least, when they used the passage in print, seemed to use the word, wonderful, in that sense that I understood it and used it, on the occasion referred to. I have no doubt that His name *is* Wonderful, and that it may be fitly so expressed at times; but in that place and on that occasion (as well as at other times), I wished to convey the idea, or rather to enforce the doctrine, that He is a *Wonderful Counsellor*, as well as "the mighty God, the everlasting Father, and the Prince of Peace." And it seems to me to be more in harmony with the rest of that passage, so to use or quote it. I desire to be preserved from needless and useless, as well as doubtful disputations, and I am not aware of being much given to it; neither is this a subject that I ever spoke of, or heard spoken of, before, that I know; and yet it is one that I have often thought of. I was under the impression that there were in that assembly such as were vainly trusting in the *name* of Christ, calling it Wonderful (as it truly is, and holy also; for His name is called, and He is, the Word of God and the Power of God), without knowing Him to be their Counsellor to instruct them, or being willing to walk in the light of His counsel. I have never thought that the punctuation and heading of the chapters, or the division into chapters and verses (however convenient), was infallibly correct. I have no doubt, that in some places the true sense has been marred or obscured, by the manner in which this has been done [by commentators], as well as by mistranslation, &c.;—although sufficiently clear, for all that; and I fully believe that the translators were even very much favored therein. But still I never like to hear the Holy Scriptures termed the "sacred *volume;*" an expression which has been very common of late, but which I have always, I believe, avoided using; they not being, according to my observation, ever so termed in the Bible; and it seems to me that the terms, *sacred* and *holy*, apply to the matter and the doctrine, rather than to the mere *book* or *volume*. . . . .

Second month, 6th.

P.S.—I returned home from Providence last evening, and found thine of the 30th ult. had arrived in my absence. . . . . . . I have had a suffering week of it physically, having been very closely employed, and laboriously too; and have returned home, feeling almost worn out in that respect, yet mercifully somewhat comforted and refreshed in spirit, which is a great favor. . . . . . Our quarterly meeting was large, for us, and I thought a favored season, though mostly held in silence. C. W. spoke first, and was followed by N. P., in a short, but sweet, appropriate, and lively testimony. No other voice was heard. I was greatly surprised, on reaching Valley Falls, third-day morning, to find that dear Rachel Thornton had been released during the previous night. I had not heard of her being more poorly, and had looked forward with pleasure, in hope of enjoying her company once more. Dear J. W. and myself visited the poor bereaved daughters that evening. We had not more than taken our seats, when a precious covering spread over us; and J. W.'s mouth was soon livingly and powerfully opened, referring to Naomi and Ruth, and to the godly resolution of the latter, encouraging them to adopt it, and to follow their dear departed mother, as she had followed Christ; expressing also a firm belief and assurance that the dear departed friend had been mercifully permitted, through great tribulation, to enter into that everlasting rest which remaineth for the people of God. On sixth-day, the funeral took place at ten o'clock at the house; and, after the body was interred, a large and solemn meeting was held in the Baptist meeting-house, near the place of interment; many Friends, who had come to the quarterly meeting, staying to the funeral, and a goodly number of the inhabitants of the village. J. Wilbur soon stood up with the words, "Mark the perfect man, and behold the upright, for the end of that man is peace;" and after briefly referring to the deceased, as a mother in Israel, and to his belief that, through faithfulness to her Leader, the great tribulations through which she had passed had wrought for her a far more exceeding and eternal weight of glory, and also speaking very weightily and pertinently to her relations and friends, he proceeded to show the great necessity which exists for all to know a living engagement to prepare an habitation for the God of Jacob to dwell in, even the perfecting of holiness in the fear of the Lord; seeing that He dwelleth not in temples made with hands, nor yet in unsanctified hearts; and proceeded to point out the work of righteousness, and the necessity of the new birth unto holiness, without which no man shall see the Lord, nor experience Him to dwell with and in him. The very pith and substance of the Christian religion—of "primitive Christianity"—was revived and borne testimony unto, and a very solemn covering prevailed over the meeting; under which I should have been glad it had been permitted to close without any addition; for to me the cup seemed full, and the service of the meeting accomplished. But there was something more attempted, which added nothing to the weight, in my view, though otherwise harmless. Surely wisdom remains to be the principal thing; and how desirable it is, with all our gettings, to get wisdom and understanding also! And silence often is wisdom; while seeking to add words without renewed divine authority, surely and always is folly. In his public communications, our dear, aged friend, J. W., surely does increase in brightness; and the weight of his spirit in private also is truly expressive of a religious awe, verifying the expressions of David, "They that be planted in the house of the Lord shall flourish in the courts of our God. They shall still bring forth fruit in old age; they shall be fat and flourishing." . . . . .

Second month, 7th.

[Alluding to his own health at this time, he says]: Many of my friends here, are and have been not a little apprehensive about it, notwithstanding I am generally about. But I can bear very little exposure, or exertion of any kind, without serious effects following upon it, being often obliged to stop two or three times in the course of a walk of a fourth of a mile. Everything, indeed, of an exciting nature, whether of pleasure or of pain, produces nearly the same effect. In the meeting at Fall River, last first-day afternoon, I think I was not on my feet in all more than twenty minutes, and the last half of that time I found it extremely difficult to utter what I had to say, from pain and exhaustion. My throat is much better, and has been, since the last occasion of my raising blood, soon after W. Waring was here. What the end of it will be, I know not; but there is a "need be" of preparation for it undoubtedly. I often think it is not far distant, and it does seem as if it might probably come very suddenly. Although the pain which I suffer in my chest, &c., is almost constant, by night as well as by day, so that I get but very little sleep, and it costs little to keep me, yet it is very much increased by exposure, &c.; and I feel it a great mercy that I was permitted to get home before this extremely cold weather came on. The thermometer, at noon yesterday, was five degrees below zero, and eleven below zero at ten o'clock last night; which is six or seven degrees colder than I ever knew it on this island before, or indeed my father either. . . . . I ventured out but once yesterday, then only to father's; it was quite too much, and I have not tried it to-day. . . . . My dear M. unites with me in love to you. . . . . .

T. B. GOULD.

TO JOSHUA MAULE.

NEWPORT, 25th of 3d mo., 1855.

MY DEAR BROTHER, J. MAULE,—

Every part of thy letter of the 21st of second month was deeply interesting to me, neither was I disappointed in the account of things; by which it very plainly appears that the bitterness of death is by no means past. A little after, I received a letter, much in the same strain as thine, from Joseph Hobson. . . . I was much interested to hear who was with you at the time of your quarterly meeting. Everything that relates to the state of things and individuals in Ohio is deeply interesting to me. Oh! how strongly I feel bound to true-hearted Friends there! And greatly, though much in secrėt, do I mourn over many who are in great danger of turning entirely away backward, through the plausible but delusive snares of an arch-enemy, who is quite content that men should possess the form, and be very zealous for the form and outward order, if he can but deprive them of the power and the life, and the substance!

I am obliged by thy sending John Vanlaw's letter; how clear and lively, and to the point it was! It was strengthening and encouraging to us. . . . . Do please tell me whatever thou hearest of Friends in Iowa. Do they still keep up their monthly meeting? I hope so, faithfully, and that they will not be discouraged, but patiently "abide their time;" and I have no doubt there will be a service in it, that a blessing will rest upon the heads of those who have been separated from their brethren, and whose names have been cast out as evil, because they could not follow a multitude to do evil. I hope they will be preserved from making any compromises with the powers that be. Oh! what harm has come of making compromises and concessions, and giving the ground to the enemies of truth, for peace' sake! I have wanted much to write to Caleb, and tell him so; not because I thought he needed instruction, but to endeavor to encourage him and his friends, and to strengthen their hands. But I have been let hitherto. . . . . My love is to N. P. and M. H., and dear little R. Oh, how truly kind they all were to us poor pilgrims and outcasts; and it is not a light or a small matter either, to be willing to be known as the "companions of such as are so used," as we were by some upon whose civility (if not hospitality), we had more than ordinary claims. But, upon them, we had not any other than ordinary ones; yet their hearts were opened to show us great kindness, not by constraint but willingly. . . .

As ever, truly yours,

T. B. Gould.

To William Hodgson.

Elmside, 4th mo., 9th, 1855.

My very dear Friend,

. . . . . . But I wanted to say, that, since the *Meeting for Sufferings*, in Ohio, has undertaken to extend their jurisdiction beyond their own limits, even within the limits of Indiana Yearly Meeting, and beyond it, and to make all Friends who may remove to that vast territory, members of Stillwater Monthly Meeting; and since the power that controls the Philadelphia "*Friend*" has seemed to endorse this measure, I think that —— —— and company ought to hold their peace respecting a minute which our *yearly* meeting has found it needful to make respecting removals or settlements within our own borders. Where was the authority, precedent, or usage, to justify the meeting for sufferings in Ohio in taking such a step? What becomes of order here? What will become of discipline, especially if your yearly meeting should continue your correspondence with Indiana? Ah, I fear that it is but as the beginning of disorder and confusion, that will follow, if those who are aiming at the same thing do not disregard consequences, and get and keep closer together, and mingle more with one another; that so the advantage of various gifts, and degrees of experience and knowledge of the truth, may be reaped from a united labor, as well as exercise at a distance; according to ancient practice, and the original design of Him who gathered us to be a people, and while the fear of Him had more place amongst us, and the fear of man less. Friends formerly spake often one unto another; many ran to and fro in the earth, not in "creaturely heat or zeal" either; and the Lord hearkened and heard them, and light and knowledge were increased. Oh! what a cruel device of the enemy it has been and is, to put and keep things in such a shape, as to keep true Friends at a distance from each other, to separate very friends, and to make them actually afraid one of another! But why should I run on in this strain? I am sure I cannot tell. Truly, thou never felt nearer or dearer to me; and as your yearly meeting has been approaching, thou hast been increasingly, almost constantly, the companion of my thoughts, in near and true unity (according to my small measure), and with tender, heartfelt sympathy; earnestly desiring that thou mayst find grace to help thee in time of need, and that neither one thing nor another, neither heights nor depths, nor principalities nor powers, things present nor things to come, nor any other creature, may be able to turn thee aside from thy integrity in the truth and to the truth; but that thou mayst be innocently bold in thy assertion of it, patient in suffering for it, firm in thy adherence to it, immovable as a rock! This much in brief I felt bound to tell thee, though not a tithe of what I feel; neither can what I feel for thee and many more up and down amongst you, in the fulness and extent of it, be by me expressed in words. Neither am I devoid of feeling on my own account; and surely it could scarcely be otherwise, with such a prospect as I have resting and increasingly pressing upon me, as the time of my departure draweth nigh; a prospect which, though not large, in a sense, yet truly it is large and heavy for me. And I do desire the help of the faithful, in a united exercise. Oh, what a blessed help and strength it was to me last fall! I was as truly sensible of the unity, and travail, and intercession, and (shall I say?) access, too, of many, who were dipped into a feeling of unity with that concern, even when far distant from them, as though I had heard them breathing with my outward ears. And I have often thought, that the degree of help and preservation vouchsafed, was, after the cause, mainly attributable thereto. . . . .

Thy true friend,

T. B. Gould.

To Ethan and Anna Foster.

Newport, 15th of 4th mo., 1855.

My dear Friends:

Since I received Charles Perry's last letter, written on his return from Boston, we had not heard a word from you, in any way, until yesterday; when, by way of East Greenwich, we learned that your beloved little Hannah had been released from all her sufferings. During her illness, I often felt as if I would like to tell you that you had our very near sympathy, but seemed unavoidably prevented from so doing; and since we heard of your close bereavement, I have felt as if I must say that much to you, although not expecting to use many words, being, I think, somewhat sensible how far short of reaching such a wound any mere words must necessarily come. And yet I have, in a somewhat similar affliction, myself realized some consolation by the expression of the near sympathy of sincere friends. But what more than this could I say, by way of condolence, that you know not already? Time and resignation may, and no doubt will, take off the sharper edges, and partially heal up the wound which has been made in one of the dearest affections of your hearts; but the memory of hopes destroyed will continue. And if this dispensation of Unerring Wisdom and Divine Providence, without whose notice not even a sparrow falleth to the ground, has the happy effect of weakening your hold on the things of time, and fixing them more firmly on those that are above, and which are both unchangeable and of eternal duration; then you will doubtless be the better prepared to acknowledge, that "affliction springeth not out of the dust, nor trouble out of the ground;" and that, although no affliction for the present seemeth to be joyous, but very grievous, nevertheless it will yield the peaceable fruits of righteousness to those that are rightly exercised thereby,—and so you may be qualified to say, "For all we bless Thee,—most for the severe;"—"The Lord gave, and the Lord hath taken away; blessed be the name of the Lord!" . . . Oh! what a blessed thing it is, to have things brought into, and kept in, their proper places; to have the vessel, whether it be more or less honorable, sanctified, and made meet for the Master's use; and so to be furnished with mouth and wisdom, tongue and utterance, which all our adversaries shall not be able to gainsay, or entirely to resist. . . . .

I remain, as ever, your sincere and affectionate friend,

THOMAS B. GOULD.

The prospect of paying a visit, in Gospel love, to some parts of New York Yearly Meeting, had remained with him ever since his visit to Ohio and Pennsylvania; but the time had not appeared to himself to be fully come for its accomplishment, until the spring of 1855; when he prepared to leave his home once more, for the fulfilment of what he believed was required of him. Writing to Charles Perry, on the 19th of the 4th month, he thus alludes to his approaching arduous engagement:—

. . . The prospect of leaving home is in itself considerable, and wears upon me, or would do so, even if that was all. But then there are trials and baptisms connected with it, which are far greater and more wearing to poor flesh and blood; so that I need the sympathy and help of the faithful, in their nearest approaches to the Lord, that the precious cause may not suffer by me; for these are indeed perilous times for any to go forth in, and especially for me. . . . .

To William Hodgson.

Lincoln, Vermont, 6th of 5th mo., 1855.

My dear Friend:

. . . I had been much more poorly for a week previous, and quite unable to sit up, most of the time, nor yet to get any adequate rest or sleep in bed, my cough was so constant and distressing, and my body so full of pain. Yet, notwithstanding this, I did so far recruit before the time came, as to set forth against both wind and tide, literally; going up the river [or bay] in a sloop, in a gale of wind; but comfortably, compared with a ride in an open wagon, seven miles further than where we landed. But we were favored to reach brother George Kenyon's in safety, before dark; and, through favor, I did not add much to my cold, and was also enabled to serve as clerk of the select quarterly meeting next day, the clerk being absent. The select meeting was small, and, I thought, a low time: the quarterly meeting the next day was to me a solid and interesting one. . . . .

On fifth-day afternoon, after quarterly meeting, we took the car to Valley Falls, and reached the house of our kind friends, Harvey and Anne Chace, just as they did, who came in their own carriage. After tea, the family and my dear Israel went to bed, and I lay down on the sofa in the sitting-room, but could not lie even there, and well bolstered up, too; and so, without a wink of sleep myself, we set out again at one o'clock that morning, to Providence, six miles, in H. C.'s carriage, with him for a driver; where, at three o'clock, we took the Boston train, reaching that city about sunrise, and at seven o'clock took the Fitchburg and Cheshire, and from that the Rutland and Burlington Railroad, and reached New Haven, Vermont, about five o'clock, P. M.; from whence, by stage, we came to Bristol, six miles, over one of the worst roads I ever travelled, in an open wagon, too, and heavily loaded. At Bristol, which is at the foot of the Green Mountains, we hired a wagon and driver, and proceeded up the mountain five miles further, to the house of our kind friends, Pelatiah and Phebe L. Gove; which we were favored to reach in safety, and without the least accident, just after dark. They live high up the mountains, and in the midst of them, on either hand, except to the north; one of the highest peaks of the Green Mountains being due east, and only about two miles to the foot of it from this house. The scenery is grand and wild in the extreme; and, although the weather is cold, corresponding with ours in the third month, and the sides of the mountains are covered with snow, yet it is truly remarkable, and cause of much heartfelt gratitude, that this air does not pinch and search me like our own: my cough is better, and so is my appetite, and I can draw a long, deep breath, without any pain in my lungs, which is more than I have been able to do for a long while before.

Our ride from Bristol to this place was all the way by the side of New Haven River, a rushing, noisy mountain stream, tumbling over a rough, rocky bed, with now and then a beautiful cascade pouring down the sides of the mountain into the main stream. But canst thou bear with me in all this? Truly, it is a liberty which is granted to me, or which I am permitted to enjoy; and such scenery as this is a source of much subordinate enjoyment to me. But that which affords me the most solid satisfaction, is the abundant evidence which has been mercifully afforded, that I am in my right place at present, in that I did break through the thick cloud of discouragements which surrounded me, and came here to visit these honest-hearted Friends. Thou little knowest how I have dreaded this part of my prospect. Scipio I could endure to look forward to, but Vermont was bitter and agonizing in prospect, in my feeble and precarious state of health. Then, again, I was told that Friends here had, many of them, removed away to Iowa, &c.; that others were going, and that such as remained were so poor that we should be almost a burden to them. The first part was too true; but there is a goodly little company left, to whom our visit has been none the less acceptable on account of their having been so much stripped. It has really seemed to do them good, for the time being, at any rate, that we were constrained to pay them a visit; and I must confess that I have been already amply rewarded for coming, if I should not receive another penny. But the draft which I felt, was so strong to this part of the heritage, that I was not to be deterred from making the attempt to visit them, either by the secret reluctance which I felt to the journey at this season of the year, or by the report which I heard, that there was "not much here to attract!" Indeed, there is much roughness of exterior in many, but underlaid with sincerity of heart, and, as I think, more genuine Quakerism, more primitive simplicity and Christianity, than is possessed by many who appear much smoother on the surface. It is not likely we shall be able to visit all the meetings in this quarter. Some of them are remote, and the roads bad, the frost not being yet out of the ground in many places. But the quarterly meeting is to be held next third, fourth, and fifth-days, at Starksborough; of which I was glad, when I heard of it, since we came, and which seemed to be confirmatory of the rectitude of the time of our coming, although we knew nothing of it before. . . . .

. . . . . The meeting here at Lincoln to-day was much larger than I expected, both of Friends and others; and yet they say it is reduced more than half in number since the separation, and quite recently, too, by deaths, disownments, and removals. . . . . The meeting, though trying and laborious, was relieving and satisfactory to me, and also to others, so far as I could see or judge. But it is an awful service, and seems to be especially so when called upon to stand, as it were, between the living and the dead, and to be baptized for the dead; and well may we say, "What advantageth it us, if the dead rise not?" The remark in thine, that thou "looked upon this undertaking as a very different service from that which was laid upon me last fall," was in exact accordance with my own feelings and views respecting it. But I could not adequately express to thee in words, even if I had time, and was not so weary, what preparatory plunges and baptisms it has been my lot to pass through, or how completely emptied I have been of anything which (so to speak) I had gathered or experienced in that journey; so that I had nothing left to lean or rely upon, but the renewed qualification; and, eventually, I received an increase of faith to believe that, as my eye was singly kept to and upon Him with whom, or in whom, are all the treasures of wisdom and knowledge, the needful portion would not be withheld. . . . . . Be assured that I am, as ever, thy sincere and affectionate friend, T. B. GOULD.

TO MARTHA S. GOULD.

SHERWOODS, 17th of 5th month, 1855.

MY DEAR MARTHA:

I wrote to sister Lydia last second-day morning, at the house of Daniel Nichols, of Peru, New York; which letter thou hast doubtless seen, and so I need not recapitulate what I stated therein. We attended an appointed meeting at Peru, in Friends' meeting-house, at ten o'clock that morning, as was expected. It was small, there being but few Friends in that place, and of this number were Burling and Lydia Hallock. . . . . The meeting was satisfactory to me, and, in some respects, rather extraordinary,—there being much tenderness and brokenness apparent in several; part of which was probably owing to its being the last time dear Lydia Hallock was likely very soon to meet with the little company who are left there, by whom she appeared to be entirely beloved, and from whom she seemed very reluctant to part, as well as they from her. We dined at the house of Phebe Hoag; and most of the members, and some other persons, went and dined with us there, making quite a large company. . . . After tea, a young Friend took L. Hallock and daughter, I. B. and myself, five or six miles in his wagon to Keesville; where we got into the stage, and rode some eight or ten miles further to Port Kent, on the western shore of Lake Champlain. Here we waited until near midnight, for the steamboat southward to Whitehall, and arrived there about sunrise; took the cars to Schenectady, and so to Auburn, about one hundred and fifty miles, which we reached about sunset. Here we lodged near the depot, and close to the great State prison, in which there are about eight hundred prisoners. I had a good night's rest, and, at eight o'clock this morning, we took stage for this place, and reached Sherwoods Post-office about noon; where we waited for the mail to be opened, and I received thy most welcome letter, written last first-day, which had come all the way in the same carriage with us, as well as one written to Job Otis by Friends in Vermont, more than a week ago, requesting him to meet us at Auburn. But the dear old man was overjoyed to see us. The situation is delightful. So is the whole country in itself; and the beauty, and so to speak, the outward glory of it, greatly enhanced by the freshness and greenness of early spring, the fruit-trees, except the apples, being in full bloom, and the meadows and pastures covered with flowers.

After dinner we went to see Joseph Chase, who is very low. . . . . . He seemed in a quiet, comfortable state of mind. . . . We have had delightful weather, all through Vermont and Northern New York, which was a great favor, where covered carriages are almost unknown, and they have been quite so to us. But it commenced raining the night before last, while we were on Lake Champlain, and rained steadily and powerfully all the way to Auburn, clearing up just before we got there, and we should otherwise have been exposed to it. Thus we have been favored, however truly unmerited, and I desire to be thankful. . . . Though I write cheerfully about the weather, scenery, &c., I am not without my exercises, peculiar exercises, adapted to the state of things here, which is peculiar; and so they were in Vermont, according to the latitude and longitude of each place, &c. . . . .

Thine,
T. B. GOULD.

TO R. S. NICHOLS.

HECTOR, N. Y., 21st of 5th month, 1855.

MY DEAR FRIEND, R. S. NICHOLS:

. . . . On awaking this morning, after having written to my precious Martha last evening, and been favored to sleep well from midnight till after sunrise, thou wast brought so sweetly and renewedly to my remembrance, that I thought I would just tell thee of it, although little more might arise. But I know that thou wilt be glad to hear, that, notwithstanding I have not been favored with such an unusual degree of strength and clearness in testimony, as was the case last fall, yet I have been mercifully enabled hitherto to answer the service required at my hands, in a manner that has been relieving to my own mind, and also, I think, satisfactory and comforting to Friends. My line of service has been more like seeking out the lost and scattered sheep of the house of Israel, than in the way of the Gentiles, or in visiting the "cities of the Samaritans," with whom now, as anciently, the Jews have little or no dealings in a general way. Yet it has sometimes been laid upon me to cry against the separate altar, which has been set up, as in Bethel or in Dan; and some of its votaries, or of those who, like Jeroboam, have been concerned in the erection and defence of this separate altar and its idol calf-worship,—or, in other words, will-worship, which remains to be idolatry,—have sometimes been present: but no one has been permitted openly to put forth his hand against me, or my unequivocal testimony, nor yet really to say, "Lay hold on him!" The preciousness of standing within the walls of Jerusalem, the quiet habitation, whither the tribes go up to worship, and where the ark of the Lord's testimony and covenant rests, and is known, and entered into, and abode in; with the beauty of the situation of Mount Zion, and the strength and salvation of its walls, have been much given me to hold forth to view; and, in short, glorious things have been given me to speak boldly concerning it; and also of the goodliness of Jacob's tents, and so to labor for the gathering of Israel to their tent; that so, as the valleys, they may be again spread forth, and flourish "like cedar trees beside the waters, and as trees of lign aloes which the Lord hath planted." And however limited in ploughing or in planting, nor yet either eloquent in speech, or mighty in the Scriptures, and so not qualified to water so extensively, and perhaps effectively as many, yet the Great Head of the Church has been pleased to own my feeble efforts in His cause, and to give some increase of strength and consolation to a remnant.

The meeting yesterday at Hector was large, quite a goodly number of Friends being in attendance, both as to numbers and appearance. Several of other persuasions came in, and my mouth was opened largely, in a close, searching testimony; wherein I seemed to have stepping-stones laid for me from one state to another, at such distances from each other that I could just reach them by carefully minding my goings, and keeping my feet, or rather by their *being* mercifully *kept;* and so I was preserved from falling into the snare of judging after the sight of the eye, or the hearing of the ear; and I think the meeting ended solidly and well. This evening we had an appointed meeting at a Methodist meeting-house, in Truemansburg; in which Truth favored with more than ordinary clearness and authority, in declaring the doctrines of the Gospel, and especially as regards the spirituality of them; and there did indeed seem to be a door of entrance mercifully opened in the hearts of a seeking, sober people; and some present, who were not for a time at all sober, were eventually solemnized in a truly remarkable manner.

We returned to the house of dear Charles and Sarah Owen to lodge, and the next morning set our faces eastward again, towards Cayuga Lake; about two miles west of which, we passed by the celebrated Taughanic Falls, in the town of Ulysses. This fall being two hundred and ten feet, and perpendicular, is sixty feet higher than those of Niagara; but the sheet of water did not appear to be more than twenty or thirty feet wide, and the volume of water is not large, but beautiful indeed. . . . .

Believe me to be thy sincere and affectionate friend,

T. B. GOULD.

TO WILLIAM HODGSON.

AURORA, N. Y., 28th of fifth month, 1855.

MY DEAR FRIEND,

After attending the meeting at Lincoln, Vt., where I wrote thee, we attended their quarterly meeting, held at Starksborough, the same week; and although it was smaller than I had expected, yet it was a good meeting, and I was well satisfied in being among them; my being there did also appear to be satisfactory and encouraging to them. But it did not appear surprising to me that they should feel somewhat discouraged; for no less than twenty-eight or thirty of their members have either gone this spring, or were about going, to the west, some of them to Iowa and some to Indiana. This has brought the remnant who are left, under very close and renewed trial; but it may be of use to them; and there is indeed a goodly little company left, with whom, some of them especially, my spirit was brought into near fellowship. We had a public meeting one evening in a little village at Starksborough, in a Methodist meeting-house; which was well in the end, though hard and trying in the commencement; and another at Ferrisburg, not far from where dear old Joseph Hoag lived. There are but two families of Friends there, and one of them, with whom we dined, was just about breaking up to go west. With these and some others of the emigrants I had some tendering labor. . . .

We set out the next morning for Grand Isle, in Lake Champlain, a distance of forty miles. . . . We crossed the lake by a bridge three miles in length, one half the distance being through a swamp, and among large trees, apparently growing in water; and the other half is built upon a sand-bar in the lake, which Friends used to ford at some seasons of the year, in going to their meetings, before the bridge was built. This last distance, one mile and a half, we had to walk the horses; and it was the roughest road, and apparently the most dangerous travelling, that I ever passed; although I thought I had endured some hardness before, in the line of bad roads. After riding five or six miles northward on the island, we came to a kind Friend's house; where we stayed the night, and the next day, being first-day, the 13th of the month, attended their meeting; which was large, public notice of our being there having been given. There are but two families of Friends on this island, and one aged woman, by the name of M. M——, living with her children, who are Gurneyites. But she is a sweet and lively-spirited minister, evincing remarkable greenness, and clearness of vision, at the advanced age of eighty-eight years. She was at meeting; and near the close of it, lifted up her voice like a trumpet, having something like a seal to set to what had been previously delivered. At the close of the meeting, on giving her my hand, holding it long and closely in hers, and viewing me from head to foot, without either of us uttering a word for some time, after a little time she said, "Thou art a stranger to me as to the outward; I never saw thee before; thou dost not *feel* like a stranger: I am glad to see thee here; and I am satisfied, satisfied, satisfied!"—shaking my hand heartily and most expressively. Her daughter stood close by, apparently watching us both. The old woman was evidently aware of it. I was deeply interested in her, and admired her shrewdness, or rather her wisdom. But, on inviting me to the house, her daughter seconded the invitation; and I conditionally accepted it, and afterwards rode four or five miles to do so. She is a very striking and interesting example of primitive simplicity and plainness, wearing a brown linen bonnet, with strings of the same material, &c. . . . . Friends and Gurneyites meet together on Grand Isle, on first-days; quite a company of friendly Hicksites came in when we were there, and many other people, forming a mixed company indeed; so that it required much careful looking, to find the stepping-stones, and to reach from one to another without slipping. But through favor the meeting ended well, and relievingly to my own mind. The next day a friendly Hicksite set us over the west side of the lake in his boat, but would by no means allow us to pay him for it, saying that he had been already more than paid.

Grand Isle is a beautiful spot; about the same size as our own dear island, and lying in the lake, much as Rhode Island lies in the blue waters of Narragansett Bay. The mountains on either side being obscured, when we were there, by a thick, smoky atmosphere, the shores of Vermont on the east, and of New York on the west, very much resembled the shores of our own lovely bay. But the shores of Grand Isle itself were in many places lined with splendid arbor vitæ trees, rendering them extremely picturesque and beautiful. We landed at Plattsburg, where our friend, Daniel Nichols, met us, and took us twelve miles to his house at Peru. The next day we had an appointed meeting there, which was small, there being only three or four families of Friends, and about as many solitary individuals scattered among those who are not members. About twelve o'clock that night we took a steamboat and ran up Lake Champlain to Whitehall; and so by the rails through Saratoga, Syracuse, &c., along the banks of the Mohawk, to Auburn, where we lodged at a hotel; and the next morning went by stage to Sherwoods, and reached the house of my old and dear friend, Job Otis, where we met with a most welcome reception. It having been many years since we had met before, the warm-hearted old man was quite overcome, and wept like a child, notwithstanding his reputed hardness. . . . . .

We attended the meeting at Hector on first-day, a week ago yesterday. It was large, and well, I think; and some choice Friends we found there, and visited, I believe, to mutual satisfaction. The next evening we had an appointed meeting in a Methodist meeting-house at Truemansburg, among a tender, seeking people, and some light and airy spirits; many Friends also coming to it for miles around. I felt much openness among them, and the Gospel of life and salvation was largely preached, in a degree, as I humbly trust, of its own power. . . . . . On fourth-day we attended their usual mid-week meeting here at Poplar Ridge, which was a good and heavenly meeting. . . . . . The meeting-house is much too small, and was very much crowded yesterday. Many Hicksites came in the afternoon, and a few Gurneyites: one of the latter, an aged, plain-looking man, stopped me, as I was passing him at the close of it, and, in a tender and feeling manner, expressed an earnest desire that I might continue faithful in the gift received, and to the testimony given me to bear, and so be made instrumental of good to multitudes, as he said had been the case to him; adding, "It is the truth, the very truth, and there is no other way of salvation."

. . . . . Both sittings [of the yearly meeting] to-day

were mercifully owned, but little expression; and the business much better conducted, and with far more dignity and propriety, than I expected would be the case, after attending the meeting for sufferings on seventh-day, which was rather trying to me. However, even that would not suffer at all in comparison with that in ——, with —— at the table.

We have a meeting appointed to-morrow evening, at seven o'clock, six miles from here, at a village called Northville. . . . . But it is near 1 o'clock, third-day morning, and I must try to get some rest; so farewell. In love unchangeable, I trust, to thee and thine.

Thy friend and brother,
THOMAS B. GOULD.

TO JOSHUA MAULE.

EAST GREENWICH, R. I., 6th month, 3d, 1855.

MY DEAR BROTHER, JOSHUA MAULE:

. . . . . . I am so lame, and in so much pain with my rheumatic affection, that I am not much in a writing mood; but I did want to let thee and dear sister Sarah know, how wonderfully we have been cared for, and favored to get along without any accident to harm us in the least, and with a remarkable improvement in my general health, as I was unable to sit up much of the time until within three days of my setting forth; which made the prospect of leaving home, and going into a cold, wilderness country, as Vermont seemed to me then to be, and especially with such lungs, and no appetite, nor strength sufficient to do anything about home, look very discouraging. But either the change of air, or some peculiarity in the mountain air, or the journey itself, or all three put together, had a very beneficial effect. I have sometimes thought it was owing to the degree of relief afforded by the consciousness of being in the way of discharging the service required of me in these parts; to which, after getting home once more (on my return from Ohio, &c.), I had felt all my usual and natural reluctance to set out and go forth again, revive. Indeed it would never have answered for me to have gone thither in the winter, or even late in the fall; so I had to carry this burden all winter, until way did clearly open, which was at length the case, and which in itself afforded some relief. And as to the time, I believe it could scarcely have been better. . . . . .

The select meeting [at Starksboro'] was a trying one to me, and nearly silent; although, towards the close, I was enabled to obtain some relief, and it ended more satisfactorily than I had expected for some time after sitting down among them. The two last-named meetings [the quarterly meeting for business, and the public meeting on fifth-day], were very satisfactory, relieving, and remarkable opportunities; the last especially so, ending in solemn, vocal thanksgiving, and praise; in which nearly or quite all present seemed prepared to unite, and many were exceedingly tendered and broken, and so continued to be until late in the afternoon, when we parted; they going to their respective places of abode, and we to an appointed meeting, at a village about two miles from Friends' meeting-house. It was held in a Methodist house, among a rather uncouth set of people, who were unreasonably long in gathering, and in other respects I was much tried. But truth at length arose for our help, and I was enabled to obtain relief, and left them with a peaceful mind. The next day we proceeded to Ferrisburg, and, in the evening, had another appointed meeting, among a more experienced and cultivated Methodist people. To them my mouth was largely opened in declaring the truth, in a good degree of its ancient and new power: the minds of many were seriously affected therewith, and the meeting ended solidly and well. On our way to this place, we passed close by Monkton meeting-house and burying-ground, in which lie the earthly remains of that good man, and able minister of the Gospel, Joseph Hoag. Monkton was the meeting he belonged to, and usually attended when at home, and his son also, in whose house he died. . . . . . The next day, being seventh-day, we rode forty miles to Grand Isle. . . . . .

Thy affectionate brother,

THOMAS B. GOULD.

To William Hodgson.

Elmside, 19th of 6th mo., 1855.

My dear Friend,

. . . . I reached my own dear home and beloved family on second-day, the fourth of this month, about noon; where I need scarcely say, I met a most welcome reception, and was rejoiced to find all as well as I could have expected. . . . .

. . . I can thankfully and reverently acknowledge, that my northwestern journey affords me, in the retrospect, inexpressible relief, and solid, peaceful satisfaction. Although I had not many meetings, and it seemed like spending a good deal of time to little purpose, in respect of the small number of meetings, &c., yet many remote corners, and solitary individuals or families, were searched out and visited, in the love, and in a measure, I trust, of the power of the Gospel; sufficiently so, at least, to give us, and the testimony given me to bear, some place in their hearts, and to convince them in whose name we came. Neither have I been able to see that I omitted, or left undone, anything that was required of me at this time. I may also say to thee, that, although I went forth truly without purse, or scrip, or any provision for the journey, yet I lacked nothing, and, as I proceeded, was most abundantly provided for, helped, and furnished every way; though I had nothing over, nothing to boast of or to glory in, and do sincerely desire that the Lord alone may have the praise of His own work: for it was His work and His doings, and it is marvellous in my eyes, especially, considering what a poor, weak, nothing creature I am. Oh! how greatly I have been and am condescended to and helped! And now my desire is, that I may be preserved alive, even in famine, and instructed afresh and continually how to suffer want, as well as how to return thanks for past favors, and humbly to hope for more, even for such, and for such only, as are convenient and proper for me.

. . . I was not without an apprehension, on entering the village [of Northville], that I should have to appoint a meeting in their Presbyterian meeting-house. . . . When third-day came, it appeared that there was no sitting of the yearly meeting that afternoon; which afforded ample time to ride down thither, and was a collateral evidence of its being the right time for the meeting; although, at the time of making the appointment, I had no knowledge of their practice to have no sitting of the yearly meeting on third-day afternoon. My cousin Benjamin and his wife were to take Israel and myself down, and did so; but when we got there, I found my Scotch cousin not a little concerned about the whole thing, although she said nothing, and was kind. But her great joy on first seeing me, appeared changed to apprehension, as to how it was to be got through with, evidently; while my aged aunt, more than eighty years of age, and who had not walked a step for two years, seemed so rejoiced at the prospect of being likely to attend a Friends' meeting once more, that she was making arrangements to be carried to it in her chair, the meeting-house being near their place of residence. And her son, who, until now, had always seemed prejudiced against Friends, seemed to have exerted himself greatly and remarkably to give notice of the meeting, and to make other arrangements for it. But his wife's Scotch pride was up, as well as some fear, evidently, for her "religious copyhold;" for she said she had never forgotten some things I said to her, on taking leave of her at the steamboat at Newport, nor her being at our silent meeting here, four or five years ago. She had always loved me dearly, since she first saw me, but she did not know what the result of this would be; though she would gladly, she said, "have gone to Poplar Ridge on Sunday," if she could have done so consistently with the rites of hospitality due to her old pastor, and her duty to him, &c. Well, we went to the meeting (when the time came), which proved to be a large one, the house, which was large, being nearly filled. My knees were ready to smite together, for the whole prospect of this meeting, among my near relatives, had been, from the first, more trying than I can express; much more so, even, than among strangers. Several Friends from the Ridge came down to attend it.

. . . The meeting was very early covered with a precious solemnity, remarkably so, considering the class of persons present; I have rarely known the like in any place: and my mouth was soon opened amongst them, having to tell them, in the first place, that I was not only led to come, but also to stand up amongst them, in weakness, and in fear, and in much trembling, and without the least expectation of doing any great thing; yet, as an advocate for that cause which is dignified with immortality and crowned with eternal life, under a strong and renewed sense and feeling of the love of the everlasting and glorious Gospel, and of its being, both immediately, and instrumentally, and renewedly extended to them. And so I proceeded to speak of the nature and character of the Gospel, its worship and ministry; how this was received and exercised, and that the true and rightly called and qualified ministers of it were enabled to teach baptizingly into the very name of Jesus, ministering a portion of the power of the Gospel, and of the Word of Life and salvation to the people,—and distinguishing between this Word, which by the Gospel was preached unto them and in them, and the words of men and man-made ministers, and hirelings, and all will-worship, which is idolatry;—and showing how this ministry was neither received of man nor taught, but by the revelation of Jesus Christ; that if any speak in His name, he must speak as the oracle of God, and if any man minister, he must do it in that ability which He giveth, that He in all things might be glorified;—and that they were of the circumcision, and they alone, who worship God in spirit, rejoice alone in Christ Jesus, and have no confidence in the flesh. After this, the main doctrines and principles of the Christian religion, as held by Friends, were opened to my view, and largely declared, even the truth as it is in Jesus, and in a measure of its own demonstration and power; which came mercifully and triumphantly into dominion in the end, for the time being at least;—and the meeting concluded, to my great relief and humbling admiration. When the people had mostly left the house, perceiving that my aged aunt, who could not walk or help herself at all, was left nearly alone, I went to her and sat down by her, while she waited to be carried out; which her son, my cousin James Gould, perceiving, he came to us, and inquired of me if I noticed a man,—describing him,—who sat in such a seat, pointing to it. Upon my answering in the negative, he said: "That is the man whom we have on trial, and think of calling to preach for us: but he is young, still studying for the ministry, only preaches occasionally, and is not yet ordained; and I thought it truly remarkable that you should have been led to speak so much upon the subject of the ministry in general, and the nature of the call to it, and the qualification for it, in particular, and especially that no assembly of people could either call or ordain a minister; that this was the sole prerogative of the Head of the Church; and that all that even the true Church could do, was to own, concur with, or acknowledge the gift, and receive the minister whom the Minister of all rightly gathered assemblies might raise up, qualify, and send amongst them. I considered it," he continued, "a striking proof of the truth of what you subsequently said, that neither divine immediate revelation, nor the spirit of prophecy, had ceased; and that when it should cease, or if it should cease, Christianity would cease to exist, because, if any man have not the Spirit of Christ, he is none of His." I told him I had been unable to tell why I was thus led, since I had been really under the impression that they had no settled minister (knowing their old one had gone), and that no such person was present; but that I dared do no other than follow my Guide; and that, if a suitable opportunity occurred, he might let his friend know this; adding, that I hoped he would not suppose me to have been invidiously pointing at him. He said, "he believed no harm had been done, he hoped some good; at any rate, he might and ought to be instructed by it, for it was deeper far than he (the minister, so called) had ever seen, known, or heard, and he was truly glad he was there;" to which my aged aunt fully and heartily responded. Her son and I took her in our arms, and carried her out of the meeting-house, and seating her in her carriage, she rode home, where I stayed the night. On reaching cousin James's house, a very different feeling was apparent in his wife, from what I had discovered before meeting. She said, the meeting was all too short for her and for the people; but that she was deeply concerned for me; that if I went on daily from meeting to meeting, at this rate, I would soon be worn out, and that I must spare myself, &c. But I showed her more fully the ground of my concern, and that I must labor, a necessity being laid upon me; and was willing to labor freely, to spend and be spent in this cause, until I could obtain relief, and in order that I might finish the work allotted unto me, and the ministry which I had received of the Lord Jesus, to testify the Gospel of the grace of God. But she still seemed to think, that I must study a great deal, and think a great deal, or I could not (as she said Israel Buffinton had told her was the case), be thus engaged nearly every day, and two or three times a day sometimes, for months together. I asked her, if she saw any signs of study or premeditation in me, during the hours I had spent with her, immediately preceding the meeting? "Why, no, she had not; she noticed how freely I had spoken of other matters, saw no signs of preparation for the service of the meeting, and was greatly concerned as to what the result would be. Still," she added, "I watched you very closely in the meeting, and the most orthodox and learned divine could not have delivered a sounder communication, or more fully proved the truth of his positions and doctrines, by numerous and copious quotations from the Scriptures;" adding, "they were as correctly given, too, as if they had been read from the book; and I had previously no idea that the Friends were so entirely sound in doctrine, or that without any premeditation they could be so," &c. And her astonishment seemed not to be lessened, when I assured her, "that even when I stood up in that meeting, I had nothing before me save my concern, the evidence that my time had come, and the sentence which I commenced with." She was full of inquiry; much opportunity was afforded for an explanation of our principles on many points; and, although they would willingly, I believe, have sat up till morning, yet, finding anchorage ground at length, I left them, and went to bed.

. . . . But truly, dear William, I had no intention of going into such a detail when I commenced, and I fear it will prove tedious and burdensome to thee; neither have I done the like before, in respect of this journey at least. But knowing and feeling how kindly and deeply thou hast been interested in my getting along, I was willing to give thee some account of one very exercising engagement, although, much as I have written, I have not told thee one-half of this, or near it; but thou canst probably, from this, form some idea of others which were constantly occurring; in which I can truly and thankfully acknowledge, that I did afresh and repeatedly experience verified the truth of a communication which dear Mildred Radcliffe made to me many years ago, to wit: that, if I were faithful to what would be required of me, the key of the treasury and storehouse would be given me, and therein I should find all sorts of instruments, skilfully and exactly adapted to every work and service whereunto I should be called. And it is only to the praise of that Grace and Power, by which I am what I am, that these things are mentioned, and if it may be, for thy encouragement also.

Nothing out of the usual course occurred in our own yearly meeting, except that many Friends who have never failed to get here before, since the separation, were detained by sickness themselves or in their families. But others came in, who had not previously attended, so that with those here from abroad, it was nearly or quite as large as common; and I thought the public meetings, as well as those for discipline, were remarkably owned, and more than usually preserved from being hurt by unsanctified and unskilful communications. Our dear friend —— —— was largely engaged on first-day morning and fifth-day. As for J. W. and myself, we were both, I believe, well satisfied to see good work well done by others, except during a visit which I was concerned to pay to the women's meeting on third-day afternoon, and some close service which he (J. W.), had in the select meeting. Several of the sittings were remarkably owned, during the time not occupied by any ministerial labor; and the business was conducted, throughout, in much unity and harmony; although some deeply exercised minds were not insensible of the need of more dedication, closer engagement, and increased faithfulness, in the support of Truth's cause and testimony. . . .

The meeting ended solemnly, silently, and well.

. . . . . Farewell.

As ever, truly and sincerely thy friend,

THOMAS B. GOULD.

TO WILLIAM HODGSON.

ELMSIDE, 22d of 6th month, 1855.

MY ENDEARED FRIEND AND BROTHER:

Thine of the 19th inst. is just received, and was truly acceptable and appropriate. I was particularly struck with thy remarks respecting my own state, in a retrospect of my late little embassy; for truly the language has been adopted again and again, before I received thy letter, and mercifully verified also: "Return to thy rest, O! my soul, for the Lord thy God has dealt bountifully with thee." This I can say and acknowledge without boasting, or any feeling like unto it. I might also truly add, "What shall I render unto Him for all His benefits?"—although I have been left to feel enough of stripping and desertion, as I trust, to keep me under a true sense, in whom and from whom are all my fresh springs of consolation, and ability to do good or communicate it; and that, when all has been done that seems to be required for the time being, I am still an unprofitable servant, having done no more than was my duty to do, and having nothing but what I also received from Him; who is mercifully pleased to accept His own work, and to reward abundantly for it, notwithstanding the weakness which still attaches to the creature, and the imperfections of the instrument employed therein. . . . . . .

In great haste, but true love to thee and the cause,

Farewell,

THOMAS B. GOULD.

To William Hodgson.

Elmside, 10th of 11th month, 1855.

My beloved Friend:

. . . . I have hastily written this much after all have retired; and although it may be too late to be availing, yet I think I shall let it go for what it may be worth. It may serve to show thee, and I hope it will convince you both, that although, so far as you have seen or could see, appearances have been all against me, yet my will has been good to write, and indeed I have tried hard to do it. And, dear William, hast thou not had some sense of my captivity, my deep captivity; of the perishing hunger and the famishing want, which I have endured? Oh, how I have been tossed! No tongue can utter it, nor the pen of the most ready writer adequately and fully describe.

And even now, I see little hope, but that things will go almost "by the board:" at any rate, such as are saved, will be a mere handful, "some on boards and some on broken pieces of the ship:" for the treacherous dealer hath dealt and is dealing exceeding treacherously; and the spoiler hath grievously spoiled, and is spoiling, or seeking to spoil, I believe, some who have hitherto in good degree mercifully escaped.

Oh! that letter from —— —— to W. W.! I was so sorry to hear he had written it!—for what good can be expected from such a time-server as he has proved himself to be? And yet how much it is to be feared, that even such out-of-door sympathy and encouragement will have a "conservative" influence and effect; and is there not reason to fear it was designed to have such an effect? Alas! how many wheels there are within wheels, in these degenerate days, these days of treading down and perplexity! Neither is it to be doubted, that some who have been in good measure *battle-proof*, are not *wheedle-proof;* especially if they "have not known," or do not know, "the depths of Satan, as *they* speak" who resort to *wheedling*, and other unworthy methods of accomplishing their ends upon the unsuspecting and unwary. Oh, for more honest simplicity and straightforwardness! although it may subject a man to the charge of "raking up old matters," and may seem to shake the very pillars upon which the house is reputed to rest; said pillars, by the way, being so very tottlish, that, although shoulder may be joined to shoulder in the effort to steady them, it will all prove eventually unavailing; for everything that can be shaken will be shaken, that only that which is immovable may remain. Don't regard being called "a disturber of the peace:" the charge seemed as familiar to me, as an household word. . . . .

Farewell. In unabated and dear love to you all, in which my dear Martha desires to be included,

Thy sincere though tribulated brother,

T. B. GOULD.

TO JOSHUA AND SARAH MAULE.

NEWPORT, 11th month, 19th, 1855.

MY DEAR BROTHER AND SISTER:

We received the letter, containing the afflicting intelligence of the sickness of dear little Henry, and the afflicting termination of it, a week ago yesterday, and sent the letter by the next mail to Greenwich. It was not for want of near and tender sympathy with you, that we have not written sooner. . . . No doubt this has been a most bitter cup for you. But what can I say that will have a tendency to sweeten it? You know as well as I do, and perhaps better, where and how to look for help to enable you to bear it, and to reap the benefit designed by this dispensation of Divine Providence, which, in inscrutable and unerring wisdom, has been meted out to you; and you are, I trust, in no danger of supposing that it is a mere "chance" that has happened to you. I have myself no doubt, that in this case the expression of the poet will apply with full force:

"In love directed, and in mercy meant,
Are trials suffered and afflictions sent."

And if it should have the effect of further refinement upon you; if it should be a means of weaning you from the world, and rendering you more meet for the kingdom of heaven, the end will no doubt be happily accomplished.

Our dear love is to you all.

T. B. G.

To C. C. G., of Vermont.

Elmside, Newport, 12th mo. 16th, 1855.

My dear Friend:

It is now more than two months since I received thy kind letter, which was very acceptable to me, and which I have often thought I would like to reply to; but I have had little time of late for writing, and even less qualification for it. Neither is it probable that I can now do much more than just let thee know that thou and thy dear parents, as well as other Friends in your beautiful country, are still had in affectionate remembrance; nor do I think it probable that either your kindness to us as strangers and pilgrims, or the grand scenery in the midst of which you live, and by which you are continually surrounded, will ever be forgotten while memory lasts. Truly I have great reason to remember my visit to you, with solid satisfaction and thankfulness; as it not only proved relieving to my mind, of a heavy burden which had long rested painfully upon it, in anticipation of many difficulties which either had no real existence, or were mercifully made easy and removed; but your mountain air, the effect of which upon my weak and irritated lungs I had dreaded so much, has seemed to prove of singular benefit to me in that respect; my lungs, since I was there, having been restored to more strength and soundness, apparently, than for a long time before; more so, indeed, than I had ever expected they would be again; although my health, in divers other respects, has been very indifferent during much of the past summer and autumn.

. . . . I never could sit down and *patch-up* what some might call a religious letter; but which I should call dry and lifeless, a mere batch of sentimentality, or a repetition of desires and supposed experiences, which, if they were ever well-founded, had become too stale and stereotyped to be worth anything. I would myself prefer to write and to receive the most ordinary and natural thoughts upon common things and occurrences, so long as they were innocent, unless something of a higher order does occur in a lively manner; and if that is the case, even children and illiterate persons have seldom found any great difficulty in giving utterance to such impressions. So that thou needed not to have apologized to me, for what seemed to thyself the commonplace character of thy letter, or for the innocent freedom used therein, for I was unfeignedly pleased with both. . . . . .

Are any more of your members likely to leave you, and go West? If so, you must try to keep up your meetings, and strengthen the things which remain. I do hope, dear young woman, that thou wilt be careful to keep close to the tendering visitations of Heavenly Good, and the manifestations of Divine Light and Grace which thou hast already received; and also be obedient to those discoveries of the mind and will of thy Heavenly Father, concerning thyself and the way of truth, which, as thou art faithful, will yet further be revealed. That so, as thou growest older in years, thou mayst also experience a growth in the truth, and in the saving knowledge of Him, whom to know is life eternal; and that others may continue to be encouraged, by thy consistent example, to maintain a faithful testimony to all those precious and peculiar principles which have assuredly been given us to hold, including those in regard to plainness both of dress and address, of speech and behaviour. Oh! there is something remarkably sweet and convincing in the conduct of those young persons, members of our poor, shattered Society, who manifest by an humble, self-denying, cross-bearing deportment, that the principles in which they were educated have not been adopted as a thing of course, or received by tradition and education merely; but are the result of heartfelt conviction, and the manifestations of that Divine Light, which is "the true Light that lighteth every man that cometh into the world," and in which there is no darkness at all, nor any occasion of stumbling whatever.

. . . This has been written in much haste, and thou

must excuse the appearance of it. I remain thy sincere friend,

THOMAS B. GOULD.

TO W. AND E. R. HODGSON.

ELMSIDE, 1st month, 19th, 1856.

MY VERY DEAR FRIENDS:

. . . . . I received recently a long, good letter, from D. H. Without having heard anything of me for a long while, he seemed remarkably dipped into a sense of my state; and it was very pleasant and acceptable to me to be thus remembered for good by the goodly in the land of the living; although it failed to raise me up, the place of my dwelling being yet "among the pots." Still, if I may be permitted to say so, I am nevertheless at times made sensible of the travail, intercession, and help of the faithful, when the sceptre is held forth unto them, although not otherwise permitted to behold its extension; and that, too, in great mercy, even when they do not tell me so in words. But I do not mean to complain, knowing that I am unworthy of the least of the Lord's mercies; and if my life is only preserved, and given me for a prey, and I am but enabled to stand in my lot to the end and at the end of the days, it is no matter how low I am brought, either in my own eyes or those of others; some of whom, no doubt, are ready to say, "Ah ha! so would we have it!"

. . . . . We had the most severe snow-storm, a week ago last first-day, that has been known here for many years; and the next third-day night, between ten and twelve o'clock, the "Truro Street House," and four or five other and smaller houses, were entirely destroyed by fire. All the buildings were of wood, the wind was high, and the scene terrific! That great house was consumed like a heap of dry shavings, and the whole town, and country round, were lighted up with a brilliancy almost equal to daylight. The heavens were overcast with a dense squall cloud, and the ground covered with snow to a depth which rendered many of the streets entirely impassable;

the thermometer only two degrees above zero, and the water scanty; so that the whole fashionable part of the town being saved from destruction, seems remarkable, and, under Providence, is mainly attributable to the great quantity of snow on the ground, and on the roofs of the houses. . . . . .

Our rocks and shores present a very different aspect now from what they did when you were here; but truly they are very fine, even in winter; and I think that you would agree with me in this remark, if you could see them now. The contrast between the long points and bold promontories covered with snow, and the deep blue sea, is very fine, and renders the scene particularly striking and truly magnificent. Last fourth-day the sea was as still as a mill-pond. I was at the south shore about a month since, directly after a great storm; the sea was then almost as white with foam as the ground now is with snow; and the foam was driven, by the force of the wind, into every little inlet, in such quantities and heaps, that we could not go very near the shore without being ourselves covered with it. . . . . It is, indeed, a great and unspeakable favor, that my health is so good, and that we are *all* preserved in health; and thou wilt not marvel, with the knowledge thou hast of my natural temperament, that it has a good effect upon my spirits. . . . . .

My M. S. G. unites with me in dear love to you all. Farewell.

As ever, your sincere and affectionate friend,

THOMAS B. GOULD.

The labors and services of this faithful watchman, and soldier in the Church militant, had been commenced in very early life; and he continued unabated in his zeal for the truth as it is in Jesus, and firm in his testimony against all innovations on it, or perversions thereof. But his Divine Lord and Master now saw it right, in His inscrutable wisdom, after he had suffered awhile in those afflictions of the body which still remained for him to fulfil, for the Church's sake, and for his entire purification and preparation for the world to come, to remove him from further conflict and trial, and receive him to Himself, as fruit early ripened for His heavenly garner.

Since his journey in Vermont and New York, his health had generally been quite as good as usual for him; but in the latter part of the first month of 1856, having taken cold, he was revisited severely with asthma, which considerably reduced his strength. After this attack subsided, on the first day of the second month he was taken with a heavy chill, followed by high fever, and subsequently by acute pain in his right side, and other symptoms of pleurisy.* He had much difficulty in breathing, and became rapidly prostrated. During the early part of his sickness, his mind was evidently deeply engaged in frequent waiting on the Almighty, yet without much vocal expression of his feelings. But about the beginning of the second week after the attack, his mouth was opened in thankfulness to the Lord for the sweet incomes of His love and life. He broke forth, that morning, in the following acknowledgment of His goodness and mercy: "Oh! the fulness of joy—the abundance of His goodness—the sweet peace—the glory that I feel! I could sing of it! Yet nothing is of myself—it is all in mercy! I have not attained to these things through a multiplicity of petitions. Oh no! All that I could do was to throw myself at Jesus' feet; and in His own time, when He saw I had nothing of my own, He was pleased to pour in the oil and the wine." He marvelled that such an experience should have been vouchsafed to him, saying that it was beyond anything he had ever conceived; that he had never asked anything but the lowest seat; yet, lo! the gates of heaven had been opened unto him, and he had been permitted to see a mansion prepared for him! Alluding afterward to his bodily sufferings, he remarked, that they were intended to bring him low, and additionally purify him; adding, "But the Lord

* This account of his sickness and death is compiled from the Memorial of him issued by Rhode Island Monthly Meeting, and from memoranda and letters from the family, addressed to the editor during his illness, or very soon after his decease.

supports me, and He will support me. My life hangs, as it were, upon a single point; I have been aware of my critical situation; and the power that supports me is the Lord's power.".

On the ninth day of his sickness he was brought very low, and for several hours appeared to be near the close; in the evening, however, he revived; but continued to have very low sinking turns at intervals during the night. On recovering from one of them, he said, "I have had a severe conflict with death; and now the sting of death is taken away." Again, in a few hours, he appeared to be sinking rapidly; but after a time revived, and exclaimed aloud, "Another victory! another victory! The grave has lost its terrors now." And once again, towards morning, on reviving from a similar great prostration, he said, "Now I have triumphed over death, hell, and the grave! These are hard words, but they are true. Christ has given me the victory."

On third-day, the twelfth of the month, his brother-in-law, George Kenyon, coming to see him, he said, on his entering the room, "Although my earthly house of this tabernacle be dissolved, I have a building of God, an house not made with hands, eternal in the heavens." Again, "My weaknesses and propensities have been as a cloud, and as a thick cloud, they have been blotted out. My sins have all been forgiven; I have been sanctified, and thoroughly cleansed."

On fourth-day morning, when asked by J. B., how he had passed the night, he said, "This has been a crowning night to me; I have seen things not lawful to be uttered!" The same day, a friend calling to see him, he said, "I seem to have been all day grasping for life, holding on to it as by a single thread; but I have been wonderfully comforted, and strengthened, and helped." Then, alluding to a time previous to his illness, he remarked, "I looked all night for my Beloved; I sought him in the streets, but I could not find Him, He hid Himself from me; but He has comforted and strengthened me now." He then exclaimed, "Great and marvellous are Thy works, Lord God Almighty!—just and true are Thy ways, thou King of saints." The same day he said, "The Lord had made all his bed in this sickness—that it was as a bed of roses." He was so low that he was desired not to exert himself too much to speak; but he replied, "When the Master is pleased to say it is enough, I can be silent:" that, although he was so very weak and low, he should be supported; then added, "This is very different from anything I ever anticipated, to have so much to say at such a time as this. There are times when words must be spoken; and if they are not spoken, the very stones would cry out."

On fifth-day evening, after lying some time in a state of great quietness and exhaustion, seeming scarcely to breathe, he suddenly revived, and exclaimed in a clear voice, "Glory! glory! hallelujah!—Oh! I could sing of redemption, of this great redemption; and of regeneration, of thorough, heartfelt regeneration." The family coming into the room, he continued speaking in this triumphant strain of praise and thanksgiving for about half an hour; during which, among other expressions, he repeated, with great emphasis, "Out of Zion, the perfection of beauty, God hath shined." After this, he again sunk very low for a time; and when a little revived, he repeated this passage: "Filling up that which is behind, of the sufferings of Christ, in my flesh, for his body's sake, which is the Church."

During the night, he said to those about him: "I am going to take a little rest now, and in that rest I may leave you; if I do, you will know that I am safe; I am going to sleep on Jesus' bosom." He then fell asleep. At another time he said: "How often, of late, have I longed for rest—rest and quiet!—Oh, how joyous would be that rest! But this desire to go, is not resignation—I must know a perfect willingness wrought in me to remain, to perform some service which has been shown me in times past, but which I shrunk from, on account of the painful nature of it. But for this unfaithfulness, I might have passed away this beautiful morning, as the day dawned, and been forever at rest." After a time, he was favored to experience an entire resignation of his own will; and said, "Now, I can truly say, not my will, but thine, O

Lord, be done." It was not until he had thus become fully resigned to perform the deeply exercising service, which he had felt to be required of him, that the will appears to have been accepted for the deed, and the work cut short in righteousness. He experienced many low seasons; and at such a time said: "I see what is for me; there is great relief, great blessing in store for me—but I am too low to receive it; *too low*. I must be raised up; I can't lay hold of it." And then, after a time of reverent silence, songs of praise and thanksgiving flowed from his lips, in clear, audible tones.

At one time, he desired all to be very quiet; and said, he wanted to be sure that the Captain of his soul's salvation was kept on board his little barque—he must not lose sight of Him. At another time, he exclaimed, "Surely, this is the house of God, this is the gate of heaven;" and repeated it several times. "Lift up, lift up, oh ye gates, that the righteous nation which keepeth the truth may enter in." Again, he repeated, "The glorious Lord will be unto us a place of broad rivers and streams, wherein shall go no galley with oars, neither shall gallant ship pass thereby." He said, "I see no danger in humiliation, but great danger in exaltation." Sometimes he would exclaim, "Glory! glory! hallelujah! praise the Lord;" and said, "he felt lifted above all things,—the moon was under his feet—his joy was full; there were rivers of joy, fountains of joy, and he was bathing in it." And the room did seem at such times to be filled with the Divine Presence. He said, he had read accounts of the triumphs of ancient worthies, but it had been mere history to him, compared with this. He could not have thought it possible for man *so* to taste the joys of heaven, and remain in the body. At times, he spoke to the states of those around him, in a manner that was to them truly memorable, seeming to have a vivid sense of their feelings and thoughts. On one of these occasions, he had been saying something so remarkable, that his brother-in-law felt a momentary doubt, whether there was not a little undue excitement of mind, but remained silent. The moment this doubt arose, Thomas suddenly stopped, and looking anxiously at him, said: "Brother George, thou art doubting! Don't doubt again: it will lead thee into difficulty. What I have said, IS TRUTH!"

At one time, when permitted to be closely tried, he exclaimed, in tones of agony, "I shall be swallowed up! I shall be swallowed up!"—but very soon afterwards he solemnly petitioned, "Holy Father, vouchsafe thine aid!"—and continued in vocal supplication for some minutes. When he ceased, the overflowings of divine consolation were so great, that he cried out, "they were all too much; that there was not room to receive all the goodness that the Lord had revealed to him, a poor worm of the dust." In speaking of this extremity afterwards, he said, "I was made more than conqueror," &c. On one occasion he said: "My faith is strong; I live by faith, yet not I, but Christ within me. It is the Lord's power, that supports me and keeps me alive."

He expressed admiration that he should be called upon to say so much, remarking, "I have not been accustomed to speak of my own attainments—Martha, thou knowest that I have not. But now I can do no other." That some had passed through these things without saying much, but that it was his duty to proclaim them; and he exclaimed, "Oh, the fulness of Divine Love! it is as a river to swim in!"—often repeating the words, "Holy, holy, holy; worthy, worthy!" &c.

On the eighteenth of the month, he had a suffering night, and said more than once in a whisper (for now his voice had much failed, and articulation was difficult), "How long, dear Saviour, *how long?*"

He was remarkably relieved of anxiety in regard to the state of the Society; far more so than usual. Speaking of its shattered condition, he said, "We must leave it in the hands of the Lord; for He *will* have the ordering* of

* Some have of late attempted to show from this saying, that Thomas B. Gould's view here was to inculcate the need of our giving up "contending for the faith" altogether to the Lord, in a confidence that He would *himself* bring about His own work *without the use of instruments;* such reasoners intending by this, to imply, that a continued holding up of the testimony through all opposition, is creaturely zeal; and so to

the battle;" repeating it many times over; and adding, "there is no cause for discouragement."

Once when he seemed to speak, being asked if he wanted anything, he replied, "I hear sweet music, rapturous music, songs of the redeemed!" At another time, during this night, he seemed somewhat restless; when a part of the 103d Psalm was repeated to him. When he heard the words, "Who redeemeth thy life from destruction," he said, "Yes, He has redeemed it, and He will redeem it."

On fourth-day, the twentieth of the month, being two days before his close, he seemed to have less to say than usual, and to be very thoughtful. When inquired of, if he felt more poorly, he replied, "My thoughts are full of immortality and eternal life."

A friend, who was frequently with him during his illness, thus writes:

"If I had a memory as some have, how many things of deep interest I could tell; but the sweet, full, overflowing sense of his perfection and everlasting happiness is more to me than all. I have read many accounts of great and good men ending their days full of hope and in great peace; but never did I dream that I should have the privilege of being a witness of the power and glory of God through Jesus Christ, being revealed in so wonderful a manner in one of His servants. Thomas said, when recounting the unspeakable favors which he had received, 'that very few in this latter day had been permitted to see what he had seen.' At one time, he thanked the Lord, that he had been counted worthy to suffer persecution for His Name's sake. Once when I went in to see him, he held my hand, and began to speak in the most sweet and prophetic strain, of great companies which should be gathered together, to hear the preaching and receive the sweet

slacken the hands of Friends. But this is evidently a perversion of his meaning; as the word "ordering" plainly implies that there are to be soldiers, or servants, in their proper allotments, to obey the Divine commands, evidently in allusion to 1 Kings 20:14: and more than once during his sickness, he clearly expressed the "unity of his spirit" with those who were still engaged in the conflict against spiritual wickedness in high places; naming several, and sending messages.

outpourings of the Gospel. He said, 'There is a new congregation to be gathered in Philadelphia.'

"He said to his wife, 'there should be such a visitation in the earth, as had never been—such a pouring out of the Spirit—but it would not be in our day—it would not be till the next century.' His mind was so filled to overflowing, with the enjoyments of heaven, that, much of the time, he hardly regarded his bodily sufferings.—When Martha and R. S. N. would urge him to take something to strengthen him, he would look them sweetly in the face, and say, 'I have meat to eat, that ye know not of.' On fifth-day, when I came from meeting, I found him restless; but, oh, how heavenly was his face! I could not see that he was dying—none of us could see it—in wisdom was it hid from us."

On the twenty-second, the last day of his continuance, he said much that could not be understood, owing to his great weakness, and the difficulty of articulation above alluded to; but several times in the course of the day, he impressively repeated the passage, "That which may be known of God, is manifest in man." Towards evening, his wife perceiving a change in him, said, "Dearest Thomas, art thou going?" After one ineffectual attempt to speak, he made another effort, and said, "Farewell, farewell, farewell!" which were the last words he uttered. But he was entirely sensible to the last, understood what was said, and responded to it by a look, only a few minutes before the close. All the agonies of death appeared to have been passed through, previous to this time; his breathing, which had been difficult, became easy, but shorter and shorter; there was now no struggle, and he quietly and peacefully passed away, about eight o'clock in the evening.

Thus did it please the Head of the Church, in His fathomless wisdom, to cut short the work, and remove, in the prime of life and the meridian of usefulness, one on whom many hopes had been placed of more extensive service in a day to come, for the comfort and strength of the remnant left of the captivity; and to whom the hearts of the living in Israel had become closely bound, in that fellowship which hath Christ, the Lamb, for its centre—the Lord Almighty for its Alpha and its Omega! But He who is the very fountain of wisdom, shall He not ever do wisely? And He that teacheth his servant knowledge, shall He not know what is best for His Church and people in their every need?

In a consideration of the calm, composed and heavenly frame of the spirit of this our brother, towards the close of his earthly pilgrimage, even under the pains of mortal illness and with the near prospect of dissolution, how clear is the evidence that his course had been acceptable to the Great Shepherd of the flock; and that he had not followed cunningly devised fables in advocating the cause of pure and primitive Christianity, and in standing unflinchingly, through obloquy and persecution, for the ancient landmarks of his profession! Well may we adore the goodness of God in making him what he was through His Grace; for to Him alone all the praise belongs. And in looking at the wonderful foretaste of the joys of Heaven, which was thus vouchsafed to him while in the body, for his own comfort and support, and for the confirmation of the faith of those whom he has left behind, truly may we acknowledge, that "this is the Lord's doing, and marvellous in our eyes!"

www.ingramcontent.com/pod-product-compliance
Lightning Source LLC
LaVergne TN
LVHW021131110826
845150LV00005B/995

* 9 7 8 1 4 2 5 5 5 0 0 9 7 *